CONTENTS

FUNDAMENTALS OF ORGANISATIONAL LEARNING AND DEVELOPMENT

FIRST STEPS TO MANAGING THE L&D PORTFOLIO

BRIAN ALLEN

Copyright.

Fundamentals of Organisational Learning and Development. First Steps to Managing the L&D Portfolio.

ISBN 978-0-473-30737-0

Brian Allen

INTRODUCTION

The learning and development field is seemingly vast. For the HR professional or the emerging L&D specialist, the vista can be daunting, even intimidating in its complexity. Each specific area within the discipline is supported by considerable specialised literature. It is more difficult however to find a practical overview of the fundamentals that are essential for a "big picture" understanding of how learning might operate within organisations. Without this holistic appreciation, newcomers to the world of L&D are likely to become mired in the technical detail of particular aspects and perhaps "fail to see the wood for trees".

This is not an academic book. It is not intended to discuss or critique the ideas of the prominent contributors to the L&D field. Its chief purpose is to capture the breadth of the L&D world at an introductory level. Consequently each component of the L&D continuum is touched on only lightly. Drilling down deeper into these areas will be a matter for the reader's personal needs, interests and professional context.

Although concepts are described at a relatively high level, many will be new even to experienced professionals. This is because the fundamentals are so often assumed to be understood and are consequently seldom explored. Beyond the basic concepts, numerous practical examples and tools are provided to illustrate L&D at work in specific organisational contexts. These are drawn from 40 years of hands-on experience across a wide range of organisations. These examples are not intended to be adopted directly, rather to be considered for possible adaptation to the reader's own organisational requirements.

There is a fairly obvious agenda here, and that is to encourage a strategic approach to learning and development. Many years of observing organisational L&D practice has revealed that it is, for the most part, piecemeal, reactive and *ad hoc*. More often than not there is little alignment to the reality of longer term organisational development needs. The result, (as so many surveys have shown), is that the L&D dollar is often wasted and any learning that occurs is ineffectual. To a large extent this has been inevitable due to the historically pervasive view of HR as a support service rather than a strategic partner to the business. Fortunately this is now changing and HR is very consciously re-inventing itself as a contributing architect of organisational development. The requirement for strategic L&D thinking is therefore increasingly critical.

Those tasked with the L&D portfolio will undoubtedly continue to struggle to make the case successfully with senior managers for a more strategic approach. That much said, the doors are now creaking open as management generally becomes aware of the need for constant change and adaptation. However, the onus lies with HR to prove itself capable of understanding the business imperatives. The opportunities are certainly there if we are sufficiently well informed and prepared. This book is intended to be a starting point in that direction by equipping HR departments with a sound foundation.

As we approach 2015 we are entering a period of sustained workforce decline and inevitable skills shortages. The battle for talent is heating up as we speak. A major strategy in that battle will be 'survival by growing our own'. To some extent at least, companies must transition to true learning organisations in order to nurture their own talent. Guiding managers, at all levels, through this seminal change, will be the greatest challenge for HR and especially for those holding the L&D portfolio. Hopefully, this book will prove to be a source of conceptual and practical guidance for taking on that task.

Brian Allen

Rotorua. New Zealand 2014.

1. WHAT IS LEARNING AND DEVELOPMENT?

Over the last two decades most large, successful organisations have undergone a subtle but significant shift in their understanding of what is needed to provide progression that is meaningful both for individual staff members and for the business. This shift has required a move from a generally unsystematic micro view, based on reactive response to business need, to a strategically-oriented macro view linked proactively to all other aspects of business activity.

The drivers for this change in approach are numerous, but leading the charge would be events such as:
- The emergence of the "learning organisation" philosophy and systems thinking, articulated most forcefully by Peter Senge. (1)This seminal work recognises that the ever-increasing pace of change necessitates a paradigm shift from formally arranged, isolated, sporadic training inputs to more informal, self-directed, continuous learning.
- The recognition that performance quality could only be assured through the comprehensive integration of business systems and processes - demonstrated through the widespread adoption of the Baldridge criteria in the US and its offspring business excellence variants that developed in Europe, Australasia and Canada. (2)
- The ongoing transformation of HR departments into "strategic business partners" to their parent organisations. HR practitioners are now increasingly the primary source of organisational development expertise within companies.
- The emergence of holistic approaches to workforce development through initiatives such as Investors in People.
- The eventual maturing of learning development systems (e.g. the Systems Approach to Training (SAT) developed by the US and UK military; Instructional Systems Design, the ADDIE model, Dick & Carey Model) to include a "front end" justification link to organisational strategic planning and a "back end evaluation to ensure that strategic objectives were indeed being serviced.
- The proliferation of alternatives to traditional classroom-based training (e.g. coaching, mentoring and buddy systems, action learning sets, E-learning, webinars, job rotation) which has led, inevitably, to a focus on "blending" and individualising development strategies. (3)

All this adds up to a vastly more complex situation for HR professionals. "Training and development" is no longer seen as an adequate description for what HR must now provide to the business. In its 1999 review of professional standards, the Chartered Institute of Personnel and Development in the UK debated this issue and eventually resolved to adopt the term "learning and development" to reflect the much broader spectrum. "L&D" has now generally usurped "T&D".

The landscape has now changed sufficiently to demand specialist skills and knowledge in the HR team, well beyond straightforward training provision. The erstwhile "training coordinator" is now the "L&D specialist" and needs a fundamental understanding of the full spectrum of development activity and how the various aspects integrate.

The key to this understanding is clarity around what these two terms actually mean. The development of our people is an organisational objective. Learning is the primary means by which that objective is achieved. So, what is learning? Expressed simply, learning is a generic term for the methods by which we acquire new information, skills, values, perhaps even attitudes, and make sufficient sense of it all to "progress" in some way. Figure 1.1 illustrates the principal learning inputs and their relationship to development.

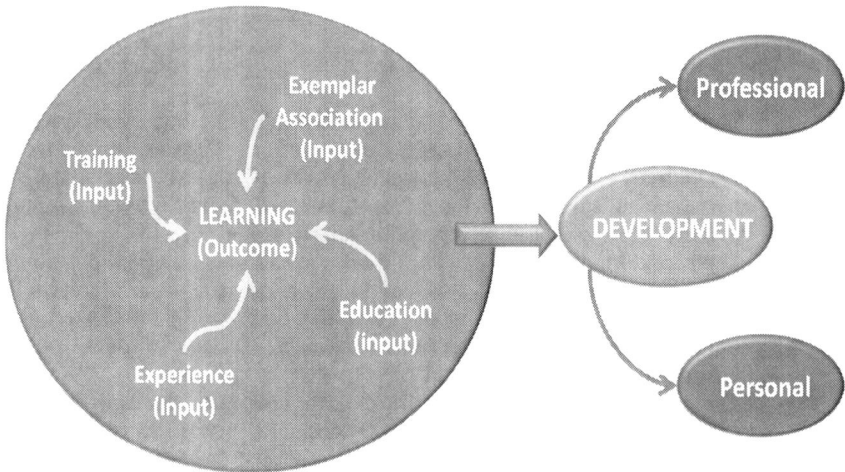

Figure 1.1 – The relationship between learning and development

LEARNING – THE PRINCIPAL INPUTS.

Training.

Taking the lid off the learning box reveals four principal inputs or learning portals. As L&D professionals we should appreciate that individual learners may bring all four to bear simultaneously as they "develop". This eventually poses problems but also presents opportunities for the development of organisational learning strategies and individual development plans. So what are these inputs?

Training, in all its forms, is learning that is focused on the acquisition or enhancement of a specific skill set, generally as a directed or managed activity within a relatively short timeframe. The learner pursues specified objectives or outcomes within a learning programme or course, with little ability or need to follow individual interests.

Education.

Education is, of course, a longer term affair. While educational programmes may well contain elements of training, the overall focus is much broader, seeking to integrate skills and knowledge into higher level competencies that enable individuals to act independently and to exercise some control over their affairs – including their own learning. Educational programmes are generally more loosely structured, allowing the learner (and the trainer / teacher) sufficient space to adjust the input to meet desired outcomes.

Experience.

According to Pliny the Elder, "experience is the most efficient teacher of all things". (4). By this he means that without direct involvement, events will inevitably remain theoretical or academic. Their true meaning (for the individual) is unlikely to emerge without the frisson of personal reality.

However, simply "having an experience" will teach us nothing unless we make some kind of sense of it. Learning does not occur until the individual evolves and attaches a meaning to each significant experience. Learning from experience refers to a very wide spectrum – from the life-changing epiphany experienced by the few, to the mundane and often minute adjustments of behaviour familiar to the many. Making sense of experience is ultimately dependent upon our ability to "reflect"; to review and to draw out principles or concepts that can then be validated through self-conscious application.

Modern educational theory acknowledges the paramount need for reflection, chiefly through models such as David Kolb's experiential learning cycle. The essence of the Kolb model is its cyclical nature. He believes that the process of learning always follows a similar pattern i.e.
- firstly we are involved with a direct, tangible experience – (concreteness).
- secondly, if learning is to occur, we consider the experience and its effects (reflection).
- thirdly, we extract core ideas, principles, concepts, beliefs or even values from the reflective activity (abstractness).
- fourthly, we test the abstracted information or ideas by applying them to other situations or experiences.

Kolb goes on to maintain that each of these stages is characterised by a "learning mode" as illustrated in Figure 1.2. The learning modes can be thought of more simplistically e.g.
- concrete experience = "feeling".
- reflective observation = "watching".
- abstract conceptualising = "thinking".
- active experiment = "doing".

It is not difficult to see how these modes align with the broad personality types that are commonly associated with established systems such as the Myers Briggs type indicator (MBTI). The relationship is further substantiated by the fact that although we all work through the learning cycle, each of us will exhibit a tendency to extract more learning from one particular mode – or perhaps a subtle combination of two modes.

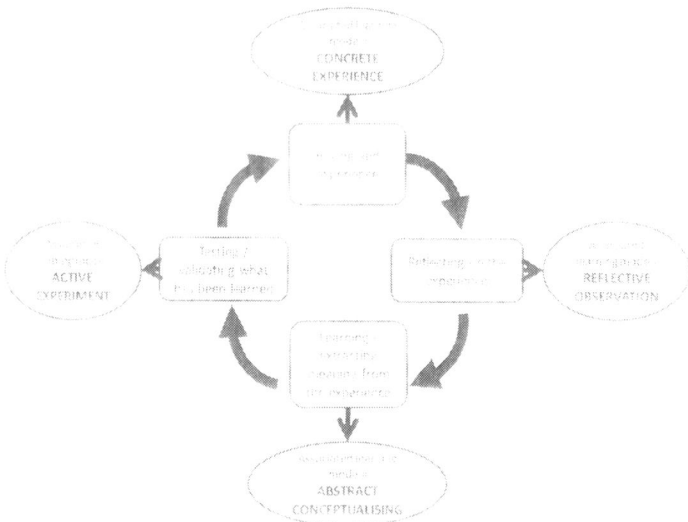

Figure 1.2 – the Kolb Experiential Learning Cycle (after David Kolb 1984)

For those of us who are tasked with the design and delivery of learning, the Kolb model provides a useful tool for questioning the quality of our products. In group learning experiences we cannot hope to accommodate all individual preferred learning styles entirely. Consequently, if we are to succeed in "pleasing most of the people most of the time" the ideal learning experience should contain elements of all four learning modes. The precise balance of these modes will naturally depend on the kind of learning involved. A philosophy seminar is likely to be heavily weighted toward "thinking" while learning to drive a forklift will undoubtedly involve a great deal of "doing". Fortunately however, if our course selection has been effective, our participants should be favourably disposed toward the predominant learning mode.

When dealing with individuals e.g. in a coaching or mentoring capacity, we can be more focused on individual preferences. Identifying an individual's preferred learning style is not difficult if you know them well. When this is not the case, there is a range of assessment tools available to assist. These are discussed in full in section 5 which deals with the design and development of learning experiences. For the present, as a general principle, we should allow that actual experience provides the most powerful learning. Being "taught" is always a second-hand affair. As Winston Churchill remarked, "I am always ready to learn, but do not much care for being taught".

Exemplar association.

Learning and development have many dimensions. Most often we interpret learning in specific terms; as a clearly identifiable "event" that can be ticked off as accomplished. Unfortunately however, these accomplishments tend to have little meaning, or fail to realise their full potential if they are not located within a larger framework of positive values and attitudes. So where do we go to acquire those larger mental models?

By and large, most of us do not consciously develop a higher level framework of principles and ethical behaviour. Nevertheless this occurs, to a greater or lesser extent, simply because we are all, from birth, at the centre of a complex hub of influences from those people in a position to provide an example – whether good or bad. Figure 1.3 below shows just how complex this web of example can be as each of us moves through life.

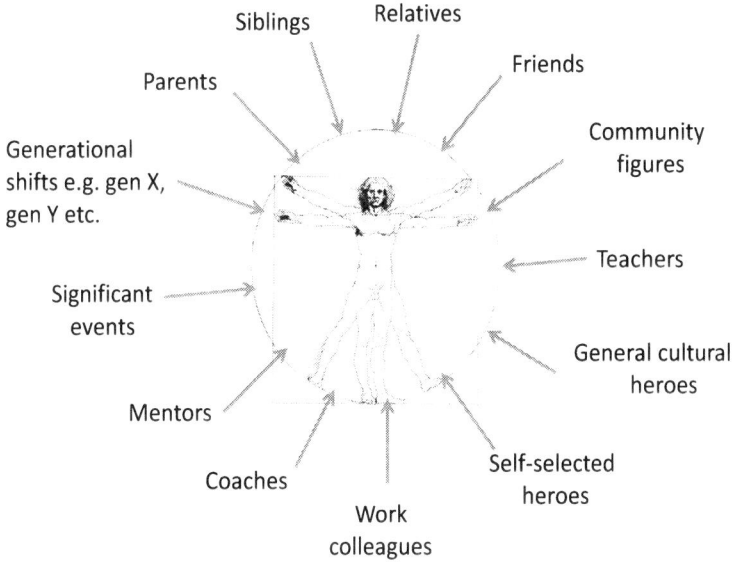

Figure 1.3 – Typical exemplar influences

The learning input from all these sources is mostly unpredictable, unmanaged and often unconsciously received. The learning outcomes emerge generally as values, morals and ethics. These are all relatively abstract concepts that are often mistakenly used interchangeably by individuals and organisations alike. It is particularly important that companies which seek to inculcate corporate values and codes of conduct should be clear about the distinctions.

In general terms, values are motivational or aspirational and are associated with what we positively try to do and with how we try to behave. Morals and ethics, on the other hand are primarily concerned with what we should not do and with restrictions on our behaviour.

Values are essentially personal, either to the individual or to an individual organisation. They may or may not be overtly stated, although it is fashionable now for organisations to do so. Values underpin every aspect of positive behaviour and are often defined as "what we hold dear – the way we do things around here".

Morals tend to derive from the individual's community or specific cultural environment and reflect what that particular group regards as acceptable behaviour.

The term "ethics" is now mostly used to indicate formally constructed codes of conduct which legally constrain the behaviour of professional bodies e.g. the medical and legal professions. Most public services are now bound by formal ethical codes.

Although so many of these influences are subliminal and consequently difficult to quantify or articulate, their effects are profound, particularly because they shape attitudes and responses to more overt learning opportunities. For this reasons many organisations now accept that to maximise their investment in training, or in professional learning programmes, they need to develop the individual in a holistic sense. Hence the move to structured mentoring systems and the shift to "learning" rather "training" as a generic reference for human resource professionals. Increasingly, the impetus now is toward L&D frameworks which will allow and encourage the integration of experience, education, training and the positive influence of role models.

So, to answer the question "what is learning and development?" we could simply define it as the wide variety of inputs, structured and unstructured, formal and informal, through which individuals acquire knowledge, skills and attributes which further their positive evolution, both professionally and personally.

The critical issue for organisations is to understand that learning in the workplace occurs continually, mostly outside the arena of the training room, in an informal manner, and that this informal learning may account for the greater part of an individual's development. Managers, and of course human resource departments, should therefore work to understand how those informal channels work, and then take every opportunity to enhance the individual's capacity for drawing the maximum learning from events and the people they associate with. This objective should sit at the heart of continuum activities such as performance appraisals, one-on-one coaching sessions, mentoring, project debriefs, team development workshops etc. This is a hallmark of a true learning organisation.

THE PURPOSE OF ORGANISATIONAL LEARNING AND DEVELOPMENT.

Superficially, the purpose of organisational L&D is to ensure that all personnel possess the knowledge and skills required to perform their present and potential roles to required levels of performance. This sounds simple enough but drilling down into this statement reveals considerable complexity. L&D is required to support organisational performance across a wide spectrum of priorities. Complexity and prioritisation can only be properly managed if managers adhere to clear guiding principles.

The defining requirement of learning and development activity in any organisation is that it should be strategic. This is not necessarily true of individuals outside the organisational context. Much of our personal learning outside working hours is driven by the need for amusement, relaxation, social interaction e.g. learning to play bridge or taking up the guitar. Yes it may well be strategic e.g. research activity to support writing a book on local history – but it does not have to be.

The workplace is seldom driven by altruistic motives. With very few exceptions, organisations invest in the development of their people only if they can anticipate some kind of return, usually in terms of the individual's capability or capacity to contribute in some way to higher levels of output, quality, safety or service provision. Requests to the company by individuals for financial support for a learning initiative must inevitably pass the acid test of the business case.

The rationale for learning and development activity derives from the strategic plan at the highest level, or from the departmental business plans (operational) that should devolve from it. Any planned significant change in activity or equipment will, most likely, result in a knowledge or skills gap in some part of the workforce. The most obvious purpose of organisational learning and development is to ensure that these gaps are adequately closed in a timeframe that ensures operational continuity.

However, defining the purpose of L&D is rather more complex than closing skills gaps. In addition to new ventures, a well-structured strategic plan will set out intentions for maintaining compliance, providing for operational and management succession, expansion (as opposed to innovation) and any required benchmarking initiatives e.g. ISO 9001 or Business Excellence. These elements of learning should be addressed (in outline at least) in the strategic plan, and in detail in departmental / operational plans, precisely because they are things any organisation must do to ensure continuing success. Figure 1.4 sets out the most common "must do" learning components of organisational strategy.

Most "must do" activities will provide directly measurable evaluation data and can offer sound metrics for ROI (return on investment). ROI for compliance training activities is always less tangible since, even with a spotless health and safety performance, it is difficult to measure the cost of events that did not occur. Compliance effectively sits outside return on investment evaluation simply because it is a "must do".

Beyond "must do" learning lies the "act of faith" realm. Providing they have sufficient resources, most organisations find themselves looking at what they *ought* to be doing. This inevitably takes them into areas where the return on investment can never be guaranteed or directly attributed to the learning activities involved. Activities like continuing professional development (attendance at conferences, institute meetings etc.) or attending a generic leadership course may bring no immediately tangible returns to the organisation. Nevertheless, the organisation believes that payback will come over the long term, and even if the knowledge and skills are not applied directly "the place is simply all the better for it".

"Act of faith" learning is seldom defined in strategy. It is most often supported through a policy statement. Not surprisingly, the business environment "Act of faith" learning is seldom defined in strategy. It is most often supported through a *policy* statement. Not surprisingly, when the business environment tightens up it is this area that falls first to the financial controller's axe.

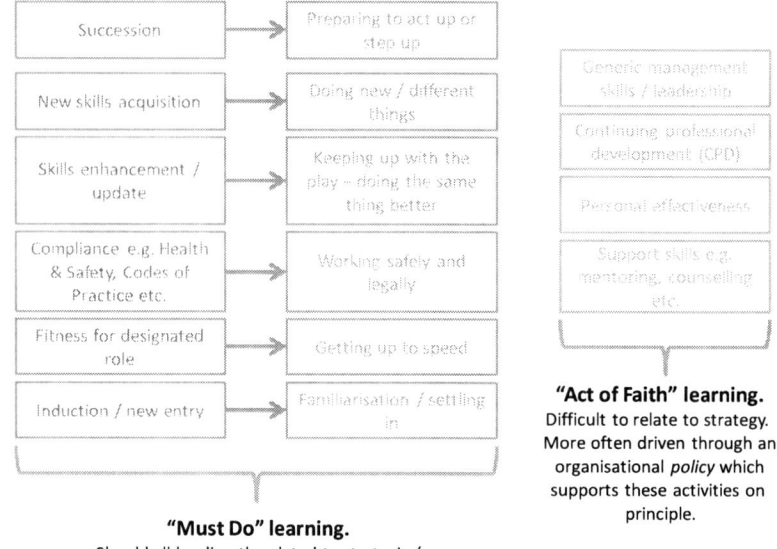

Succession	→	Preparing to act up or step up
New skills acquisition	→	Doing new / different things
Skills enhancement / update	→	Keeping up with the play – doing the same thing better
Compliance e.g. Health & Safety, Codes of Practice etc.	→	Working safely and legally
Fitness for designated role	→	Getting up to speed
Induction / new entry	→	Familiarisation / settling in

Generic management skills / leadership

Continuing professional development (CPD)

Personal effectiveness

Support skills e.g. mentoring, counselling etc.

"Act of Faith" learning.
Difficult to relate to strategy. More often driven through an organisational *policy* which supports these activities on principle.

"Must Do" learning.
Should all be directly related to strategic / operational / business plans

Figure 1.4 – Major areas of organisational learning activity

THE ROLE OF HR IN LEARNING AND DEVELOPMENT.

We have come a long way from the days of the "personnel department" which focused primarily on recruiting and payroll. As late as the 1970's many organisations regarded employees primarily as a "resource" to be used up and replaced. The rationalist approach to management persisted and tended to view people in the same light as equipment or consumables.

However, events were unfolding that effectively displaced the notion that human beings should be regarded as a resource. Unlike, equipment or consumables, people are not fixed entities. They always have the potential to change and develop to meet emerging organisational needs. The rise of strategic management coincided with the realisation that employees are best treated like any form of capital investment. To grow the business you need to invest in the capital of expertise.

During the 1980's strategically oriented managers began to understand that recruiting, developing and retaining high quality people ensures competitive advantage. At the same time the management gurus e.g. Tom Peters, were pointing out that organisations flourished when they created and cherished distinct cultures which their people could identify with and "belong to". In 1995 Charles Greer noted the transition.
"In a growing number of organisations, human resources are now viewed as a source of competitive advantage. There is greater recognition that distinctive competencies are obtained through highly developed employee skills, distinctive organisational cultures, management processes and systems. This is in contrast to the traditional emphasis on transferable resources such as equipment. Increasingly it is being recognised that competitive advantage can be obtained with a high quality workforce."(6)

Concurrent with the advent of strategic management, Japanese management techniques such as TQM and Kaizen clearly demonstrated the fundamental importance of enabling and empowering staff to contribute to their highest potential. The astonishing success of Japanese industry from the 1960's onward has compelled Western businesses to completely revise their understanding of their human "resources" to one of infinite potential - providing sufficient investment and support systems are developed. This is the contemporary concept of "human capital" that has displaced the more basic human resource concept in more progressive, strategically managed organisations.

Major organisations are now becoming aware that on-going success depends, to a critical extent, on the quantum, quality and strategic relevance of the human capital they are able to access. They also understand that capital, in this sense, means so much more than know-how. Of course knowledge, skills and experience provide the bedrock, but a broader and deeper examination reveals the importance of aptitudes, attitudes, personal ethics, creativity, potential for leadership etc. These aspects represent latent potential which can only be released through the vision of strategic management. Most major corporations are now expanding their vision of the learning and development function and working to integrate it with all other strategic business systems.

"The perception of the learning function is shifting from being an operating cost to becoming a strategic lever that can add value at multiple levels of the organisation. Learning's focus is moving from training and certification to all facets of learning including collaboration, knowledge management, analytics and performance improvement. Once pushed at workers in their silos, learning now pulls in everyone in the firm's value chain. Highly skilled, more engaged employees and partners have become the ultimate competitive advantage. For corporations, getting this right has become a critical issue. Talent has become scarce and competency has become a competitive weapon. It's clear that learning now warrants strategic management. Effective learning governance strengthens an organisation's ability to adapt and even thrive in a dynamic environment."(7)

So, in a very real sense, the role of HR, (and its L&D specialists in particular), is to work with senior managers and key stakeholders within the business, to unlock and develop human capital to meet the strategic needs of the organisation. Recruiting new staff is now seen to be a lesser option for the acquisition of talent. Investing in the development of existing staff can return handsome dividends, particularly since it is proven to assist the retention of key personnel, and continues the accumulation of human capital. Fulfilling this role is no easy feat. HR staff will need rigorous strategies and proven methods to do so. Appropriate rigour and method can be assured through the use of a strategic organisational learning and development approach. One purpose of this book is to describe that approach in depth.

LEARNING AND DEVELOPMENT – A MODEL

Figure 1.5 gives a schematic overview of a strategic L&D model. In essence, this is a cyclical process that begins and ends with the organisation's strategic plan.

An absence of strategic planning essentially means that learning and development have no direction or clear objectives. This does not mean that the rest of the model (stages 3-9) is of no use. On the contrary, adherence to structure and sequence will at least allow for the generation of an effective learning product – but it may well be the wrong product, unsuited or irrelevant to where the organisation eventually finds itself! For the purposes of this book we shall assume that organisations do strategise and plan sufficiently to provide HR with a practical vision of the future.

It will be clear to most L&D professionals that this model is an extension of existing instructional design paradigms e.g. IDS or ADDIE.(8) These are, in turn, evolutions of the systems approach to training (SAT) developed by the US and British military in the 1960's. They propose a systematic process logic that will ensure quality design of training / learning activity – but they are not conceptually linked to organisational business strategy or to the increasingly important human capital strategy of alignment to external qualifications. The strategic model draws these critical factors into the mix and in so doing re-organises the process somewhat.

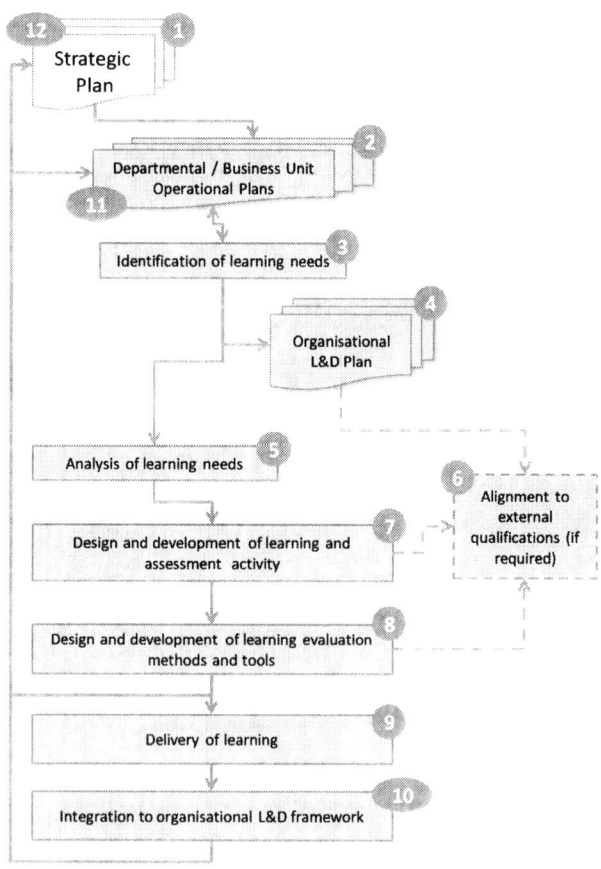

Figure 1.5 – A strategic model of organisational learning & development

2. IDENTIFICATION OF LEARNING NEEDS

BASIC CONSIDERATIONS: THE STRUCTURE OF STRATEGY.

Effective learning and development planning is never the easiest of exercises. There are a number of reasons for this e.g.
- Lack of appropriate expertise in the HR department.
- Lack of clarity around organisational strategy.
- Limited access to appropriate managers for detailed consultation around strategic intention.
- Lack of senior management will or determination to do things properly – preferring the "quick and dirty" approach.
- The compelling instinct to be seen to "do" rather than to "think".

Any combination of these factors can lead to the abandoning of meaningful planning activity in favour of the scattergun approach, where the training dollar is sprayed around to little substantial effect. Under these circumstances the "squeaky wheels" are quick to take advantage.

The last two decades have seen responsive HR departments fully embrace the concept of acting as a strategic business partner. Broadening the traditional roles in this way demands that HR professionals fully understand the strategic dynamics of their organisation and reflect them in all areas of their practice. Ideally, HR managers, possibly even L&D managers will have an active presence on the Board or the organisation's lead team. This enables first hand involvement and awareness of strategic imperatives.

If organisational learning and development is to be fully aligned, the L&D plan should be very deliberately tuned to the strategic planning structure. This will involve reflecting a number of constants e.g. declared company values, but also the continuing adjustment to strategic variables generated by the shifting sands of business needs. When producing their own annual operational plans, HR departments should always ensure that they are indeed drawing the links and joining the dots across to the business planning framework. Essentially this means accessing strategy in its structural detail and then interpreting what this means in terms of learning requirements.

Larger organisations, both public and private sector, now adhere to a planning framework that devolves from an overarching vision. Terminology may vary but the planning function is essentially similar across the spectrum. Figure 2.1 illustrates this hierarchy and some of the common variations in nomenclature that occur between public and private sector organisations.

Public sector strategic plans are generally required to be publicly accessible, usually through the organisation's website. There are many excellent examples available. A thoroughly worked example of the public sector planning structure cited above can be found at the site of the New Zealand Fire Service (1). Corporate plans are inevitably commercially sensitive and therefore not usually accessible in the same way.

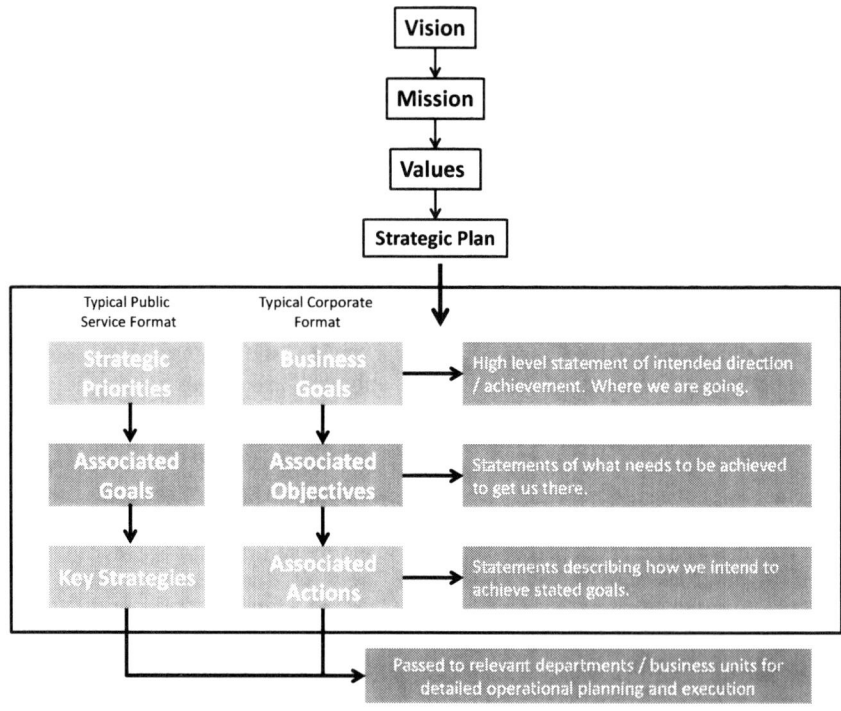

Figure 2.1 – Standard strategic planning hierarchies

When trying to align learning and development, HR professionals often miss the essential first principle i.e. you must be strategic about being strategic. It is always so tempting to engage immediately with the "tangible", with the detail of what business managers say they want or need. Leaping out of the trenches in this way may mean that you lose sight of what the campaign is all about.

If senior managers have gone to the trouble of developing a fully modelled strategic plan, those of us in HR should use this as our alignment template – beginning with the big picture stuff – vision, mission and values. Understanding what these high level statements mean, and are supposed to do, is crucial for alignment.

ALIGNING LEARNING WITH ORGANISATIONAL VISION.

Vision is often confused with mission. Let's be clear about it. Vision is what we want the future to look like. The mission statement describes what we do, to the best of our ability, in our journey to the future.

That future must be defined as a good place, otherwise why would we bother with it? The vision statement needs to be inspirational in tone and succinct enough for everybody to understand and instantly recall. The bold simplicity of Microsoft's vision is a case in point –"A personal computer in every home, running Microsoft software". Other companies choose to put more flesh on the bones but in so doing run the risk of reducing memorability. Coca Cola's vision statement is a prime example:

"To achieve sustainable growth, we have established a Vision with clear goals:
- People: Being a great place to work where people are inspired to be the best they can be.
- Planet: Being a responsible global citizen that makes a difference.
- Portfolio: Bringing to the world a portfolio of beverage brands that anticipate and satisfy peoples' desires and needs
- Partners: Nurturing a winning network of partners and building mutual loyalty
- Profit: Maximising return to shareowners while being mindful of our overall responsibilities."

While all these ideas are certainly worthy, what is the essential, key message here? Most managers and employees would probably struggle to recall this level of complexity. Arguably, some of these statements would be more at home further down the strategy chain e.g. as values?

There are numerous examples of much more complex vision statements, all of which have little lasting impact. Nevertheless, without vision we are confronted by a workplace that is essentially meaningless. Senior management may define the vision but unless it can be shared by all, as a common bond, it will most likely sit on the shelf and gather the dust of neglect.

In The Fifth Discipline, Peter Senge articulates this issue clearly.
"When there is a genuine vision (as opposed to the all-too-familiar 'vision statement'), people excel and learn, not because they are told to, but because they want to. But many leaders have personal visions that never get translated into shared visions that galvanise an organisation. What has been lacking is a discipline for translating vision into shared vision - not a 'cookbook' but a set of principles and guiding practices.(2)

Truly exceptional leaders may appreciate the need to communicate the vision across the whole organisation, but are seldom able to do so without assistance. One of Senge's "principles" should surely be that all managers should constantly be asking the essential question for and with their staff "how does what we are doing in this department, today, tomorrow, next month, next year, move us closer to our vision?" If a manager cannot answer that question with some conviction, something is wrong.

HR managers have a special role to play here. First of all they can take positive action to ensure that the learning programmes they develop or sanction clearly support the drive toward organisational vision. There are a number of practical ways in which this can be done. They can:
- Ensure that all learning programmes commence with a direct reference to vision and an explanation of how this particular learning supports to it.

- Ensure that learning materials always carry the essential vision statement as a motif.
- Design summative programme activities and evaluation materials that investigate the perceived success of the learning in supporting organisational vision.

Secondly, HR can and should take the lead in coaching other managers at all levels, (as part of their ongoing leadership development) in the techniques needed to stitch vision awareness into the fabric of departmental interactions e.g.
- By integrating reflective comment into formal team meetings.
- By relating individual performance to the bigger picture during staff appraisals.

Thirdly, through being primarily responsible for staff induction processes, HR is in a unique position to ensure that appropriate weight is given to vision awareness throughout the employee's initial learning about the organisation.

ALIGNING LEARNING WITH THE MISSION.

Many organisations are guilty of conflating vision and mission. This can cause confusion among managers and employees alike. As we move down the strategic planning hierarchy, aligning learning and development should become a more tangible process. This will be problematic if the mission statement is clouded by purely aspirational elements. Properly crafted mission statements should step back from the inspirational tone of vision to offer a more pragmatic summary of what the organisation does, day in, day out, to achieve the long term vision.

As with vision, a succinctly expressed mission statement will always be more memorable and therefore more useful. However, the tendency is for the statement to provide an insight into function and this generally requires somewhat lengthier description. The US Department of Labour's Occupational Safety and Health Administration provides a good example of the clear difference between vision and mission. Its vision is stated as:

"Every employer and employee in the nation recognises that occupational safety and health add value to American businesses, workplaces and workers' lives."

Its mission statement is:

"OSHA's mission is to assure the safety and health of America's workers by setting and enforcing standards; providing training, outreach, and education; establishing partnerships; and encouraging continual improvement in workplace safety and health."

For HR's learning and development specialists, clearly articulated high level statements like this provide a very useful set of priorities to target and service. If we can link learning strategy to what the organisation explicitly exists to do, the justification of the L&D spend becomes a whole lot easier.

Using the OSHA example above, to achieve a truly conscious alignment will involve a degree of "interrogation" of senior managers in order to elicit a genuine consensus on what is actually meant by "setting standards, providing training, outreach, establishing partnerships, encouraging continual improvement etc." Then the question can be asked "is there likely to be any learning need associated with these requirements and, if so, how do we provide the most appropriate solution?" This is always a useful exercise, and ideally should be done on a regular basis to refresh thinking at all levels. Significant shifts can occur and a general understanding can become fragmented very quickly. Mission statements may not change much over the years at first glance, but what the individual functional references mean in terms of contemporary solutions may change radically. For example "outreach" in the OSHA mission statement above may have started life as a reference to the work of field operatives, but when managers are questioned at a later date might also include web-based support programmes. This kind of "creep" is inevitable and consequently mission statements need to be regularly reviewed to ensure clarity and consensus.

Of course what the HR department fervently hopes for is that senior managers are completing the planning cycle to full depth. If so, changes of emphasis around core functions will show up in detail in the key strategies / associated actions level and finally in departmental operational planning.

ALIGNING LEARNING WITH ORGANISATIONAL VALUES.

If vision is about aspiration (what we finally hope to achieve) and mission is about core functions (what we do to get us there), values are about the standards we set ourselves when carrying out those functions. They are therefore statements about expectations of behaviour and often drive follow-on definition in the form of highly specified codes of conduct. Values define the working ethic of the organisation.

Some organisations work hard to distil their fundamental behavioural principles into an apparently simple (and memorable) creed e.g. WalMart:
- Respect for the individual.
- Service to our customers.
- Strive for excellence.

Others will offer greater definition, or just a longer list e.g. Microsoft:

"As a company, and as individuals, we value integrity, honesty, openness, personal excellence, constructive self-criticism, continual self-improvement, and mutual respect. We are committed to our customers and partners and have a passion for technology. We take on big challenges, and pride ourselves on seeing them through. We hold ourselves accountable to our customers, shareholders, partners, and employees by honouring our commitments, providing results, and striving for the highest quality."

What is immediately evident here is that value statements invariably contain abstract nouns which may be understood quite differently by individuals or even different cultures. "Respect" will certainly have different connotations for the average US or Japanese citizen. And what exactly is "excellence?" Once again, if employees are to live the company values, they must absorb them thoroughly through the induction and follow-on mentoring processes. Aligning learning to values is achievable if a clear definition is available. Often we find that company leaders step up to clarify meaning and drive home a common understanding. For example Don Soderquist, Senior Vice Chairman of WalMart Stores expanded on "Respect for the individual" as follows:

"When we say that our people make the difference, this is not a meaningless slogan – it's a reality at WalMart. We are a group of dedicated, hard- working, ordinary people who have teamed together to accomplish extraordinary things. We have very different backgrounds, different colours and different beliefs, but we do believe that every individual deserves to be treated with respect and dignity."(3)

As a corporate leader Soderquist recognised the absolute need to reinforce corporate values constantly, well beyond initial rote learning.

"Some companies put their value statement in the back of the policy manual. It is good to have a set of values, but most people wouldn't be drawn naturally to the policy manual in their desk drawer when they are wondering what to do. We all need to be reminded constantly in order to maintain the culture. We used to reserve one Saturday morning meeting per month just to focus on the company's values. I would ask a different person each month to prepare something for our Saturday morning management meeting on how our values could be seen in action. We would talk about them when we met in the stores. We would post them prominently."(4)

Organisational learning initiatives present the perfect vehicle for reinforcing values. HR's responsibility here is multi-faceted e.g.
- To work with senior managers / leaders to ensure that values are clearly articulated.
- To ensure that all learning activity, materials, and methods, from induction onward, are required to overtly relate what is learned to organisational values.
- To train or equip all facilitators, trainers, coaches, mentors to ask the key questions "what does this learning tell us about our values?" or vice versa, "what do our values tell us about this learning?"
- To ensure that all learning and development processes live the values e.g. for WalMart learning must be designed to support at the level of individual need, its primary focus must be on developing the highest customer service standards and the quality of learning activity itself must always be subject to continuous improvement. For L&D this is no more than "walking the talk".

SERVICING THE STRATEGIC PLAN.

Vision, mission and values provide the strategic constants in organisational life. They are what Soderquist calls "the core". Changes tend to be subtle rather than radical. Providing we refresh our understanding of these essentials, and adapt when necessary, alignment of learning in these areas should not need constant re-working.

This is not the case with the strategic planning cycle. Most organisations will plan ahead on a five year basis. However, for fast-moving industries such as IT this may be too far out to make sensible decisions. Local government organisations must provide longer term guidance and consequently generally plan out to ten years.

Regardless of the projected scope of the strategic plan, once published it must be regularly revisited and progress against it carefully examined. This may lead to adjustments to the original plan, causing reciprocal adjustments to departmental operational plans further down the chain. Reviews are usually scheduled on an annual basis resulting in annual business or operational plans at department level. In addition to achieving a full depth appreciation of the parent document, HR departments need to track changes emerging from the review cycle.

HR departments are, of course, business units themselves and should therefore be active participants in the organisation's planning cycles. In practice this means that the HR department will produce its own annual business plan. However, because HR provides such a wide range of key services to the organisation, its annual business planning must follow on from departmental business planning and is ultimately dependent on departmental heads for the quality of those plans.

Figure 2.2 illustrates a standard model of corporate planning cycles. Annual reviews usually generate adjustments or additions to the overarching 5 year plan and these in turn drive reciprocal adjustments to departmental business plans. HR planning then adjusts its own annual business plan after analysing departmental plans.

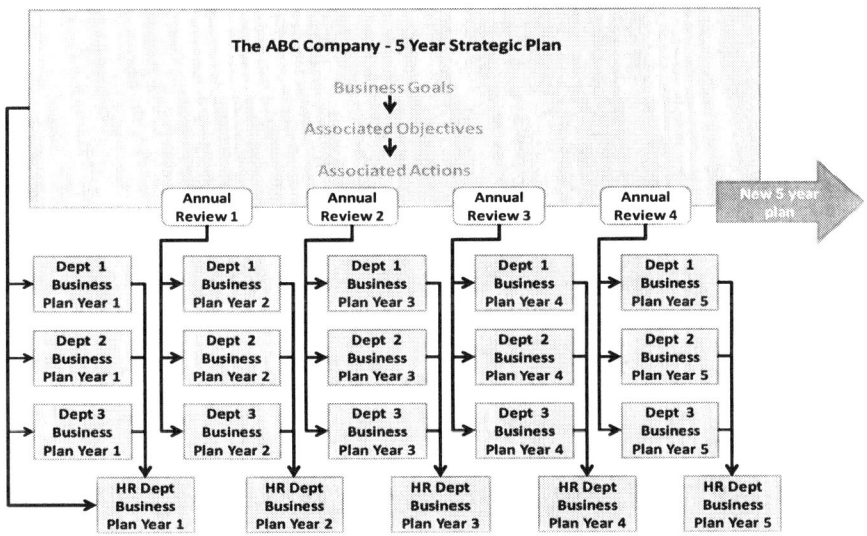

Figure 2.2 – A typical corporate planning cycle (HR focus)

Significant time and energy can be saved if an HR representative is able to sit in on departmental planning and "interrogate" decision-making directly for the potential range of HR support required, including of course, learning and development. Unfortunately, HR departments are seldom staffed to do this. Consequently the HR team finds itself analysing the completed departmental plan and then going back to appropriate managers for clarification.

Focusing specifically on L&D, what are the process steps we need to follow to ensure the L&D contribution to the annual HR plan is properly aligned to the strategic plan? Providing the overall strategic planning process has been carried out professionally, we should be able to focus directly on the objectives articulated in departmental business plans. These objectives derive expressly from the higher level strategy and the higher level alignment may therefore be assumed. The primary target for the L&D specialist is the departmental objectives for the year(s) ahead.

As a worked scenario let us suppose that the one of the business goals in the *ABC Widgets Company* strategic plan is: "To increase overall output by a factor of 5% with current plant and equipment levels." This in turn might spawn the following associated objectives:
- "To identify realistic but attainable production targets for existing plant and equipment levels".
- "To review and if possible improve work processes in all production areas."
- "To minimise shut down time."
- "To ensure employee understanding and commitment to achieving production targets"
- "To improve production monitoring and reporting procedures".
- "To improve employee commitment to increased production."

At this level of "drill down" the potential need for new learning (up-skilling or new skills) begins to emerge. Nevertheless, these needs are no more than latent. These objectives need to be further opened up and specified before learning needs finally announce themselves. For example, "To review and if possible improve work processes" sounds like a straightforward process mapping and possible re-engineering job – but if significant changes are deemed necessary, a training intervention of some kind might be needed. Most likely, training of this kind will be developed internally and delivered in a very short timeframe. L&D's role may be strictly advisory in this context.

On the other hand, we should be able to recognise that objectives such as "improve employee commitment to increased production" are pregnant with potentially larger scale learning implications. The third level of associated actions for this objective might look like this:
- "Review and improve communication and feedback procedures to ensure employee understanding of production targets and schedules".
- "Review and (if necessary) improve systems of employee performance management."
- "Review and improve the leadership capability of managers at all levels of the company".

The wording here reveals something of the analysis that has gone into the planning process. It seems clear that both the communication procedures and the general leadership capability have been found wanting. The directive is quite clear i.e. "review and improve". This is not the case for performance management where improvement will only occur "if necessary" i.e. the systems here may not be at fault.

GAP ANALYSIS.

All three of these associated actions call for two responses; review and, if needed, improvement. Reviewing and improving inevitably imply firstly that you know where you are starting from, and secondly you know where you want to go. In terms of learning and development this means that we need an understanding of existing skill / knowledge levels and a clear idea of the new levels we wish to achieve. In the case of entirely new roles, accurate in-depth scoping will be needed.

The planning process will now delegate associated actions to the most appropriate departments at the operational level. Having been advised of what needs to be done, departmental managers and teams must set about planning the how. This is the tactical level of the planning process and is inevitably a much more in-depth event. Operational level plans, often referred to as departmental business plans, may task individuals or teams with servicing associated actions from the strategic plan, or perhaps set up specific projects with their own governance structures. In the event of insufficient internal expertise, consultants may be called in to deal with the issue. In any event, individuals, project teams or consultants must eventually ask the question "Is there a gap between the skills our people currently have and those they will need to meet the new requirements?" This is gap analysis and successful completion will identify whether or not there is an actual learning need. Performing this analysis with any certainty will ultimately depend on the skilled selection and use of key tools and documentation e.g.
- Role maps
- Competency frameworks
- Auditing matrices e.g. cross team training matrices.

LEARNING NEEDS AND THE CONCEPT OF 'COMPETENCE'.

Underpinning the entire process of training needs analysis is the notion that the individual learner will be able to "do the job properly" on completion of the programme or training event. Unfortunately however, doing the job 'properly' is an inexact term that might be variously interpreted by everybody in the workplace. The absence of clarity here often leads to significant issues around performance expectations and assessment. Avoiding these issues requires general agreement on what the individual is expected to do (functions) in a given role and the 'standard' to which they should do these things. Agreement may also be needed on how the individual should go about performing their role (behaviours) within their specific organisational culture.

Once we introduce the idea of an accepted standard we can talk meaningfully about "competence". To be competent is a more precise idea than simply "doing the job properly". A competent individual is able to carry out a function to an agreed minimum standard. It may also allude to behaving in accordance with overtly stated organisational norms. These standards (particularly in relation to skills and knowledge) are often assembled to form competency frameworks or qualifications. Organisations cannot effectively carry out TNA unless they examine the idea of competency and what it should mean, specifically, for them. Training provision is necessarily focused to a stated outcome, usually framed in terms of a minimum or benchmark standard. The traditional view (certainly among managers who are looking for demonstrable ROI) is that once this standard is achieved the individual may be deemed competent. However, experience shows that while this may be true in many instances, achieving competence is not necessarily a finite process and may often need to be viewed as a continuum of improving performance. Furthermore, achieving that initial minimum standard may simply be a 'license' to do the job but true competence is only achieved through the consolidation of experience and integration with related knowledge and skills. The obvious analogy here would be driving. The learner driver passes a driving test and is allowed to drive unaccompanied. Everybody understands however that the newly qualified driver still has much to learn and only continued experience will teach him.

Understanding that achieving competence is often a progressive process was formally recognised in the 1970's by Noel Burch of Gordon training International. He developed the 'conscious competence model' which has proven to be a useful aid to organisations seeking to position the measure of competence or qualification at the most appropriate point in learning development. If we take the training of a production worker who will operate very valuable plant, we can immediately understand that managers might feel reluctant to allow him to run the plant unsupervised immediately on completion of training. It is unlikely that training would have encompassed all the scenarios (breakdowns, maintenance interventions etc.) that would be experienced over the longer term. Managers here would naturally look for consolidation over time before they would be confident about signing off on 'competence'.

Shown at Figure 2.3 is an interpretation of Burch's model by Professor Will Taylor. The model shows the learner progressing through the following stages:
1. **Unconscious incompetence**. At this stage learners "don't know what it is that they don't know". Referring to our driving analogy this might be the teenager who has taken to driving the family automatic 4x4 around the paddock and innocently believes they can drive.

2. **Conscious incompetence**. The rude awakening stage. The learner comes face to face with the reality of the task and realises that in fact they know very little. Our teenager ventures on to the open road for the first time, in traffic, driving a manual change car and quickly realises that they have a great deal to learn about driving! As Taylor's model suggests, this is a 'discovery' process, and often a very sobering one.

3. **Conscious competence**. The learner works through the training to a pre-determined minimum performance standard. He is able to do the job but consciously concentrate to do so. Our teenage driver has passed his driving test but when on the road is still actively focusing all his attention in order to drive safely.

4. **Unconscious competence**. By this stage the leaner has achieved true mastery. He no longer has to think about what he is doing and responds instinctively / intuitively to issues as they arise. Our driver has now progressed to a level of expertise such that he is able to drive safely while thinking about other things. Typically he finds that he has arrived at his destination and cannot quite remember how he got there.

Taylor's model includes a fifth element, reflective competence which he cites as the key to mature practice. He justifies this additional component as follows:
"We revisit conscious incompetence, making discoveries in the holes in our knowledge and skills, becoming discouraged, which fuels incentive to proceed (when it does not

defeat). We perpetually learn, inviting on-going tutelage, mentoring and self-study (on-going conscious competence). We continually challenge our 'unconscious competence' in the face of complacency, areas of ignorance, unconscious errors, and the changing world and knowledge base: We challenge our unconscious competence when we recognize that a return to unconscious incompetence would be inevitable. We do this in part by self-study and use of peer review - such that mature practice encompasses the entire 'conscious competence' model, rather than supersedes it as the hierarchical model might suggest." (5)

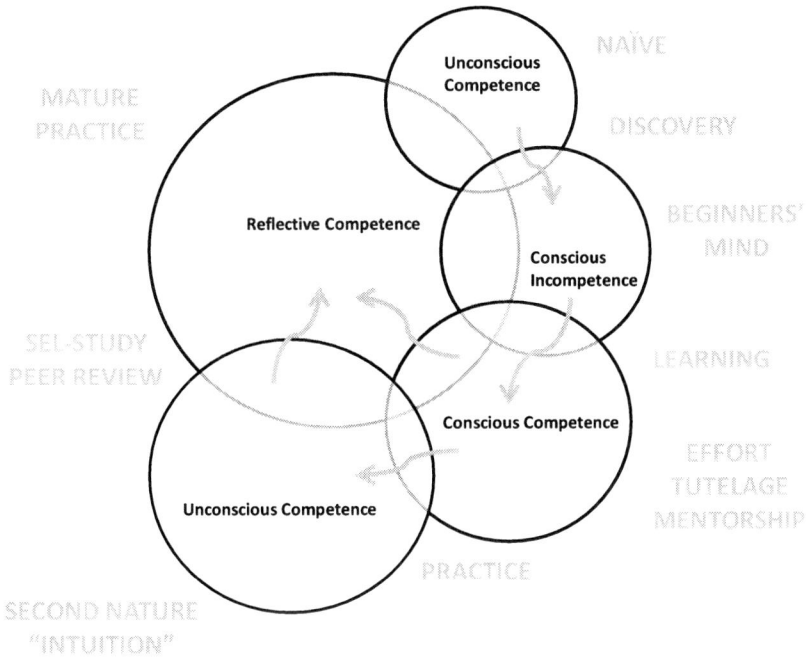

Figure 2.3 – Competency Model. Courtsey of Will Taylor, Chair, Department of Homeopathic Medicine, National College of Natural Medicine, Portland, Oregon, USA, March 2007

With this model in mind the implications are clear. A decision must be made, for each role, as to where to place the bar for the recognition of competency, and also how the individual should progress toward it. For example, after completion of initial training should we grant 'conditional' competency that allows the individual to operate plant with on-going supervision through a period of consolidation prior to final sign-off. Perhaps we should schedule training to be delivered in progressive phases?

Linked conceptually to this model is the progressive scheme for skills acquisition put forward by the Dreyfus brothers in 1980 and which is now very much part of the lingua franca of the L&D world. With this model the learner progresses in five stages through to a level of true expertise. The concept of competence here is again shown to be cumulative and increasingly less conscious. Michael Eraut (6) describes the five stages as follows:

Level of competence	Characteristic Behaviours
Novice	• "rigid adherence to taught rules or plans". • no exercise of "discretionary judgment".
Advanced Beginner	• limited "situational perception". • all aspects of work treated separately with equal importance.
Competent	• "coping with crowdedness" (multiple activities, accumulation of information). • some perception of actions in relation to goals. • deliberate planning. • formulates routines.
Proficient	• holistic view of situation. • prioritizes importance of aspects. • "perceives deviations from the normal pattern". • employs maxims for guidance, with meanings that adapt to the situation at hand.
Expert	• transcends reliance on rules, guidelines, and maxims • "intuitive grasp of situations based on deep, tacit understanding" • has "vision of what is possible" • uses "analytical approaches" in new situations or in case of problems.

Competence, in the Dreyfus scheme, clearly aligns with conscious competence. Nevertheless, setting the bar for signing off competence will depend on specific context and criticality. In complex roles, true expertise generally takes considerable time to acquire and it would be unrealistic to insist on any equation of competence with the expert role. Raising the bar to the level of proficiency might however be reasonable in some circumstances. This is a discussion that should occur between HR / L&D operational management and expert role incumbents.

BEYOND FUNCTIONAL COMPETENCE

The Burch and Dreyfus perspectives on competence were largely focused on what people do in their jobs – on functionality. Over time however, most organisations have come to realise that competence is a more complex creature and should also account for the range of expected behaviours. Consequently the work of David McClelland dating from the 1960's has been increasingly influential.

Significantly, in 1973 McClelland published work which promoted a shift from testing for functional competence and "intelligence" to aligning and assessing people against the behaviours, traits and qualities of acknowledged expert performers in specific roles. His approach is therefore a broadening of the concept of competence to the more qualitative description that we now refer to as competency. Consequently we have seen two contrasting approaches developed in parallel. The essential differences are shown in the table below.

Competence-based approach	Competency-based approach
Function / skill based.	Focused on behaviours.
Assessed against acknowledged standard.	Assessed against observed exemplary behaviours.
Measurements of the "what" is done.	Measurement of "how" things are done.

The need for clarity around performance expectation has led to the birth of the 'competency statement' in various forms and their accumulation into 'competency frameworks' for specific professional or vocational areas. The process of role mapping (already described in section 2) could be regarded as a competency framework of sorts, but these are most often rooted in functional description. They serve to inform the development of comprehensive frameworks.

These frameworks exist in a variety of formats but are essentially matrices which set organisational levels / roles against competencies and then infill with descriptors which interpret what the competency means at each specific level.

OCCUPATIONALLY SPECIFIC COMPETENCE - ROLE MAPPING.

The purpose of the basic role map is to provide a detailed specification of what the incumbent is expected to do (role functions) in a specific role, in a specific organisation, at a specific time. In that sense they are unique and do not transfer *holus bolus* to other organisations. They are therefore fundamentally different from generic competency frameworks which will be discussed later.

A role map should also describe the relative importance of the required functions (criticality). Fully developed maps may go on to identify other requirements such as enabling skills and aptitudes. These are extremely useful for recruiting or promoting into the role. Mapping roles is a time-consuming process and requires a level of expertise that can prove costly where it is not available internally. Consequently, very few organisations are comprehensively mapped. However, those that are fully mapped are much better placed to drive key management and HR processes.

There is no standard format or template for a role map, but due to the common sense logic involved, the variants are inevitably very similar. The mapping process first identifies the primary functions associated with the role. These are simple, high level descriptors, generally few in number and are perhaps best thought of as the basic skeleton or framework of the role upon which all the detail is suspended. For example, if we look at the role of an airport security supervisor we might identify the following:

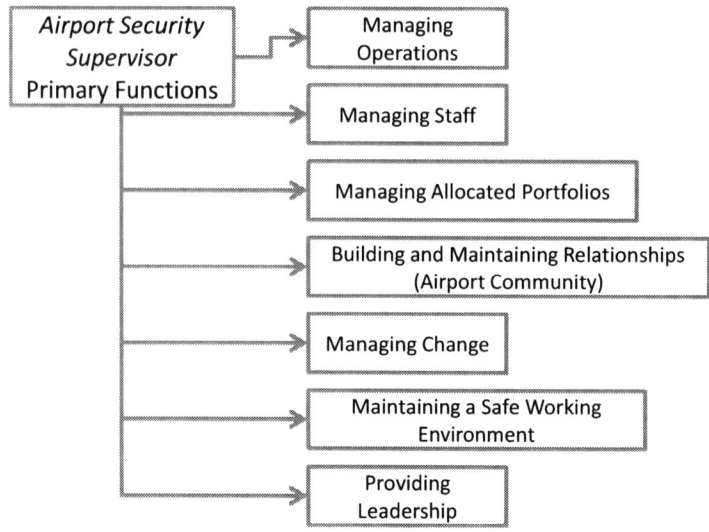

Figure 2.4 – Example of role breakdown to primary functions

Each of these primary functions must then be opened up to reveal the associated tasks i.e. what those primary functions translate to in terms of definable task areas. This analysis takes us down to the second level of the hierarchy. So, if we look specifically at the "managing operations" primary function, we might find the following breakdown:

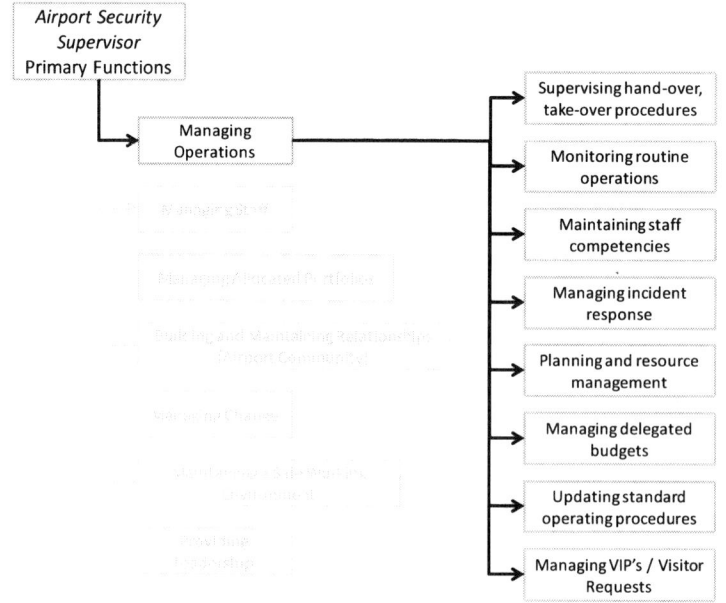

Figure 2.5 – Example of specific primary function breakdown to associated tasks.

The third, (and usually final) level of "drill down" analysis involves opening up each of the associated tasks to identify associated actions i.e. the various procedures required to complete a given task. It is unusual and often difficult to drill down further. To do so will most likely result in an unnecessary quagmire of detail, quickly consigning the document to the "too hard basket" where it will languish indefinitely. Figure 2.6 illustrates this third level.

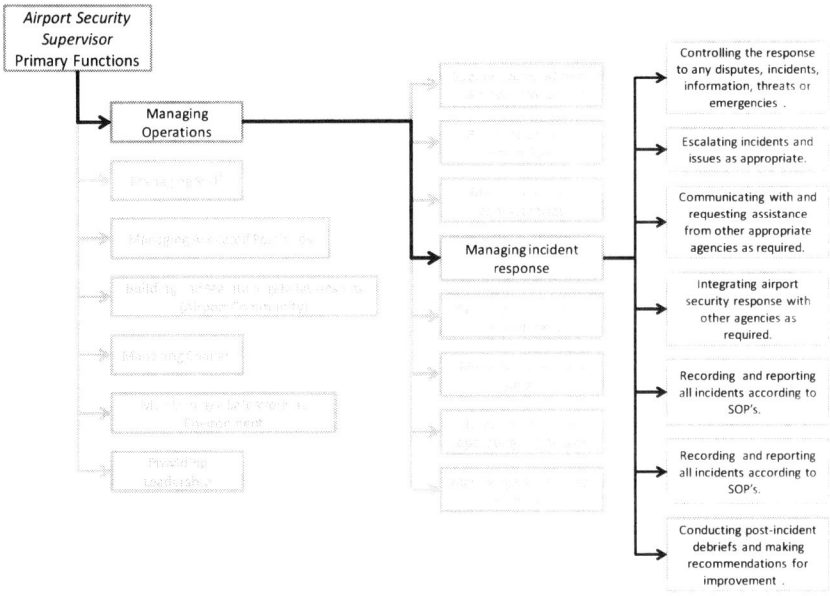

Figure 2.6 – Example of associated task breakdown to associated activities.

Getting role incumbents to identify all the associated actions can be a difficult process. By far the best method is to encourage the individual to work through the task as a process, step by step. This will then reveal the activity involved and enable sensible judgements to be made about what to include. Analysing the associated task "managing incident response" we might find the associated actions shown in figure 2.6.

The next and usually final stage of the mapping analysis is to consider the criticality of each component. Although role incumbents are often loath to admit it, not everything they do is of critical importance. Much of what they do may actually be routine and unlikely to impact significantly if delayed or perhaps not done at all. This is the fundamental rationale that supports the prioritisation of workloads, providing a more strategic approach.

Identifying relative criticality also underpins all those management functions previously discussed, especially performance management. Assessment of performance should be aligned primarily to the critical aspects of the role. This is the stuff that really matters. Focusing unduly on the non-critical is irrational and unfair if the individual is performing well in the critical areas.

So how is the assessment of criticality done? There are a number of methods currently employed. Companies using the balanced scorecard approach to measuring performance might favour "weighting" by the allocation of percentages – but this can become very complicated and difficult to apply practically. Simple rating systems are always the best option. An example is that developed by the US Department of Labour where required performance levels are categorised as follows:

- **Mastery (M)** – this indicates the highest level of performance. The need here is for 100% familiarity and compliance to standards or protocols. The individual should not need to approach others for assistance or to consult procedural manuals. Mastery indicates activity critical to task achievement. The individual should be capable of doing it right first time every time – virtually without thinking. We could think of this as "unconscious competence". There are very obvious examples e.g. Cardio-Pulmonary Resuscitation (CPR) is clearly a mastery level skill for a paramedic. If the casualty has no pulse and has stopped breathing there is obviously no time to consult the manual!

- **High Conformity (HC)** – this indicates a high level of performance but the need is not absolutely critical. In these situations the individual can be afforded some scope and time to adjust her approach and eventual performance on matters of detail, either through further attempts or through taking advice. In this sense they are conforming, to a high degree, to best practice. Referring again to our paramedic, high conformity would be expected in the application of bandages and dressings. However, getting this "text book" right first time is seldom critical and the patient is unlikely to suffer if several adjustments are made. We could think of this as "conscious competence".

- **Low Conformity (LC)** – this indicates a relatively low level of required competence. Typically this might be allocated to background knowledge, peripheral skills or additional expertise that individuals might acquire through refinement of technique. These areas have little or no impact on the successful achievement of the task in hand. For our paramedic, understanding the long-term treatment of diabetes is a good example of low conformity. In terms of processes and compliance to procedures we would not expect anything beyond basic understanding or familiarity.

When categorising performance requirements in this way we also have to be aware that it must be done across the three dimensions of primary function, associated task, and associated activity. This simply recognises that while an activity might be critical for the achievement of a task, that task might actually be a low conformity item. Being clear about these things ensures that the team member, the manager and the L&D staff will be sharply focused on the key areas of performance and learning need.

Figure 2.7 illustrates a single page extract from a role map using a typical basic template. Note that the performance level of primary function, associated task and associated activities are assessed and categorised for the required performance level.

Role Ref.	Primary Function	Perf. Cat.	Associated Tasks	Perf. Cat.	Associated Activities	Perf. Cat.
	Role – Shift Manager (Re-Cycle Plant)					
	Primary Function: Assuring continuity of production.					
1.	Assuring continuity of production.	M	1.1 - Planning shift production.	M	1.1.1 - Liaising with the previous shift to understand the current situation (Hand-over, take-over).	M
					1.1.2 - Confirming throughput requirement for the shift.	M
					1.1.3 - Assessing manning levels, skills, raw stock etc .required for the shift.	HC
					1.1.4 - Identifying and planning to address the issues / risks that may impact on the ability to complete the plan	
					1.1.5 - Communicating the plan to the team through face-to-face, one-on-one meetings, Email and logbooks.	HC
					1.1.6 - Providing the appropriate information to ensure an effective shift hand-over.	HC
			1.2 - Ensuring conformity to operational and production standards.	M	1.2.1 - Ensuring plant is running according to SOP's.	M
					1.2.2 - Ensuring operators fully understand plant functionality and requirements.	HC
					1.2.3 - Monitoring plant management systems for non-conformity.	M
					1.2.4 - Communicating with operators to assess and monitor any potential non-conformity.	M
					1.2.5 - Assessing impact of any non-conformity and assisting affected operator when required.	M
					1.2.6 - Monitoring the general state of the plant.	HC
					1.2.7 - Monitoring progress against the plan and communicating any changes to operators and other stakeholders.	M
			1.3 – Problem solving.	HC	1.3.1 - Assessing problems and their potential impacts on production and the effective working of the plant.	HC
					1.3.2 - When required, re-organising production factors (production rate, product type, people etc.) to maximise production or assist with problem resolution.	HC
					1.3.3 - Forming action plans appropriate to the severity of the problem and the current state of the plant.	HC
					1.3.4 - Implementing action plans.	HC
					1.3.5 - When appropriate, delegating responsibilities to the relevant Technical Manager.	HC
					1.3.6 - Reporting on incidents that have impacted (or have the potential to impact) quality or quantity of production.	HC
			1.4 - Routine review and forward planning	HC	1.4.1 - Participating in production meetings to review previous 24 hours and plan for the next 24 hour period.	HC
			1.5 – Routine reporting	HC	1.5.1 - Completing 24 hour shift report accurately and on time.	HC

Figure 2.7 – Single page extract from a typical role map using a basic template.

In this example "assuring continuity of production" is understandably categorised as mastery – but this is not the case for all the associated actions. This is particularly true for the problem-solving activities - presumably because this is a shared activity with the team and, if necessary, could be conducted in a trial and error fashion.

The great benefit of categorising expected performance is that it provides additional clarity around proper work focus for both the role incumbent and the manager. With the role map in place it is a relatively simple exercise to compare it with any new functional requirements signalled by the strategic planning process and then to identify any apparent gaps. If an entirely new role is required the map will need to be developed from scratch.

When we bear in mind that figure 2.7 is only a one page extract, it becomes clear that the mapping of all roles within an organisation can be a time consuming process that will require significant senior management determination over the long term if it is to succeed. Nevertheless, those organisations that have achieved comprehensive mapping have been able to go on to build learning and development frameworks that are accurately focused on the learning gap. This quickly returns huge dividends and ensures that learning is indeed strategically "lean". So what is the mapping process? Given the complexity of the task it is always tempting to take shortcuts, but the following process remains an ideal approach.

Step 1	Identify and establish a contributing survey group i.e. those with a legitimate view of the role, for example, managers, peers, subordinates, unions, health & safety representatives, impacted departments etc. In some cases, customers might be included in this group.
Step 2	Carry out initial discussions with relevant managers and role incumbents to identify the primary functions.

Step 3	Confirm primary functions by survey of the most appropriate wider contributing group. At the same time ask contributors to categorise required performance for these i.e. mastery, high conformity, low conformity.
Step 4	Select a focus group to identify associated tasks and associated activities for each of the primary functions – together with related performance categories.
Step 5	Compile draft map. Present to wider contributing group for confirmation. At this stage contributors should be invited to add associated tasks or activities which may have been missed by the focus group. It may also be useful to ask for comment on aspects such as the frequency of involvement in given tasks and perhaps on the perception of training / learning priority for the organisation. This information helps to define the role more acutely. Organisations which sustain roles that may be potentially dangerous often use the role map to identify and rate tasks for risk. Once again, this assists with the prioritisation of training.

Role maps are essentially a framework in which the tasks and activities associated with the role are identified in detail and the required level of performance assigned to each. As a result they provide a matrix for specifying "performance" against a notional level or standard. When we are able to apply a map to a complete class or group (e.g. infantrymen), the role map becomes generic to that group. Every soldier will be bound by the same expectations of functional performance.

The most highly developed role map systems have evolved into full blooded competency frameworks, offering extremely detailed guidance. Unsurprisingly perhaps, the best examples are those developed by the military. The role maps relate the concepts of mastery and high conformity to specific learning / training objectives and assessment criteria which may be used to define the required standard precisely. These sit as a sub-reference to what it actually means to be "competent". As a consequence, measuring the gap between existing and desired learning is relatively straightforward and is based on hard data.

As an example, the role map for an infantryman might cite 'navigating expertly across all forms of terrain" as a primary function. This might then be broken down to include the associated task of "locating own position" which in turn might yield the associated activity "using a prismatic compass to fix own position". At this point the map will indicate a training reference which (most often) spells out, as a behavioural objective" the real detail of the standard expected before an individual can be considered "competent". An example is given below:

Objective	Test conditions	Test standards
The infantryman will be able to fix his own position in open / remote country.	Given good visibility, a 1:50000 topographical map, prismatic compass and mils protractor.	To within 100 m square i.e. a 6 figure grid reference, + or – 1 figure in the 3rd and 6th figures.

Precise specification of this kind standardises the meaning of competence and renders training, assessment and evaluation completely transparent. Skills such as navigation are commonly referred to as "hard skills". They are visible, tangible, and easily defined. The parameters are easily determined and fixed. "Soft skills" on the other hand will always elude exact prescription. These are the skills that depend on personality, specific situations and culture e.g. management and leadership.

The only useful way of describing the soft skill functions is by way of higher level descriptors that can be applied universally in a more abstract manner. This has led to the development of generic competency frameworks which most, if not all organisations or individuals can access if they so wish. They are "transferable".

GENERIC COMPETENCY FRAMEWORKS.

For all intents and purposes, generic competency frameworks fall into two distinct categories:

- **Standard frameworks** i.e. can be applied as a standard to all those fulfilling the same role. Perhaps the best examples would be the framework applicable to all police officers of the same rank operating within the same police force. Similarly we would expect all train drivers operating on the same rail system to have the same knowledge and skills. These frameworks are applicable to classes of employees. They are not universally transferrable.

- **Universal frameworks** i.e. can be applied in any organisational context. In practice these are invariably linked to what are often referred to as core or key skills e.g. management, leadership, communication, information technology, inter-personal skills etc. Although they are universal in potential, organisations will often adopt a framework and then focus on selected competencies according to perceived needs at a given time.

Universal frameworks also differ significantly in terms of scope and range. For example, management and leadership competency frameworks usually attempt to define, in graduated terms, what a particular competency means at all levels of management to which it might be applicable. This can lead to some issues around adequate differentiation between the levels.

Competency frameworks of this kind are big business. Many are marketed globally (e.g. PDI Ninth House; Lominger; Margerison-McCann; the Leadership Practices Inventory etc.). However, even though they represent a comprehensive analysis, each is inevitably based on a favoured philosophical position and therefore focuses critical emphasis differently. An organisation will select a particular framework because the underpinning philosophy suits its particular view of the world, its culture and values. Despite the undoubted quality of the analysis present in many of these frameworks, organisations generally find themselves "interpreting" the individual competency descriptors in order to find a more localised meaning and thus able to identify development needs more accurately. Many will successfully adapt the "bought in" product. Others will become frustrated by the high level, non-specific descriptors and move on to developing a variant framework of their own.

The identification of learning needs does not end with the servicing of the strategic planning process. By definition, planning focuses principally on the future and seldom addresses on-going business as usual activity (for which plans should already exist). Learning and development professionals must be mindful of the fact that an exclusive focus on the future may sell the present short. When core operations have not apparently changed (business as usual) it is all too easy to assume that the learning we put in place last year will suffice for this year.

A regular review (usually annual) is the best way to avoid this pitfall. Figure 2.8 provides an overview of the typical annual review concepts.

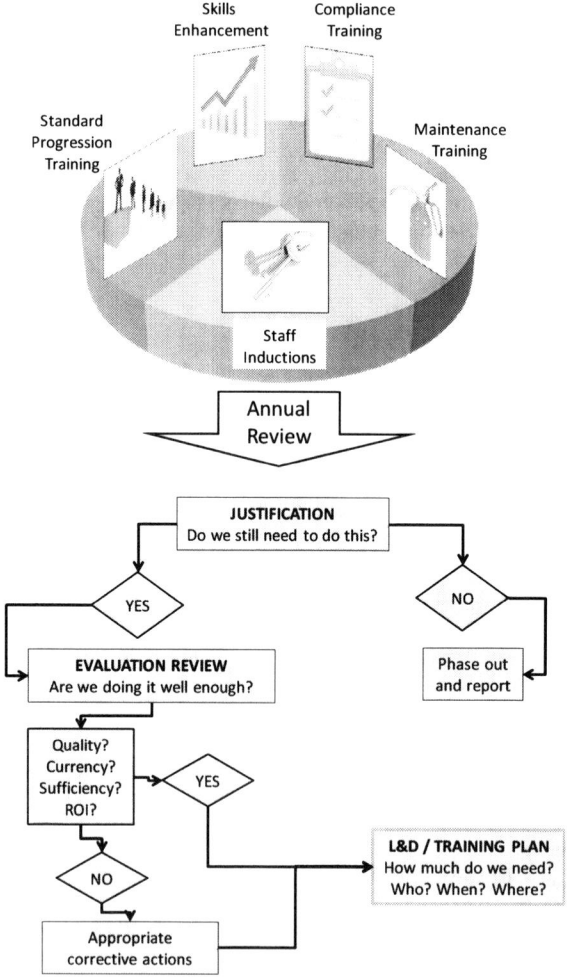

Figure 2.8 – Business as usual learning needs annual review

BAU learning activity typically falls into the following categories:

- Staff inductions – for new employees or for staff transferring to new departments
- Compliance training – mandatory learning or recertification associated with legislative requirements, codes of practice or company policy e.g. workplace
- First aid provision, confined space working, handling dangerous goods etc.
- Maintenance training – typically this would be refresher training intended to keep the less-often used or critical skill sets up to required performance standards e.g. physical fitness training, evacuation procedures etc.
- Skills / knowledge enhancement – typically needed when procedures, processes or equipment is upgraded rather than significantly altered e.g. detail changes to legislation or a component upgrade that requires changes to standard operating procedures.

In most organisations BAU learning activity makes up the bulk of learning activity and consumes most of the L&D budget. Consequently it deserves on-going attention through regular review. The review process should be driven by HR as a best practice activity, particularly in terms of ensuring an appropriate return on investment (ROI).

Currency of material is perhaps the biggest concern. Continuing to deliver out of date material is a common cause of disenchantment with training. In the context of safety, out of date materials could of course have serious consequences.

The key considerations for the L&D staff are:

- **Justification** – the need for this particular learning activity has been identified and substantiated in the past, but does the need still exist or has it changed in any significant way? These questions seem obvious enough, but so often it is left to the front line employees to tell management that a particular training event is now irrelevant and no longer needed. Methods for gathering this information systematically will vary according to organisational structures, but consultation with appropriate managers and stakeholders should be a standard (albeit critical) third quarter L&D activity.
- **Evaluation review** – this is a summative review of evaluations carried out during the year. Kirkpatrick level 1 and level 2 data should be available more or less immediately following completion of the learning event. Availability of Level 3 and 4 data may be a longer term issue (see section 7 for a full explanation of Kirkpatrick and other evaluation systems). The review should reveal whether the learning event or programme:
  - Has achieved the required outcomes and been delivered in an appropriate manner – quality
  - Remains up to date in content and relevance - currency
  - Has been delivered to all staff designated as requiring it - sufficiency
  - Has added value, either qualitative or quantitative – return on investment (ROI)

- **Corrective action** – these are the steps taken to rectify deficiencies in quality before the learning activity is repeated.
- **The annual L&D plan** – this is the summary of all learning planned to take place in the forthcoming year. It will include both the BAU requirements and the additional new learning requirements identified through analysis of the strategic planning process. These new requirements may of course become BAU in following years. The draft plan must then be costed and an approved budget signed off to support it.

ALTERNATIVES TO GAP ANALYSIS.

Thus far we have focused, more or less exclusively, on identifying organisational learning and development needs through gap or discrepancy analysis referencing the strategic planning process. This will certainly provide a stringent rationale for how the training dollar is spent. Nevertheless, relying only on this formal approach may define learning and development too narrowly.

Gap analysis is a precision tool, rather akin to a surgeon's scalpel. It will identify, and hopefully eventually cure issues clearly evidenced. However, the long term health and well-being of the patient depends on taking a more holistic view of needs which, in practice, means looking beyond overt organisational business strategy to focus in on the development needs of individual employees. Only then can we ensure that key issues such as succession and retention are properly addressed. This is particularly critical when dealing with critical longer term "pipeline" issues such as leadership development. Focus at the individual level reveals a wide range of tools and techniques for consideration.

IDENTIFYING AND PROVIDING FOR INDIVIDUAL LEARNING NEEDS.

As a general principle we are entitled to say that the identification of individual learning needs is the joint responsibility of the individual in question and his line manager. It is not the responsibility or the prerogative of the HR department. All well and good, but the reality encountered in most organisations is one of general ignorance. So often, neither the individual nor the manager has any real understanding of how to go about it. Worse still, one or perhaps both have little inclination to engage in the process. The annual round of discussion around personal development plans may be regarded as a thankless chore by managers, or perhaps even dreaded by those who are at least conscious of their ineptitude in this respect. Individual development planning becomes a whole lot easier (and more rewarding) once a few key "rules of thumb" are taken on board and understood by both parties. So what are they?

First principle – We may all prefer to think that we are unique but, by and large, groups or teams of people conform to well-established norms. What does this mean in practice? Essentially it gives the manager some license (albeit loosely) to apply the normal curve of distribution when thinking about who is seeking or may be ready for development. It is not unusual to find managers "beating themselves up" because they cannot seem to inspire every member of their team to plunge headlong into personal development. Misguidedly, they may see this as a failing of their personal leadership, when in fact they are simply dealing with normal variations in individual attitudes and personal circumstances. Conversely, managers may opt to demonise those individuals who may, for the present, be content with their current role, as negative, uncooperative and unsupportive of team goals.

Of course we should never rush to fit people into neat statistical templates. Nevertheless it is certainly useful to have a mental model of what constitutes normal behaviour. This allows us to keep things in perspective. Figure 2.9 offers such a model.

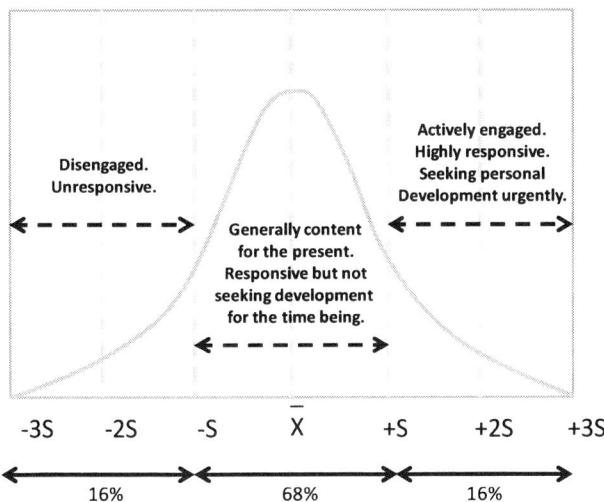

Figure 2.9 – "Normalised" model of typical team reaction to personal development opportunities.

This tells us that in any sizeable team or department we should expect a small percentage of staff to be beating a path to the manager's door with constant requests for personal development. Equally we should anticipate that a small percentage will, for a variety of reasons, be disengaged and even perhaps resentful of any pressure to develop themselves further. Between these two extremes are the majority who are largely content with their present lot and, for the time being, are not actively seeking development opportunities.

Alternatively, staff may be keen to progress but be at a stage in their private or working lives where they cannot take on any additional loading e.g. those with young families that demand attention or those engaged in significant long-term work projects. These are people who possess the capability but not the capacity. If managers truly need to develop these individuals then they must find ways to improve their capacity. This is a mental model only and should not be taken too literally. Its usefulness lies in providing managers with a pragmatic perspective.

Second principle – Managers, and those they manage, should avoid leaping to formal, structured training or learning opportunities as the best solution for individual development planning. Reaching immediately for the course handbook may signal a degree of pro-activity, but unless it is preceded by analysis of the alternatives, the result may ultimately be a waste of time and money. The prevalence of formal courses as a solution to development planning is most likely due to:

- Managers having insufficient time to consider the full range of options.
- Managers and staff being unaware of the range of alternative strategies available.
- Traditional "pathway" associations i.e. the acceptance that individuals moving to certain roles always attend certain course or programmes.
- "Flavour of the month" pressures i.e. the assumption that what is new is necessarily better and must be tried
- Well-chosen formal learning is, without doubt, immensely valuable. Nevertheless, research tells us that formal learning actually drives a relatively small percentage of individual development. Once again, a mental model is a useful backdrop to identifying the most appropriate solutions for individual learning needs. The 70/20/10 principle is useful here, but once again should not be interpreted prescriptively.

The 70/20/10 model was originally developed by Lombardo, Eichinger and McCall at the Centre for Creative Leadership as a means to meet the learning and development needs of emerging managers. Consequently, its context was relatively specific to management development. However, since its introduction the concept of meeting learning needs through an appropriate balance of formal learning, informal / social learning, and on-the-job experience has migrated to a wide variety of organisational environments. The original model was based on extensive research and found that for the western world management context approximately 70% of learning occurred through challenging experiences gained directly in the workplace, around 20% occurred through interaction with others via relationships, networking or feedback, and only around 10% occurred through formal training inputs. Although research shows that the actual ratios vary somewhat according to particular contexts, the message is clear i.e. when looking at individual learning and development needs managers should seek to provide an appropriately balanced blend of learning opportunities. Figure 2.10 illustrates the 70/20/10 concept.

With this model in mind, managers must ask two key questions and attempt to reconcile the answers:

- What learning / development does the organisation need this individual to undergo? This should derive ultimately from the strategic planning process but may be driven by unforeseen developments.

- What learning / development does the individual believe they need or simply want to undertake? This is likely to be driven primarily by longer term career aspirations and may or may not be relevant to current organisational need.

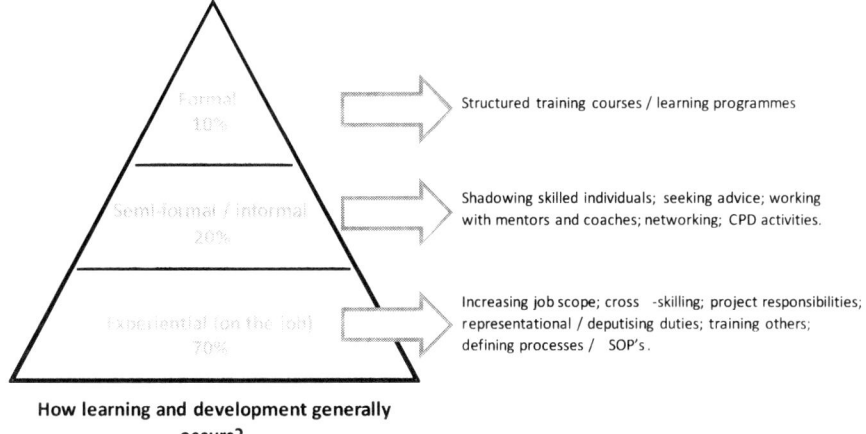

Structured training courses / learning programmes

Shadowing skilled individuals; seeking advice; working with mentors and coaches; networking; CPD activities.

Increasing job scope; cross -skilling; project responsibilities; representational / deputising duties; training others; defining processes / SOP's.

How learning and development generally occurs?

Figure 2.10 – the 70/20/10 model

We have seen that, in a properly functioning organisation, learning needs for individuals will mostly devolve from the strategic planning process. Nevertheless, even in the best-ordered environments unforeseen events will occur that drive the need for additional knowledge or skills. For example, unexpected resignations may result in a "shuffling of the pack" as an individual steps up or across into the vacant role. In such cases line managers must move quickly to identify and provide the appropriate level of support to enable the individual to expand into the new role – perhaps through role shadowing, mentoring, or one-on-one coaching.

In situations like these, a simple gap analysis to identify required skills may not be enough. If the new role is different in kind as well as degree, questions need to be asked about behavioural change and the type of learning or guidance the individual might need to accomplish the shift. We see this often with individuals moving out of the team into their first supervisory management role, perhaps as shift leader or charge hand. While they can quickly absorb the additional administrative skills, many will experience great difficulties in "letting go" and acquiring sufficient detachment to succeed in the new job. This means of course that line managers must be prepared to revisit and perhaps update any development plan put in place for individual staff members.

This would certainly be the case for individuals falling short of the organisational performance requirements. If the shortfall is directly linked to key accountabilities or performance objectives then the development plan created to support the desired performance may be inadequate.

The danger here is that managers will rush too quickly to L&D as a solution. A shortfall in performance may result from a variety of causes. Throwing people into further training, when skill levels are not actually the issue, will inevitably make things worse. The dilemma faced by managers here is an ethical one i.e. distinguishing appropriately between *poor performance* which is seldom related to skills and *under performance*, which usually is.

To accuse an individual of poor performance when they are in fact under-performing through no direct fault of their own is unethical. People under-perform largely because they are not sufficiently enabled, perhaps through poor equipment, insufficient resources, personal issues such as illness or indeed lack of appropriate training. Poor performance is most often related to lack of motivation resulting in the individual choosing not to perform to the best of their ability.

Organisations generally have clear expectations for performance levels. When individual employees fail to live up to these expectations, managers must look carefully at what is actually going on before leaping to the training budget. A useful tool here is the performance analysis quadrant (Jones 1993) shown at figure 2.11 overleaf.

Effective managers will have a range of strategies for gleaning information on individual performance e.g.

- Personal observation of the individual at work.
- Frequent informal discussion on progress and issues.
- Planned formal feedback sessions e.g. quarterly one-on-ones.
- Feedback from the individual's workmates or team members.

Taken together, this information should allow the manager to answer the two key questions shown in figure 2.11, concerning job knowledge or skills and attitude. Feeding answers into the matrix promotes clear thinking about the probable issue and its solution.

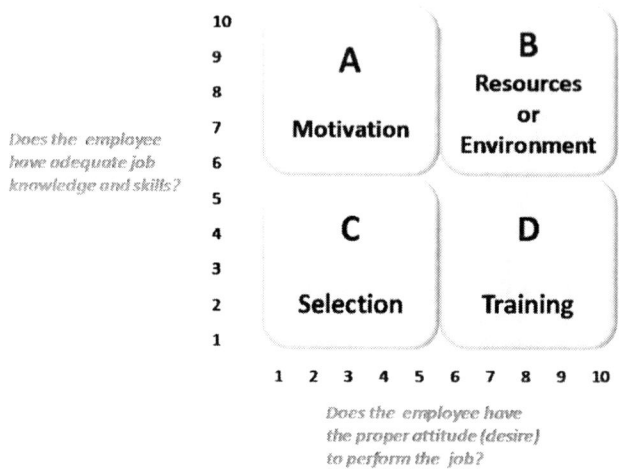

Figure 2.11 – The Performance Analysis Quadrant (PAQ)

Quadrant A (Motivation issue) When an employee clearly has sufficient knowledge and skills to do the job (i.e. he has already demonstrated adequate performance) but is now displaying an inappropriate attitude, this is most likely to be a motivational problem, and may be classed as poor performance. The solution will be rooted in behavioural adjustment – not training. Care must be taken to isolate the cause of the fall-off in motivation. After all, it may be the manager's own poor leadership!

Quadrant B (Resource or environment issue) On occasion we will find that performance is unsatisfactory even though the individual's attitude and skill levels are more than adequate. In these situations the issue generally lies with inadequate resources (tools to do the job) or negative environmental issues (which may include people) that impact negatively on the ability to perform. The solution here, obviously, is to identify the impacting factors and correct them.

Quadrant C (Selection) We should never encounter individuals in this situation – but of course it does happen. An individual with a poor attitude and no skills simply should not be in the job. He needs to be moved to something more suitable, or, if the attitude cannot be improved, performance managed out of the organisation.

Quadrant D (Training) Only when we encounter the individual who clearly wishes to perform to his full potential (a positive attitude) but is lacking in skills or job knowledge, should we move to a training / learning intervention of some kind.

To summarise, effective identification of learning needs will depend on the clarity and currency of role descriptions and the ability of managers to use simple conceptual tools to focus their thinking on the real issues. The next step in the strategic approach is to analyse the identified need in order to determine what kind of intervention is most appropriate and so provide the learning development team or external providers with a full and clear brief.

SELF-IDENTIFIED LEARNING NEEDS.

Proactive and ambitious individuals will regularly review their careers and adjust their goals. They may do this privately or in consultation with family, friends, career advisers and perhaps even their managers. As a result they may identify a learning or developmental need and then look to their manager for support.

For the most part these requests are usually reasonable i.e. they do have some relevance to organisational strategy. However, most managers will be familiar with the staff member who insists that the flower arranging course really would be good for company profits and consequently having to turn down such requests! This is a stereotype of course, but individuals will not necessarily view their own development needs entirely in alignment with departmental business needs. Perhaps they are seriously considering a change in direction, or see themselves as future managers. Occasionally they may just have spotted a course that seems vaguely interesting and will get them out of the office for a few days.

Either way, managers need to have a clear mental process for dealing with these self-identified needs rationally and fairly. Without a clear process in mind they may find themselves subject to pressures they find difficult to resist. The "squeakiest wheel gets most of the oil" is an all too familiar scenario. The table below provides a simple set of questions which managers can use to evaluate these self-identified requests.

Staff initiated requests			
1	Does the request have an obvious alignment with business strategy (short or long term)? *If no* – examine the individual's motives through further discussion to identify any potential indirect ROI e.g. long term motivation and retention of a skilled employee. Wider consultation may be needed before a final decision on support is made. *If yes* – move to question 2.	Yes	No
2	Is the request aligned to a well-conceived career development strategy on the part of the individual? *If no* – advise the individual that more thought should be given to how the request supports his / her career progression. *If yes* – go to question 3.	Yes	No
3	Does the request align to the department's view of ideal career progression for the individual? *If no* – advise the individual that the request will fall into a lower priority category and will be further considered after all higher priority development has been accommodated i.e. requests that do align with the departmental view. *If yes* – got to question 4.	Yes	No
4	Can the required development be provided without undue impact on the business? i.e. appropriate expertise and resources are available and any required time off-job is reasonable. *If yes* – go to question 5. *If no* – advise the individual that the request cannot be accommodated at this time. Wider consultation may be needed before a final decision on support is made.	Yes	No
5	If actioned, how will the approved request be viewed by other members of the team? Would this result in any friction or animosity? *If yes* – advise the individual that the request will be approved providing an appropriate balance can be achieved across the department / team. *If no* - advise the individual that the request will be subsequently action-planned.	Yes	No

3. TRAINING AND LEARNING NEEDS ANALYSIS

It is worth emphasising that identifying a learning need and analysing that need are two distinctly different processes. Clarity is important here because the two processes are so often thrown together as "TNA" – usually with the "analysis" component ending up as a poor relation. So many needs analyses do a good job of gap analysis and building an overall picture of needs for planning purpose, but often fail to examine those needs to work out exactly what kind of learning we are actually dealing with. Identifying needs is akin to the "Houston we have a problem!" scenario. Needs analysis is the business of finding out what kind of problem.

Effective analysis, as always, depends on referencing against established models or techniques – whether they are generally established (e.g. educational principles) or organisationally unique systems. The L&D analyst uses those models to categorise need in order to provide a proper brief for development or selection from existing provision.

STRANDING.

The base level of analysis is "stranding". Essentially this is no more than the identification of the categories or classes of learning with which the organisation engages. Given the sheer diversity of organisation types, it is not surprising that there is no standard model. Nevertheless, there will certainly be broad similarities of learning activity between kindred organisations e.g. manufacturing, professions, service industries, emergency services etc.

The first level of analysis revolves around establishing the range of learning activity supported by the organisation. Typically, this will extend from easily justified "must do" induction and compliance training applicable to all or to large groups and driven by legislation or company policy, through to individualised development that is much more difficult to justify. Close inspection usually reveals a surprising number of permutations between the extremes. Understanding the graduations between these strands is essential for prioritising development and allocating budget. Figure 3.1 shows fairly typical stranding for a large commercial organisation.

These strands reflect the range of formal learning that goes on. However, we should never forget or undervalue the various types of informal learning that occurs on a daily basis. Informal mentoring, coaching, learning via organizational culture – these are difficult, if not impossible to analyse in a structured format, but are probably significant enough to merit a separate and distinct analysis.

As a general rule, the lower strands tend to be more "complex" i.e. there is a greater number and greater variety of learning events, often on a continuous turnover basis. However, these events also tend to be of shorter duration than those from the upper strands. By the time we get to strand 5 we will inevitably be dealing with small numbers of specially selected employees. However, regardless of stranding, once a learning gap has been identified, the same fundamental questions have to be answered if we are to complete the learning needs analysis. These are:

- What is the nature of the learning gap required?
- How would an acceptable level of competence or understanding be demonstrated?
- What kind of learning event will achieve the required competence or understanding most effectively?

The information gathered here provides the development team or the provider with a solid foundation. Without it, the sourcing of appropriate training or learning events leans toward the best guess scenario.

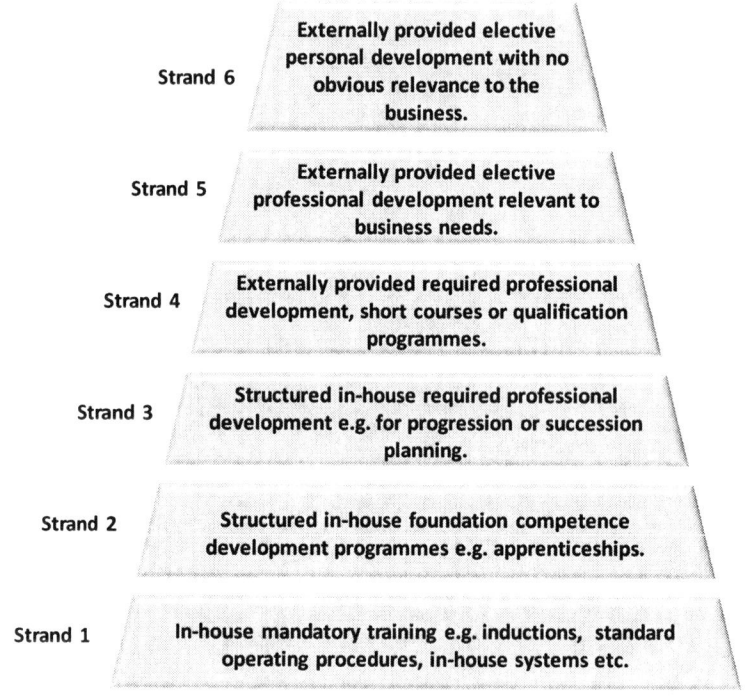

Figure 3.1 – Typical "stranding" of organisational learning activity.

THE NATURE OF THE LEARNING GAP – TAXONOMIC DESCRIPTION.

Learning cannot be simply defined. Even a cursory examination reveals progressive levels of engagement, input and output. Well designed learning activity will deliver content at the appropriate level of demand. To identify what is appropriate, the L&D specialist must be familiar with the range or "taxonomy" of options available. Considerable research has been done in this area and there are now a number of taxonomies or hierarchies currently informing the world of learning and development. Perhaps the best known of these in Benjamin Bloom's Taxonomy of Learning Domains dating from 1956. Bloom's analysis still provides a useful method of screening and filtering the learning gap to find out what is really involved and his scheme has been recently updated by Anderson and Krathwohl.(1)

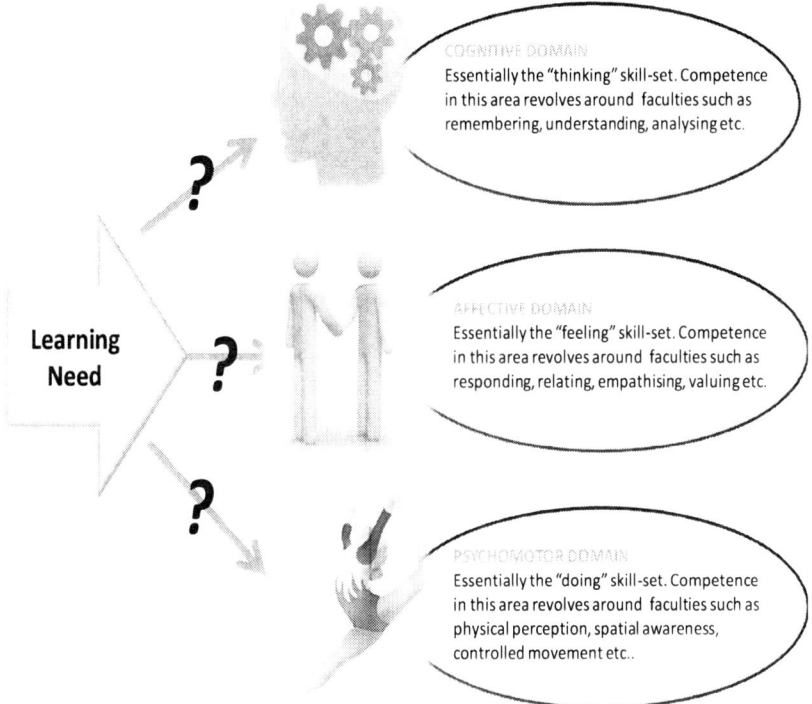

COGNITIVE DOMAIN
Essentially the "thinking" skill-set. Competence in this area revolves around faculties such as remembering, understanding, analysing etc.

AFFECTIVE DOMAIN
Essentially the "feeling" skill-set. Competence in this area revolves around faculties such as responding, relating, empathising, valuing etc.

PSYCHOMOTOR DOMAIN
Essentially the "doing" skill-set. Competence in this area revolves around faculties such as physical perception, spatial awareness, controlled movement etc..

Learning Need

Figure 3.2 – Bloom's Learning Domains

Figure 3.2 illustrates the foundation concept of Bloom's analysis i.e. that human learning can be classified into three "domains". These are not learning styles. The domains simply indicate classes of skills that specific learning activity will primarily target. The domains are not separate and isolated. They will frequently, if not always, interact to some degree. For example a dancer learning a new routine may focus primarily on the physical skills involved in executing the movements required but, as she masters the steps, shift the focus to the feeling engendered by movement and music. Thus she shifts from the psychomotor domain to the affective. Similarly an artist may be struck with awe before a great landscape and then, over time, come to understand the principles of colour and composition that combined to create such a powerful effect. Thus he moves from the affective domain to the cognitive. High level concepts such as this are of little practical use to the analysis of learning need. We have to go deeper to find concepts and a vocabulary that will help us identify the true nature of particular learning events. Bloom provides that depth by identifying the learning levels within each domain. Figure 3.3 shows Bloom's original scheme for the cognitive domain and the subtle revisions made by Anderson et al which are now accepted as being more in tune with current learning philosophies.

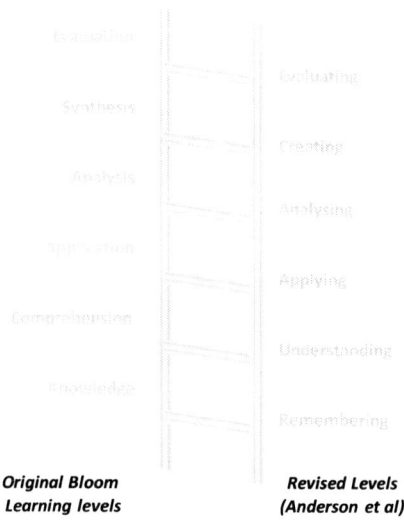

Original Bloom
Learning levels

Revised Levels
(Anderson et al)

Figure 3.3 – Bloom's taxonomy (cognitive domain)

The premise here is that while there is certainly a need for it, simple learning through memory is the least valuable since it is not necessarily a precursor to understanding. The highest (and most demanding) level of learning is evaluation. Learning of this kind equips the individual with the ability to compare, contrast, and draw appropriate conclusions about the relative value of ideas, systems etc. Figure 3.4 provides descriptors for the six cognitive levels.

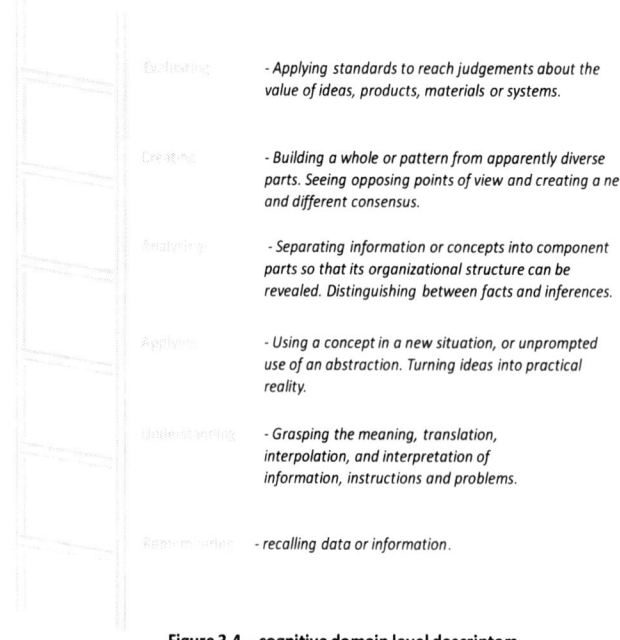

Evaluating   - *Applying standards to reach judgements about the value of ideas, products, materials or systems.*

Creating   - *Building a whole or pattern from apparently diverse parts. Seeing opposing points of view and creating a new and different consensus.*

Analysing   - *Separating information or concepts into component parts so that its organizational structure can be revealed. Distinguishing between facts and inferences.*

Applying   - *Using a concept in a new situation, or unprompted use of an abstraction. Turning ideas into practical reality.*

Understanding   - *Grasping the meaning, translation, interpolation, and interpretation of information, instructions and problems.*

Remembering   - *recalling data or information.*

Figure 3.4 – cognitive domain level descriptors

The cognitive domain generally receives the greatest attention in terms of analysing learning needs. This simply reflects the common understanding of learning as an essentially intellectual /mental activity. This view has been somewhat encouraged by the emphasis given to cognitive learning by the research community. Bloom himself focused primarily on this area, leaving detailed exploration of the affective and psychomotor domains to his followers.

The perceived importance of affective domain learning has expanded exponentially with the emergence of the emotional intelligence movement and the ever-increasing demand for "soft skills" within the manager's portfolio. Much of the current debate around "mindfulness" and "being in the moment" has its origins in the acceptance of the need for affective learning and competence. Figure 3.5 illustrates Bloom's analysis of the affective domain.

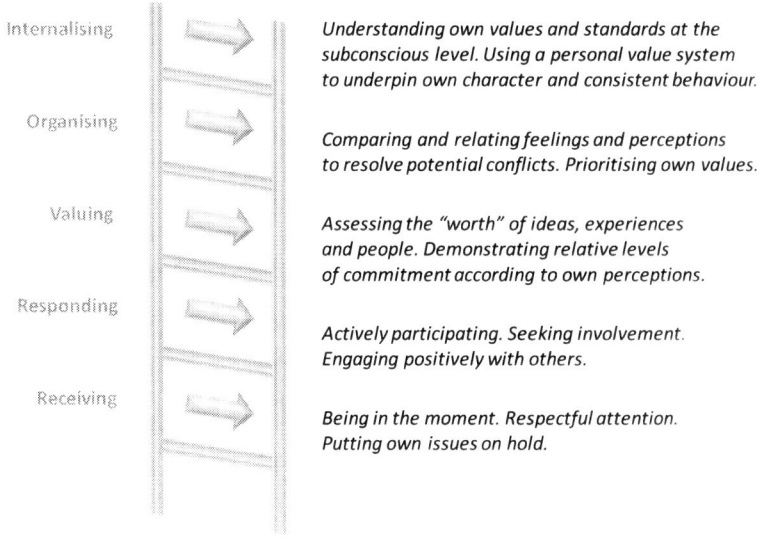

Figure 3.5 – Bloom's taxonomy (affective domain)

It is easy to see why learning of this kind is so difficult to specify, design and deliver. For the most part we are dealing with abstract, even indefinable learning that has different meanings for all concerned. For these reasons formal learning programmes seldom move beyond receiving and responding. Typically, learning at these levels occurs in programmes such as negotiating skills, interviewing skills, conflict resolution, performance management, assertiveness etc. Realistically, the levels above inhabit the realm of personal experience and reflection. "Valuing" might be addressed within learning activities such as leadership development.

Bloom's committee did very little work on psychomotor learning. We should remember that this work was done well before the era of multiple intelligence theory or the concept of emotional quotient (EQ). The psychomotor domain has subsequently been explored and populated with several schemes. Perhaps the most useful and accessible is that put forward by R.H. Dave. His scheme is illustrated at figure 3.6.

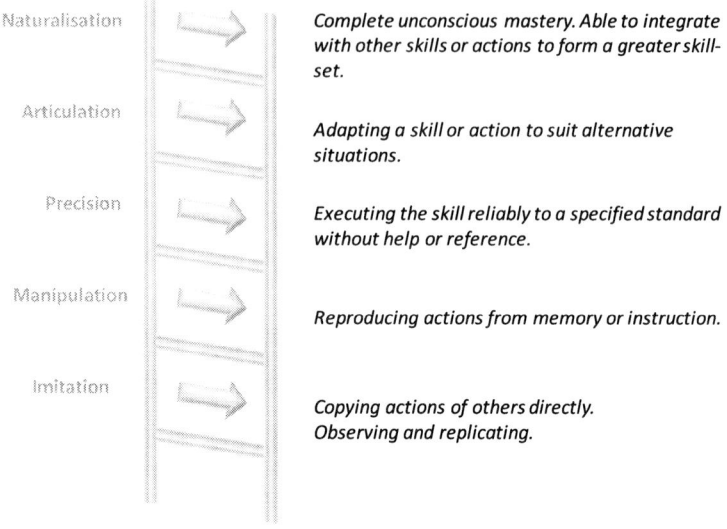

Figure 3.6 – Bloom's taxonomy (Dave's description of the psychomotor domain)

As with the affective domain, formal learning generally focuses at the three lower levels. We are all familiar with learning physical skills through direct observation e.g. a child's first foray on the skateboard. Formal learning tends to focus on the manipulation level, leading hopefully to precision. EDIP, the traditional structure of practical skills training (explanation, demonstration, imitation, practice) illustrates this principle well. Moving to skill levels beyond recognised competence requires specialised coaching e.g. adapting the basic golf swing to accommodate variations of topography or weather conditions. Naturalisation moves skills on to the "unconscious competence" plane where performance is virtually instinctive.

The usefulness of this scheme for analysing and defining our learning needs should be immediately apparent. The domain descriptors allow us to ensure that learning will be pitched at the right level and will use appropriate methods for delivery. The descriptors have been extended beyond simple behavioural examples to offer descriptions of related evidence of learning occurrence and then to appropriate language for specifying the learning and assessment activity. Examples from the three domains are shown below.

Cognitive domain (level 1)

Learning Category	Typical Behaviour Description	Typical evidence of learning	Appropriate active verbs
Knowledge	Recalling or recognising	Recounting facts or statistics, recalling a	Define, describe, label, list,

	information	process, quoting rules, providing definitions; quoting laws or standard procedures	memorise, reproduce recognise, relate, , select, state, arrange

Affective domain (level 2)

Learning Category	Typical Behaviour Description	Typical Evidence of learning	Appropriate active verbs
Responding	Reacting constructively to learning input, participating fully.	Willing participation in activity, active in group discussions, supporting group actions enthusiastically, questioning and examining ideas, obviously interested in outcomes, becoming animated	Responding, clarifying, interpret, offering alternatives, contributing, reacting, questioning, performing

Psychomotor domain (level 3)

Learning Category	Typical Behaviour Description	Typical Evidence of learning	Appropriate active verbs
Precision	Executing a skill reliably, without assistance	Consistently performing a task or activity with expertise to the standard required without assistance or instruction; able to show others how to do the task	Completing, performing, carrying out, demonstrating

Familiarity with the full taxonomy should be fundamental knowledge for an L&D professional. It will focus thinking acutely and allow learning needs to be fully articulated for the next stage in the strategic L&D process i.e. development.

When applying the taxonomy criteria we need to feed in two fundamental questions i.e.

- What do we expect the individual to know and be able to do following the learning event?
- What kind of learning (or blend of learning) is needed to achieve this and at what level?

Let us work through a typical (fictitious) scenario.

The case of ABC Widgets Ltd.

ABC Widgets Ltd is a manufacturer of a wide range of domestic hardware items. The last 2 years have been characterised by unacceptable down time on a number of production lines, and growing quality issues resulting in unacceptable rates of rejection at QC sampling. Despite the sampling process, faulty items are getting through, leading to mounting complaints, returned product and three cancellations of significant orders from long-standing customers. Senior management has addressed this issue at the strategic planning level, setting in motion the following chain of planning requirements:

Business Goal 1: To maximize production through the constant reduction of production down time to an acceptable level i.e. 0.5% annual average.

Business Goal 2: To build customer trust and confidence through maximized quality of product delivered.

Associated Objective 1.1: To employ effective problem-prevention and problem-solving at the point of origin.

Associated Objective 2.1 To improve quality controls throughout the production chain.

Associated Action 1.1.1: To ensure that appropriate problem identification and problem-solving techniques are built into production routines and facilitated at production team level.

Associated Action 2.1.1: To identify stages in production where faults are occurring and to institute appropriate improvements.

Discussion with production managers indicates that the preferred problem-solving approach is 8D (Eight Disciplines) using RCA (root cause analysis) at the identification stage. Consulting the shift manager role maps confirms that these skills have not been required previously and therefore expertise cannot be assumed. A focused skills audit rapidly confirms the learning need. The audit revealed good levels of understanding around managing a team since this had always been a pivotal part of the role. Further development was not deemed necessary in that respect.

Moving to the analysis phase we can employ Bloom's domain descriptors to define the need more precisely. Even a cursory glance at the 8D methodology begins to reveal the required learning input levels e.g.

- **Discipline 1 – Planning to solve the problem** i.e. defining what has to be done and who should be involved. The emphasis here is on the planning skill set – requiring primarily cognitive input at the application level. We need to bring the shift manager to the point where he not only understands planning but can actually apply the skills in his own unique situation. This is level 3 in the cognitive domain and naturally assumes achievement at levels 1 and 2.

Learning Category	Typical Behaviour Description	Typical Evidence of learning
Cognitive – Applying.	Putting theory into practice, using knowledge in response to real circumstances.	Adapting concepts, principles and processes to particular situations, using theory as a tool.

- **Discipline 2 – Identify and use an appropriately skilled team e.g. skilled, experienced production operatives.** Although it is likely that no training is required here, the emphasis would be on affective input. This is leadership. Consequently, all the affective skills would be needed through to level 4. It would probably be wise to discuss each individual shift manager's leadership ability with the relevant line manager to highlight any isolated shortcomings for specific treatment through one on one coaching.

- **Discipline 3 – Describe the problem e.g. who, what, where, when, why, how and how many?** This involves clarifying the nature of the problem from a number of different perspectives but stopping short of finding a solution. Consequently this is level 4 cognitive learning i.e. analysis.

Learning Category	Typical Behaviour Description	Typical Evidence of learning
Cognitive – Analysis.	interpreting elements, organisational principles, structure, construction, internal relationships.	Identifying and breaking down to constituent parts or functions of a process or concept, making qualitative assessment of elements, relationships, values and effects; measuring requirements or needs...

- **Discipline 4 – Develop interim containment measures i.e. isolate the problem or prevent it from becoming worse.** This is not simply the application of containment measures. The key word here is "develop" i.e. the individual would be expected to create adequate solutions for very specific situations based on the knowledge that he possesses. Essentially, this is synthesis learning at level 5. It is typically characterised by "what if......?" and "suppose that" and "what could we do to......?"

Learning Category	Typical Behaviour Description	Typical Evidence of learning
Cognitive – Synthesis	Developing new unique structures, systems, models, approaches, ideas; thinking creatively; bringing disparate or opposing elements together.	Designing solutions, integrating ideas or methods; creating teams; developing new approaches, developing protocols or contingencies

- **Discipline 5 – Identify the origin / cause of the problem using RCA.** Of course this is the direct application of a learned method, but the real level of required learning is evident in the term "root cause analysis".

- **Discipline 6 – Identify permanent corrective actions (PCA's).** This is essentially the same creative process as discipline 4 but moves on to solutions that can be accepted as permanent. So once again this is level 5 synthesis. If several feasible options are available they would need to be evaluated thus taking learning to level 6.

- **Discipline 7 - Prevent recurrence through modification of processes, equipment or people (up-skilling).** This discipline is linked directly to discipline 8. It requires the highest order learning i.e. evaluation after monitoring performance of solutions.

Learning Category	Typical Behaviour Description	Typical Evidence of learning
Cognitive – evaluation	Assessing effectiveness or "value" of whole systems or concepts, in terms of outputs, viability etc; thinking critically; comparing and reviewing positives and negative aspects.	Reviewing options, plans, systems; Assessing return on investment or cost-effectiveness; Assessing sustainability; performing a SWOT or PEST analysis to assess viability and identify issues; performing a detailed risk analysis.

- **Discipline 8 – Monitor, evaluate solutions and report.** As for discipline 7 above.

There are no physical skills to be acquired here so the psychomotor domain is not engaged. While there may be some individualised affective learning around leadership, this is not likely to be significant. The main focus of the new learning will be cognitive.

So where does this take us? We can now move to drawing up a learning needs statement that will serve as a brief for the developer. As a general principle we assume that each of the required levels may include learning at the lower levels. This concept (for the cognitive domain) is illustrated at figure 3.7.

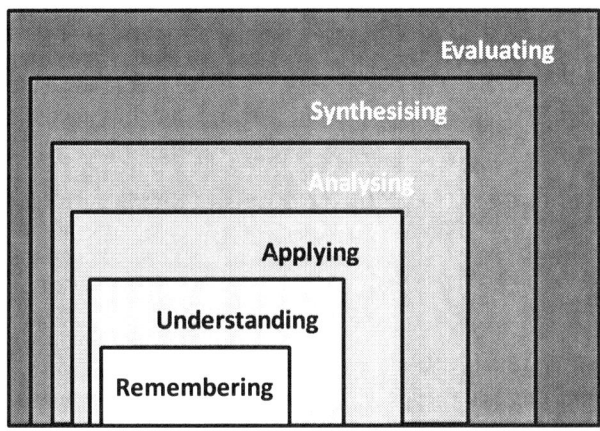

Figure 3.7 – The progressive inclusion of the cognitive domains.

ABC Widgets Ltd. Learning Needs Analysis – Summary Statement		
Requirement.	General: Problem-solving skills.	
	Specific: 8 disciplines methodology (including root cause analysis) as company standard technique.	
Target learners.	Operational shift managers.	
Existing knowledge levels.	From nil to limited. All concepts and techniques involved should be covered in depth.	
Required learning level.	Overall: <u>Application</u>. After training, shift managers will be able to use the 8D problem-solving technique effectively and proactively in the context of all foreseeable operational situations.	
	Specific: The main content components should achieve the following levels of learning:	
	Topic	Level
	Discipline 1 – Planning to solve the problem.	<u>Cognitive Level 3</u> : <u>Application</u> - the shift manager will understand planning requirements for this process and be able apply the skills effectively in his / her own unique situation.

	Discipline 2 – Selecting and leading an appropriate team.	Not required in this programme.
	Discipline 3 – Describing the problem.	<u>Cognitive level 4 : Analysis</u> – the shift manager will be able to isolate the actual problem from the general issue environment and be able to describe it succinctly and accurately so that it can be generally understood by the team.
	Discipline 4 - Developing interim containment measures.	<u>Cognitive level 5 : Synthesis</u> – the shift manager will be able to draw information and observation together from multiple sources and create feasible temporary options for problem containment.
	Discipline 5 – Identifying the origin or cause of the problem.	<u>Cognitive level 4 : Analysis</u> – the shift manager will be able to track problem manifestations back to origin using team resources.
	Discipline 6 – Identifying PCA's (permanent corrective actions)	<u>Cognitive level 5/6 : Synthesis/ Evaluation</u> – the shift manager will be able to create options for problem solution or containment that are sufficiently robust to be permanently adopted.
	Discipline 7 – Prevent recurrence through modification or processes, equipment or people (skills)	<u>Cognitive level 6 : Evaluation</u> – the shift manager will be able to monitor adopted measures and make appropriate adjustment to optimise performance.
	Discipline 8 – Monitor, evaluate solutions and report.	<u>Cognitive level 6 : Evaluation</u> the shift manager will be able to carry out formal evaluations of selected permanent corrective actions and report fully on findings.

Given that leadership development is not required here, the focus is entirely focused around cognitive skills. If it had been a requirement, a separate summary statement would have been appropriate. Leading teams is a significant affective domain learning intervention and would certainly warrant its own analysis and programme development. Needs of a lesser dimension, emanating from the different domains, can be blended into the same summary statement.

Summary statements of this kind form the basis of the design brief for learning development. Armed with this kind information developers can proceed with confidence, knowing to what level they must take the learning for each topic or component. The various learning levels will largely define the kind of learning activity that must be built into programmes if they are to hit the mark precisely.

4. PROGRAMME OR COURSE DEVELOPMENT

Following needs analysis, the strategic approach moves on to answer a very significant question i.e. "Are we going to "outsource" the development of the required learning – or should we attempt to do this ourselves?" Getting to the right decision is not necessarily a straightforward matter. An apparently simple question can be seriously obfuscated by a host of variables e.g. historical practice, "we've always done it ourselves".

- Lack of confidence, "we just don't have the expertise! The last time we tried this it was a complete stuff up!"
- Pressure of work, "we need a quick result – we simply can't fit it in!"
- Justifying existing resources, "we have a training development team therefore we must use them!"
- Legal requirement, "it's a compliance issue. We have to use a ministry approved package."
- False perspectives, "it's what these people specialise in – they're bound to be better than us!"
- Legacy mentality, "We've always used them. Why make changes now?"
- Lack of technical resource, "We just don't have the equipment or the software to take this on".

Internal or external development? If we have a choice, which way should we go? Are there any clear guidelines? The short answer is no. Just because your company has an HR department with a development team does not mean that they should tackle every learning need that arises. Similarly, small organisations with no development capacity should not rule out taking on the challenge. Every scenario needs to be evaluated on a cost / benefit / capability basis. This analysis needs to be supported by a clear view of the advantages or disadvantages that the internal and external solutions offer. So what are they?

Internal v External Development – issues comparison		
Issue	**Internal**	**External**
Cost	Up-front cost apparently significantly lower, especially if in-house capability exists (development team). However, any hidden costs should be accounted for e.g. • Expert staff being taken "off line" to assist development i.e. non-production or costs to cover absence.	Up-front costs apparently higher. However, when internal hidden costs are accounted for the final cost may be significantly reduced.

	• Need to develop specific skills for staff tasked with development. • Purchase or hire of equipment or software needed for specific development project. • Office space costs e.g. power, heating, IT etc.	
Quality	Hugely variable, depending on the expertise of those tasked with development and of the subject experts they consult. The organisation has to live with the results or invest further to put things right.	Variable but more predictable if monitored properly through the process. Company does not have to accept a sub-standard product.
Capability	Can be high (if a professional development team is in place) – if not, this may have to be developed or contracted in. Capability tends to be "one-eyed" i.e. views things from a narrow organisational perspective.	Should be excellent (that's why they were chosen). Tend to bring a broader perspective to the learning need and to possible solutions.
Timeframes	Can be very protracted. Contributing staff have their normal jobs and are therefore subject to constant distraction. Internal funding can easily be redirected causing hold-ups or stagnation.	Generally much shorter. External providers have a vested interest in completing on or before time. Funds and staff committed by contract cannot be withdrawn, therefore less chance of disruption or hold-ups.
Disruption	Can be very significant if not planned for e.g. subject experts are withdrawn from strategic projects etc. Distraction of HR and operational staff to scope and manage development can be very disruptive if there is no in-house L&D capability.	Insignificant if provider has own sources of expertise or it is their specialist area. Can be a major issues if dependent on client for specific expertise i.e. experts may be not be available when required.

Reception	Generally very well received – providing quality is good. Seen to much more in tune with the reality of the company, its culture, equipment or processes.	May be judged more harshly due to the knowledge that funds have been expended on "outsiders". Any failure to relate to the workplace will invite immediate criticism.
Alignment to other systems	"Knock-on" impacts quickly recognised and assessed due to internal familiarity.	Unlikely to be noticed, therefore leading to possible follow-on internal work – an extra cost.
Unique skills	Highly specialised skills or commercially sensitive learning is generally only be developed internally. For example, the infantry would not be able to contract out its tactics training. Neither would the intelligence services outsource training in interrogation techniques.	Generally less able to function in this area. If pursued, contracts likely to come at high cost.
Shelf-life	Content detail easily maintained at low cost providing structure remains largely unaltered.	Can be easily maintained if a long-term relationship is developed – but at a cost.

There is often considerable pressure to move too quickly through this most fundamental decision-making process. This may be due to simple urgency e.g. there has been a serious failing in a critical procedure and perhaps safety or quality is compromised. Analysis of the issue and re-training is considered essential. In these circumstances most organisations will outsource to ensure a quick fix. But can they be sure of getting the quality and shelf life that an internal design might provide?

It is tempting to believe that once a decision is taken to outsource development, the external provider is wholly responsible for everything that follows, through to handing over the final package for delivery. Unfortunately nothing could be further from the truth. In order to safeguard themselves and to ensure an effective production to brief, providers will usually return to the client at a number of key stages for confirmation and sign-off. The implication of this is clear i.e. while the client company may not be doing the work, it still needs to provide expertise capable of reviewing the provider's efforts. This means that somebody (probably from HR) needs to possess the same fundamental knowledge and skills around development as would be required if they were developing internally. This is a hard truth, but a truth nonetheless.

So what is this fundamental knowledge? Essentially, it is an understanding of the key process steps attached to the development of learning experiences. The required depth of such understanding will vary according to circumstances i.e.

- If outsourcing – the HR professional will need to understand the process at least at a conceptual level. This will allow him to "interrogate" the progress made by the contracted developer.
- If developing in-house – HR will need highly developed L&D experience which includes the full development process in depth.

Figure 4.1 illustrates the ideal process required to select the most appropriate delivery methodologies for a given topic, course, or programme.

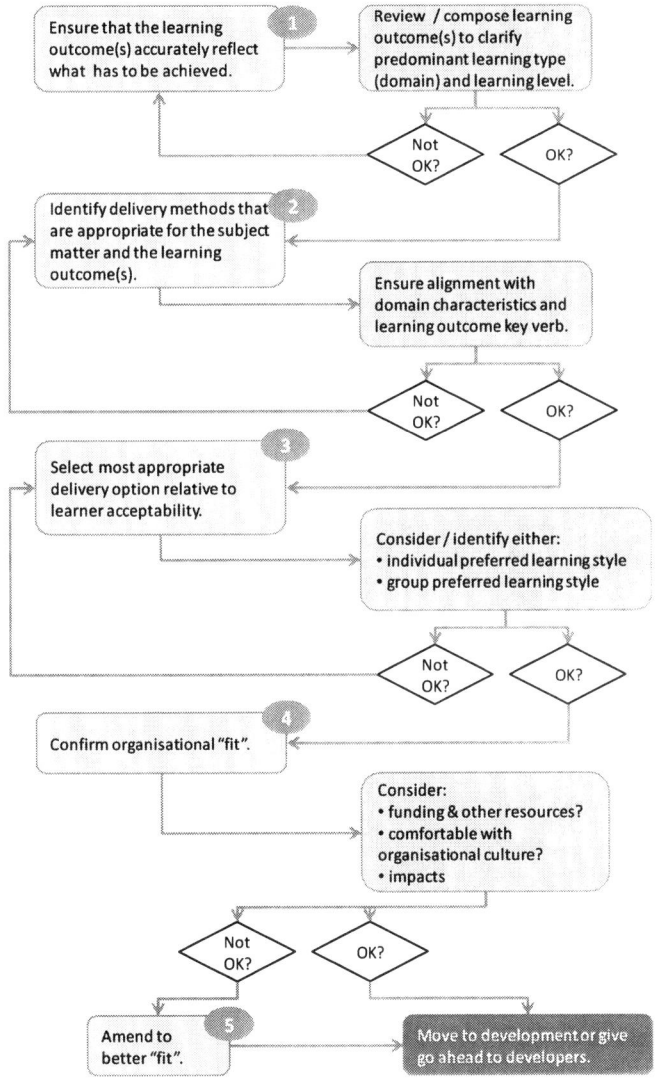

Figure 4.1– Development process steps

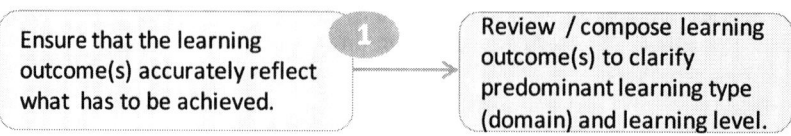

In a perfect world the learning programme developer will always be provided with a learning needs analysis statement by the client, internal or external. The real world is rather different. More often than not, developers have to take a step backwards and do the needs analysis themselves or simply go ahead on the basis of experience or intuition. For present purposes we will assume the ideal and move directly to the specification of the learning content.

In most cases, accurate and comprehensive specification is critical. It is the blueprint that drives the development process and keeps it firmly on track. This is particularly important when working with subject matter experts (SME's) who so often want to "blow out" the content beyond what is actually required. Ongoing reference to the programme specification ensures good discipline and focus from everybody involved.

AIMS, OBJECTIVES AND LEARNING OUTCOMES.

The advent of competence-based education and training (CBET) in the 1980's provoked something of a re-think on how learning should be specified. Until then specification was essentially a two-stage process involving a broad statement of intent for the outcome of the whole course or programme – the "aim", and an accompanying set of more narrowly focused statements that defined specific behavioural or knowledge gains to be achieved – the "objectives". Since the objectives largely described new or changed behaviours they were commonly referred to as "behavioural objectives".

While there is a definite art to writing good objectives, this dual layer approach was relatively simple to understand and work with. Unfortunately, since the 1980's the situation has become rather muddied and confused. The ongoing evolution of CBET brought with it an apparent need for greater precision i.e. to describe precisely what "competence" meant for a given skill. As a consequence many educational and training organisations, including some universities, moved to a three layer system i.e. programme aims, objectives and learning outcomes. Others have preferred to retain the old language but have likewise moved to three layer system e.g. aim, general objectives and specific objectives. A rose by any other name – they amount to the same thing and the language used largely reflects organisational style as much as anything else.

Highly detailed specification certainly has its place, but has often resulted in a quite unnecessary muddle where it is patently unnecessary. There has been something of a backlash against drilling down too far and becoming entirely prescriptive. This is particularly true of vocational qualifications where industry has finally rebelled against the impossible strait-jacket of over-specification. We now find that most competence-based vocational programmes are characterised by learning outcomes that are more flexibly specified, allowing participating organisations some "wriggle room" with which to fit the qualification to their operational needs. Courses or learning programmes that are designed specifically for one organisation can and often do specify very precisely, because their requirements do not transfer or overlap elsewhere. For example the Armed Services of many countries have taken specification to an extreme form. The rationale for this is often linked to the fact that the learning is so often linked to critical functions such as weapon handling, or navigation skills where there is little or no room for error and everyone must be trained to exactly the same standard. To achieve this level of precision, a highly developed version of the behavioural objective is used as a learning outcome. An example (infantry map reading) is illustrated at figure 23 overleaf. The approach shown here is ideally suited to training environments where there is no expectation that the learner will deviate in any way from intended behavior and the outcome is entirely predictable.

In practice, the two layer system is usually quite adequate for specifying what should eventually be achieved by short courses. It is fair to say however, that long duration programmes such as we find in the world of tertiary qualifications may need the modern three level approach (aims, objectives, learning outcomes) but this tends to apply in the main to technically oriented programmes. A cursory examination of tertiary specification reveals some variation in the way the terms "objective" and "outcome" are understood, with most universities providing their own customised guidance to staff on how to specify their programmes. Nevertheless, semantic differences seldom distort the fundamental descriptions of what the programme is intended to achieve and what the student will know and be able to do. Cambridge University's on-line Educational and Student Policy document is a very clear example of how aims and learning outcomes are to be used within that institution:

The aims of a course should represent the intentions of the teacher. They should:
- *Encapsulate the purpose of the course and what the institution is trying to achieve in providing it.*
- *Indicate the audience for whom the course is intended, or the kind of career or future study for which it might be designed.*
- *State whether the course is broad-based or taught as a series of specialised options, and explain the rationale. It is the kind of statement that might go into a prospectus to advertise the course.*

Learning outcomes tell students and prospective students the kinds of knowledge that they will be given the opportunity to acquire during the course.

Learning outcomes are:
- *Distinct from programme or course aims since they are concerned with the achievements of the learner, rather than the intentions of the teacher.*
  Iincluded in the programme specification at the level of award (e.g. the Tripos, MPhil) or at a major subdivision (Part of the Tripos, MPhil option).

Attempts are made to distinguish learning outcomes from old-fashioned objectives – but in practice they are essentially the same. If there is a difference, it is one of degree rather than kind. Learning outcomes are often somewhat more flexibly expressed but nevertheless, like objectives, they articulate what the learner will know and be able to do as a consequence of completing the learning successfully. Whether we choose the contemporary term or the traditional, what really matters is that the outcome or the objective is well written.

WRITING EFFECTIVE LEARNING OUTCOMES / OBJECTIVES

The HR / L&D professional who is not proposing to become directly involved in the development of learning activities or programmes may be tempted to ask "Why do I need to know how to write learning outcomes?" The answer is quite straightforward i.e. if you assume any responsibility or accountability for commissioning development work, whether through outsourcing or through an internal development team) you must be able to satisfy yourself that the proposed programme will actually meet the stipulated learning needs. Consequently you need to know what you are looking at.

The table that follows is an excerpt from a military training manual. As an example of classic behavioural objectives, it is "performance oriented". Its purpose is to describe precisely what the soldier will be able to do once he is successfully trained. This particular objective deals with prismatic compass skills and is structured to detail how the accomplishment of learning for each specific skill will be measured. It does not detail how learning will occur. The conditions under which assessment takes place are carefully detailed as are the exact standards to be met. Consequently what we see here is a definitive judgment concerning "competence" relative to compass skills for the Infantry. There is no ambiguity here. Both the learner and the trainer know exactly what has to be achieved – what the outcome must be.

When we consider that the detail shown here is just an excerpt from a training manual we can begin to appreciate the sheer hard work that has to go into producing such detailed objectives for the whole learning programme. This may explain why such depth of specification tends to be limited to organisations that are able to commit extraordinary resources and time to training. Such investment becomes a more attractive proposition when learning is unlikely to change significantly and to be repeated on a continuing basis.

For most other situations, learning outcomes are rather more lightweight. Nevertheless, whatever the depth of detail, writing learning outcomes should adhere to the same basic principles.

There is a very real value here for the trainee as well. Best practice organisations will always include the course or programme objectives with the initial learning materials. This allows the student to focus sharply on exactly what is required as a minimum level of competence. Without such clarity of performance expectation individual trainees who might fail the test could, with some justification, claim that the system was 'unfair".

The most difficult aspect of formulating objectives is not actually the writing task, after all the structure is clear and standardised. The hard work is getting agreement on the test conditions and test standards.

Course Aim: To equip the recruit soldier with land navigation skills to Infantry Standard 2.		
General Objective 4: To enable the recruit soldier to perform all prismatic compass skills required at Infantry Standard 2.		
Specific objective.	**Test Conditions.**	**Test Standards.**
4.1 – The soldier will be able to calculate a grid bearing using the mils protractor from maps of varying scale.	Given a mils protractor, a 1:25000 map and a 1:50000 map.	To within + or – 100 mils. 10/10 correct responses required.
4.2 – The soldier will be able to convert a grid bearing to a magnetic bearing.	Given a 1: 50000 map allowing access to variation detail.	To within + or – 100 mils. 5/5 correct responses required.
4.3 – The soldier will be able to march accurately on a magnetic bearing for a stipulated distance using the prismatic compass.	Given a prismatic compass. Having established own pacing for 100 metres.	For a distance of 700 metres. Finishing within + or - 30 metres in any direction from target destination. 2 performances required.
4.4 – The soldier will be able to determine the magnetic bearing of an object / location in relation to his own position.	Given a prismatic compass. Own position identified. Target object / location pointed out.	To within + or – 100 mils. 5/5 correct responses required.
4.5 – The soldier will be able to convert a magnetic bearing to a grid bearing.	Given a 1: 50000 map allowing access to variation detail.	To within + or – 100 mils. 5/5 correct responses required.
4.6 – The soldier will be able to plot a grid bearing on maps of varying scale.	Given a mils protractor, a 1:25000 map and a 1:50000 map.	To within + or – 100 mils. 10/10 correct responses required.
4.7 – The soldier will be able to perform a resection to fix own position.	Given a prismatic compass, mils protractor and a 1:50000 map.	Selected reference points to be clearly indicated. Position fixed to within 1 figure either way in 3rd and 5th figures of 6 figure reference.

First principle – start with the end in mind.

Learning outcomes (or objectives) specify the "what" not the "how". Keeping this in mind will avoid the common tendency to stray into the methods that will be used to deliver the learning.

Properly constructed, the learning outcome should:

- Inform the learner, the trainer, assessors, employers and other stakeholders of the knowledge, skills and (sometimes) attitudes that will be acquired on successful completion of the learning component.
- Inform learning and assessment developers of precisely what must be covered (content and level) in the course or learning component.
- Assist the learner to "self-assess" and measure formative progress.

Second principle – focus on ABC.

A well written learning outcome is built around:

- A clearly identified specific AUDIENCE. For entirely generic "off the shelf" programmes this is not always possible. Inevitably therefore, we do come across outcomes which are directed to "the learner" "the student" "the participant" etc. If however, you are designing in-house, or buying in development, then the outcome should target a specific job title or occupational function e.g. "the laboratory technician will .... "the shift manager will......."
- A performance focus on a single aspect of BEHAVIOUR. The purpose of a learning outcome is to specify what new skills (physical or mental) will be acquired. Ideally, the desired behavior should be defined in a measurable way. The old adage "you can't manage what you can't (or don't) measure" applies even at this very specific level. For example "the shift manager will be able to deal with interpersonal conflict between team members in a satisfactory manner" is meaningless. What is the meaning of "satisfactory' in this context? A far better statement would be "The shift manager will be able to deal with interpersonal conflict between team members in full accordance with the procedures and protocols set down in the staff management handbook".
- A specific CONDITIONS element. This is probably optional, depending on the level of "up-front detail" required. However, it is particularly important in the context of "hard skills" mastery learning where there is no room for error or individual approach at time of assessment. Learners, trainers and assessors need to be entirely confident of what is expected. Outcomes with condition elements often begin with "given a ...... the learner will ...." As in "Given access to the relevant safety data sheet and a mobile or field telephone, the operator will, within 5minutes, be able to identify and initiate the appropriate accidental spill response to the chemical in question."

Third principle – select the most appropriate active verb.

More than any other word in the outcome statement, the active verb establishes how success is to be measured. The validity of an assessment outcome depends heavily on the appropriateness of what the learner is asked to do. Given the sheer number of verb choices available in any language, the potential for confusion is obvious. For example what precisely is the difference between "identify" "indicate" "explain"? Understanding such subtleties can be a nightmare for all concerned, unless guidance is forthcoming in the shape of a glossary or set of exemplars.

Fortunately, for the learning developer, help is available in the form of verb lists selected for their appropriateness to the Bloom learning levels. In particular, Bloom's analysis of the cognitive domain provides us with a comprehensive verb catalogue. Providing we are confident of the cognitive learning level required, we can narrow down the verb field considerably by consulting Bloom's tables. Typical cognitive domain verbs are suggested below. These lists can of course be expanded if a more precise fit is needed.

Cognitive Domain – level 1 (Remembering) verbs					
Tell	List	Define	Name	Recall	Identify
State	Know	Relate	Reproduce	Memorise	Order
Remember	Repeat	Recognise	Label	Recite	Match
Cognitive Domain – level 2 (Understanding) verbs					
Transform	Change	Restate	Describe	Explain	Review
Paraphrase	Relate	Generalise	Contrast	Classify	Summarise
Describe	Discuss	Interpret	Infer	Justify	Report
Sort	Translate	Select	Indicate	Illustrate	Represent
Formulate	Express				
Cognitive Domain – level 3 (Applying) verbs					
Apply	Practice	Employ	Use	Demonstrate	Illustrate
Show	Report	Predict	Instruct	Compute	Calculate
Perform	Choose	Schedule	Sketch	Interpret	Allocate
Cognitive Domain – level 4 (Analysing) verbs					
Dissect	Organise	Analyse	Distinguish	Examine	Compare
Differentiate	Solve	Contrast	Appraise	Survey	Investigate
Calculate	Categorise	Separate	Criticise	Classify	Discriminate
Deduce					
Cognitive Domain – level 5 (Synthesising) verbs					
Create	Combine	Invent	Summarise	Compose	Restate
Generalise	Construct	Design	Conclude	Modify	Arrange
Imagine	Assemble	Formulate	Propose	Plan	Prepare
Write	Set up	Synthesise			
Cognitive Domain – level 6 (Evaluating) verbs					
Judge	Appraise	Assess	Argue	Decide	Attack
Select	Choose	Justify	Compare	Evaluate	Estimate
Critique	Predict	Debate	Rate	Verify	Score
Recommend	Value	Support	Determine	Defend	

Although the same verbs re-appear at different levels, this is quite natural because they will refer to different objects and modifiers. The same applies to the affective and psychomotor domains.

Bloom's cognitive domain is increasingly thought of in simpler terms as "cognitive lower level" relating to levels 1 and 2, and "cognitive upper level" relating to levels 3-6. It is also accepted that adult learning should always be pitched at level 3 and above, although it will naturally encompass remembering and understanding.

So, returning to our ABC Widgets Ltd scenario, the learning needs summary statement tells us that learning will be firmly rooted in the cognitive domain. The skills are primarily (but not exclusively) intellectual and the active verbs should be selected from, or be akin to those shown for the relevant cognitive learning levels 3 and above. Looking at the learning needs analysis summary statement we find the following overall learning level requirement for topic 1 (planning).

Cognitive Level 3: Application - the shift manager will understand planning requirements for this process and be able apply the skills effectively in his / her own unique situation.

This statement might serve very well as a general objective in the old-fashioned format, or as an aim for the topic delivery around "planning to solve the problem". Accurate specification now requires that a set of learning outcomes be drawn out of this general statement. This set might look like this:

Topic Aim:
The shift manager will understand planning requirements for this process and be able apply the skills effectively in his / her own unique situation.

Learning outcomes:
Without guidance or the need to consult, the shift manager will be able to:
<ul><li>(apply) information and data gathering skills sufficient to (predict) the scope of the problem</li><li>(deduce) the likely resource requirements from the problem scope e.g.<ul><li>staffing / expertise</li><li>financial</li><li>time</li><li>technical / equipment</li></ul></li><li>(assemble) sufficient expertise to (interpret) problem scope and to (choose) most appropriate solution path</li><li>(use) team expertise to (schedule) tasks to milestones to fit the designated timeframe</li><li>(allocate) appropriate individual expertise and resources to tasks</li><li>(report) on plan to manager and obtain approval</li></ul>

Once again, we can see that writing the learning outcomes for the whole course or programme will be a time-consuming affair and requires a thorough, logical mind. HR staff tasked with L&D responsibilities may elect not to tackle this themselves, but they should know what to look for before signing off on any outsourced development.

Typical affective domain verbs are suggested below.

Affective Domain – level 1 (Receiving Phenomena) verbs					
Ask	Choose	Describe	Follow	Give	Hold
Identify	Locate	Name	Point to	Select	Erect
Reply	Use				
Affective Domain – level 2 (Responding to Phenomena) verbs					
Answer	Assist	Aid	Comply	Conform	Discuss
Greet	Help	Label	Perform	Practice	Present
Read	Recite	Report	Select	Tell	Write
Affective Domain – level 3 (Valuing) verbs					
Complete	Demonstrate	Differentiate	Explain	Follow	Form
Initiate	Invite	Join	Justify	Propose	Read
Report	Select	Share	Study	Work	
Affective Domain – level 4 (Organising) verbs					
Adhere	Alter	Arrange	Combine	Compare	Complete
Defend	Explain	Formulate	Generalise	Identify	Integrate
Modify	Order	Organise	Prepare	Relate	Synthesize
Affective Domain – level 5 (Internalising) verbs					
Acts	Discriminate	Display	Influence	Listen	Modify
Perform	Practice	Propose	Qualify	Question	Revise
Serve	Solve	Verify			

Although our ABC Widgets shift managers are supposedly trained and capable leaders, we might suppose that a refresher element would be included around the critical function of managing the project team. If so, the learning outcomes would certainly be rooted primarily in the affective domain. The outcome set might look something like this:

Topic Aim: – the shift manager will identify and use an appropriately skilled team e.g. experienced production operatives.

Without assistance or the need to consult, the shift manager will be able to:
- (select) most appropriate team members for specific tasks.
- (modify) own preferred leadership style sufficiently to maintain effective working relationships
- (differentiate) between poorly-performing and under-performing team members.
- (formulate) and (present) consensus conclusions to the satisfaction of the team.
- (integrate) individual working methods of project team members toward an agreed joint working practice

Bloom did not examine the psychomotor domain in any depth. There are a number of current analyses (Simpson 1972, Harrow 1972, Simpson 1975). The suggested verb lists below reflects Simpson.

Psychomotor Domain – level 1 (Perception) verbs					
Choose	Describe	Detect	Differentiate	Distinguish	Identify
Isolate	Relate	Selects			
Psychomotor Domain – level 2 (Mindset) verbs					
Begin	Display	Explain	Move	Proceed	React
Show	State	Volunteer			
Psychomotor Domain – level 3 (Guided response) verbs					
Copy	Trace	Follow	React	Reproduce	Respond
Psychomotor Domain – level 4 (Mechanism) verbs					
Assemble	Calibrate	Construct	Dismantle	Display	Fasten
Fix	Grind	Heat	Manipulate	Measure	Mend
Mix	Organise	Sketch			
Psychomotor Domain – level 5 (Complex overt response) verbs					
Assemble	Calibrate	Construct	Dismantle	Display	Fasten
Fix	Grind	Heat	Manipulate	Measure	Mend
Mix	Organise	Sketch			

Note: Although the active verbs are the same as Mechanism they will have adverbs or adjectives that indicate that the performance is quicker, better, more accurate, e.g. assemble rapidly, sketch confidently etc.

Psychomotor Domain – level 6 (Adaptation) verbs					
Adapt	Alter	Change	Re-arrange	Re-organise	Revise
Psychomotor Domain – level 7 (Origination) verbs					
Arrange	Build	Combine	Compose	Construct	Create
Design	Initiate	Make	Originate		

Problem-solving is primarily a cognitive skill. Consequently we can easily fall into the trap of assuming that psychomotor skills may not be required for our shift managers. However, when we examine the training needs analysis summary statement more closely (see pages 68 and 69) and focus on disciplines 5 and 6, the possibility of psychomotor skills becomes apparent. Disciplines 5 and 6 are about tracking problem manifestations and coming up with permanent corrective actions. If the problems stem from errors in human physical performance the shift manager and his team will need to demonstrate psychomotor understanding at least to level 5, thus bringing into play those key verbs we see above; adapt, alter, change, re-arrange, re-organise, revise etc.

Fourth principle – avoid unnecessary complexity.

In the same way that "complex question" is a logical fallacy to be avoided in argument, learning outcomes that actually specify several achievements generally cause confusion for all concerned. The following example demonstrates a lack of understanding of this basic principle:

"The Shift Manager will be able to select, brief and use an appropriate team to conduct root cause analysis".

The presence of the three verbs here (select, brief use) should sound the alarm bell. They refer to three quite distinct skills and should therefore be treated uniquely. If they are not, then difficulties may arise in designing and delivering training, but more importantly perhaps, may lead to construct invalidities in assessment. This is discussed in detail in section 5. This outcome should be broken into three individual outcomes e.g.

"The Shift Manager will be able to select appropriate staff to form a team to use the root cause analysis technique".

"The shift manager will be able to brief the problem solving team effectively using the standard organisational format".

"The shift manager will be able to use team skills and expertise to conduct root cause analysis of a problem".

Fifth principle – select and use language and format that is appropriate to the end-user organisation.

Variations in style and format of learning outcomes have evolved to reflect firstly the level and type of learning, and secondly the environment in which they have to function. Low level, mechanistic learning involving "hard skills" can be very precisely specified. Higher level "soft skills" mostly cannot. For example, the processes involved in changing a wheel on a car are entirely predictable. Counseling a distressed employee is not a predictable process and trying to specify a fixed sequence will probably end in frustration all round.

Language and format must also vary according to environment and organisational culture. What is appropriate and necessary for military training would certainly be out of place, for example, in the training of palliative carers. For hard skills the full behavioural format is generally appropriate i.e. using the three desirable specification components:

Outcome = Conditions + Performance + Criteria	
Conditions:	Usually an opening clause such as "given "x" … without "y" etc.
Performance:	Generally "the learner will (appropriate verb)…" or "will be able to".
Criteria / Standards:	Usually closes the outcome statement with a definition of required accuracy / quality,

	quantity (e.g. number of repetitions) or time limitations (e.g. "within one minute').

For soft skills we may be limited to the performance element only e.g. "The counsellor will be able to take a full case history from the client". We could hardly add "within 30 minutes" or "by the end of the first interview".

SELECTING APPROPRIATE DELIVERY STRATEGIES.

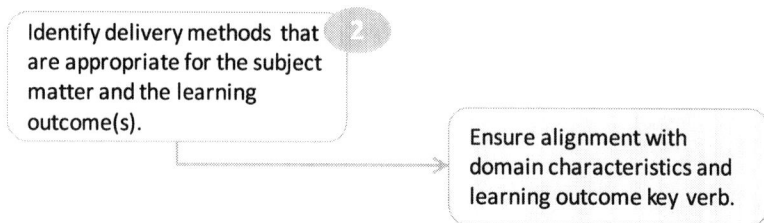

Identify delivery methods that are appropriate for the subject matter and the learning outcome(s).

Ensure alignment with domain characteristics and learning outcome key verb.

Armed with well-constructed learning outcomes, the developer can now move on to considering how these outcomes might best be translated into a learning or development experience. The first task is to screen out the possibility of learning being achieved through channels other than formal structured learning. Returning to the big picture illustrated at figure 1 it is always useful to remind ourselves of the alternatives, particularly of broad "experience".

Selecting the learning mode.

If formal, planned learning is deemed to be appropriate for the subject and particular learning outcomes, a wide range of options are available for consideration. The field will be reduced considerably once it becomes clear whether individual or group learning is needed. Of course many programmes may have elements of both e.g. distance learning programmes with elements of block attendance offered by many universities.

In simple terms, formalised learning is delivered in one of the following basic modes:

- Individualised remote learning. – the learner works through material at own pace possibly with the support of a distant tutor / assessor.
- Individualised face to face learning.
- Small group face to face learning.
- Large group face to face learning.
- Group / individualised learning.

	Individualised remote learning – the learner works through material at own pace possibly with the support of a distant tutor / assessor e.g. • Directed study of identified sources e.g. texts, film archives etc. • Tutored self-instruction e.g. correspondence courses • Computer-based learning (CBL or "E" learning) • Distance learning assignments or individual projects
	Individualised face to face learning – the learner is coached one on one to achieve outcomes e.g. • On job training (OJT) • Off-job coaching
	Small group face to face (FTF) learning – typical examples • Traditional training courses • Seminars and workshops • Group projects • Games • Simulations
	Group – individualised learning • Remote CBL learner groups (virtual classrooms) • Pod / Web casts

The table below summarises what these various modes offer the developer. Each mode is typically accompanied by predictable and necessary behaviours from the trainer and the learner. At this stage the paramount concern must be the subject matter and the learning outcomes i.e. which is the most effective way for this topic to be delivered?

Learning Mode	Typical role of trainer.	Typical role of learner.	Advantages	Disadvantages
Individualised remote learning	If involved, limited to written feedback or pre-arranged verbal feedback.	Largely independent learning.	Cost effective. Flexible (learning can be done at times to suit the learner). No need to consider needs of other learners / group members.	Often accompanied by a sense of isolation. High levels of self-discipline needed. No social extension Limitations of distant feedback.
Individualised face to face	Direct and intensive. Style of input	Usually dependent at the outset.	Generally highly effective and efficient.	Relatively expensive. Results may not be good if trainer /

learning.	varies according to subject and learner personality.	May quickly develop to greater independenc e as trainer "lets out the string'.	Learner makes rapid progress therefore good for "quick fixes". Immediate feedback and corrective action. Trainer only has to "read" one personality.	learner personalities do not gel. Learners can be fazed by one–on–one intensity.
Small group FTF learning	Direct and intensive but may use group members to reduce own impact. Generally a mix of expository and negotiated styles. Engages on the individual and the group level.	Collegiate and highly social in successful groups. Individuals required to contribute in a manner acceptable to group.	Often the most effective mode as long as group dynamics are positive. Relatively easy to judge learning uptake and make rapid adjustments to delivery style.	Still relatively expensive – particularly if training does not go well. Trainer has to "read" and manage several personalities.
Large group FTF learning	Generally expository, limited engagement possible.	Largely passive. Inputs, queries limited by the size of the group.	Very efficient method of imparting factual information. Trainer has high level of control.	Can be difficult to judge learning uptake. Little or no engagement or development of relationship with group. Control focused, therefore often inflexible.
Group-individualised learning	Very much focused on technology and maintaining functional control. Little or no personal engagement with learners. Often facilitative in nature – providing a	Generally contributive – depending on self-confidence with technology. Must be prepared to observe protocols to allow others sufficient space to participate.	Can bring together learners from wide ranging backgrounds and diverse locations. Large numbers can participate. Once established, can be very cost effective - no travel or accommodation costs etc).	Dependent on successful technology solutions and availability. Will not appeal to "technophobes" or social learners. Session timings may be a significant issue for some. Difficult to manage requiring high levels of trainer expertise.

	managed environment for learners to engage at a distance.			

As a general rule, learning which requires direct engagement, either with people or equipment, will need a high proportion of face to face involvement. Practical skills need practical training, as close to the "real world" situation as possible. Theoretical elements can be taught at a distance by way of preparation but practical skill can only be acquired through "hands on" experience. If we take a course in electric motor repair as an example, this principle is obvious, but not necessarily so in the case of basic counseling techniques. We often see learning of this kind individualised through a distance approach, but, eventually it is a practical technique involving high levels of engagement and a face to face element will certainly be needed for learning to be effective.

Conversely, material that is entirely theoretical or conceptual can be successfully delivered at a distance, but questions always have to be asked about the additional perspectives that face to face engagement might bring. Learning such as the study of literature or philosophy, because it is rooted in personal interpretation, epitomises individualised acquisition of knowledge. However, even here, learning institutions will usually bring students together because the additional perspectives of discussion, debate and embracing the views of others are best acquired in that way.

Selecting the learning method(s).

Once a decision on the most appropriate mode has been made, more detailed design can begin. This will involve a switch of focus to the range of methods that are available and known to work well within the chosen mode. It will also mean adjusting focus down to the individual or clusters of learning outcomes.

Scaling down from the course level to individual learning outcomes, the same basic questions have to be asked. Each outcome needs to be examined for its essential nature, and delivery methods should, if possible reflect that. This may result in a variety of methods and techniques within a single course – but that of course is no bad thing. The tables that follow list the typical methods used for the various learning modes.

Mode	Typical Methods	Potential Advantages	Potential Disadvantages
Individualised remote learning.	Directed study of identified sources e.g. texts, film, archives etc.	Viewed as and when learner wishes. Possibility of repeat viewings. Can be professional quality and so meet exacting expectations.	May contain irrelevant material. Possible technology compatibility issues.

Individualised remote learning continued.	Computer-based learning (CBL or "E" learning).	As above plus: High level of learner control. Potentially endless web linkages. Material selected for targeted learning, therefore efficient use of learner time. E Learning programmes easily kept up to date.	Availability of web may encourage distraction activity e.g. surfing. Not possible to update CD based materials. High quality E learning very expensive to develop. Dependent on individual user access to relevant technology.
	Tutored self-instruction e.g. correspondence courses.	Material selected for targeted learning, therefore efficient use of learner time. Can include a wide range of material. Generally have some access to "tutor" feedback (distant). Relatively cheap to produce.	Learner may feel restricted. Learner may feel isolated. Dependent on leaner discipline and motivation. Dependent on efficient course administration. Dependent on quality and motivation of distant tutor. No opportunity to network
	Web / Pod casts	Available anytime/anywhere for students. Easy to create, distribute, and download -- no professional equipment is required. New podcasts are auto-downloaded. Can restrict podcasts to students enrolled in the course. Power of audio over text -- students can listen and learn while walking, riding, waiting in line, etc.	Entire file is downloaded to students' computer/device. Need sufficient bandwidth to download the podcasts in a timely fashion. Limited usefulness for hearing impaired people. No interactivity - audience cannot participate, etc. Intellectual property issues.
	Directed reading.	Material selected for targeted learning, therefore efficient use of learner time. Low cost	May not suit younger learning styles Availability may be an issue if

		development and provision.	materials not provided.
	Distance learning assignments or individual projects.	Can be highly motivating and liberating for some learners. Able to evidence a wide range of skills. Can be tailored to reflect individual strengths and learning styles (if known).	Can be frustrating if expectations are not absolutely clear. Learners need to be confident self-starters. Difficult to control. May take learners down unforeseen pathways.
Individualised FTF learning.	On-job training "Sitting by Nellie".	Cost effective "Real world, real thing" practical basis. Simultaneous absorption of associated workplace culture. Acknowledges the 70/20/10 principle. Supports the esteem of the selected workplace trainer. Learner may be more readily accepted into the workplace team on completion of training.	Selected workplace trainer may not be effective. Bad habits can be perpetuated. "Nellie" may not be a suitable trainer.
	Off-job coaching.	Useful for rapidly addressing specific shortcomings	Relatively expensive e.g. need to provide cover, distraction for coach etc.
	Mentoring	Useful for helping induction and settling in to new organisations or roles. Very useful for "steering" and motivating individuals who may have lost their direction.	Often confused with the coaching role. Relationships can distort into dependency. Hard to find people with true mentoring capability. Can be difficult to sustain.
Small group FTF learning	Traditional EDIP training— Explanation, Demonstration, Imitation, Practice.	Sound, proven approach provides predictable structure for developers, trainers and learners. Numerous specific methods can be appended to the process. Provides a good mix	Only suited to practical skills training.

		of activity to suit a range of individual learning styles.	
	Pair work, syndicate work with feedback to whole group.	Excellent for shifting the learning focus on to the learners.	May allow dominant characters to push their own views forward
		Does not allow the poor learner to hide so easily. Allows trainer to shift group dynamics by mixing individuals among syndicates. Allows trainers to engage with individuals.	Syndicates may drift "off task" when trainer is busy elsewhere. Some individuals may resent this approach feeling that their role should be to simply listen.
	Open discussions.	Useful for opening up a topic and exploring group knowledge levels, attitudes etc. Obvious vehicle for the Socratic technique.	Needs firm control from trainer to avoid straying off topic. Hard to ensure everybody contributes.
	Debates	Excellent vehicle for getting learners to "assemble" their thinking around a topic sufficient to present an argument. Can be structured to ensure that everybody contributes something.	Needs to be formally structured according to traditional rules. May be time consuming to set up.
	Seminars	Very effective for highlighting or scrutinising an individual's work within a group context. Useful for training individuals to be supportive group embers.	Individuals can feel threatened by this level of exposure. Immature or irresponsible group members could be vindictive, therefore strong control needed from trainer.
	Role plays	Absolutely essential for some learning e.g. conflict resolution, interviewing skills etc. Active involvement appeals to active learners.	Hard to organise and manage. Can be "dangerous" if things get out of control. Genuinely loathed and dreaded by many learners.
		Can provide rich "shared experience"	Needs general maturity to work

		material for subsequent examination by whole group.	well.
	Case study and in basket exercises	Excellent for consolidating chunks of information and theory input in an applied format.	Need to be piloted and validated. Trainer needs to be expert with the solutions
Large group FTF learning	Formal traditional lectures low level learning aids e.g. whiteboard.	Low cost re trainer / learner ratio No technology to malfunction. Simple to organize and run. Suited to certain cultures.	Totally dependent on trainer skill and personality. Less acceptable to younger audiences Little or no interactivity. Little opportunity for the individual voice.
	Lecture-forum i.e. with extended Q&A session designed in.	As above but design must anticipate and prepare for a possible wide range of questions.	Trainer must be expert on the topic
	Film / video presentations	Low cost re trainer / learner ratio. Content can be precisely selected. Allow the trainer to organize other learning administration etc. Can be high quality i.e. professionally produced.	Trainer must be able to handle difficult questions and the occasional "ambush". Some of the material may not be relevant, therefore pre-editing or on the spot adjustments. Learner attention span may not match the duration of the film. Content may need frequent updating
	Presentations with designed listening assignments / reaction panels.	Useful for maintaining learner focus and attention. Reaction panels can be used to provide a full re-interpretation of the material, so consolidating learning for all.	May offend traditional passive learners.
Group-individualised learning.	Remote virtual classrooms.	Often the only way of gaining some level of learner interactivity – with facilitator and other learners. Can be across	Learners need to be computer savvy. Dependent on multi-site technology working in an

		cultures, organisations, time zones etc. Can include other web-based technologies, therefore limitless referencing possible.	integrated fashion. Trainer / facilitators need to be very highly skilled in the use of the technology. Topic can get lost among the technology issues. Learners can get frustrated if things do not work well first time.

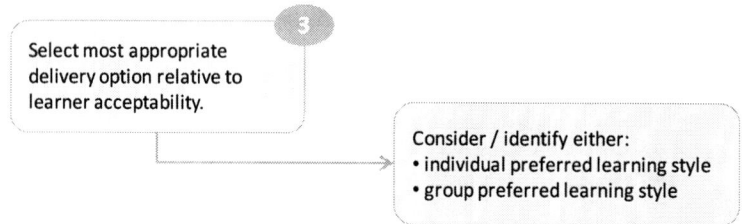

3

Select most appropriate delivery option relative to learner acceptability.

Consider / identify either:
• individual preferred learning style
• group preferred learning style

Extensive research over the last forty years has substantiated what educators and trainers have always instinctively understood i.e. that individuals prefer to learn in ways that accord with their basic personality types. Good teachers and trainers have always been distinguished by their ability to "tune in" to individuals and make adjustments that help them to absorb information, theory and practice.

Does it follow therefore, that if we are able to identify "preferred learning styles" for each of the participants attending a course we will be able to design programmes that are truly "learner friendly"? This is certainly the principle that has informed much of the research that occurred through the 1970's and 1980's. During that period a number of theories and models emerged to advance the preferred learning style concept. While this is not the place for an exhaustive review, it is certainly worthwhile summarising the principal models and then, more importantly, to discuss their potential application and their likely limitations for programme design.

Individual learning styles – the Kolb model.

We have already touched on David Kolb's experiential theory of learning in the introductory section. Kolb's model of preferred learning styles is a logical extension of his early work. Fundamentally Kolb maintains that we prefer to grasp experience through a range of approaches on a continuum between "concrete experience" (immediate, hands-on, direct involvement) and "abstract conceptualisation" (standing back, considering, imagined or remote involvement). He calls this the "processing continuum". Making sense of that experience or "transforming" experience into meaning, occurs on another continuum, from "active experimentation" through to "reflective observation". This is the "perception continuum". Kolb maintains that truly effective learning will involve all of these approaches to varying extents. For example, when learning to lead or manage people, the most meaningful progress is achieved if we:

- experience what it feels like to be a leader – concrete experience.
- reflect on what we have experienced and observed – reflective observation
- construct beliefs about what it means to lead or manage well – abstract conceptualisation.
- test how these beliefs stand up in new situations – active experimentation.

This is a picture of the truly mature learner. However, despite this ideal, as they develop and mature, individuals will, if given a choice, consistently gravitate toward a combination of these two continuums that aligns with their personality. This combination is their preferred learning style. Many programme developers and educators maintain that if this gravitation toward a preferred learning style is a fact of life, it makes sense to work with it than fight against it. The Kolb model is illustrated at figure 4.2 below.

The learning styles emerge from the combinations of adjacent continuum options e.g.

- active experimentation + concrete experience = the "accommodating" learner.
- concrete experience + reflective observation = the "diverging" learner.
- reflective observation + abstract conceptualisation = the "assimilating" learner.
- abstract conceptualisation + active experimentation = the "converging" learner.

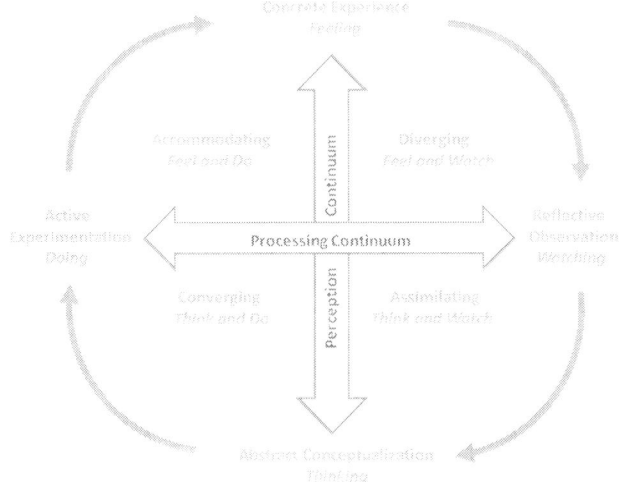

Figure 4.2 – Kolb's model of preferred learning styles

Kolb went on to develop the Learning Styles Inventory (2) as a means of diagnosing an individual's preferred learning style and describes the chief characteristics of each type.

The diverging learner tends to be both imaginative and emotional in the responses. They are willing and able to see things from a range of perspectives and then to build these different views into a "gestalt" or a view that is more than the sum of its parts. The generation of ideas, brainstorming and mind-mapping comes naturally to them. Typically they do well in the humanities and the arts, with wide ranging cultural interests.

The converging learner approaches the world with an opposite strategy. Convergers are "no nonsense" people who prefer things to be clear cut with one clear answer or obvious method. Typically, they are deductive thinkers, honing problems down and focusing in on specifics. They prefer process and rational order to overtly emotional situations. Consequently they tend to avoid people-centred environments which can be muddied by difficult emotions. Their interests are far narrower than the diverger and they tend to excel in science and engineering.

The assimilating learner is a watcher and thinker. His fundamental approach is inductive reasoning. Consequently he is likely to construct theoretical models and concepts from specific observations – it is his way of making sense of the world. They are lovers of order, structure and predictability, generally preferring systems to social interaction. They excel at distance learning because they do not need the social aspect of face to face group environments. They are typically found in the sciences and mathematically oriented occupations.

The accommodating learner is a "doer". They are much more likely to plunge into things, to experiment and to adapt to what they discover. They are not likely to enjoy formal lectures or extended theory sessions and they would empathise entirely with the Nike philosophy i.e. "Just do it!" In learning groups they can exhibit impatience and may express boredom when things are not moving fast enough for their liking. Not given to extended reasoning, their problem-solving is rooted in trial and error rather than analysis.

Individual learning styles – the Honey and Mumford model.

A glance at Honey and Mumford's learning styles model (figure 4.3 below) shows that it is essentially similar to Kolb's and is similarly rooted in the earlier work of John Dewey and Kurt Lewin. Its chief attraction for many is the relative simplicity of the language. It is not difficult to project the behaviour of activists, reflectors, theorists and pragmatists.

The model is driven by a questionnaire which elicits the individual's preferred learning style. Conceived essentially as a management tool, the model is intended to assist managers and educators in strategizing to develop under-utilised learning / information processing styles in an attempt to 'round out' the individual's skill set.

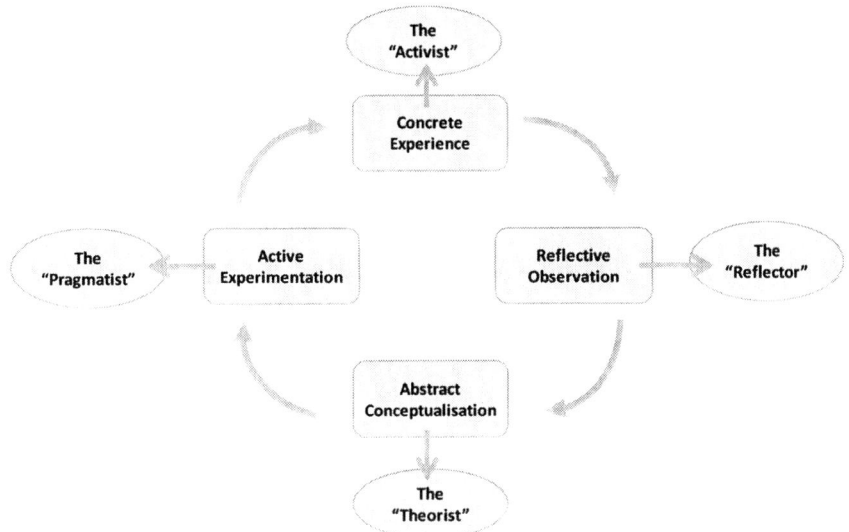

Figure 4.3 – Honey and Mumford's Learning Styles Model

Individual learning styles – the Gregorc model.

The work of Anthony Gregorc offers a subtly different way of looking at learning. His theory evolved from the "energic" model of learning first posited in the 1960's and brought to maturity in his Mind Styles Model of 1984. Fundamentally, he maintains that all individuals take in and "perceive" information through concrete mechanisms i.e. through tangible apprehension provided by our senses, and through abstract mechanisms provide by mental processes such as reason, intuition and imagination. We can see here a relationship to Honey and Mumfords "concrete experience" and "abstract conceptualisation".

Having taken in information the individual must make sense of it. Gregorc calls this the "ordering" function. We either process information sequentially, working in a more or less strict, step by step manner, or we process randomly, with no particular pattern in mind, often taking unconnected leaps. This leads to the now familiar intersection of continuums, producing four basic learning styles. These are:

- concrete sequential (CS)
- abstract random (AR)
- abstract sequential (AS)
- concrete random (CR)

The CS Learner

He is firmly rooted in the soils of clarity, structure and order. He learns best when he:

- is dealing with predictable situations
- is working within a highly structured environment
- is able to apply ideas aimed at a pragmatic outcome
- is able to rely on others having a similar outlook to their own

He likes:
- order
- clear, logical steps to follow
- unambiguous directions
- predictability

He dislikes:
- having to work in "buzzy" creative groups
- discussions that don't seem to lead anywhere
- working with high level abstract ideas or concepts
- having to work alongside disorganised people
- having to work in a cluttered environment

The AS Learner

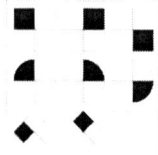

She learns best when she:
- is allowed to work alone
- is challenged to find order and structure in things
- is able to refer to expert knowledge to support own ideas

She likes:
- to be able to think things through thoroughly before committing to action
- to be able to use logical methods
- to see the links and relationships between things

She dislikes:
- being rushed to conclusions
- needless repetition
- having to express emotions
- having to be diplomatic with those who don't think the same way

The CR Learner

He learns best when he:
- is allowed to "suck it and see" (trial and error)
- is allowed to just get on with it without too many rules

- is allowed to take risks

He likes:
- intuitive people
- competing
- being able to change course or approach
- changing environments
- having options available

He dislikes:
- being restricted
- repetition or routines
- following strict procedures
- keeping records or filling in forms
- having to explain how he reached a conclusion or decisions

The AR Learner

She learns best when she:
- feels that learning is personalised
- sees participants socialise and get on well together
- is able to build strong relationships
- is able to focus on issues in a constructive, cooperative group manner

She likes:
- listening to the views of others
- harmony / absence of conflict
- working in teams or groups
- taking a broad rather than deep focus

She dislikes:
- working with challenging people
- being unnecessarily restricted
- working in an unfriendly atmosphere
- being made to be precise
- criticism

Individual Learning Styles - The VARK Model.

This model of learning styles is perhaps the most widely used in education and training. The reason for this is undoubtedly that it is the simplest to understand and use for all concerned. Based on a simple questionnaire, it identifies 4 variants of learning styles.

V = visual learners

A = aural (or auditory) learners

R = read / write learners

K = kinesthetic learners

Visual learners acquire and process information most effectively through the visual channel. Given the opportunity they will naturally turn information into graphical form. They respond readily to illustrations, diagrams, charts, graphs, videos film etc. They are not keen on reading lengthy texts or being subjected to extended lectures – unless they are accompanied by good graphics of course.

Aural learners depend heavily on listening skills to take in information. They are perfectly happy to sit through long lectures, to listen to extended radio broadcasts. It is not unusual to find these learners recording lectures rather than writing notes.

Reading and writing learners prefer to take in information in text format. They will also re-order information to suit their own preferred text structures. Often this will involve the painstaking rewriting of texts. Characteristically we will often hear this type of learner saying "I need to write it down, then I've got it!"

Kinesthetic learners are alternatively referred to as "tactile" learners because they need to "get hands on" in order to grasp things fully. Consequently they can become frustrated and bored if they have sit through long presentations or are asked to read lengthy texts. They are essentially practical people.

As with all models, the VARK system is defined by its polarities, but this does not mean that learners are entirely polarised into one style. Most will have a primary tendency but will combine this with elements of another. For example, an aural learner may also prefer to have a lecture summarised periodically with a good graphic and a reading writing learner may well introduce visual notes to assist written work. There are very few people who would learn entirely without use of the visual channel. Occasionally, the questionnaire reveals that an individual has no preferred style and is quite happy to accept learning in any form. These individuals are known as "multimodal" learners.

Individual learning styles – practical applications?

If we suppose that it is always possible to gather information on the preferred learning styles of our learners (through the various questionnaire and inventory systems), we are still left with a very large elephant in the room i.e. what do we do with this information? How can we put it to good use?

The value of understanding how an individual prefers to learn is obvious in the context of one-on-one coaching. Providing the subject matter is not compromised, the trainer can take positive steps to adapt delivery to suit the individual. However, the moment we move to group situations such adaptation becomes altogether more difficult. With the average learning group, the trainer will most likely be faced with a range of styles that need to be accommodated. It is relatively easy to accommodate "monocultural" groups which have predictably similar attitudes. For example, we could assume that a group of recruit firefighters will be fundamentally physical, hands-on people who will respond positively to the "doing" components of learning. As a group they are more likely to find the theoretical elements harder to work with. Nevertheless, even with groups such as these there will be, at any one time, a number of individuals who are not in their comfort zone.

Teachers within the general education system may have the advantage of working with the same learner groups over extended periods. Consequently, they have an opportunity to analyse their learners and "differentiate" them into groups with the same or similar learning styles. Debate continues as to whether this is actually beneficial since it may deprive children of the opportunity to "learn to learn" across the styles. Recent research questions whether trying to accommodate individual preferred learning styles actually has any positive effects., (3) (4) (5) Most trainers operating in the adult learning field do not have the opportunity to research their learners preferred styles and must, pragmatically, base their design and delivery on "pleasing all of the people some of the time". This is the simple reality of the trainer's world.

Recognising this stark reality, researchers such as Bernice McCarthy now maintain that the first principle of learning design and delivery should always be to take learners on a journey that systematically addresses the needs associated with perceiving and processing identified in all the various models. Along with many contemporary educationalists she maintains that learning is actually enhanced when learners come to perceive and process in ways that are not necessarily "natural" to them. Indeed. We might say that learners are not fully "mature" until they are able to respond positively to all learning events, no matter how they are presented. McCarthy developed this thinking into a solution which makes more practical use of the learning style concept.

Individual learning styles - the 4Mat system.

McCarthy's approach utilises the work of Robert Sperry who classified human beings as being either essentially left or right brain thinkers. Sperry maintained that the two hemispheres of the brain perceive and process information differently. A person who is "left-brained" is likely to be more logical, analytical and objective. The converse holds for a person who is "right-brained", and likely to be more intuitive, thoughtful and subjective. Typically left brainers "stand apart" from experience; functioning through the application of structure and sequence, precise use of language and number. They seek to break down information and analyse perception. Right brainers prefer to be "engaged" to be "in the moment". They are inclined to look for patterns, metaphors and to think in images. Their instinct is not to analyse but to synthesise.

While we may all have a preference for left or right brain functioning, there is a constant interplay between the two polarities. McCarthy maintains that a balance between right and left is the ideal solution to learning and thinking at a higher level. Bringing both perceptive modes into play initiates deeper and broader understanding and inevitably leads to more creative thinking and problem solving. Figure 4.4 illustrates the concept that has become established as the "4 MAT system" (6).

The system promotes an essentially practical way of designing and delivering any learning event is such a way as to engage all learners through their preferred learning style at least some of the time, while ensuring that they are taken through a complete learning experience which adequately meets subject matter needs. This is a process that helps the individual mature as a learner, rather than continually attempting to indulge immediate preferences.

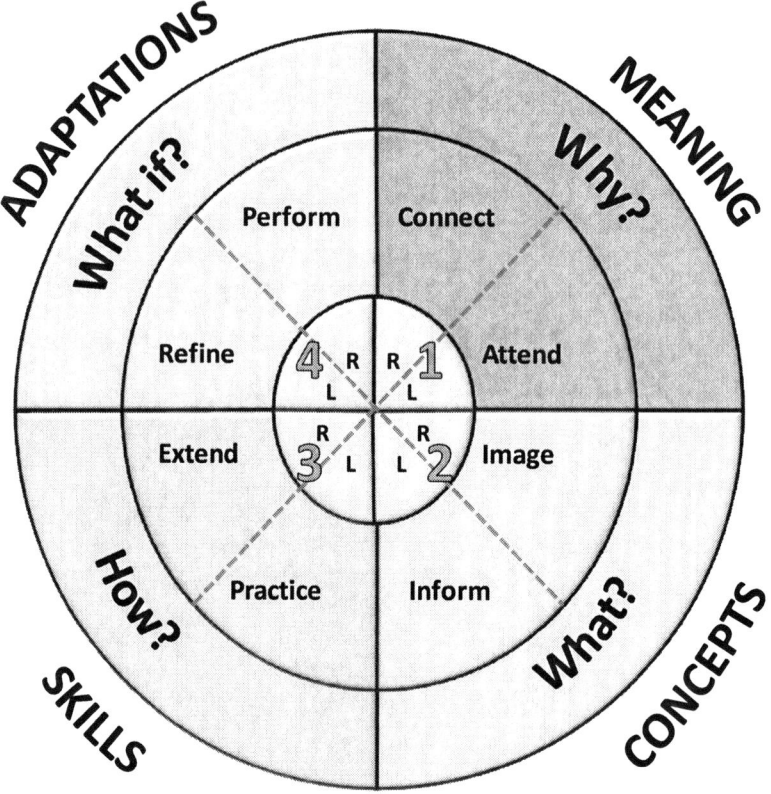

Figure 4.4 – McCarthy's 4MAT system

In a similar manner to Kolb, Honey and Mumford and other Jungian oriented theorists, McCarthy identifies 4 types of learners:

- **Type 1**: These are individuals that need to establish what the learning means for them. At a subliminal level they are constantly asking the questions "why?" "How is this relevant to me?" If these questions are not satisfactorily answered they are unlikely to engage in the process. They will not be tempted with learning for learning's sake. Once engaged and persuaded of the value for them personally, they can learn effectively in most modes.

- **Type 2**: These are individuals drawn strongly to facts, concepts and underlying principles. The key questions for them are "What is this all about?" "What is going on here". Consequently they excel at analysis, research and probing the views of associated experts.

- **Type 3**: These are typically active experimenters who not inclined to stand aside and study the facts of the situation. Their first response is always to get hands on and give it a try. They are typified by the adage "when all else fails – read the instructions!" They are generally the first to try anything practical or to volunteer to lead the group.

- **Type 4**: These are individuals primarily geared to taking the learning and extending it into other dimensions or uses. They are truly individual in that while they accept input from those around them they are self-directed. Consequently, type 4 learners need little motivation, making excellent independent learners. However, they do not always end up where the trainer / teacher intends them to.

The model goes on to offer a systematic approach or process for design and delivery that will capture all four types in the net. Successful learning should:

- Deal firstly with the WHY. This enables the learners (particularly type 1) to "Connect" and provides a rational for individuals to "attend".

- Move on to the factual substance – the WHAT. This is where the trainer builds the conceptual and factual "image" through "informing". This does not have to be expository in nature – the Socratic technique of eliciting understanding through questioning would be just as appropriate. This will satisfy the type 2 learners in particular.

- Follow up on the essential facts with the HOW. This is the stage characterised by demonstration and "practice" sessions aimed at "extending" understanding. Type 3 learners will relish this.

- Finally, type 4 learners can be fully engaged through invitations to consider how the techniques, concepts, skills could be used in a range of circumstances or be adapted for other uses. This is the WHAT IF? Extension of the system.

For trainers who cannot realistically differentiate learners for a given course, the 4MAT process offers a reliable formula for designing well-constructed learning that will engage most learners to a satisfactory degree and remain true to the subject matter. The HR professional who commissions work rather than designs it can use this "blueprint" to question the efficacy of what is being offered by the contractor.

CONSIDERING ACCEPTABILITY FOR THE ORGANIZATION.

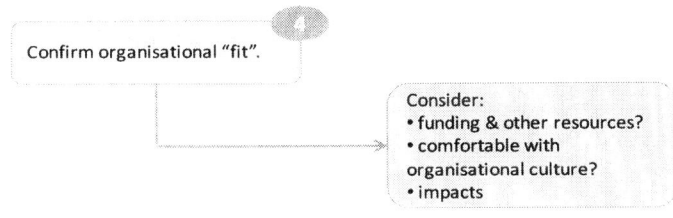

Confirm organisational "fit".

Consider:
- funding & other resources?
- comfortable with organisational culture?
- impacts

Organisational approval may seem to be an obvious prerequisite for embarking on a new learning delivery initiative, but the range of considerations required is often less so. Failure to address the key concerns before committing to a design strategy may lead to eventual failure on a number of fronts.

Top of the list will always be financial resources. The cost of training or learning programmes varies hugely according to mode, methods, duration and the support resources required. Identifying the true costs of providing training is not a simple process due to the wide range of variables involved and the degree of variance within each variable. Organisations that deliver training on an ongoing basis usually develop spreadsheet tools that help pin down costs to an acceptable level of accuracy. The major costs components are:

- Design and development
- Delivery
- Associated assessment
- Evaluation

Design costs.

These are almost always under-estimated. Organisations with their own training departments may not have to justify costs in detail. As long as costs are not seen to be excessive relative to cost history, the training department may simply be left to get on with learning development as business as usual. However, once development is outsourced, costs will inevitably be scrutinised more fully. It is important to understand that outsourcing is not necessarily more expensive. Contractors may be able to provide greater expertise, technical resources and the dedicated time that enables them to work much faster.

Internal or external, the costs associated with design and development can be sobering and should be projected to a reasonable estimate before any commitment is made. The $ cost per hour of development will vary according to developers salaries, profit margins imposed by external contractors and the type of work being done. More technically demanding design (e.g. high end simulation) will command higher costs per development hour. The most useful estimator of costs is always the average number of hours required for the different modes and methods. The table below illustrates the development time for the most commonly occurring delivery modes.

Type of learning activity	Development time
Basic text materials. Includes research, review, editing and sign-off.	12 hours per 1 hour of learning activity.
Traditional face-to-face instructor led classroom training. Includes learning specification, delivery design, lesson plans and associated presentation and learner materials.	34 hours for 1 hour of learning activity.
Standard E learning. Includes on-screen presentation elements, audio, some embedded video, basic assessments. Time varies according to level sophistication. The E-learning Guild provides	

the following estimates:	
• Simple synchronous learning (static HTML pages with text and graphics)	86 hours per 1 hour of learning activity.
• Simple asynchronous learning (static HTML pages with text and graphics)	117 hours per 1 hour of learning activity.
• Medium complexity synchronous learning (as above plus Flash, Java scripting, animated gifs etc.)	147 hours per 1 hour of learning activity.
• Medium complexity asynchronous lerning (as above plus Flash, Java scripting, animated gifs etc.)	191 hours per 1 hour of learning activity.
• Complex synchronous learning (as above plus audio, video, interactive simulations)	222 hours per 1 hour of learning activity.
• Complex asynchronous learning (as above plus audio, video, interactive simulations)	276 hours per 1 hour of learning activity.
Conversion of in-house PowerPoint material to basic E-Learning format.	33 hours per 1 hour of learning activity.
Distance learning through correspondence type course or assignment work.	Similar to costs for basic text materials but may increase if CD Rom or E-learning elements are included.

While E-Learning may eventually offer significant savings, it will only do so if it is effectively designed. Learners now demand very high quality which drives up development costs still further. However, it is possible to reduce costs significantly if organisations work consistently with one development partner and development standard practices and template libraries. This allows content to be dropped into standardised "branded" formats.

The development times shown above are drawn from the work of Bryan Chapman of the Brandon Hall Group. They are averages and consequently some development work would come in well under the indicated investment, but conversely, work of particularly high complexity would come in much higher. The first principle when outsourcing is always to demand a full breakdown and justification of estimated costs, within a fixed price contract. It is then the responsibility of the developer to ensure that he has a full and accurate specification signed off by the client.

Delivery costs.

The costs associated with training delivery are certainly more predictable than those for design and development. Nevertheless there are costs that can sneak through under the radar of the unprepared, only to come as an unpleasant surprise at a later date. The most obvious example would be the cost of lost production due to trainees being off job.

As with development, most, if not all, of delivery costs would be absorbed as business as usual by an internal training department, but in most cases would still need to be aligned to departmental budgets. When using external providers all costs would certainly need to be carefully tracked. The typical delivery costs that need to be considered are:

- Venue hire.
- Equipment hire e.g. data projectors, computers etc. training aids.
- Materials e.g. workbooks, hand-outs etc.
- Facilitator fees.
- Train the trainer costs.
- Travel e.g. flights, motor mileage allowances etc.
- Accommodation
- Meals
- Administrative support costs.
- Lost production costs
- Provision of cover (for trainees released)
- Payment for trainees attending in own time (if applicable)
- Post course assessment costs (if applicable)
- Post course evaluation costs (if applicable)
- Registration or certification fees (if applicable)

Setting these costs up as a spread-sheet is a relatively simple matter. The spread-sheet can then be populated for each different course or programme delivered and a cost per learner calculated. This information is obviously invaluable for budgeting purposes but also for calculating return on investment (ROI).

Organisational culture.

Organisations are driven by people, and people generally have an inherent need to belong to a community. In the workplace this means conforming to the "way we do things around here", to the norms, positive or negative, that have developed as the organisation matures. Some aspects of culture are overt and obviously linked to the occupations concerned. We would be very surprised, even disappointed, to find that a military unit did not have a "macho", highly conformist culture. Similarly, we would generally expect our schools to be founded on a nurturing, individualising culture. Other aspects of culture are less obvious, even subliminal and difficult to define or describe.

In larger organisations culture is also often horizontally and vertically differentiated. Managers and employees in different departments will often develop significantly different ways of working together. The HR department for example might operate quite differently to finance or planning. This is horizontal differentiation. Managers might have to adapt their behaviours as they move from their department setting into the management team environment and senior managers adapt again as they move to the board room. This is vertical differentiation.

All this adds up to up to a complex mix which can be further clouded by the need to accommodate associated cultures e.g. trade union relationships. So what does this mean for the HR professional or the L&D specialist within the company? In simple terms, learning activity is of little use if it is not acceptable or credible to its audience. This means that while the subject matter may not be negotiable the means of delivery must always be open to verification against positive cultural norms. Negative norms should never be appeased. When design is outsourced there is a very real danger of the specifics of organisational culture being overlooked. Consequently the commissioning agent (usually from HR) needs to vet:

- Delivery and assessment methods
- Materials – especially language use
- Trainers / facilitators – in some instances even gender can be an issue e.g. for religious reasons

Impacts.

Systems thinking is the name of the game here. It is extremely unlikely that a training event will have no effect on other aspects of organisational life. Training often addresses new techniques, policies, processes or equipment and the "knock-on effects" need to be traced through to ensure that everything realigns. The impact may simply be personal e.g. as a result of completing a qualification course the individual may be entitled to a salary increment. This obviously impacts on payroll systems.

Running a training course is rather like throwing a pebble into a pond, the ripples spread outward at a rate proportionate to the size of the pebble i.e. the significance and novelty of the training event. Training that supports particularly important initiatives may need extensive change management planning to ensure that all impacts are fully traced and accounted for.

ADJUSTING TO ACHIEVE ACCEPTABILITY.

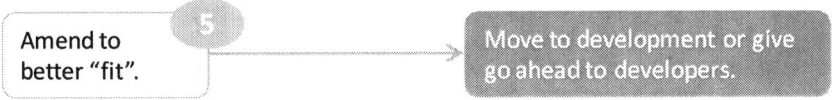

This is self-explanatory. Assuming that aspects of training design are found to be unacceptable or "uncomfortable' for the organisation, changes will have to be made until a better fit is achieved. This may simply be a matter of achieving savings on design or delivery costs or perhaps phasing in training to allow other systems to be adjusted alongside. Sound training design can eventually falter for want of fine tuning.

Building content – the selection and use of subject matter experts (SME's).

Whether you are tasked with developing the content of the programme yourself, or you are outsourcing, you will probably need to gather accurate and current material from somewhere. Unless, by chance, you possess undoubted expertise and experience in the subject, you will need to find subject matter experts to help you identify, build and validate the content. Even if you are an expert, you would be foolish not to enlist the critical eye of others in field that might bring alternative perspectives to the project.

The first task is to find your SME's. This is not as simple as seeking out people with long experience who are highly respected for their technical know-how. All organisations have these people – how else would they be successful? Getting access to them can be difficult however, usually because their expertise makes them very valuable commodities with little time to spare. It is always worth approaching their managers to get approval and support for the SME's involvement before approaching the individual directly, because there are other critical criteria that should be satisfied before engagement. These are:

- **Reputation** – how is the SME regarded across the company / industry? This is important because the credibility of your course or programme will suffer if your SME's are not highly respected.
- **Previous experience** – if SME's have little or no experience of assisting with content development you will have to invest a good deal of effort in "setting them up" e.g. with a basic understanding of learning concepts and strategies.
- **Ability to work in a team** – unfortunately, high levels of expertise often go hand in hand with large egos. Groups of SME's will often waste significant amounts of time bickering over niceties and possibly over fundamentals. The ability and willingness to work to consensus is essential.
- **Ability to see things from the learner's perspective** – most experts take their knowledge and skills for granted and many fail to understand why others might struggle with basic concepts or techniques. The developer so often finds herself reminding SME's to empathise with the struggling novice.
- **Willingness to accept guidance / direction** – inevitably, experts are passionate about their subject. They may fail to understand why learners might not want to learn everything about the subject, all at once. Without clear and consistent guidance SME's will often try to pile everything into a course; too much material, often at too high a level. They must be able to focus themselves on the required learning outcomes.
- **Self discipline and work ethic** – developing course content is a time consuming and expensive business. This means that SME meetings must remain focused and determined to be productive. With every gathering of SME's there is always the danger of drifting off target into peripheral arguments or perhaps into bouts of "war stories".

So, in summary, the perfect SME is a highly respected individual, able to work in a focused and participative manner with others. He is able to resist overloading the content and able to empathise with the learner's actual needs. As a professional, he is mindful of the hidden costs and able to deliver to agreed deadlines.

Having found such a creature, the developer needs to get the best out of him through building an effective working relationship based on mutual respect. How do we achieve this? There are a few simple guidelines.

Before requesting a first meeting:

- Research the SME's background. Find out what they have been involved in that has contributed to their expert status?
- What is the current involvement? You need to understand something of workload, tasking etc. Are there any obvious synergies between current involvement and the projected programme content?
- Research the subject yourself – to the extent that you can at least frame sensible questions. This will earn you some respect and allow you to maintain an appropriate level of control.

When requesting a first meeting:
- Provide a succinct overview of the development project; what, why, who, timeframes etc.
- Explain that he has been recommended etc. as a source of knowledge and expertise that will assist with creating a focused, high quality programme. Specify his scope of work e.g. either
  - To act as sole SME for the whole or a specific part project
  - Or to join a SME group for whole or part of the project
- Outline his anticipated time / travel commitment – be honest about this. If demands are too great further down the track, the relationship is bound to suffer.

A few days prior to first meeting:
- Send through programme aims, objectives / learning outcomes for initial familiarization.

At first meeting (may be within a SME group setting):
- Provide detailed account of project history to date and current status in terms of learning outcomes to be achieved, qualification alignments etc.
- Clarify and confirm your own role i.e. to ensure that the project remains on track and that emerging group efforts remain aligned and restricted to learning outcomes.
- Clarify and confirm roles of others who may be involved e.g. project sponsor, key stakeholders etc.
- Clarify and confirm commitment and ways of working; discussion, recording, drafting of selected information, consultation and sign-off etc.
- Set out tasks to be achieved and approximate timetable. Task 1 should always be a final review of learning outcomes.
- If possible tackle first tasks at this meeting in order to establish working practices.

Ongoing throughout the development project:
- Maintain prompt and effective communication with all SME's. Always bear in mind that you are in their debt and responding rapidly to their queries or submissions will acknowledge that debt.
- Provide SME's with regular progress updates and draft versions. This will keep them focused on their contribution.
- Focus on the coordination function. Ensure that SME's are able to communicate with each other and with other stakeholders as required.
- At the end of the day your role is to manage SME's effectively. Content and construct validity can easily be undermined if you do not do so.

Key materials.

Successful interaction with SME's should produce most, if not all the raw material necessary for training delivery. The task now is to craft the raw content into the key materials that make up the training package. Final package configuration will of course vary according to the subject and audience but most successful learning will be supported by the following key materials:

- A trainer guide – containing session delivery plans and an outline of how to present the material.
- Participant materials – prepared notes or note-taking facilities, handouts, workbooks etc.
- Assessment materials if required.
- Learning / training aids

The trainer guide.

We would normally expect a trainer to be expert in the subject, or at least more so than the participants. Even so, a well-designed course will provide designated trainers with detailed guidelines on how to frame delivery to the best effect. The trainer guide is primarily intended to ensure that all the required material is covered, with appropriate emphases, in a more or less standardised fashion. Experienced trainers will inevitably internalise these guidelines and add their own anecdotes and personal touches, but each course delivered should nevertheless be predictably similar. The level of detail provided will depend largely on the criticality of the subject and the degree of standardisation required. For example, we would expect trainers to follow more or less exact guidelines when training medical students in potentially dangerous invasive procedures. Conversely, an evening class in digital photography will be much more loosely handled.

There is no set template for laying out a trainer guide, but certain components are mandatory if they are to function effectively. Layout may also be dictated or conditioned by organisational "style guides" which assure both the required level of quality and a look and feel that aligns with company branding. The guide should be "chunked down" into discrete sessions and these in turn should be punctuated with regular breaks to refresh participants. While adults possess greater powers of concentration than younger people they should nevertheless not be subjected to sessions longer than 90 minutes. Exceptions can sometimes be made for practical or physical training which may be more engaging than theoretical presentations. The essential components for each session plan are:

- The relevant learning outcome
- References to any external standard, code of practice, or internal standard operating procedure.
- Expected session duration
- A delivery narrative (not to be delivered word for word). This would include details of all activities, exercises and perhaps even appropriate questions to ask. Some guides will anticipate participant responses and provide the trainer with tips on how to deal with these.
- A running schedule to help the trainer keep on track.
- A reference to the accompanying learning aids.

- Examples of completed assessments etc.

An excerpt from a typical trainer guide follows. In this example the training is dealing with the hazards of working in confined spaces. This involves critical safety knowledge and consequently the level of guidance to the trainer is considerable. Note that learning aids are indicated by icons, selected as a part of the company's style guide.

Trainer guides are of greatest value to the inexperienced. Once a trainer becomes thoroughly familiar with a specific course or programme she will probably choose to work without it. Inevitably, she will also add her own touches in terms of delivery style. Nevertheless, delivery should be monitored against the requirements of the trainer guide in order to ensure that content and focus needs are being adhered to.

TOPIC: HAZARD AWARENESS AND IDENTIFICATION

Estimated duration: 60 min

Learning Outcome: The learner will be able to explain how risk assessment and risk management procedures associated with confined space working comply with the requirements of health and safety legislation. Ref: Unit Standard 18426 / 2.1, 2.2, 2.3 and 2.4		
Sub-topic and approximate schedule	**Delivery suggestion for trainer**	**Training Aids**
Duties of employer and employee (HSE Act 1992) **1130-1150**	Explain that safety in the workplace cannot be left to chance. Experience shows that without external controls, employers and employees are likely to cut corners and engage in unsafe working practices to get the job done faster. The removal of machine guards is the classic example. Consequently all work places in New Zealand are governed by the Health and Safety in Employment Act (HSE) dating from 1992. This sets out the legal responsibilities of both the employer and the employee in regard to health and safety. Everybody in the workplace needs to understand what their responsibilities are. Show slides 28-30 and work through the key duty statements. Field discussion about what these mean in practice.	 **28-30**
Definition of a hazard (recap) **1150-1200**	Explain that in this session we will be looking closely at the typical hazards that can be encountered in confined space working. Explain that it is always useful to remind ourselves of what is meant by a "hazard".	

	Ask generally for the official definition. Confirm by showing slides 31-32 and clarifying "harm" v "serious harm" etc.	**31-32**
Introduction to typical confined space hazards **1200-1230**	Divide the group into 6 syndicates. Issue each with a photo-board showing a confined space environment plus a written description. Task each syndicate to think about the specific confined space allocated to them and to list the hazards that might occur within them. Ask each syndicate to note their identified hazards on flip chart paper. Allow 5-10 minutes for the exercise.	**Picture Boards 1-6**
	Show matching slides, asking each syndicate in turn to post their flipcharts and talk to the slide. Invite comment from other syndicates. Summarise and critique for each syndicate in turn– expanding the list as required.	**33-38**

Naturally, the guidelines need to be tested before general publication, particularly the suggested scheduling. This will never be precise. Inquisitive, proactive learner groups will stretch the schedule. Unresponsive groups may leave the trainer "stranded". Good trainers are generally able to average out schedule variations over the day to bring things back on track.

Whether you outsource programme delivery, or take it on yourself, you should always aim off to cover those situations where the expert trainer is not available but the course must still go ahead. This is when you need that extra depth in the trainer guide. It is always a good tactic to task your developer with producing a guide that any experienced trainer (not necessarily expert in the subject) could pick up and, with a little preparation, make a reasonably good job of delivery.

Learner materials – text format.

Learning can be enhanced by wide range of devices. It would be a truly exceptional trainer or facilitator that could rely purely on their charisma and command of the spoken word to guarantee effective learning. Once we go beyond short verbal descriptions or summaries we are faced at least with the problem of factual retention, and perhaps with the learner's wish to review information or concepts over a longer timeframe. Good designers will always consider learning as a broader continuum than the conventional face-to-face component. With access to appropriate aids, learners can be "primed" before the course, assisted during it and provided with ongoing support afterwards.

Other than the trainer, the basic instrument of learner support is always the written word, perhaps assisted by graphics or illustrations of some kind. The commonly encountered formats are:

- Pre-course reading via selected texts.
- Designated web-based sources.
- Course hand-outs / notes.

These are all within the design ability of most HR/L&D staff. The interactive or CDROM based materials call for more specialised skills and, if justified, is best outsourced to professional studios. The key questions to be answered before embarking on development of learner material are:

- What purpose will it serve? e.g.
  - To provide an introduction to the subject before the course begins.
  - To provide a factual summary of topics covered – thus freeing participants from the task of note-taking.
  - To extend the participant's understanding by providing reading material not actually covered in the course.
  - To provide full depth coverage of the subject, perhaps accumulating as inserts into a file over the life of the programme.
  - To provide essential key facts for examination purposes.

Pre-course reading material can be a simple matter of directing the learner to specific texts or web sites. In this case it is important to provide precise instructions and to limit the reading to what is absolutely necessary. Participant goodwill will quickly evaporate if they come to realise half way through the face to face course that much of what they had to read has no actual relevance. Don't overburden them. Those that are particularly keen will do further research anyway. Alternatively, trainers may wish to put their own material together for mailing out. If this involves copying and reproducing significant chunks of other people's work, care should be taken not to infringe copyright or intellectual property laws which will vary from country to country. Selected texts should always be accompanied by an introduction, explaining their relevance and value, and possibly by a follow-on question set or self-assessment exercise to ensure that the learner has captured the target content.

Designing effective handouts.

Participant handouts are perhaps the most frequently abused form of learner material. As often as not they end up in the waste bin as the group leave the training room. While this might well be due to lack of learner interest or motivation, it might also be a comment on the quality of the material and how it is presented. Vast tracts of block text are unlikely to be well received. Similarly, diagrams or photos with no annotation may prove frustrating. Good layout and use of "white space" is important because it helps the learner navigate and digest the materials. While predictable, the classical design rules are the most reliable here. The most fundamental is the principle of the golden ratio, observed in nature thousands of years ago by the Greeks and since absorbed into mathematics as the Fibonacci sequence. Because the proportion appears constantly in nature, human beings are "hard wired" to respond favourably to it. For Leonardo it was the "divine proportion". When used to layout print materials it guarantees a pleasing effect. It is no accident that books are generally formatted in proportions that approximate to the golden ratio. The commonest paper sizing system is the "A" series. This has evolved somewhat from the divine proportion due to the need for constant halving with loss of proportion and the ability to scale down images without loss of aspect ratio.

Fundamental use of space.
The precise ratio is 1:1.618, often loosely translated as the "rule of thirds". This is a sound approach to simple design problems. Using this elegant principle you can divide your white space (paper) into a series of rectangles each proportionately related to each other (more or less) on the basis of the ratio. As shown in figure 4.5.

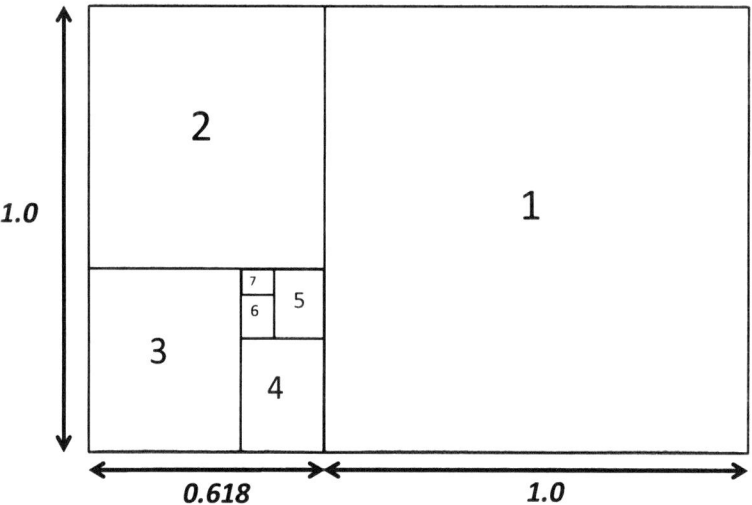

Figure 4.5 – The Golden Ratio

The various rectangles can then be used to locate graphics, text or titles, or simply be left as white space. Figure 4.6 shows a double page from a university prospectus where this golden ratio has been used very obviously to arrange the content. The proportion would seldom be slavishly followed but even used approximately will certainly assist successful layout.

The overlaid spiral demonstrates the mathematical unity of the ratios. It is also a foundation of natural design, of which the best known and most perfect example would be the shell of the nautilus.

The layout in figure 4.6 is probably more the territory of the graphic designer, but the basic principles can be exploited by trainers who need to prepare workbooks or simple handouts.

Figure 4.6 – Example of page layout using the golden section.

Inserting material.

Using the golden ratio you can divide your white space (paper) into areas that strike the eye as harmoniously proportioned. The combination and arrangement of rectangles is almost infinite. Larger graphics can be set in the larger sections (two thirds division) and smaller figures or illustrations will fit into the smaller spaces.

References to further reading or citations can also be inserted into the smaller space directly opposite the relevant discussion in the main text, as shown here. Use italics to differentiate references from the main text.

Learners need to be able to find their way through information, and to be able to refer to it with ease in discussions, seminars etc. Your workbooks or handouts should therefore follow a clear and consistent structural formula. The design can be entirely yours but the general layout rules should easily detectable to the reader.

Use titles in a hierarchical manner to organise your material and information into discrete, bite-size "chunks". Main topic titles can be clearly differentiated by the exclusive use of capitals and the lower level sub-headings by reducing font size. All titles should be differentiated through colour if possible. Figure 4.7 overleaf illustrates some of these simple principles. The use of borders to separate areas of information is another useful technique to assist navigational clarity.

These are very simple principles which, if followed, will reliably produce effective handouts for learners. If there is a general rule it is "avoid clutter". Edward Tufte has done extensive work on how information, (especially graphical data) should be laid out or displayed, both in paper-based and in electronic formats. His ideas, while complex at first sight are, in effect, classically elegant. He maintains that excessive simplification is a design sin because detail provides the deep substance of learning. However, detailed that is provided in a thoughtless manner is also a grave error. Perhaps his best known mantras are: "To clarify, add detail" and "Clutter is a failure of design, not an attribute of information".

Lifespan of handout materials.

If you have made the effort to design and produce good handouts for your learners then it is certainly worthwhile asking the question "what will they do with them once the training is completed". Of course you hope that they will cherish them and continue to refer to them in the future. They are unlikely to do this unless there is a clear signal that the handouts are worth keeping and some mechanism is provided for keeping them out of harm's way.

Even for a short duration course it is good practice to provide an attractive soft cover file into which the handouts can be inserted, perhaps together with a note-taking pad. For longer programmes, professionally produced participant folders, with tabulated sections, should be provided together with a briefing on their use and their importance for future success. Some individuals will do this for themselves, but they will certainly be in the minority. Consequently course designers should accept this as part of their overall responsibility.

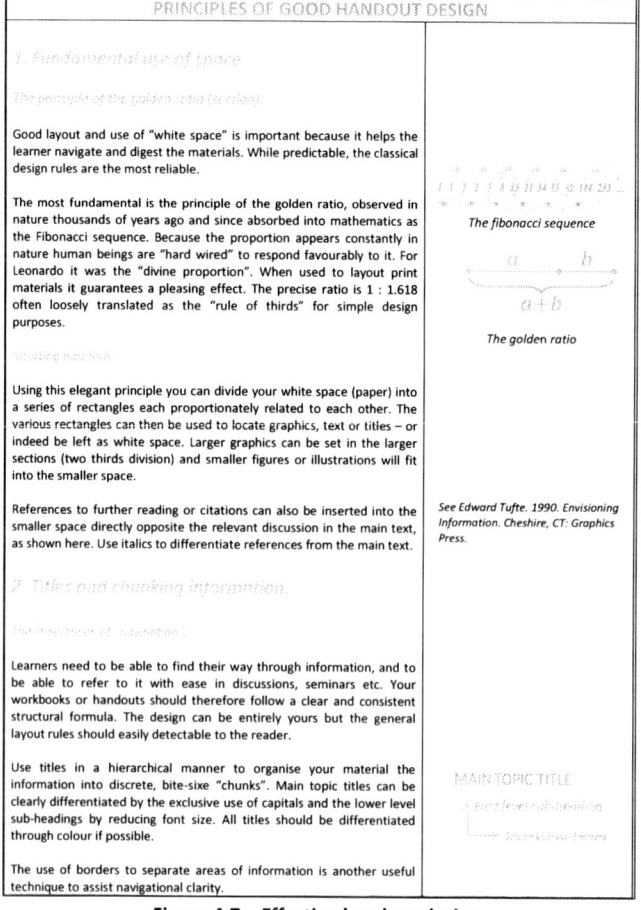

Figure 4.7 – Effective handout design

Workbooks.

Course workbooks provide a means of bringing together all the materials required by the learner in one package. For courses that are built on numerous activities and supporting handouts, the bound workbook format offers real advantages. Managing one document is obviously so much easier for the learner and of course the trainer does not have to produce and manage the distribution of separate piles of handouts or assessment materials. However, despite these advantages, workbooks require a considerable investment of time, energy and financial resources if they are to be worthwhile. Before opting for the workbook format should ask themselves the following questions:

- *"What is the likely longevity of the course / programme?"* Quite rightly, the client is unlikely to support the development expense for a one-off course. Repeatability brings with it a greater return on investment.

- *"Am I sufficiently certain of the stability of the material?"* Has the course been piloted sufficiently to ensure that the materials work well and are therefore unlikely to be changed? If there is any uncertainty here a ring binder format is should be used so that individual sections can be amended. Bound formats, while more professional in appearance, should be avoided unless stability can be guaranteed.

- *"How much release control do I need?"* Bound workbooks allow learners to "get ahead" of training delivery and may cause significant distraction. Trainers must think carefully about how they wish learning to be built up and accumulated during the course. If the course requires tight control, a bound workbook is not a good idea.

So, assuming that the course in question will be delivered on a continuing basis, is supported by proven and stable materials, and has no significant release control requirements, we could opt for a bound workbook format. All that is required now is to design the document effectively.

The look and feel of the workbook should conform to the client organisation's style guide. This will set down clear principles and provide templates for all documentation. If a style guide is not available then efforts should be made to align the visual design to the organisation's branding. Consistency of presentation is more than cosmetic; it gives the learner confidence in the professionalism of the product and in organisational ownership.

Structural design will vary according to the type and level of learning involved. Nevertheless there are certainly some standard requirements:
- An attractive cover with a suitable graphic and course title.
- Document control page – giving version number, amendment details etc.
- Table of contents.
- An introduction outlining what the course is about (course aim), any alignment to internal or external qualifications, any assessment requirements, learning pathways etc.
- A listing of the learning outcomes.

- Topic dividers / tabs for each discrete section / component of the course.
- Designated materials, exercises, assessments etc for each section. These might include print-outs of PowerPoint slides etc.
- Sufficient blank sheets or space for note-taking in each section.
- A glossary – if the course has a technical content.
- Separate section for suggested references / further reading.

The layout of materials should conform generally to those that apply to handout design. We all know that "a picture is worth a thousand words" so graphics should be used to support text whenever possible – but they need to be of good quality and free from copyright issues.

PowerPoint presentations.

A training environment without data projection and PowerPoint is now virtually inconceivable. Microsoft's presentation format is now globally dominant to the extent that it is often the first port of call for the training developer. The question is – does it deserve such pre-eminence? The short answer would be "No!" A more considered response would be "No – but it can play a significant part in learning delivery, especially when integrated with other formats and technologies".

Criticism of PowerPoint is generally unjustified. After all, it is simply another tool available to the trainer. The often caustic comments made about PowerPoint would be better directed at those who use it badly. We have all suffered "death by PowerPoint", dozing off in our seats during a seemingly endless parade of soporific text extracts probably accompanied by banal clipart. This is not the fault of the medium itself. Nevertheless there are some genuine concerns that the designer and presenter must deal with when using PowerPoint as a delivery strategy. These are:
- The PowerPoint "page" or screen by screen delivery is essentially linear. This can make it very directive since the learner must take in information in a totally managed fashion. This may suit the presenter – but often irritates the learner.
- It is a poor method of displaying more complex charts, tables or graphs – especially if these have to be directly compared.
- The wealth of "whizz bangs" or "PowerPoint Phluff" encourages poor designers to include hordes of wearisome animations and template devices.
- The PowerPoint presentation often takes centre stage, encouraging the presenter to retreat to the sidelines
- Each screen can only carry limited amounts of information and therefore encourages a level of information précis that may dilute real learning.

The truth is that Powerpoint has evolved now to a level of sophistication that its actual potential as a learning tool or learning medium is seldom fully explored. In the hands of an expert it can offer:
- Relatively sophisticated graphic design facilities at a "built in" price. Probably around 80% of PowerPoint's tools go unused. This includes the ability to build up layered animations e.g to demonstrate mechanical or electrical principles.
- The ability to carry embedded video.

- The ability to carry narration and talking head commentary.
- The ability to hyperlink directly to internet or intranet sites and files.
- The ability to be packaged as on line learning units.
- Compatability with a wealth of software (much of it inexpensive or freeware) that allows material to be transformed for the web or for mobile phone.

However, it is as a presentation tool that PowerPoint is primarily encountered. Whether the HR professional is presenting herself or monitoring the quality of trainers, there are a number of well-known pitfalls to avoid.

Too much detail:

Probably the commonest error. So often presenters ignore the golden rule – keep it simple. Either people cannot read it – or there is just too much to take in in one go. Appreciation of detail can be achieved by separating out sections into separate slides or by building up item by item.

Poor use of colour / lack of contrast:

Given the frequency with which colours are combined inappropriately we could be forgiven for believing that most presenters are colour blind! Look for effective contrasts, light and dark or use the colour wheel to find what will work

Use of outdated, banal clipart and Wordart.

Stay well away from stock clipart. Almost certainly they will have seen it all before and even if they haven't, it's so boring! Also, try to avoid the standard design templates. It's easy enough to make your own. Think about what you are trying to say and then look for fresh imagery that will reinforce. Try to develop your own style.

There is a wealth of images freely avaiable on the web via the various search engines. Try always to use images to reinforce the key message or learning.

Use of difficult, hard to read fonts or mixed fonts:

Standard computer systems provide us with a wealth of fonts but in reality very few of them are used. There is a very good reason for that i.e. most of them are difficult to read!

Stick to trusted no nonsense fonts such as Calibri, Arial etc. and avoid mixing fonts on the same screen.

Use of underprint images:

Underprint images are a graphic design convention that can be very effective if well done. They serve little purpose (other than confusion) in a PowerPoint presentation.

If used, keep them for Intro slides and make certain that the brightness of the underprint image is sufficiently reduced to ensure adequate contrast for the superimposed text.

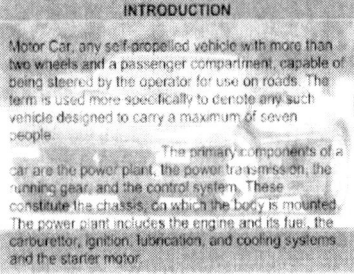

Overuse of animation:

Animation can certainly be helpful but it must be used sparingly. Avoid the 'whizz bangs' – they pall very quickly. Probably the most useful animations are those geared to bringing up items in succession and fading down to allow the audience to focus on one topic at a time.

Reading for the audience:

This is the cardinal sin. Training or presentation is about engagement and communication with an audience. This cannot occur if the trainer has his nose deep in notes or, worse still, insists on reading the slide content for the audience. This is not only tedious, it is insulting for the audience who, we must assume, can actually read. Most often, presenter faults of this kind are a sign or nerves or simple lack of preparation.

Sales Performance YTD
* Northern = 20% increase
* Midland = 6% increase
* Southern = 2% decrease

* **Northern = 20% increase**
* **Midland = 6% increase**
* **Southern = 2% decrease**

Just too many slides!

Natural attention spans are getting shorter with each successive generation. Around 40 minutes seems to be the limit without some kind of activity change. It is important to limit slide numbers to the minimum, especially if they contain a good deal of text. Far better to provide detailed text information as a handout. PowerPoint should be thought of as primarily a vehicle for the presentation of core concepts backed by visual stimulus.

The issues highlighted above are all genuine issues – but all can be overcome within a proper design framework. Firstly we should remember that "presenting" is a very poor method of delivering learning. Presentation of information and ideas should always be accompanied by other strategies e.g. discussion, participation activities etc. If we go back to EDIP, the most basic instructional format, (explanation, demonstration, imitation, practice), we can see that PowerPoint might be useful for the explanation phase, but could never be adequately substituted for the others.

Secondly, the linearity inherent in PowerPoint can be overcome by "blending" in other media e.g. allowing your audience access to more extensive documentation before and during the session.

Thirdly, use of the default templates and woeful clipart is not actually mandatory. Those who use PowerPoint should take the time and trouble to develop a style of their own that acknowledges the principles of sound design. Learning to put good PowerPoints together is relatively easy. There is now a wealth of guidance on good

PowerPoint design. The quickest route to effective design is to understand what not to do. For amusing, but absolutely pertinent advice see Don McMillan's skit on YouTube www.youtube.com/watch?v=lpvgfmEU2Ck or for positive tips see the LACS Training Blog at: http://lacs trainingblog.com. For an in-depth analysis of PowerPoint and what it offers the trainer see Dave Paradi's book *Present It So They Get It* available as an Ebook or in hard back from Amazon.

Fourthly, putting yourself at the centre of the presentation can be achieved by a number of simple devices e.g.
- Keeping your slides simple so that you have to expand on them verbally.
- Building in regular pauses (use B button) to return the focus to you as the presenter.
- Arranging the venue so that the screen is to one side and your position is central to the audience.
- Using a remote so that you are not "chained to the laptop". This allows you to move around naturally and to focus on that all important direct engagement.

Fifthly, don't expect PowerPoint to carry huge amounts of detail. It should be used to summarise and emphasise key points. Provide detail via handouts or other forms of text or through open discussion.

Lastly, and most important of all is preparation. Good trainers are familiar with the flow of the presentation material and have worked through how they will expand on each slide. By all means use the notes pages facility in PowerPoint for preparation but never refer to them during the actual show.

A case for E-learning?

"E-learning" has now evolved to such a level of reliability and potential sophistication that its undoubted benefits cannot be ignored. Nevertheless, the experience of the last two decades has shown that it is rarely the magic bullet that the training department is desperately seeking. The trick, as always, for the HR / L&D professional is to know what you want to buy and to make sure that you get what you want.

Why consider E-learning? Technology has not just given us additional means of access to knowledge. It is busy re-defining what we consider to be knowledge and what we think of as learning. Younger generations are increasingly leaning to the view that "knowledge" is more to do with knowing how and where to find out than it is with knowing the "thing itself". For them, learning is "anytime, anywhere" and inextricably bound up with the on-line world. So, if this is the way things are we would be foolish not to engage technology whenever it might be appropriate.

Therein lies the problem – when is it appropriate? Technophile or technophobe, making sound judgments about E-learning relies on a dispassionate appreciation of the advantages that it might offer for organisational learning strategy.

E-Learning - Key advantages for the organisation.

If you are really convinced that E-learning is the way to go for a particular learning programme, you will have to provide senior management with some convincing arguments, particularly of the cost-benefit kind. Getting into E-learning for the first time, or embarking on new E-learning initiatives can generate significant up-front costs. You will certainly be asked to demonstrate how those costs will be recouped, and how quickly. Ultimate costs savings should certainly be one of your major sales pitches, but there are undoubtedly others that will assist e.g.

- **Significant reduction in traditional training costs**. By definition E-learning strategies do not require a face-to-face component. Consequently the disproportionate costs of travel, accommodation and meals disappear.
- **Simultaneous training of large numbers**. Traditional training solutions are generally limited in the participant numbers they can handle at any one time. Not so with E-learning.
- **Reduction in time away from the workplace**. Being able to log on and follow a course at work (or at home) offers a company huge advantages. Not only is the individual available if needed, he or she is not "disengaged" as often happens when required to attend off-job traditional programmes.
- **No need for face-to-face trainers / facilitators**. Yet again, another potential significant cost saving.
- **Can help to develop individual's accountability for own learning**. Participant learners cannot sit back and wait for the trainer to drive things forward. They must continually motivate themselves and be prepared for defending their position if they do not complete.
- **Consistency of message and delivery**. Multi-site, geographically dispersed organisations are faced with the prospect of varied approaches and possibly even different standards being adopted in their various locations. With an E-learning solution everybody gets exactly the same, time and time again.
- **Customisation.** Modularised programmes can be variously 'packaged' to suit individuals. This has obvious appeal when dealing with groups that have differing levels of experience or knowledge of the subject matter. Another potential cost saving.

E-Learning - Key advantages for the learner.

- **Flexibility**. This is probably the single most attractive aspect for the learner. The reality of the workplace, and of our family and social lives is that they are rarely highly structured and seldom entirely predictable. Being able to vary the pace is hugely valuable to many learners.
- **Individualisation and privacy**. Although we are social creatures, some learners do not enjoy the open nature of learning progress and assessment in the traditional training room. That anxiety does not arise in the privacy of the E-learning forum.
- **Repeat access**. Many E-learning programmes will allow learners to return to learning (and perhaps assessment modules) as often as they wish until they feel that they have grasped the material sufficiently well. This is not possible in a traditional setting.
- **Proximity to support learning**. The very act of being on-line means that if a particular aspect of a course interests the learner, he can immediately do further research on the topic.

E-Learning - Key advantages for the trainer.

- **Ease of management**. Updating of material is rapid and straightforward.
- **No production labour or costs**. E-learning is essentially paperless at the trainer end. Learners may choose to print out materials but the cost of doing so is usually borne by their departments rather than the training budget.
- **Useful data and ease of record keeping**. Providing the E-learning is supported by an adequate learning management system (LMS) – either in-house or hosted, the training manager or HR department can access useful training data for reporting and management purposes.

Why discount E-learning?

Despite the wonders of technology there are many reasons why E-learning may have little to offer the course developer. The most obvious of these is that it may simply be inappropriate for the subject in question. The training of essentially practical skills or learning that needs intensive exposure to "the real thing" is clearly not suited to E-learning delivery. Unfortunately this has not deterred some organisations from trying to achieve this in the past. Theoretical elements of primarily practical learning can certainly be delivered via E-learning in a blended design. Driving is a very good example. Knowledge of the highway code and basic mechanical knowledge would be prime candidates for E-learning delivery, but mastering the actual driving skills is quite definitely a "real world" experience.

Aside from the obvious issue of appropriateness there are other important considerations that may lead the developer to discount E-learning.

- **Sense of isolation**. Many learners will react negatively to working alone. For them there is no substitute for face-to-face interaction with an expert trainer or facilitator. Dissatisfaction may be voiced as feeling cheated or being given a second rate product.
- **Motivation.** E-learning will certainly suit highly disciplined individuals who prefer to plan and structure their lives. Unfortunately, these individuals tend to be a minority. The majority will miss the momentum that is built into face-to-face learning and may struggle to keep to required schedules on their own.
- **Interference factor.** Being removed from the workplace for face-to-face training ensures that the individual has dedicated time and space to learn. In contrast, E-learning in the workplace or at home can easily be disrupted unless the individual learner can devise a limited access regime that other will respect.
- **Demand for high quality**. The quality of electronic media presentation and materials (video, film, computer games etc.) is now so good that high quality is the norm. E-learning must live up to these standards if it is to be taken seriously. We have moved well beyond the point when the "jazzed up PowerPoint" was acceptable. Quality comes at a cost.
- **Up-front costs**. Adopting E-learning for a one-off programme makes little sense for an organisation. Costs can only be reduced to an acceptable level if a full-blooded E-learning strategy is developed and implemented. This allows organisations to work with developers to create templates,

learning objects (re-usable chunks of material) and standardised approaches.

- **Technological angst.** We should never assume that everybody is "computer savvy". Technophobes are surprisingly common especially among the older generation. This can lead to significant additional costs if learners have to be trained to use the training.
- **Cultural issues.** Communication and learning in many cultures is grounded in the values of face-to-face interaction e.g. the *kanohi ki te kanohi* custom of New Zealand Maori. In these situations it is not unusual to encounter resistance, even outright rejection of E-learning methods.

E-learning design principles: know your pedagogies?

Even if all the factors outlined above are accommodated and a decision to go with E-learning is taken, the issues do not end there. It would be rare for an HR department (even with L&D specialists in the team) to possess sufficient technical skill to develop E-learning programmes. Development is therefore generally outsourced to specialist companies and this is where things can go badly awry. These companies may possess the technical expertise and the latest hard and software capabilities, but they are not always able to deploy appropriate educational knowledge to the development project. The result may well be a disconnect between what the client actually needs and what is eventually provided. As with traditional training, the client organisation must take responsibility for providing an accurate brief. With E-learning this is not straightforward.

If we assume that a proper needs analysis has been carried out, a summary statement will be available. This will indicate very clearly the kinds of learning required and the levels involved. If E-learning is deemed then to be appropriate, a professional E-learning development studio will be contracted. The majority of these will be relatively small in scale and usually are linked to a particular brand of authoring software. This means that what they produce is likely to reflect their particular technology at least as much as the client's brief. The studio's standard output will also reflect (perhaps unconsciously) a particular pedagogy in the sense of how the learner is expected to learn. In most cases the pedagogical slant of the studio stems from the founding partners and their own understanding of how learning occurs.

So, before commissioning E-learning development work we should confirm, as far as possible, where the studio stands in terms of its pedagogical slant and the authoring technology it proposes to use. This requires the L&D professional to have a working knowledge of the various pedagogies currently driving E-learning development. Armed with that basic understanding the developer's plan can be interrogated sufficiently to ensure that it aligns appropriately with the brief.

Most managers working in HR or L&D have not grown up in a truly digital world. They are "digital immigrants" arriving on the shores of the digital universe in a piecemeal manner as necessity has dictated. Until fairly recently, this has also been true of the learners they have engaged with – but no longer. Increasingly the targets of organisational learning are "digital natives". They have no memory of a non-digital world. Digital devices, in all their variety, are simply part of the landscape, as is the fact of ever accelerating digital progress. So we have two quite different players on the stage and there is no question as to who will take the lead role. Managers at all levels have to come to terms with the way our digital natives, think, act and engage with learning. The changes occurring in the learner population have been huge and swift. Marc Prensky in his 2001 paper *Digital Natives, Digital Immigrants* makes this point very clearly:

"Today's students have not changed incrementally from those of the past. A really big discontinuity has taken place. One might even call it a singularity – an event which changes things so fundamentally that there is no going back. This singularity is the arrival and rapid dissemination of digital technology in the last decades of the 20th century. Our digital immigrant instructors are struggling to teach a population that speaks an entirely new language. Today's teachers have to learn to communicate in the language and style of their students... going faster, less step-by-step, more in parallel, with more random access."

To cope with this very rapid shift, E-learning itself has had to transform from the early, clumsy attempts at simple replication of traditional learning methods, to the provision of connected environments in which learners can largely make their own decisions about how they progress their learning. Consequently we have seen an expansion of pedagogy, the design principle that underpins learning, as illustrated in figure 4.8.

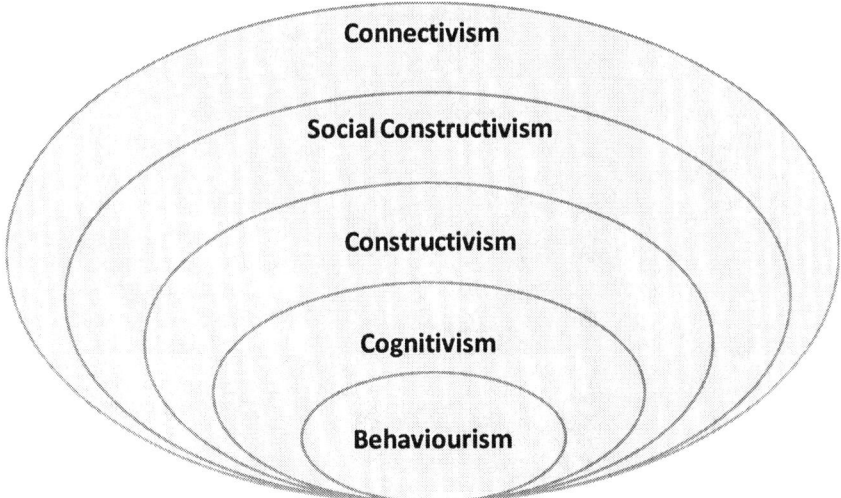

Figure 4.8 – the expansion of E-Learning Pedagogy

It is just possible to make a case for all of these pedagogies having a part to play in learning – but even a cursory understanding of each indicates some of their limitations:

- **Behaviourism:** the most basic form of learning, linked to stimulus and response and to the lower Bloom levels. Early E-learning design was heavily criticised because it seldom managed to go beyond simple behaviourist techniques. Behaviourism takes little account of the learner's experience or predisposition, viewing him very much as an empty vessel into which "knowledge' could simply be poured.

- **Cognitivism**: an approach that is anchored at the level of understanding rather than simply remembering. Greater demands are made on the learner through on-line trainer-led activities. Learning is still very much trainer or teacher focused. Learners have little or no control over what they choose to learn or over the method. Greater variety of learning activity goes some way to accommodating individual learning styles.
- **Constructivism**: a model much more in keeping with the Socratic approach to teaching in the sense that the trainer / teacher facilitates learning through stimulation rather than active direction. The underlying principle here is that what constitutes knowledge is ultimately subjective and is "constructed" by the learner through the filters of their own experience and beliefs. The fundamentals were developed by Piaget in the 1970's (7) who maintained that this construction occurs via two principal processes:
    - **Assimilation** – whereby knowledge is readily added and integrated into the individual's existing understanding.
    - **Accommodation** - whereby adjustments are made (re-construction) to existing understanding and mental models in order to accept ideas and concepts that are initially uncomfortable. This leads to a higher level of understanding. The intellectual unease that often accompanies learning in this mode is often referred to as "cognitive dissonance".
- **Social Constructivism**: essentially a variant of constructivist theory that builds on Vygotsky's research into the advantages enjoyed by the social learner.(8) He maintains that the quantum and quality of learning will be enhanced through interaction with other learners and with others who may have an interest or stake in the subject matter. This concept has driven the move to virtual classroom and connected E-learning groups. It has also given added weight to integrated face-to-face block courses within distance learning programmes driven mainly by E-learning methods.
- **Connectivism**: this is the recent acknowledgement of the effects of emerging Web 2.0 technologies and tools. The new breed of learner now grazes much further afield than the constraints of the actual programme he is signed up for. The advent of social media, blogs, wikis, discussion forums etc. means that the learning process is far more organic and much more in the control of the learner. Much will therefore depend on the learner's ability to build these web connections.

However, "connectivity" more accurately refers to the web's ability to immediately reference related areas of knowledge, largely through search engine association. Its chief proponent, George Siemens maintains that learning requires the connecting of the various levels of data provided by the web. He defines these as:

- Data: raw elements (simple facts etc).
- Information: data elements linked by intelligent appraisal.

- Knowledge: information that is understood in context and internalised as pragmatically useful.
- Meaning: drawing out the values and implications of knowledge.

We can see the obvious links with Kolb here in as much as true learning only really occurs when meaning is extracted from mere knowledge or experience. What has changed so radically in the last two decades is that learning is no longer an end in itself but a continuous process of connecting and extrapolating from one "node" or information source to others and intelligence is increasingly seen as the ability to connect creatively.

However, Siemens' connectivity is not limited to the digital world. He links to social constructivism when he acknowledges that learning will be greatly enhanced in a social or community setting. Individuals within a community act as nodes, each connected to others. As information is processed and updated by one individual the ultimate effect is that the whole network gains.

"A community is a rich learning network of individuals who in themselves are completed learning networks. As these elements update, the entire network structure similarly gains and benefits. In a sense the network grows in intelligence."(9)

So what is the HR or L&D professional to make of all this when considering E-learning as a potential solution for learning delivery? The implications are clear, the way forward less so. It seems certain that the role of traditional trainer-focused learning is fast diminishing. It is being usurped by a distinctly learner-focused emphasis which is based more and more upon a network of influences, conscious or unconsciously received. Hand in hand with this development goes ever decreasing structure and control. L&D "managers" must come to terms with the fact that (in conventional terms) they will come to manage less and less. Training at the lower levels within the domains e.g. compliance training, safety training etc. will at least retain a semblance of structure, but even here we can be certain that the formal training event will only be one of a number of inputs, and perhaps not the most significant. At the higher levels, formal, structured direction of learning is no longer possible.

"The connectivist view that learning is a network creation process significantly impacts on how we design and develop learning within corporations and learning institutions. When the act of learning is seen as a function under the control of the learner, designers need to shift the focus to fostering the ideal ecology to permit learning to occur. By recognising learning as a messy, nebulous, informal, chaotic process, we need to rethink how we design our instruction."(10)

What we are witnessing here is social change of a fundamental nature driven by an elemental force largely beyond any strategic control i.e. technological advance. It is not something we could successfully fight against. Therefore, the sensible solution is to work with it. When outsourcing the design and development of higher level learning (and E-learning in particular) we should now be concerned about the "ecology" being created to enable networks to be built and exploited by the learner. Of course we need to ensure that the developer addresses the specified learning outcomes at an appropriate level, but, at the same time, we should be asking "what have you done to enable the learner to "break out" from his initial isolation and join a networked community which will enable richer learning experiences?"

It is always worthwhile questioning potential developers about their views on an appropriate learning pedagogy for your specific brief. This should reveal to you how engaged they are with emerging learning issues. You do not need to have mined the depths of educational theory. You simply need to know enough to be reasonably certain that they know enough.

The case for applied learning.

Perhaps the surest sign of effective learning or training delivery is the successful transfer to the real world of work. This is Kirkpatrick's level 3 evaluation (see section 7). Disenchantment is inevitable if the individual leaner cannot apply principles and practice directly in his own workplace world. Consequently HR / L&D staff must focus in on this critical requirement, especially when outsourcing training delivery. No matter how skilled external trainers may be they will always struggle to align and relate delivery to the workplace. This difficulty becomes greatly accentuated when learners are drawn from numerous backgrounds on a public course.

We have seen that Bloom's taxonomy cites application as the first meaningful level of learning. This is the 'bottom line' of learning. If we cannot cross this threshold the return on our investment will be very low indeed. In a very obvious sense, applied learning has always been with us. Of course there are many for whom learning for learning's sake is as vital as breathing, but they are perhaps the minority in any society. For the majority, learning is eventually linked to doing, and the doing to something purposeful in their lives. This majority position has been heavily reinforced by the clarion call from industry (and consequently from governments) that learning should be "mission critical". It is a point of view succinctly articulated by Bob Mosher (2009) at the height of the global financial crisis:

"The reason why a lot of learning departments are struggling right now is because they are focused on knowledge gain. That sounds like a noble thing, but the reality is that a lot of organisations are shifting to productivity, not knowledge gain. There is not a middle manager who would argue that knowledge is a bad thing, but we live in a world now where knowledge for knowledge's sake is not helping." (11).

So, as HR / L&D professionals we must surely acknowledge the overriding need for applied learning – but what should we be looking for when critiquing the proposed delivery of external trainers? The first consideration must always be the treatment of our people as 'adult' learners. Learning design and delivery must align to the fundamentals of adult learning. Malcolm Knowles researched and set out these fundamentals as long ago as 1970. His perspective can be summarized as follows:

- Adults are internally motivated and self-directed
- Adults bring life experiences and knowledge to learning experiences
- Adults are goal-oriented
- Adults are relevancy-oriented
- Adults are practical
- Adult learners need to be respected (12)

Self-direction, experience, goal-orientation, relevancy orientation, practicality and the need for respect all point inevitably to applied learning. The principles of applied learning (AL) have evolved naturally out of the adult learning framework and now stand alone as discrete theory. There are numerous iterations of AL first principles but perhaps the most succinct can be found in the Australian education system, specifically supporting the Victorian Certificate in Applied Learning (VCAL). The concepts here can, and should be applied as far as possible to all workplace training. They are:

- Start where the learners are at;
- Negotiate the curriculum. Engage in a dialogue with learners about their curriculum;
- Share knowledge. Recognise the knowledge learners bring to the learning environment;
- Connect with communities and real life experiences;
- Build resilience, confidence and self-worth - consider the whole person;
- Integrate learning. Learning should reflect the integration that occurs in real life tasks;
- Promote diversity of learning styles and methods. Different learning styles require different teaching methods; and
- Assess appropriately. Use the assessment method that best fits the learning content and context (13)

The implications are very clear here. It is unlikely that the end of course 'happy sheets' would reveal the abuse of any of the above principles in any articulate sense but one on one follow up conversations with learners probably would. Far better to make providers aware from the outset that the company's expectations are firmly rooted in adult and applied learning principles, and requiring those providers to outline just how they plan to embrace these fundamentals.

5. DESIGNING ASSESSMENT

A broad definition of "assessment" would most likely use the word "judgement" (or something similar) to describe a process by which a decision is made concerning a current state. In any organisation this might apply to people, plant, processes or product. However, in the context of organisational learning its meaning is more precise. Assessments associated with courses or programmes are measured activities, behaviours, designated processes or required products, which enable a decision to be made as to whether specific outcomes or standards have been sufficiently mastered by an individual participant.

The essential component is of course the standard. Without clarity around the performance level to be attained, assessment is a meaningless activity. This applies even to diagnostic assessments which are designed to find out how far short of a desired standard individuals may be prior to a course – usually as an aid to focusing design and development.

Measuring performance against a standard may seem obvious enough. What is less well understood is the sheer range and variety of assessment methods and tools available to course designers. The spectrum covers everything from formal written examinations, through skill proficiency demonstrations, to auditions and long-term portfolio building. We will examine this spectrum at a later stage in this section.

There will be numerous situations in which learning undoubtedly takes place but there is no need for assessment. A typical example would be management's quarterly presentation to staff on company performance and the state of the market. We would not assess learning here because there is no standard to be achieved; the presentation is intended only to inform. Indeed if there were an assessment many employees might find good reasons for being unavailable! For most learning situations however, there are many valid reasons for assessing. These are best described in terms of stakeholder interest.

- **The learner**. While many learners may not enjoy the process of assessment, the great majority will be very keen to know the results. Human nature predisposes us to want to know "how we measure up", against a standard and perhaps against other participants.

  More importantly perhaps, learners also need to know where they have fallen short and what they should do to put things right. This requirement helps to put a positive spin on assessment and the learner can then regard it as part of the learning process rather than an angst-filled experience at the end of the course.

  The learner's need is without doubt the principal justification for structured, rigorous assessment. "In order for learners to gain insight into their learning and their understanding, frequent feedback is critical:

students need to monitor their learning and actively evaluate their strategies and their current levels of understanding." (1)

- **The trainer / facilitator**. Learners are often quite unaware that their trainer or facilitator may well be just as anxious as they are about assessments. Poor results are just as likely to stem from poor trainer input as they are from poor learner effort or attitude. Trainers are naturally concerned to maintain a reputation for good results but are also likely to be genuinely involved in their learner's success.
- **The course designer**. With standards-based courses, designers will tend to build courses with the assessment in mind. As a consequence they will be very keen to know if they have pitched things correctly. Assessment results detail will allow them to revisit and amend their design appropriately. Of course they must take care to consider the other variables in play such as trainer performance, delivery integrity or venue characteristics.
- **The assessment designer**. Assessment design at any level requires considerable skills. For that reason, the design of learning, and of the associated assessment, are often handled separately. Assuming that learning activity has been properly specified, developed and delivered, the assessment designer needs to know whether he has reflected the required level and type of learning adequately (Bloom) and has covered the full range of the learning.
- **The organisation**. Return on investment is an obvious significant concern for the company. While learning can return benefits beyond straightforward achievement, formal end of course assessments producing newly qualified staff provide readily available "hard" data to justify L&D policy. This is level 2 evaluation on the Kirkpatrick model which will be discussed in section 7.

Organisations, particularly HR departments, will have other interests in course results e.g.
- **Course design** – did this work well? If externally developed would we use that company again?
- **Trainers / facilitators** – were they successful in achieving learning outcomes to the standard required?
- **Assessment design** – are the results obtained comfortably within the required margins e.g. pass rate too high or too low, can they be relied upon as a useful indicator of competence?
- **Promotion / succession planning** – learning and development's primary role within organisation is to support succession planning by providing suitably qualified people for potential "pull through" to higher level roles. Consequently, for some courses or programmes, assessment results will be carefully scrutinised.
- **Institutional / Government / professional bodies** – if the course is linked to national, university or institute qualifications, there will be considerable interest in the integrity of assessment results. Accreditation to train and assess may be withdrawn from organisations failing to follow prescribed assessment standards.

There is a temptation to assume that the selection and design of assessment tools must follow the development of learning materials. In a practical sense this is generally true, but the higher level strategic decisions concerning what assessment should achieve need to be made earlier on, or perhaps simultaneously. Without real clarity of intent it is all too easy to select methods that eventually prove to be of little value.

The most fundamental question is always *"what do we want this assessment to do for us?"* The answer is inevitably broader in scope than simply *"to measure the extent of the learning".* We should be able to define an assessment in terms of its purpose. To do this we need to work through something of a labyrinth of possibilities and permutations.

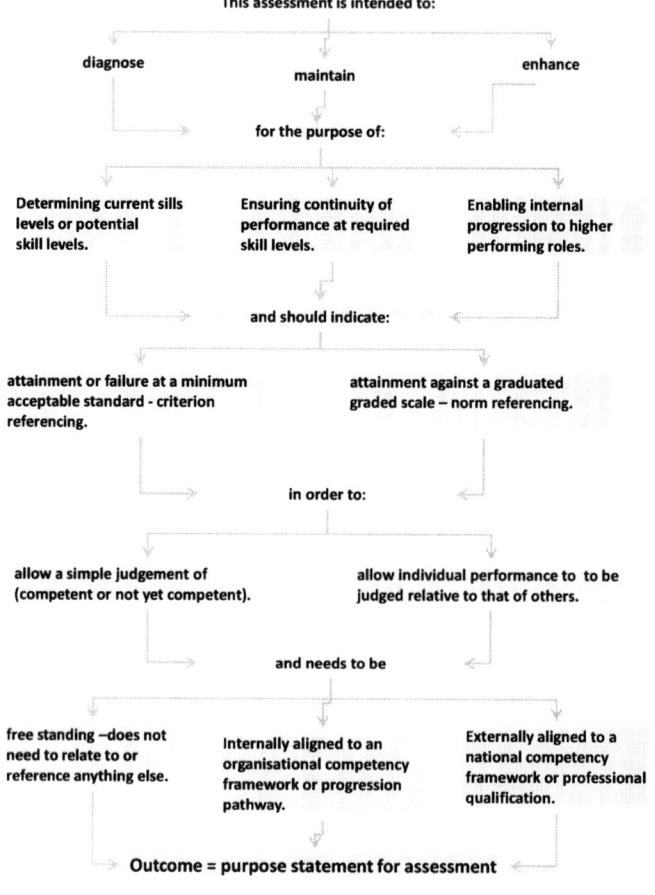

Figure 5.1 – Developing assessment strategy

Figure 5.1 above maps out the various pathways we might take to arrive at a purpose statement for a given assessment. So, for example if we are considering introducing management training which carries credit toward an external qualification we might end up with a purpose statement like this: *"This assessment is intended to diagnose current skills and will indicate skills against a graded scale to enable comparison of individual abilities to the Institute of Management standards at level 1."*

As another example, the introduction of an assessment at the conclusion of a confined space working refresher course might read: *"This assessment is intended to measure and confirm the maintenance of confined space working skills against a minimum acceptable standard, enabling a simple judgment of 'competent' or 'needs improvement'. The assessment will provide the required evidence for sign-off against the relevant standard on the national qualifications framework."*

As always, the purpose of this "drill-down" thinking is clarity. Being clear about assessment purpose allows us to start with the end in mind and thus to maintain a strategic focus.

THINKING SPECIFICALLY – SELECTING THE MOST APPROPRIATE ASSESSMENT METHOD OR TOOL

Having defined *what* an assessment is intended to achieve, the next stage is to consider *how* to go about it. Fundamentally there are three or perhaps four high level 'how' strategies: we can assess either formatively, summatively, authentically or quite possibly through an appropriate blending of all three principles.

We may need to gather information on learner progress as the course proceeds. This allows the trainer to adapt pace, content and style to meet learner needs and to maximise effectiveness. This is known as formative assessment and generally consists of a series of tests or assessment tasks, usually positioned at the end of discrete modules. Results can be accumulated to form or contribute to a final achievement rating. Formative assessments are essentially part of the delivery phase. It would be unwise to deliver lengthy programmes without formative assessments. Both learners and trainers need regular feedback to satisfy themselves that they are on track.

Alternatively, the course may lend itself to straight-through delivery with a single assessment at the end. This strategy is really only suited to relatively short duration learning, or to close off specific phases - otherwise we run the risk of assessing memory rather than understanding. This reservation aside, summative assessment provides an insight into the learning that an individual has accumulated and, perhaps more importantly, into what has been retained.

All employers will insist that the true test of learning success is whether the individual can transfer knowledge and skills to the real world of the workplace – doing the job for real. This is known as "authentic assessment". It is generally difficult to set up assessment of this kind in a training environment, but well-designed simulations, scenario assessments, in-tray exercises etc. can get very close to the real thing. On-job training does of course allow for authentic assessment where operations are predictable. Where predictability cannot be guaranteed e.g.

for ambulance operations, authentic assessment may not be a feasible option. Real heart attacks or epileptic seizures cannot be laid on to plan. Consequently, to insist on authentic assessment might result in the individual trainee never having the opportunity to demonstrate competence.

The range of assessment tools available to select from is huge. However, this diversity quickly narrows once a few essential questions are asked. The assessment purpose statement will sit in the background and the selected tools must align with it. When considering which techniques and tools to use we should ask:

- "Do I want to gather evidence straight from the learner?" This is known as direct assessment. "Or do I want to gather evidence from other source e.g. the employer?" This is known as indirect assessment.

- "Do I want an accumulating stream of assessment evidence related to specific topics within the programme?" This is formative assessment. "Or am I happy with a single end of course assessment?" This is summative assessment.

- "What kind of learning evidence can be gathered with this technique? Is this the kind of evidence that we need?" This relates directly to the Bloom domain and level descriptors.

- "Using this technique (or combination of techniques) will we gather enough learning evidence to support a pass / fail or graded performance decision?" This relates directly to the course learning outcomes.

- "Do I need learning evidence that is based on a "real world" demonstration?" This is authentic assessment.

- "How will this technique (or combination of techniques) be received by the learner group? Is it something they are obviously comfortable with or are they likely to be anxious when confronted with something new?"

- "Do we have the skills and resources to conduct this kind of assessment?"

- "What particular advantages or disadvantages does this type of assessment offer? Are they likely to be significant for us?"

The tables that follow illustrate something of the wide range of assessment tools and the characteristics which we should consider before electing to use them.

Assessment Tool	Application Direct / Indirect	Assessment Type Formative / Summative / Authentic	Potential Advantages	Potential Disadvantages	Cognitive Learning levels (Bloom)
Standardised cognitive tests using traditional item designs e.g. • Short answer • Matching block • Missing item • Naming of parts • Listing • Rating options • Ordering	• Direct	• Formative • Summative	• Can be built into item banks • Easy to analyse and validated • Generally easy to score • Easy to standardise e.g. stanining • Can integrate varied item formats into single assessments	• Generally not suitable for assessing higher level learning	• Knowledge • Comprehension • Application (if item is well designed)
Multi-choice / multi-response.	• Direct	• Formative • Summative	• Can be built into item banks • Easy to analyse and validated • Generally easy to score • Easy to standardise e.g. stanining • User friendliness • Can be optically scored, producing instant result and analysis • Easily adapted for on-line • Can be adapted and used to support other	• Tests need to be lengthy in order to ensure reliability e.g. 40+ questions each with a minimum of 4 responses • Needs good design skills • Can be difficult to find required number of distractors	• Knowledge • Comprehension • Application, Analysis, Synthesis or Evaluation (if item is well designed)

Assessment Tool	Application Direct / Indirect	Assessment Type Formative / Summative / Authentic	Potential Advantages	Potential Disadvantages	Cognitive Learning levels (Bloom)
Interpretive exercise	• Direct	• Formative • Summative • Authentic	• Excellent for assessing comprehension (understanding) and application through extrapolation or adaptation	• Can be difficult to design – often need to be paired with other tools e.g. with case study or scenario	• Knowledge • Comprehension • Application, • Analysis, (if item is well designed)
Essays	• Direct	• Formative (in longer courses or programmes) • Summative	• Excellent for assessing analytical and synthesising skills	• Can exhibit questionable validity e.g. testing language and planning skills as much as understanding of the subject • Difficult to mark • Subjectivity issues if more than one assessor used.	• Knowledge • Comprehension • Application, • Analysis, Synthesis or Evaluation (if item is well designed)
Diagrammatic representations / flowcharting	• Direct	• Formative • Summative	• Can be adapted and combined with other tools to assess higher learning levels	• Can exhibit questionable validity e.g. testing visualisation and drafting skills as much as understanding of the subject	• Knowledge • Comprehension • Application, • Analysis, Synthesis or Evaluation (if item is well designed)
Debates	• Direct	• Formative • Summative	• Excellent vehicle for assessing depth of knowledge, critical thinking and ability to react to opposing ideas	• Can exhibit questionable validity e.g. testing communication skills and personal confidence as much as	• Knowledge • Comprehension • Application, • Analysis • Synthesis • Evaluation

Assessment Tool	Application Direct / Indirect	Assessment Type Formative / Summative / Authentic	Potential Advantages	Potential Disadvantages	Cognitive Learning levels (Bloom)
Debates continued.			required content checklist.		
Presentations	• Direct	• Formative • Summative	• Excellent vehicle for assessing ability to analyse, distil and structure information • Excellent for assessing communication skills and personal confidence • Easily marked against required content or behavioural checklists • Can reveal learning at all levels	• Can exhibit questionable validity e.g. testing communication skills and personal confidence as much as understanding of the subject • May be inhibited by inadequate or under-performing technology	• Knowledge • Comprehension • Application, • Analysis • Synthesis • Evaluation
Real world problem solving	• Direct • Indirect	• Formative • Summative • Authentic	• Excellent vehicle for assessing higher level critical thinking	• Can be difficult to design – needs all potentially relevant information • Marking can be problematic because methods and solutions may not be predictable	• Knowledge • Comprehension • Application, • Analysis • Synthesis • Evaluation
Case studies / scenarios / simulations	• Direct	• Formative • Summative • Authentic	• Often the only substitute for the authentic	• Need a lot of thought and careful design – lack of authenticity is	• Knowledge • Comprehension • Application,

Assessment Tool	Application Direct / Indirect	Assessment Type Formative / Summative / Authentic	Potential Advantages	Potential Disadvantages	Cognitive Learning levels (Bloom)
Performance / practical demonstration	• Direct	• Formative • Summative • Authentic	• Only valid method for assessing practical or psychomotor skills • Easy to identify areas for further practice • Assessor can observe, and re-align performance if required. • Generally straightforward to mark / grade	• Assessment should ultimately be authentic i.e. using the "real thing" • Can be time-consuming or expensive in terms of resources / materials	• Knowledge • Comprehension • Application Higher levels can be explored if the individual is required to amend or adapt. Psychomotor domain descriptors may be needed to assist definition.
Reports	• Direct	• Formative • Summative • Authentic	• Ideal for assessing structured thinking and compliance to organisational formats • Can reveal evidence of learning at all levels	• Can exhibit questionable validity e.g. testing written communication skills as much as understanding of the subject • May not produce evidence in a predictable manner	• Knowledge • Comprehension • Application, • Analysis • Synthesis • Evaluation
Capstone projects	• Direct	• Summative • Authentic	• Ideal for drawing all learning and skills together to conclude a programme • Can reveal evidence of learning at all levels	• May require extensive coaching in requires support skills • May require arrangement of substantial support resources	• Knowledge • Comprehension • Application, • Analysis • Synthesis • Evaluation

Assessment Tool	Application Direct / Indirect	Assessment Type Formative / Summative / Authentic	Potential Advantages	Potential Disadvantages	Cognitive Learning levels (Bloom)
Team projects	• Direct • Indirect	• Formative • Summative • Authentic	• Can provide multi-dimensional evidence e.g. opinions views of team members on the performance of others • Allows for a wide range of assessment tools to be integrated	• Assessment of the individual can be obscured by the team • Individuals may be disadvantaged by team dynamics and personality issues	• Knowledge • Comprehension • Application, • Analysis • Synthesis • Evaluation
Self-assessment / reflective activities	• Direct	• Formative • Summative	• Can indicate the real nature of learning for the individual • Enables meaningful design of follow-on activities or development planning • Can reveal evidence of learning at all levels	• Disadvantages the activist / pragmatist learners who are not given to reflection • Difficult to marl or grade	• Knowledge • Comprehension • Application, • Analysis • Synthesis • Evaluation
Interview / viva	• Direct	• Formative • Summative	• Allows for in depth pursuit of issues as they arise with particular individuals • Learning can be explored to the highest levels	• Can be intimidating for some learners • Success may be dependent on relationships • Can exhibit questionable validity	• Knowledge • Comprehension • Application, • Analysis • Synthesis • Evaluation

121

| Assessment Tool | Application | Assessment Type | Potential Advantages | Potential Disadvantages | Cognitive Learning levels (Bloom) |
	Direct / Indirect	Formative / Summative / Authentic			
Employer interviews	• Indirect	• Authentic	• Best evidence of transfer to the workplace • Promotes employer engagement • Can help with adjustments of employer expectations • Can help with review of training programme	• Employer needs to be "up to speed" with the course and the anticipated skills profile. • Learner may be anxious about the process • Hard to gather consistent data • Employer views may be subjective and invalid e.g. related to own historical abilities • Employer feedback tends to centre around the application level	• Knowledge • Comprehension • Application,
Portfolios	• Direct	• Summative • Authentic	• "Big picture" evidence of professional progress. Can reveal the learner "in the round" • Increasingly demanded by new employers • Can reveal evidence of learning at all levels	• Take a great deal of time to prepare • Disadvantages those who lack structure and rigorous method essential to portfolio-building • Completed portfolio may be inappropriately balanced.	• Knowledge • Comprehension • Application, • Analysis • Synthesis • Evaluation

Traditional tests.

The traditional tests, with which we are all familiar, can be built from a combination of test "items", seemingly simple in terms of design input. They are still the most commonly encountered assessments for theoretical courses or the theory components of practical skills training. Good training delivery is often let down by poorly designed assessment because good assessment design requires significant expertise. Consequently most HR departments will contract this out, generally to the specialists who have designed the delivery. Nevertheless, the onus remains with the buyer to check the quality of the product – *caveat emptor* applies. Despite their apparent simplicity, design errors are all too common and it is worthwhile drawing attention to the most common faults.

- **Poor internal weighting**: Looking at the whole test (or section of a test) numbers of questions and marks available should reflect the learning input in terms of relative significance. This is best achieved by planning the content of the test using a specification table. This acts as a "health check" when composing tests. Shown below is an example for chemistry test on hydrochloric acid.

Aspect	Cognitive Level (Bloom)			Total %
	Knowledge	Comprehension	Application	
Physical properties	12	12	3	27
Chemical properties	6	12	2	20
Preparation guidelines	7	14	5	26
Uses	6	3	18	27
Totals	31	41	28	100

- **Short answer questions**: Common failings are:
  - No indication of what a "short answer" is. Guidance should be offered in terms of a word count, or visually through an appropriately sized answer box.
  - Fallacy of complex question. If the question requires responses to more than one issue the learner will be uncertain as to which issue might attract more marks. The usual rule is "one issue per question".
  - Inappropriate scale of question. For example "Explain the third law of thermodymics" is just too much for a short answer. However, if we were to ask "In the space below give the standard definition of the third law of thermodynamics" a short answer will be more than adequate e.g. "The third law of thermodynamics states that the entropy of a system approaches a constant value as the temperature approaches zero".

- **Missing item questions**: these are questions in which a key word or phrase has been omitted from a sentence. The learner is required to insert the missing word or phrase. To be effective, and fair to the learner, missing item questions should adhere to the following guidelines:

- Precise guidance on how to respond should be provided e.g. "Complete the statement below by filling in the gap. Only one word is needed."

- The question should have no more than one missing item per sentence and ideally no more than one sentence per question.

- The sentence should be structured so as to make it clear what kind of word is needed e.g. "Blood flowing in the veins is generally _____ in colour".

- The blank space should be indicated by a continuous line, not dashes. Learners can be drawn into assuming that the number of dashes equals the number of letters in the required word.

- **Matching block questions**: this is a technique used mostly to introduce variety and to capture sets of generally low level information. A typical example, testing knowledge of the capital cites of South East Asia is shown below.

Match the capital cities in the left hand column to their countries by placing the city's number in the appropriate box on the far right.	1	Phnom Penh		North Korea	
	2	Vientiane		Malasia	
	3	Rangoon		Myanmar	
	4	Seoul		China	
	5	Kuala Lumpur		Thailand	
	6	Manila		Laos	
	7	Hanoi		Cambodia	
	8	Bangkok		Philippines	
	9	Djakarta		South Korea	
	10	Taipei		Vietnam	
	11	Pyong Yang			
	12	Ulan Bhator			
	13	Port Moresby			
	14	Beijing			

Best practice here ensures that there are always more options than items to be matched. This weakens the effect of the learner matching the ones they know and then engaging in a process of elimination. The additional items must be reasonable distractors e.g. in the example above Oslo or London are likely to be immediately discounted.

- **Naming of parts**: this is a classic device for measuring the level of familiarisation with equipment, control panels, storage layouts etc. It is a variant of the matching block question. The absolute rule here is that validity depends upon the presentation of a current visual of the real thing; asking them to recall from memory is not acceptable. If the object has several model variations or is updated regularly it is essential to update the visual to what the learner has been trained on. A typical example is shown below:

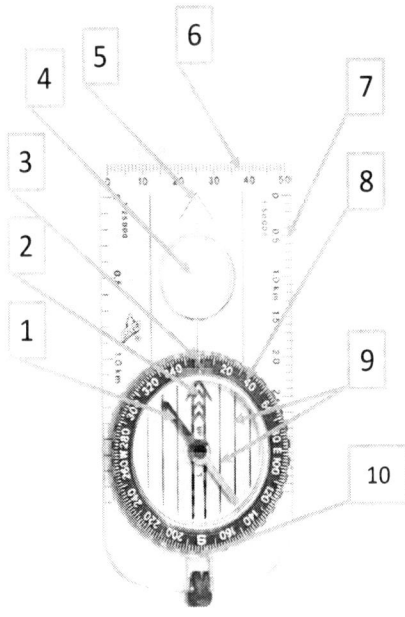

"In the boxes provided below, name the parts of the Lightweight Silva compass."

1		6	
2		7	
3		8	
4		9	
5		10	

Figure 5.2 – Example of 'naming of parts' question

A less satisfactory alternative is to present the learner with a list of parts and ask him to annotate the accompanying diagram or visual.

- **Ratings or ordering exercises**: these are typically used to assess the learner's retention of key processes or procedures. A typical example for emergency evacuation procedures is shown below.

  "If you discover a fire in your building you should take action according to the site evacuation procedures. The various steps in this procedure are shown below but are deliberately set down in the wrong order. Write down the steps in their proper order in the boxes provided.

  - *Evacuate via your closest safe exit (look for the exit signs).*
  - *Close all doors, if safe to do so.*
  - *Shut down equipment and processes.*

- *Check for any sign of immediate danger.*
- *Warn anyone in immediate danger*
- *Proceed to assembly area.*
- *Shut down equipment and processes.*
- *Fight the fire or contain the emergency, if safe and trained to do so.*
- *Activate the 'Break Glass' alarm.*
- *Report the emergency to the Control Room.*

Step	Action
1	
2	
3	
4	
5	
6	
7	
8	
9	
10	

N.B. The marking guide for this type of question needs to indicate that the marker should focus on identifying clusters of correctly sequenced items rather than the precise number sequence, because just one incorrect choice can throw the number sequence out.

- **Simple listing:** these questions do no more than test simple factual knowledge (Bloom level 1) and are therefore of limited value. A typical example would be:

"In the space below list, in any order, the 10 most important items that should be found in a home first aid kit."

- **Multi-choice** (MC): perhaps the most widely-used question format in standard testing. It is popular with learners because they are not required to write at length and popular with assessors because it is so easily marked and analysed.

It is also often maligned as being unreliable i.e. due to the "getting it right by guessing" potential (random selection). Research shows that this criticism is entirely unjustified if the test adheres to the principles of good design. For the HR / L&D professional it is essential to insist on MC test conforming to an appropriate balance between numbers of questions and numbers of choices per question. In simple terms, if you reduce the number of questions you must increase the number of choices for each question.

Following these guidelines ensures that the test is statistically reliable i.e. the chance of passing by guessing is remote. This has been clearly demonstrated in the work of Robert Brown. (2) His analysis is shown in the table below:

Number of	Percent Pass by Chance			
	Two	*Three*	*Four*	*Five*
Questions	*Choices*	*Choices*	*Choices*	*Choices*
1	50	33.3	25	20
2	75	55.6	43.8	36
4	68.8	40.7	26	18.1
6	65.6	32	16.9	9.9
10	62.3	21.3	7.8	3.28
20	58.8	9.2	1.39	0.26
30	57.2	4.4	0.275	0.023
40	56.3	2.14	0.057	0.002
50	55.6	1.1	0.012	0.0004

Consulting this table we can see that a 10 question test with 3 choices for each question allows a 21.3% chance of passing by guessing. This would be quite unacceptable. Doubling the number of questions to 20 reduces that percentage to 9.2 and increasing the number of choices to 4 per question reduces it further to 1.39. This would certainly be acceptable. Consequently, we can assume that if our test has a minimum of 20 questions with 4 choices, it will be statistically 'safe'.

Robert Brown has also demonstrated that the reliability of multi-choice assessments can also be improved through "negative marking". A typical method of applying this tactic is to award one negative mark for each incorrect choice in the question and a positive mark equal to the sum of the negative marks. So, for example, in a five choice question the correct answer would be scored at 4 marks. The effect of this is to shift the distribution to a mean of zero, meaning that the individual who randomly guesses may well score a negative total, although in practice this is unlikely because it is likely that he will guess some correctly.

Unfortunately, statistical safety is not sufficient to guarantee good design. We frequently hear learners complaining that "you couldn't really choose between some of the answers" or "some of the choices were obviously wrong". This kind of complaint stems directly from poor question design. Writing good MC questions depends first of all on understanding the structure of the question. This is shown at figure 5.3:

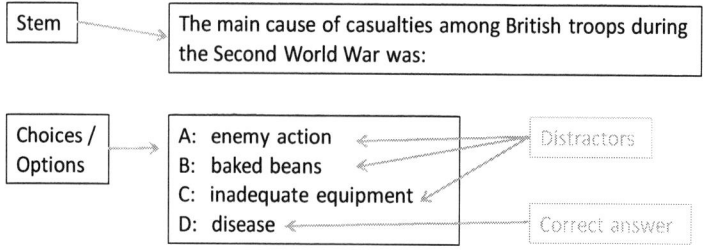

Figure 5.3 – Multi-choice question components

The rules that must be observed are:

- All choices should flow grammatically from the stem sentence.
- All choices should be more or less of the same length. Learners may be subconsciously drawn to or may unwittingly reject the "odd man out".
- All distractors must be feasible. If not, the reliability of the question diminishes. Choice B in the above example is clearly a poor distractor.
- The correct answer should be obvious to those who know. Ensure that there is no discernible pattern to the letter allocation of the correct answer across the whole test.
- If possible, avoid negative expression in the stem sentence e.g. "which of the following is NOT a cause of casualties at the battle of the Somme."
- Adjust the language level to that expected of the target audience.
- Avoid testing more than one idea in a single question.
- Avoid writing questions with answers that are subject to on-going change within short periods of time.
- Check to ensure that the content of one question does not assist learners to answer other questions. This tends to occur when there is a sequence of questions around the same topic.

- **Multi-response**: this question form takes multi-choice to a higher level because the learner must "assemble" a correct answer from a number of variables. An example is given below:

"Immediate treatment for serious arterial bleeding from a limb should include: (select 3 options from the following)
- A. raising the limb
- B. applying a tourniquet
- C. giving water
- D. applying pressure to pressure points
- E. keeping the casualty conscious
- F. treating for shock
- G. monitoring pulse, pallor and pupils
- H. sending for medical assistance

- I. confirming the casualty's blood group
- J. applying direct pressure by means of a field dressing

The multiple choice format is also often criticised for being "simplistic". However, while the format is certainly simple, its application can be extremely sophisticated. The best example of this is the use of a multi-choice / multi-response test in conjunction with a complex scenario or case study. This is common practice in the assessment of medical students.

Multi-choice is frequently combined with other techniques in examination settings. In these situations the multi-choice format is used to sample a wide range of knowledge and understanding, providing an assessment of breadth while other techniques are used to focus on specific areas in more depth.

Multi-choice assessments offer huge advantages to organisations that require on-going assessment of learners in the same topic at the same level. Once a multi-choice question or "item" has been created and found to work well it can be "banked". The item bank can be continually expanded to create a repository or proven questions from which assessments can be randomly generated. The format works extremely well on-line and can be immediately marked providing prompt feedback to the learner. Alternatively, by using proprietary answer grids, assessments can be marked by optical scanning which also provides immediate results.

- **True / false**: these have no assessment value and should never be used.

Higher Level Assessment – Case studies.

The familiar assessment tools discussed above are generally used to assess lower level learning i.e. Bloom's knowledge, comprehension and possibly application. If we wish to assess the higher levels i.e. analysis, synthesis and evaluation we need to employ more complex formats. At these higher levels, the complexity of the format will either show itself in the framing of the question or in the requirement for sophisticated marking schemes. So, for example, setting an essay question is a relatively simple matter, but marking an essay diligently is a time-consuming and complex process fraught with potential issues of subjectivity. Conversely, assessing by case-study or scenario requires a great deal of effort being put into the question design but will generally allow a tight and objective marking scheme to be developed that makes the scoring or grading a simple matter.

Choosing the actual assessment tool at this level depends of course on organisational need. Realistically, the essay format is the preserve of tertiary education and more specifically of the arts / humanities curriculum. While it is an excellent vehicle for the demonstration of learning at the very highest level, it is generally unsuited to business needs. Organisational learning and development is much more likely to be rooted in the acquisition of the systems, processes and policies needed to ensure business or service continuity. Consequently, scenario or case-study assessment tools tend to be the preferred option for assessing organisational requirements at the higher level. This means that considerable investment of time and expertise must go in "at the front end" in order to produce assessments that are easy to use and will be accepted as relevant, objective and properly focused. Shown below is an example of a typical scenario question that might be found in an assessment of people management skills in the context of applying organizational policy around sexual harassment.

"Read the following case study carefully and then answer the questions that follow.

Situation:
You are an experienced departmental manager. 3 months ago your department recruited Jenny Wright, a young female junior accountant who has been assigned to a team headed by Peter Lewis, an old hand for whom you have always had the greatest respect. As far as you can tell Jenny seems to have settled in well. Consequently you are somewhat surprised when she requests an urgent interview with you.

At that interview she informs you that she has been receiving lewd, sexually suggestive messages from Peter Lewis via his company Email. She has print-outs for you to look at. These clearly indicate Peter as the source. Jenny has approached you for advice because she doesn't want to get on the wrong side of Peter if she can avoid it. More importantly, she feels instinctively that he would not behave in this way and she does not want to damage his career unnecessarily. At this stage she is not making a formal complaint. She just wants the harassment to stop.

You decide to discuss the matter informally with Peter. He categorically denies that he had anything to do with the harassment. Knowing Peter as well as you do, you are inclined to believe him. If he is innocent, then somebody else must have obtained his personal login ID and password. While this may be somebody's idea of a joke, it is in fact illegal behavior and an outright contradiction of company HR and IT policies."

Questions.
Consult Company policies POLIT6.2 (Electronic Mai) and POLHR 1.9 (Sexual and Racial Harassment) provided as appendix 1 to this question. Then answer the following questions.

Question 1.a
If Peter Lewis did not send the Emails, the person who did is clearly guilty of 2 serious infringements of POLIT 6.2 and at least 1 infringement of POLHR 1.9. What are these infringements? Give your answer in the space below. A maximum of 4 Marks are available for this question.

Question 1b.
It is unlikely that the guilty person could be traced, but you feel that some action should be taken. Both Jenny and Peter are looking to you for leadership. In the space below describe what actions you believe you should take to deal with this situation locally and to prevent it escalating beyond your control. A maximum of 8 marks are available for this question.

Question 1.c
If, following these actions, the harassment continues in the same manner, what would be your conclusion? Give your answer in the space below. A maximum of 2 marks is available for this question.

Question 1d.
What action would you now take and which company policy gives you the authority to take that action? Give your answer in the space below. A maximum of 6 marks is available for this question.

It should be immediately evident from this example that designing assessment items such as this requires a great deal of imagination and effort. However, once completed we have a template of sorts into which we can insert variations on the theme. A simple marking guide can be devised and agreed between assessors to enable marks to be awarded objectively and fairly. In terms of the learning levels addressed, we can see that level 1 knowledge is ignored i.e. the policies are provided. We are not testing recall here. Level 2 (comprehension) is certainly addressed but more importantly, the questions assess the ability to interpret and apply. The need to assess events also calls for analytical skills. This question is therefore taking the assessment into the higher levels.

Best practice points to note here are:

- The provision of appropriately sized boxes in which to answer. This indicates to the learner the length of answer anticipated. We do not want an essay.
- An indication of the marks available. This provides a guide to the relative importance of the individual questions, thus allowing the learner to "balance" his responses appropriately.

Higher Level Assessment – Process Questions.

Well-designed scenarios or case studies will allow assessment to be taken through to synthesis and evaluation. Provided sufficient detail is made available, it is possible to assess complex process learning on the back of one situation. An example is provided below. This question is assessing a Fire Officer's tactical command knowledge and skills.

"Question 1: Strategy and Tactics. Study the scenario below and then answer the questions that follow."

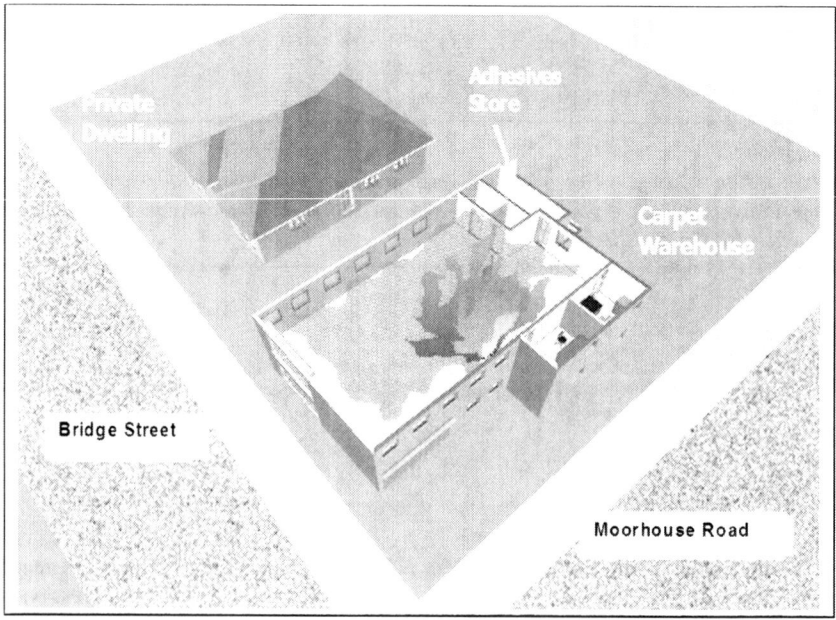

Situation:
You are the Officer in Charge of a crew that has been responded to a fire at a carpet warehouse. The warehouse is located at the junction of Bridge Street and Moorhouse

Road. The area is a mix of retail outlets, warehousing and occasional older style private houses in a small town. The area immediately surrounding the carpet warehouse has recently been cleared for development, with the exception of a private house immediately next door on Bridge Street. There are shops of various kinds across the road on both Bridge Street and Moorhouse Road.

It is mid-morning on Wednesday of a normal working week. Traffic is flowing steadily on both Bridge Street and Moorhouse Road. The shops opposite are busy, and a good number of their customers and staff have come out on to the pavement to observe the fire.

On arrival you are met by the warehouse manager (who is also the Fire Warden) for the premises. He tells you that he has evacuated everybody from the building and they are all accounted for. He also tells you that the fire has started at the rear of the upper floor and is spreading rapidly through carpet stocks toward the adhesives store. The adhesives are mostly petroleum-based and potentially explosive. The whole of the upper floor is filled with dense toxic fumes from the burning carpet. Police are on the scene and are anticipating that you will take charge as Incident Controller. They are awaiting your instructions.

You have a standard 6/3 appliance and an experienced crew. A second pump should be with you within 5 minutes. A third pump from the adjoining Volunteer Brigade has been turned out but is unlikely to arrive for another 30 minutes. The area is fully reticulated.

Questions:

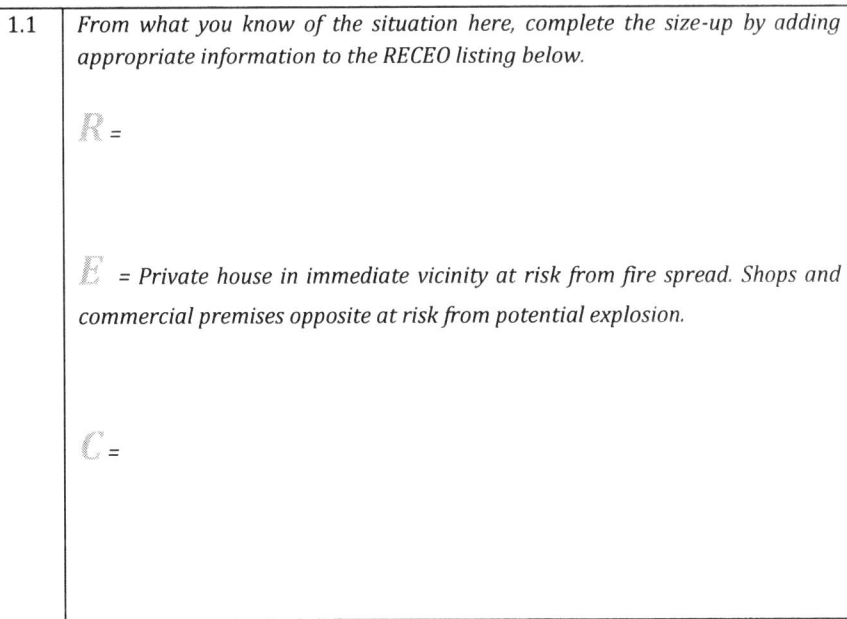

1.1	From what you know of the situation here, complete the size-up by adding appropriate information to the RECEO listing below. *R* = *E* = Private house in immediate vicinity at risk from fire spread. Shops and commercial premises opposite at risk from potential explosion. *C* =

	E = O = *A maximum of 10 marks is avaklable for this question.
1.2	*What should be your* AIM *in this situation? Write it in the space below.* *Try to do this in* **one short sentence.** *A maximum of 6 marks is avaklable for this question.
1.3	*In the space below briefly explain why you believe this should be the AIM rather than something else.* *A maximum of 6 marks is avaklable for this question.
1.4	*To achieve your aim what* STRATEGY *would you adopt? Describe this briefly in the space below.* *A maximum of 10 marks is available for this question.

1.5	*To carry out your strategy what TACTICS would you use? Describe these briefly in the space below.*
	*A maximum of 10 marks is available for this question.
1.6	*If you used these tactics, which TACTICAL MODE would you be operating? Write your answer below.*
1.7	*In this situation what might cause you to SWITCH TACTICAL MODE and why? Give an example in the space below.*
	*A maximum of 10 marks is available for this question.
1.8	*Incident ground operations are always accompanied by some degree of RISK. If you pursue your chosen strategy and tactics what, potentially, are the hazards to you and your firefighters? List them below.*
	A maximum of 10 marks is available for this question.
1.9	*Refer to the definitions of LIKELIHOOD. Now list three of the potential hazards you identified above. Next to each write down what you consider to be the likelihood of them occurring in this situation.*
	A maximum of 3 marks is available for this question.

1.10	*Refer to the definitions of* CONSEQUENCE. *Now list the potential hazards you identified above and next to each write down what you consider the consequences might be if they occurred in this situation.*
	A maximum of 3 marks is available for this question.
1.11	*We know that* RISK = LIKELIHOOD x CONSEQUENCE. *Refer to the matrix for defining level of risk. Once again, listing the potential hazards you identified above, write down the level of risk associated with each one.* *Level of risk =* *Level of risk =* *Level of risk =* *A maximum of 3 marks is available for this question.*
1.12	*Given the potential hazards and the associated levels of risk you have identified above, would you change your strategy or selected tactics?* *Yes No (Please tick appropriate answer)* *If "yes" describe briefly how you would adapt your action plan.* *A maximum of 4 marks is available for this question.*

Once again, the design input is significant. The scenario must be recognised as realistic and credible. Good graphics must be provided to ensure that all learners have a similar understanding. A better solution still would be to provide a walk through simulation e.g. via a computer-based simulation tool or a video sequence Once the scenario is set up it is possible to "milk" it to reveal all levels of learning. Again we are not seeking factual recall so things like the risk assessment matrix is provided. We are looking for evidence that the Fire Officer is able to work professionally through the complex processes associated with incident management. Consequently the range of questions requires him to show comprehension and application but also the ability to analyse information, to synthesise ideas in order to create a workable plan and to evaluate outcomes.

Questions like these are often referred to as process questions because this approach is often used to measure a learner's ability to work through procedures. It is easy to see how the approach can be adopted for any kind of procedural thinking.

IS IT DOING THE JOB? – VALIDATION OF ASSESSMENT.

At the outset it is essential to distinguish between the terms validation of assessment and evaluation because the two are often used interchangeably with inevitable ensuing confusion. Because so much can depend on the assessment outcome e.g. qualification, promotion, pay increments etc. we need to be sure that the assessment is effectively measuring what it is supposed to measure. If it is, then it is a valid assessment. If it does not, then it isn't. So, in a nutshell, assessment validity equals fitness for purpose.

Evaluation is quite different. The key to its meaning is the concept of "value". The process of evaluation determines to what extent the organisation has benefited from a particular learning intervention, a measurement of how much "value" has been added. Of course value can be either quantitative or qualitative, even perhaps both.

Assessment validity is a complex concept in as much as there are a number of issues to be considered. To be sure that the assessment is doing the job properly we need to examine:

- **Face validity** – do the various assessment items actually make sense to an expert? This is relatively easy to determine providing you can find an expert. The key is to brief the subject expert carefully on the programme, the learners, the learning outcomes and the intended level of learning. He should then be able to scan the assessment and provide feedback on the accuracy, weighting, level and sufficiency.
- **Content validity** – does it fully assess the learning outcomes? Is other "illegitimate" content included? Again, this should be relatively easy to determine. It is primarily a matter of direct comparison between the learning outcomes and the assessment content. If there is material over and above the learning outcomes it should be removed since it was not originally intended to be there.
- **Construct validity** - does it allow the required learning to be revealed or are there internal barriers potentially preventing this e.g. complex question, ambiguity, enabling skills that were not taught in the programme etc.? It boils down to "are we actually measuring what we think we're measuring?" This is not just about subject matter. We also need to ask "Is the assessment set at the appropriate level (degree of difficulty)?" This is trickier to ascertain but is worth the effort because this is certainly a major cause of assessment failure.

The most blatant example here must be the provision of assessment in something other than the learner's first language. This occurs frequently in officially multi-lingual societies. If, for example, a New Zealand Maori whose first language is *Te Reo* is forced to sit an entrance examination in English, that assessment might be considered invalid. Its "construction" is actually testing proficiency in English as much as the true subject of the examination. New Zealand is officially bi-lingual so the examination should also be provided in *Te Reo* if this is requested. Exceptions might be made if, for example, English is the operational language of the organisation and fluency must therefore be an absolute requirement.

Construct problems also occur very obviously in practical skills testing. Often, for convenience or to condense the assessment process, individual skills will be grouped together and become dependent on one another. As an example, a land navigation assessment might decide to task individuals with marching accurately on a bearing to reach a checkpoint where they will be tested on translating map to ground. At first glance this seems eminently sensible until we find that some individuals were not skilled enough at marching on a bearing to reach the checkpoint. Consequently they were not assessed on their map to ground skills and failed the test overall. Had the learning outcomes been assessed separately these individuals might well have passed the map to ground component and gained sufficient marks to pass.

- **Criterion validity** – do the results correlate readily with an external analogue or to real world performance? Returning to our map readers we might find that the results they obtain in their assessment are highly predictive of their performance when they join their scout groups or mountain rescue teams. High scorers will prove to be excellent navigators in "real" situations. Likewise, low scorers are very likely to get themselves, and others lost.
- **Reliability** – largely a measure of consistency i.e. if we gave the same assessment to similar groups of learners, who had been similarly trained, would we get similar results? There are a number of techniques that can provide useful statistical evidence of reliability both at the whole assessment level and at the level of individual questions or "items". Item analysis is particularly useful in the context of the traditional tests discussed earlier. It allows us to identify and weed out "rogue" questions that potentially distort otherwise perfectly sound assessments. The most frequently used item analysis techniques are examined in detail below.
- **Fairness** – an aspect of reliability that is often overlooked. This generally relates to the conditions under which assessments are conducted. Unless elements such as time, resources, equipment, environment and grading are standardised, assessment results will not be reliable.

Whole assessment analysis – basic data.

Assessments that produce scores allow us to apply a wide range of analytical techniques that will tell us whether an assessment is doing the job we need it to do. Some of these involve complex processes that are really the province of professional statisticians or educational psychologists, but in most situations some fairly basic techniques, easily set up and managed by internal HR / L&D staff, are all we need. The minimum basic data we need to collect at the level of the whole assessment is:

- Simple achievement i.e. number passing / % pass rates
- Mean (average) level of achievement / score
- Distribution – the "shape" of the results (reliability)
- Test – retest (reliability)
- Split half (reliability)

Whole assessment reliability analysis – achievement data.

Basic achievement data is simple to collect and analyse. It is also essential for level 2 evaluation, as we shall see in section 7. When tests are used continually it makes sense to set up a spreadsheet into which scores are entered and compared with previous tests – thus providing a commentary on achievement history and an insight into apparent trends. This is often the information that management is primarily interested in i.e. how many of our people are actually "succeeding". However, to be sure that a test is reliable we need to go beyond simple pass rates and average scores.

The mean, or average achievement is of course a simple calculation. It is probably the result that trainers are most interested in because, perhaps more than anything else it comments on their performance.

Whole assessment analysis – frequency distribution.

Perhaps the most useful, and user friendly way of monitoring assessment performance is the ongoing comparison of "shape" presented by the raw score results each time the test is used. This shape is produced by plotting the frequency with which scores occur across the full range of results i.e. a frequency distribution. Generally speaking, we should design tests to produce scores that distribute themselves "normally". Normal distribution is based on the fact that all things being equal (or 'normal'), very similar results will be attained and they will be distributed in a predictable manner across the range. So, a very similar groups of learners, trained under the same conditions, using the same techniques and assessments should produce very similar results. With a well-designed test we would normally expect to find a few individuals doing poorly, a few doing very well and the majority achieving somewhere in between. This pattern would also be revealed in most other aspects of life e.g. a survey of heights attained at maturity, body weight, physical performance, daily calorie intake etc. Traditional thinking is that assessment results should mirror reality and therefore be distributed "normally" across the range.

Statistically, a normal distribution is one in which 68% of the learners have scored within 1 standard deviation + or - from the mean, 95% within 2 standard deviations from the mean and 99.7 within 3. So, if our test had a score range of 0-100 the normal distribution of scores would look like this:

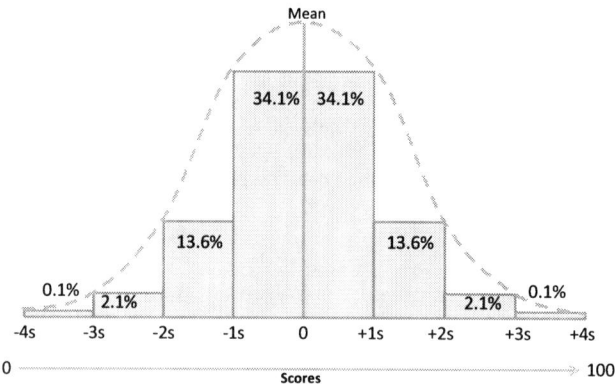

Figure 5.4 - the normal curve of distribution

In any distribution the mean is the midpoint of the range and the degree to which scores are dispersed either side of the mean is measured in standard "deviations" signified by the Greek letter sigma (σ). When a curve is drawn over the normal distribution it produces the familiar "bell curve". Test results are unlikely to reproduce this distribution exactly, but, in most cases, it represents an ideal. The actual shape of the bell curve depends on two factors - the mean and the standard deviation. The mean of the distribution determines the mid-point of the curve, and the standard deviation determines its height and width. If the standard deviation is large, the curve will be short and wide. If the standard deviation is small, the curve will be tall and narrow.

The normal distribution is in all respects symmetrical. Most tests will produce results which deviate to some degree from this symmetry. This is known as "skewed" distribution. Skewness is a measure of the lack of symmetry in a distribution. This may indicate that the assessment is faulty but, alternatively, it may be acceptable if the degree of difficulty is deliberately set high or low. Figure 5.5 below depicts a negatively skewed distribution.

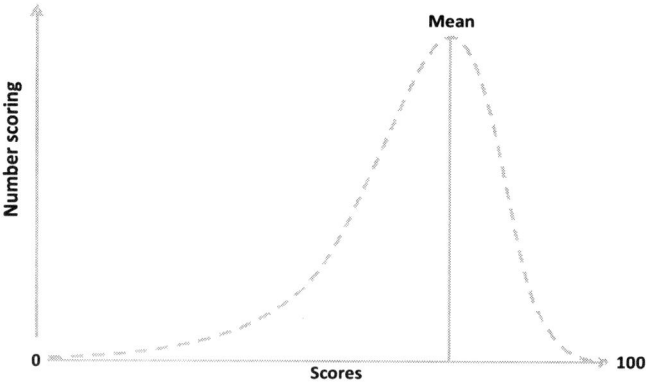

Figure 5.5 – Negative Skew

The "shape" of the test results here tells us immediately that the majority are scoring highly with the mean being around 70%. We therefore have to ask ourselves whether we are happy with that or do we need to increase the level of difficulty. It all depends on what we want the assessment to do. For example if the assessment is being used as a filter for acceptance on to a full programme then we may well wish to raise the bar, in which case we would be looking for a positive skew, as shown in figure 5.6 . This clearly shows that the majority of individuals are scoring poorly; allowing high scorers to be clearly identified.

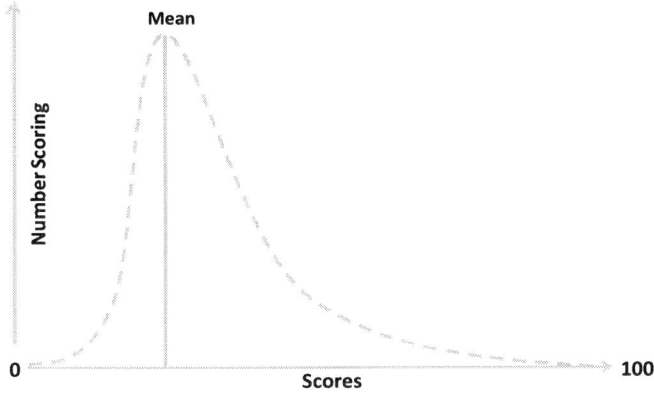

Figure 5.6 – Positive Skew

Occasionally, the distribution of scores may result in two clear central tendencies; negative and positive skewing. This is known as bimodal distribution. An example is shown below at figure 5.7.

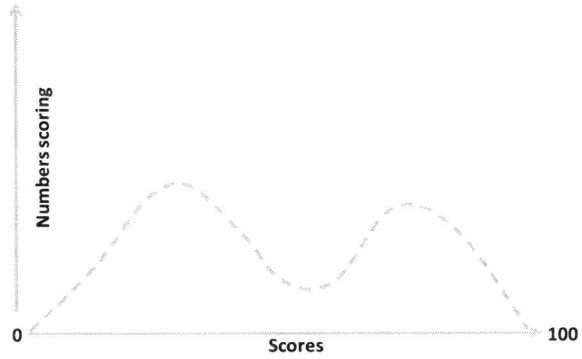

Figure 5.7 – Bi-modal Distribution

While there may be acceptable explanations for this, bimodal distribution is usually a sign that there is a lack of progression in the difficulty of the test items. A significant proportion of the learner group is scoring highly, while another large group is scoring poorly, with very few scoring in the mid-range. This may be a deliberate device to separate out the high performers but it does not provide useful data across the whole group. It can also be an indicator of confusing elements within the test items. If you need to grade your learners progressively across a range, A+ to E- for example, then this test is clearly not doing the job for you and needs to be abandoned or re-designed.

So how do we obtain distribution data? In practice there is no need for complex statistical calculations. All that is required is a simple Excel spreadsheet.

Interval	No. Scoring
1 to 5	0
6 to 10	0
11 to 15	1
16 to 20	2
21 to 25	4
26 to 30	6
31 to 35	6
36 to 40	8
41 to 45	10
46 to 50	14
51 to 55	23
56 to 60	38
61 to 65	34
66 to 70	27
71 to 75	19
76 to 80	14
81 to 85	8
86 to 90	3
91 to 95	0
96 to 100	0

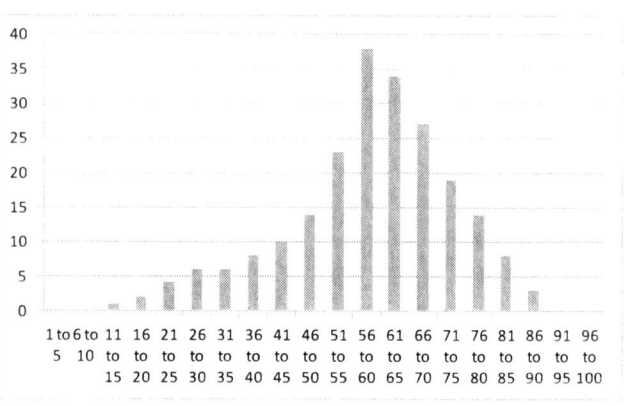

Figure 5.8 – Simple frequency distribution "test shape" using Excel.

The first step is to decide which frequency intervals to use. This will depend largely on the level of detail you want. If we take the example of a test with a maximum score of 100 we may decide that 5 marks intervals will be sufficient. A total of 217 individuals have sat the assessment. On completion of marking, their scores are allocated to the frequency intervals. We then simply use the graphing functionality in Excel to immediately extract the "shape" of the test as shown in Fig 5.8. If this distribution aligns with the purpose of the assessment it becomes the norm. Entering the raw scores each time the test is used subsequently will allow us to monitor events and to investigate if the shape departs significantly from the norm.

Whole assessment reliability analysis: test-retest.
If an assessment is reliable we should see very similar results occurring if it is administered on several occasions under precisely the same conditions i.e.
- The same group of learners.
- The same assessment.
- The same procedures.
- The same assessment conditions and environment.
- The same assessors.

The interval between test and retest should be short, preferably no more than a few days at most. A longer interval may lead to error due to the falling off of factual, conceptual retention. The individuals involved should not be advised of their first test results because this may cause them to change their responses in the retest. Test retest is an indicator of reliability over time. Ideally we would have a perfect correlation (1) but a number of intrusive factors make this unlikely. For practical purposes a correlation less than .75 is unacceptable.

So how do we calculate this correlation? Once again there is no need to wade through complex statistics "manually". Excel will do this for us. All we need to do is to enter the scores obtained for the test items in each test as two separate "arrays" as shown at figure 5.9.

	A	B	C	D	E	F
1						
2			Q.No.	First Test	Second Test	
3		Totals by question	1	52	50	
4			2	48	46	
5			3	44	46	
6			4	56	50	
7			5	40	38	
8			6	48	48	
9			7	44	46	
10			8	36	36	
11			9	38	36	
12			10	44	42	
13			11	48	44	
14			12	38	40	
15			13	54	54	
16			14	60	58	
17			15	44	44	
18			16	30	32	
19			17	38	34	
20			18	32	30	
21			19	52	48	
22			20	30	28	
23						
24						

Figure 5.9 – Test-retest data arrays

Then we select more functions from the function library bar at the top of the spreadsheet.

Figure 5.10 – Function library bar (Excel)

This will reveal a short drop-down menu from which we select "statistical" which provides a further drop-down. From this list we select Pearson. This will bring up the function arguments box. All that is needed now is to insert the cell references for the two arrays, in this case D3:D22 for the first test and E3:E22 for the second. Clicking OK calculates the coefficient and inserts into the spreadsheet.

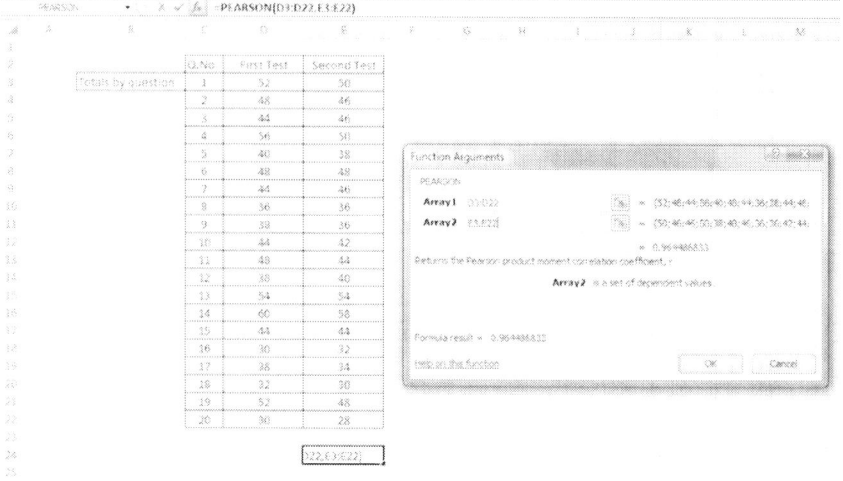

Figure 5.11 – Selecting the Pearson formula

In this case the result is 0.964 which is very good

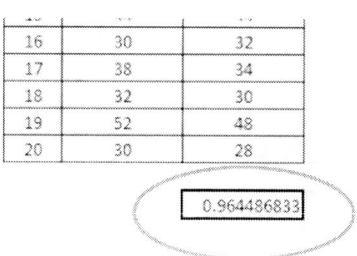

16	30	32
17	38	34
18	32	30
19	52	48
20	30	28

0.964486833

Figure 5.12 – Test-retest result

While test retest is a useful measure of reliability, it is problematic in that learners may resent having to sit the same test twice. Fortunately, there is seldom any need to carry out this procedure more than once – unless you suspect that some aspect of the second test was out of kilter with the first test.

Whole assessment internal consistency – split half analysis.

It is also useful to measure the consistency of the individual items acting as a whole. The split half method is a useful tool when we are dealing with tests composed of equally weighted questions i.e. carrying the same mark value. It cannot be used successfully for tests with widely varying marks per question (e.g. the classic short answer test) or for tests in which the questions are designed to become progressively more difficult. Consequently the best use of split half analysis is for questionnaires or multi-choice tests with an even marking schedule.

The method itself is relatively simple. If the test is reliable we should see an acceptable correlation in scores between any two half combinations. The usual technique is simply to divide the test into "odds and evens". A score for each half is then calculated for each participant and the correlation between the two scores computed using the *Pearson r formula*.

	Learner	Odd Half Total	Even Half Total
	A	22	24
	B	18	20
	C	16	17
	D	21	19
	E	23	21
	F	11	14
	G	12	13
	H	18	19
	I	16	21
	J	21	21
	K	23	24
	L	9	11
	M	12	13
	N	11	10
	O	23	19
	P	20	18
	Correlation		0.889181238

Figure 5.13 – Split half reliability using Pearson's r

As with all statistical calculations, the greater the sample population, the more reliable the result. Consequently, split half reliability analysis will be questionable for short tests. In these cases it is useful to apply a "correction" which extrapolates the result to give a more reliable result. This is the Spearman-Brown prophecy or predictive. This kind of calculation takes us into the realm of the statistician and is usually beyond the capacity of HR departments, even with an L&D specialist. Unfortunately Excel does not yet provide a formula for Spearman-Brown, but an excellent calculator has been created and generously made available by Del Siegle. This can be found at:

http://www.gifted.uconn.edu/Siegle/research/Instrument%20Reliability%20and%2 0Validity/reliabilitycalculator2.xls.

This tool also provides several other functions not available in Excel. Shown at figure 5.14 is an example of Siegle's calculator in use for a 10 question test. All that has to be done is to enter the marks attained for each learner and the statistical results appear in the top left cells. The Spearman-Brown result is ringed.

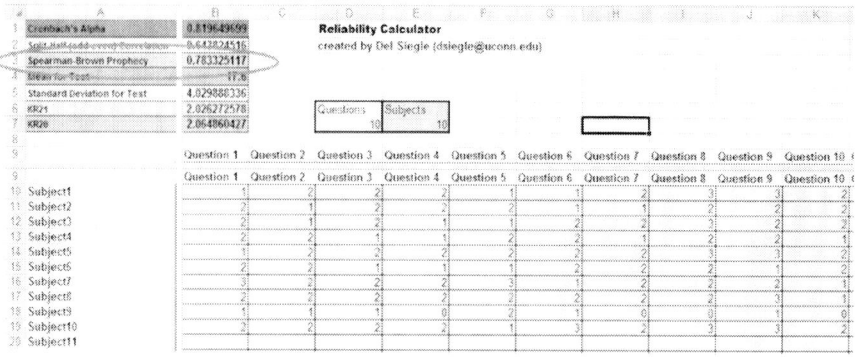

Figure 5.14 – Siegle's calculator

Siegle's calculator also allows us to calculate Cronbach's Alpha. This is generally regarded as a more reliable variant of simple odd-even split half analysis. This calculation is based on the fact that there are a number of alternative ways to split tests in half, and each of these might produce somewhat different results. Although it is a relatively complex calculation, Cronbach's Alpha simply provides an average of all the splitting methods. We can see from the results that a straightforward odd-even split for the 10 questions gives a correlation of 0.64. Cronbach Alpha corrects this to 0.81 and Spearman-Brown gives us 0.78. Consequently this test would seem to have good internal consistency.

Item analysis – facility value (FV).

When we move away from whole assessment analysis to the consideration of individual questions there are two essential analyses that need to be carried out, ideally on several successive occasions, to ensure that each question is doing what we want it to. The first of these is facility value (FV), which calculates how difficult the learners found each specific question. This calculation is ideally suited to questions that have a simple marking schedule and the answers can be adjudged either right or wrong. However, it can be used for long answer questions which have an extended mark schedule if a nominal "pass mark" is assigned. For example a complex question that attracts a possible total of 15 marks might be assigned a pass mark of 10 i.e. 66% to be considered a "right answer". In practice FV is most often used for simple test items such as multi-choice.

The calculation is simple and historical FV's are easily obtained by setting the calculation up in a test analysis spreadsheet. Facility is found by calculating the percentage of students form the whole group who answered the question correctly. So, for example if the learner group is 35 strong and only 12 answered correctly, the facility value = 12/35 x 100 = 34.3%. An FV of 0.5 is generally desirable because it ensures that learners across the whole ability spectrum will be tested. If the FV shifts significantly higher or lower then it contributes little to the overall assessment. Nevertheless there are valid arguments for departures such as these. For example questions related to mastery learning may well return a high FV because significant effort will have gone into the training related to the specific issue and we expect learners to get this right.

Figure 5.15 shows a typical matrix that is easily set up in Excel.

No. of Learners	20									Scores by Individual Learners											Facility Values Test X	
	Q. No.	A	B	C	D	E	F	G	H	I	J	K	L	M	N	O	P	Q	R	S	T	Total correct	FV
	1	1	1	1	1	0	1	1	0	1	1	0	0	1	1	0	1	1	1	1	0	14	0.7
	2	1	0	0	0	1	0	0	0	0	1	1	1	0	1	1	1	0	0	1	0	9	0.45
	3	1	1	1	1	1	1	1	0	1	1	1	1	0	1	1	1	1	0	0	1	16	0.8
	4	0	0	0	1	1	1	1	0	1	1	0	1	1	0	0	1	1	1	1	0	12	0.6
	5	1	1	1	1	1	1	1	1	1	1	1	1	1	1	0	1	1	1	1	0	18	0.9
	6	0	0	0	0	0	1	0	0	0	1	1	0	0	1	1	1	1	0	1	1	9	0.45
	7	1	1	0	1	0	0	1	1	0	1	1	1	0	0	1	1	0	0	1	1	12	0.6
	8	1	1	1	1	1	1	1	1	1	1	1	1	1	1	1	1	1	1	1	0	19	0.95
	9	0	0	0	0	1	1	0	1	1	1	0	1	1	0	0	1	1	1	1	0	11	0.55
	10	1	1	1	1	1	1	1	1	1	1	1	1	1	1	0	0	1	1	1	0	16	0.8
	11	1	0	1	1	1	0	1	0	1	1	0	1	0	1	1	0	1	0	1	1	13	0.65
	12	1	0	1	1	1	0	1	0	1	1	1	1	0	1	1	0	1	1	1	1	15	0.75
	13	1	0	0	1	1	0	1	0	1	0	1	1	0	1	1	0	1	1	1	0	11	0.55
	14	0	1	0	1	1	1	1	0	1	1	1	1	0	0	1	1	1	1	1	0	14	0.7
	15	0	1	0	1	1	1	1	0	1	1	1	1	0	1	1	1	1	1	1	0	15	0.75
	16	1	0	0	0	1	0	0	0	1	1	1	1	0	0	0	1	1	1	1	0	12	0.6
	17	1	0	1	0	1	1	1	0	0	1	1	1	0	1	1	1	1	1	1	0	14	0.7
	18	1	0	0	1	1	1	1	0	0	1	1	1	0	1	1	0	0	1	1	0	12	0.6
	19	1	1	0	0	0	0	0	0	1	1	1	1	0	0	0	1	1	1	1	0	10	0.5
	20	1	1	1	0	1	0	0	0	0	1	1	1	0	0	0	1	1	1	1	1	12	0.6
	Learner totals	15	10	9	14	16	15	13	5	12	19	16	18	8	12	15	13	17	14	19	6		

Figure 5.15 – Using Excel to calculate facility values

In this case the matrix records data for a 20 question test for 20 learners. The entries are either 1 or 0, (1 for a correct answer, 0 for incorrect). Given that an FV of 0.5 is generally the ideal, we would want to investigate question 8 (FV = 0.95) and question 10 (FV = 0.8). The great majority of the learner group has found these questions to be easy – or they have been particularly well-drilled in this topic. The issue here is that these questions are doing little to separate out the high achievers from the lesser. Where the assessment is simply related to a standard (criterion referencing) this does not matter, but if we wish to rank or grade individual performance (norm referencing) then this issue is important. Similarly, if we found questions returning a very low FV we would need to investigate. If the level of difficulty is set too high, we find that while we can distinguish the very top echelon, the question generates nothing useful concerning the majority. This brings us to the concept of discrimination.

Item analysis – index of discrimination (ID).

Whenever we are assessing to a minimum standard, or testing what is known as "mastery" learning, there is little point in trying to discern how individuals have performed relative to their peers. All that matters here is that the individual has met the standard or shown the requisite grasp of the material. However, when we need to produce a spread of scores to reveal differences in achievement, we need questions to discriminate between those who really know and understand from those that do not.

What this means in practice is that, ideally, a properly discriminating question should reveal that the top learners are all able to answer correctly, the lower achievers are all unable to answer and the middle group return a mixed performance. To calculate the degree of discrimination we ignore the middle group, focusing on the contrast between the top and bottom thirds of the learners.

Top third		1	2	3	4	5	6	7	8	9	10	11	12	13	14	15	16	17	18	19	20
	Learner S	1	1	0	1	1	1	1	1	1	1	1	1	1	1	1	1	1	1	1	1
	Learner J	1	1	1	1	1	1	1	1	1	1	1	0	1	1	1	1	1	1	1	1
	Learner L	0	1	1	1	1	0	1	1	1	1	1	1	1	1	1	1	1	1	1	1
	Learner Q	1	0	1	1	1	1	0	1	1	1	1	1	1	1	1	1	1	0	1	1
	Learner K	0	1	1	0	1	1	1	1	0	1	0	1	1	1	1	1	1	1	1	1
	Learner E	0	1	1	1	1	0	0	1	1	1	1	1	1	1	1	1	1	0	1	1
	Learner O	0	1	1	0	1	1	1	1	0	0	1	1	1	1	1	1	1	1	1	0
	No. Correct	3	6	6	5	7	5	5	7	5	6	6	7	6	7	7	7	7	5	7	6
Bottom third	Learner H	0	0	0	0	1	0	1	1	1	0	0	0	0	0	1	0	0	0	0	0
	Learner T	0	0	1	0	0	1	1	0	0	0	1	1	0	0	0	0	0	0	0	1
	Learner M	1	0	0	1	1	0	0	1	1	1	0	0	0	0	1	1	0	0	0	0
	Learner C	1	0	1	1	1	0	0	1	0	1	1	0	0	0	0	1	0	0	0	1
	Learner B	1	0	1	0	1	0	1	1	0	1	0	0	0	1	1	0	0	0	1	1
	Learner I	1	0	1	1	1	0	0	1	1	1	1	1	1	1	0	0	0	0	0	0
	Learner N	1	1	1	0	1	1	0	1	0	1	1	0	0	1	0	0	0	1	1	0
	No. Correct	5	1	5	2	6	2	3	6	3	5	4	4	1	2	4	1	2	1	2	3
	Variation	-2	5	1	3	1	3	2	1	2	1	2	3	5	5	3	6	5	4	5	3

ID Q1	-0.2857143		ID Q11	0.28571429
ID Q2	0.71428571		ID Q12	0.42857143
ID Q3	0.14285714		ID Q13	0.71428571
ID Q4	0.42857143		ID Q14	0.71428571
ID Q5	0.14285714		ID Q15	0.42857143
ID Q6	0.42857143		ID Q16	0.85714286
ID Q7	0.28571429		ID Q17	0.71428571
ID Q8	0.14285714		ID Q18	0.57142857
ID Q9	0.28571429		ID Q19	0.71428571
ID Q10	0.14285714		ID Q20	0.42857143

Figure 5.16 – Using Excel to calculate index of discrimination

So, using the example of the matrix above, the group of 20 learners is divided to reveal top and bottom thirds of 7, ignoring the middle group of 6. The correct and incorrect responses for these two groups are then entered into the spreadsheet. The discrimination is then calculated by subtracting the number getting the question right in the bottom group from the number getting it right in the top group and then dividing by the number of learners in each of the groups, in this case this is 7. So for example if look at question 1 we can see that 5 out of 7 of the bottom group answered this correctly while only 3 out of the top group were able to do so. Subtracting bottom from top gives a variation of -3 and dividing this by 7 gives a discrimination of -0.28 which is clearly unacceptable. There is obviously something seriously wrong with this question and it should be discarded or re-written. There are a number of other poorly discriminating questions that will need examination. Maximum discrimination will of course be equal to 1.

Clearly there is a dynamic relationship between facility and discrimination. If the facility value is at the high or low end of the scale the ability to discriminate will be negatively affected. Conversely, if we push for maximum discrimination the facility value will fall. High ID = low FV and vice versa.

In conclusion, an assessment may sometimes be valid but not reliable, or reliable but not valid. The driving examiner who always omits the assessment of reversing skills, could not be accused of conducting an unreliable driving test. His results would be consistent, but they would not be valid because a proper test of driving must include reversing skills. Conversely, if the same assessor covered all the required skills but, because he liked a change of scene, regularly varied the environments in which he tested them considerably, this would produce valid assessment but would probably not be reliable. To be acceptable, assessments must be valid, reliable and fair.

Higher level complex assessment – use of rubrics.

There will always be numerous kinds of learning that cannot be assessed by the types of 'hard data' techniques outlined above. For the most part this learning will involve higher level, complex understanding that can be demonstrated in a range of ways, and consequently for which there are no hard and fast answers or responses. In these situations, the central issues tend to be consistency, fairness, and standardization of what factors should be considered and evaluated.

Typically, an assessment rubric takes the form of a matrix with one axis listing the criteria to be considered and the other a range of levels with differential descriptors. Figure 5.17 shows a typical assessment rubric, in this case designed for a university level assignment. The three broad assessment criteria are aligned to 4 level descriptors which tell the assessor what to look for and the student what they should be seeking to provide as evidence of their understanding. In this instance we can see that the student has demonstrated capability at level 3 against two of the criteria and level 4 against the other.

Figure 5.18 illustrates a variation that offers a greater range of performance differentiation (0-10) and a weighting facility. This allows for a sharper focus on the more critical elements.

The use of rubrics is probably limited in the context of workplace learning but they certainly do have value, particularly for long term development programmes where they can be applied to a group or individuals. Rubrics are of obvious assistance to the assessor, but they can greatly assist learners if they are provided well ahead of assessment. This provides for clarity of expectations for all concerned.

Criteria	Level 4 4 points	Level 3 3 points	Level 2 2 points	Level 1 1 point	Score
Identification of a suitable area in your workplace/situation where applied learning has the potential to improve learning outcomes to students/learners.	The proposal reflects a very thoughtful consideration of a suitable area in your workplace/situation where applied learning has the potential to improve learning outcomes f students/learners.	The proposal reflects good consideration of a suitable area your workplace/situation where applied learning has the potenti to improve learning outcomes f students/learners.	The proposal reflects some consideration of a suitable area in your workplace/situation where applied learning has the potential to improve learning outcomes for students/learners.	The proposal reflects limited consideration of a suitable area in consideration of a suitable area in your workplace/situation where applied learning has the potential to improve learning outcomes for students/learners.	4 points
Development of a program outline, including reference to expected outcomes; learning strategies and approaches to assessment.	The proposal outline includes a very well-planned framework fo assembling applied learning experiences, including referenc to expected outcomes; learning strategies and approaches t assessment.	The proposal outline includes a good overview of applied learnin experiences, including reference to expected outcomes; learning strategies and approaches to assessment	The proposal outline includes a limited reference to expected outcomes; learning strategies and approaches to assessment	The proposal includes some reference to learning outcomes and activities but lacks suitable detail.	4 points
Analysis and critical reflection on how the program's learning objectives will contribute to the students': personal growth; academic enhancement and civic development.	The proposal reflects a very thoughtful level of analysis and critical reflection on how the program's learning objectives w contribute to the students': personal growth; academic enhancement and civic development. It makes excellen reference to the literature to support arguments	The proposal reflects a good lev of analysis and critical reflection on how the program's learning objectives will contribute to the students': personal growth; academic enhancement and civic development. It makes suitable reference to the literature to support arguments	The proposal reflect limited analysis and critical reflection on how the program's learning objectives will contribute to the students': personal growth; academic enhancement and civic development. It makes limited reference to the literature to support arguments	The proposal reflects a very minimal analysis and critical reflection on how the program' learning objectives will contribute to the students': personal growth; academic enhancement and civic development.	4 points
MaxLevel Scores	12	9	6	3	**TotalScore**
ActualScore	4	6	0	0	10 points

Figure 5.17 Example of an assessment rubric (tertiary level assignment).

Criteria	Poor (Band 1) 1 - 2	Satisfactory (Band 2) 3 - 4	Good (Band 3) 5 - 7	Excellent (Band 4) 8 - 10	Marks Weightage
Subject Knowledge	Subject knowledge is **not evident**. Information is **confusing, incorrect, or flawed.**	**Some** subject knowledge is evident. **Some** Information is confusing, incorrect, or flawed.	Subject knowledge is evident in **much** of the project. **Most** information is clear, appropriate, and correct.	Subject knowledge is evident **throughout** the project. **All** information is clear, appropriate, and correct.	30%
Creativity (Multimedia)	Presentation demonstrates a **poor** level of creativity. Media types used for presentation is **lacking in variety and/or appropriateness.**	Presentation demonstrates a **moderate** level of creativity. **Lacking in variety** in its use of media types.	Presentation demonstrates a **good** level of creativity, and uses a **limited variety** of appropriate media. **Two or lesser media** types are used.	Presentation demonstrates a **high** level of creativity, and uses a **wide variety** of appropriate media. **More than 2 media** types are used, for e.g. text, sound, photos and video.	30%
Citing Sources	**No** sources are properly cited.	**Few** sources are properly cited.	**Most** sources are properly cited.	**All** sources are properly cited.	10%
Organization	The sequence of information is **not logical**. Menus and paths to information are **not evident.**	The sequence of information is **somewhat logical**. Menus and paths are **confusing and flawed.**	The sequence of information is **logical**. Menus and paths to **most** information are clear and direct.	The sequence of information is **logical and intuitive**. Menus and paths to **all** information are clear and direct.	10%
Originality	The work is a **minimal collection or rehash** of other people's ideas, products, and images. There is **no evidence** of new thought.	The work is an **extensive collection and rehash** of other people's ideas, products, and images. There is **little evidence** of new thought or inventiveness.	The project shows **some** evidence of originality and inventiveness.	The project shows **significant evidence** of originality and inventiveness. The **majority** of the content and many of the ideas are fresh, original, and inventive.	20%

Figure 5.18 – Example of an assessment rubric for a multi media presentation assignment

6. DELIVERY OF LEARNING.

WHAT DO WE NEED TO DO?

Having reached the point where we have obtained a well-designed course or programme, with valid, reliable and fair assessment, we have to take the product to market and deliver the service. To guarantee a good outcome for that service we need to apply rigorous management processes that will ensure a high level of control.

Perhaps the most frequent comment on the end of course "happiness sheets" is that the course was badly organised. This is either due to poor planning and preparation, or poor execution on the day. Effective management of learning delivery is a chain of interdependent events. If the chain breaks at any point we are likely to have problems in the training room or the learning environment. So, are there any hard and fast rules around managing delivery of learning? Probably not – but there are certainly some crucial guidelines. All good procedures stem from solid concepts or paradigms. We have to answer two key questions here:

- What management functions do we need to apply?
- What should we apply those functions to?

Figure 6.1 presents a useful paradigm.

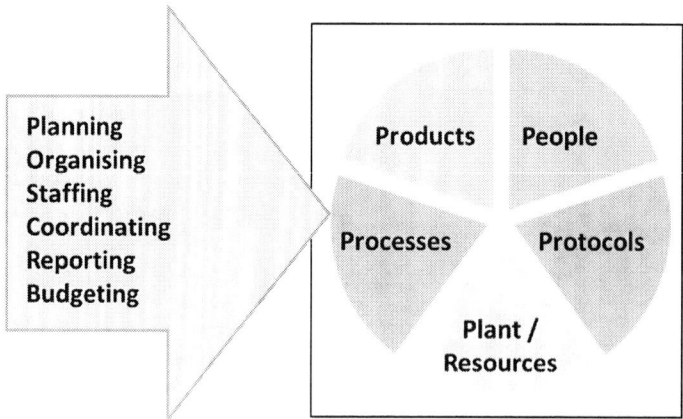

Figure 6.1 – Basic Management Paradigm

The key management functions here derive from the traditional view identified by the acronym POSDCORB, first put forward by Gulick and Urwick as long ago as 1937. Old-fashioned it may be, but it still offers a useful structure in the context of managing learning deivery. The original analysis identified the following as the core functions of management:

- Planning
- Organising
- Staffing
- Directing
- Coordinating
- Reporting (and Recording)
- Budgeting

The notion of "directing" is a little too authoritarian for today's tastes and is now understood to be subsumed within the coordinating function. Directing is therefore removed. In its place we really need to add 'leading'. While there are certainly managers that are not tasked with leading e.g. managers of processes, leadership is now generally regarded as a primary function of management.

The question of what these functions should be applied to is neatly solved by introducing the project management referencing tool, the 5P's. Pretty well all the issues that arise will stem from:
- **Products:** the final outcome or achievement.
- **People**: getting the right people and managing their performance to plan.
- **Processes**: selecting and maximising the most effective working methods.
- **Plant** (or resources / equipment): the essential tools needed to get the job done.
- **Protocols:** ensuring that organisational or client policies and procedures are complied with or adhered to.

Applying this paradigm allows us to develop a useful matrix to guide overall management of learning delivery. This is shown overleaf. While most of the emerging tasks are self-explanatory it is worthwhile investigating some in depth and identifying any useful tools. In practice, the POSDCORB acronym does not conform to the natural functional sequence here. For example, after evolving an initial plan it would be unwise to proceed further without costing out and ensuring that the final bill would sit comfortably within any allocated budget. Consequently we will deal with the functional issues in a slightly amended order.

Planning.

It is important, from the outset, to understand the difference between planning and organising. Planning is about deciding what is to happen, to whom, how, with what and when. Organising is about putting things in place to ensure that it actually happens. So planning is primarily about thinking – organising is about doing. Unfortunately, thinking and doing do not always come pre-packaged in the same person, which is why these functions are often separated out into the roles of L&D manager and L&D / HR administrator.

Referring to the matrix above we can see that most of the issues associated with planning are resolved through the ILN and LNA processes. Nevertheless, there are some aspects that merit emphasis or closer attention.

Managing Learning Delivery

	Product. (Output – what will be delivered?)	People. (Who will be involved?)	Process. (How will this happen?)	Plant / Resources. (What equipment, materials do we need?)	Protocols. (What procedures, policies need to be followed?)
Planning	• Name of programme / course • Level • Associated qualification?	• HR/L&D • Target group? • Individual participants? • Line managers? • Other stakeholders? • Staffing for cover purposes?	• Overview of delivery method e.g. On-job / off-job. Internal / external trainers. On-site/ off-site venue etc. • Timeframes and delivery structure?	• Access to production equipment / machinery? • Learning aids / materials? • IT / on-line access? • Personal protective equipment etc.?	• Company L&D policy • Company planning templates? • Departmental business & operational plans? • Programme verification (external providers)
Budgeting	• Accurate costing forecast	• HR / L&D • Managers with delegated authority • Providers	• Course cost calculator	• New equipment spend? • Additional resources? • Training venues / locations?	• Approval and sign-off on course costings from appropriate managers
Organising	• Admin activity check list inc joining instructions, booking of travel, accom, meals, venues etc.	• HR/L&D • Line managers • Training admin staff	• Meeting(s) to identify administrative tasks and deadlines. • Update / review of process as required	• Availability of equipment and resources?	• On time communication with affected line managers • Full briefing of admin staff
Staffing	• Competent delivery and assessment team • Support staff as required	• HR/L&D • Departmental managers • External providers	• Identify appropriate internal expertise • Ensure availability • Confirm external team	• Trainer guides • Personal requests?	• Train the trainer as required
Coordinating		• HR/L&D • Line managers • Training admin staff • Trainers • Participants • External providers	• Planned status checks and follow up on issues as required		
Reporting	• Level 1&2 evaluation report (Kirkpatrick) immediate. • Level 3&4 evaluation report (Kirkpatrick) later date. • ROI report – later date.	• Participants • Managers • HR/L&D • External provider (if used) • LMS?	• Phased evaluation	• Loss or damage reporting?	• Company evaluation policy

People: Line managers. We should never forget that these are often the people that identified the learning need in the first place. As such they are more than a stakeholder, they are a customer, and along with the learners, must be at the forefront of our minds.

In the context of L&D, line managers undoubtedly have "rights" but they also have responsibilities. They have a right to good service. In the main this means ongoing communication; about what is happening, about how their people are doing, and about what can be expected of them in terms of new knowledge and skills post-course. Communication is especially important during extended learning programmes or when staff are being trained externally.

While being very vocal about their rights, line managers are often inclined to overlook their responsibilities. This is particularly true in relation to post course events. High quality training often founders on the rock of indifference when individuals return to the workplace routines. Working with the L&D professional, the line manager should seek out and progress the changes necessary to allow the returning individual to step up and use the new skills. Failing to provide follow-on opportunities ultimately means very poor return on investment and demoralisation for the individual.

People: other stakeholders. To varying degrees, all learning should bring about change. The level of change is usually directly related to the level of learning. Thus extended learning programmes often bring about multi-faceted shifts in the way organisations and the people within them function. Effective learning is often disabled by a failure to track the complexity of impact on key stakeholders i.e. those with an interest (a stake) or with an ability to influence what happens subsequent to the learning input. Stakeholder mapping and management is an essential change management tool that should be part of the L&D and HR specialist's armoury.

The table that follows shows a typical layout for identifying and analysing the potential significance of stakeholders. It is always worth doing this as a team effort if possible - a single perception invariably misses somebody or encourages a skewed perspective. Stakeholder mapping is rather like throwing a pebble into a pool; the immediate ripples are immediately visible but as the energy moves away from the centre its effects are more difficult to define.

After identifying stakeholders, we develop a "stakeholder management map" by working through the following steps:

1. **Define the level of interest**. Look at the learning event from the stakeholder's point of view. How involved are they likely to become? Rate their interest on a 1-5 scale; 1 being more or less indifferent, 5 being full on, constant interest in everything that is happening.

2. **Define the level of influence**. Interest on its own is important but marginal until it is combined with the ability to influence what is happening. This relationship is often referred to as the "power-interest equation". Stakeholders who are deeply interested and have the ability to influence events become "key" stakeholders and may need high levels of

"management" going forward. Influence is again rated 1-5 and the two ratings multiplied together give a "significance rating" out of 25.

3. **Define required support**. To do this we need to think carefully about each stakeholder and ask "what level of support do we need from this person / these people?" Generally speaking, we would at least want stakeholders to be neutral. However, we may need certain individuals to be positive and fully engaged or even to act as champions for us. Having decided on the level of support needed we record this by means of a red tick in the appropriate column.

4. **Map current support level**. Next we ask ourselves where individual stakeholders currently sit in terms of support. We mark this with a black tick. We now have a clear indication of the work that has to be done across the stakeholders. Looking at the example map that follows we can immediately see that considerable effort has to be put into the shift managers. We need them all to be champions, but most are either neutral or negative. The engineering managers are positive but, as yet, are taking no active interest in events. The issues now are tactical i.e. what particular measure do we adopt to move individual stakeholders to the required level of support.

The stakeholder map needs to be updated regularly as the learning project unfolds. Once again, this should really be a team exercise. Mapping of this kind may not be necessary for one-off short courses, but it should at least be a mental exercise.

Staffing.

We are all capable of confronting new subject matter and (to some extent at least) learning unaided. This is proven continually by those legions of solo distance learners. We should ask then why we would ever need to go to the additional expense and inconvenience of removing learners from the workplace to attend face to face courses delivered by a trainer or facilitator. There are several very good reasons e.g.

- Efficiency – the face to face course is generally more intensive and is delivered to tight timeframes. Consequently the client organisation gets its people "across the line" predictably.
- Learner preference – the majority of learners still prefer the social context of face to face courses.
- Peer learning – the presence of other learners undoubtedly broadens the learning experience. Other learners will ask questions that may never occur to the solo learner or may demonstrate different ways of applying learning.
- Enrichment, clarification, inspiration and example – no matter how well designed, the e-learning or distance learning package cannot fully emulate the enthusiasm and flexibility of a fully engaged trainer / facilitator.

Stakeholder Mapping

Programme / Course: Six Sigma Fundamentals.   Mapping Update: 12 Jan 2012

Stakeholder ID	Role Incumbents	Contact	Interest 1	2	3	4	5	Influence 1	2	3	4	5	Significance Rating	Negative Engaged	Negative Not Engaged	Neutral	Positive Not Engaged	Positive Engaged	Champion
Commercial Manager	John Smith	Ext 04532	2								4		8			✓			
Manufacturing Manager	Harry Brown	Ext 04563					5				4		20					✓	
Manager Strategic Projects	Alan Green	Ext 04521	2							3			6			✓			
Engineering Managers	Brian Jones	Ext 04333			3	4				3			12				✓		
	Keith Jenkins	Ext 04328				4				3			12				✓		
Technical Managers	Larry Walker	Ext 04243			3					3		5	9			✓			
	Ian Dewar	Ext 04241	2							3			6			✓			
Receiving Shift Managers	Fred Langley	Ext 04012	1									5	5		✓				
	Glyn Morris	Ext 04013					5					5	25						✓
	Shane Hope	Ext 04014			3							5	15			✓			
	Malcolm Grey	Ext 04015			3							5	15			✓			
	Gary Warner	Ext 04016				4						5	20		✓				
	Keith Harding	Ext 04017	1									5	5		✓				
	Vernon Castle	Ext 04018	2									5	10			✓			
	Paul Yarrow	Ext 04019	2									5	10			✓			
	Steven Drew	Ext 04020				4						5	20					✓	
Qualifications Manager Engineering Training Organisation	Alex Williams	06 828 3935					5			3			15					✓	

Example of a stakeholder mapping template

157

The trainer or facilitator is the interface between the subject matter and the learner. Precisely how that interface functions will be depend on the particular mix of subject, learner group, required organisational outcomes, accepted cultures etc. If that interface is poorly established or dysfunctional, effective learning design can be entirely wasted. So when we are selecting trainers or facilitators the most important skill we should be seeking is the ability to compute all those variables and set up the most appropriate interface between subject and learner.

This interface is defined largely by trainer "style". A good trainer researches the target audience and builds a picture of how it is likely to respond to different training tactics and methods. Without this basic research effort things can go horribly awry. A group of very busy engineers are not likely to be impressed by being given koosh balls to squeeze and being rewarded with lollies for correct answers. They might not object overtly but privately they are probably thinking "stop wasting my time and get on with it!" Other learners might respond favourably however. One thing is certain; it can be very difficult to recover from misreading the learner group or failing to adapt delivery style.

Apart from this fundamental sensitivity what are the other critical skills and aptitudes that a good trainer should possess? In no particular order they would certainly include:

- **Enjoyment of people** – training is an intensely interactive undertaking. Success is only possible if the trainer positively engages with the learner group and with fellow trainers. Effective face to face learning is built upon the interpersonal skills of all involved – but especially those of the trainer.

- **Subject expertise** – we have a right to expect a trainer to know what they are talking about. Learners may come to a course knowing very little about the topic but they are nevertheless able to spot when the trainer is "winging it". Once this happens, credibility is impossible to recover. Consequently, whether we use contract trainers or internal expertise, we should check credentials very carefully.

- **Energy and enthusiasm** – subject expertise is not enough to convince an audience. If the trainer cannot bring conviction and an obvious interest in the subject matter, learners will struggle to become engaged. Subject experts will tend naturally to be enthusiastic – how else did they acquire their expertise? Nevertheless, anybody asked to deliver the same training over and over again is likely to become "stale" and end up just going through the motions. Once again, learners inevitably pick up on this, as if by osmosis, and will quickly become equally lethargic. On the other hand, energy is undoubtedly contagious. There can be no doubt that successful training or facilitation of learning is hard work and that is precisely because good trainers make their energy available for learners to "plug into".

- **Good communication skills** – perhaps the most obvious requirement for the effective delivery of learning in any mode. Obvious, but certainly not straightforward. With face to face training, written communication is generally a minor issue for trainers because text materials will have been prepared beforehand. It is obviously more significant with distance learning that involves written feedback. Much more significant for "live" training are verbal and non-verbal communication skills linked to active listening and the management of communication dynamics.

- **Verbal communication** – the foundation of verbal communication is of course linguistic fluency. This involves so much more than the simples quantum of vocabulary. As well as having the variety of words with which to describe and define, "fluency" includes being able to adjust the subtleties of language level, verbal tone, pace and pitch to meet the emerging needs of the learners. Adjustments of this kind are inevitably geared to the trainer's powers of observation and sensitivity to the verbal and non-verbal cues constantly provided by the learner group that indicate the level of reception.

- **Non-verbal communication** – at least as important as what we say, how we say things is always accompanied by complex physical signals that provide the "wrap-around" for the message. Good trainers are self-aware to the extent that they are able to watch and hear themselves, watch and hear the learner group, and then make the subtle adjustments needed to ease the communication process.

- **Creativity** – unfortunately the best laid plans often go awry. What works for one group may not work for another. In these situations, trainers need to think on their feet and come up with alternative solutions that suit the particular circumstances. Pre-thinking alternatives is the mark of a true professional.

- **Discipline** – an unlikely consideration perhaps, but lack of discipline often shows itself in the failure to follow session plans or indulging personal preferences. This is ultimately a failure of quality, since quality is ultimately defined as "delivering or performing to specification".

- **Working with diversity.** – There are certainly organisations that present the trainer with more or less 'mono-cultural' learner groups i.e. selected from similar backgrounds, of a similar age and having similar predispositions. In practice however this is relatively rare. Workplaces are increasingly multi-cultural and diverse. Good trainers are able to recognise and work with the additional value this brings to the learning event, but of course it does require the willingness to research an audience and the skills to encourage individuals to share and value each other's experience and viewpoints.

- **Professionalism** – all of the above qualities and skills could be wrapped up in the term "professionalism" – but being professional is more than this. It also must include behaviours and standards. What is expected will vary somewhat, according to organisational culture, but will always centre around integrity and respect for the learner and the client organisation.

So how can we guarantee that contracted trainers will meet these demanding criteria. In practice we can't, but we can certainly take steps to minimise risk. Training providers should be prepared to identify designated trainers and appropriate references or the names of organisations where they have been used for delivery. Following up on these should provide a reasonable picture of trainer suitability.

Coordinating.

Coordination is of course an aspect of organising - but it is specifically related to the synchronisation and integration of events and responsibilities. Life is neither simple, consistently consecutive nor one dimensional; it is usually complex, often simultaneous and multi-dimensional. Even the simplest training event will exhibit a necessary inter-relationship of people, processes, products and protocols. More complex events will often impact on other events e.g. through shared facilities or resources. These interactions need to be thought through and managed. This is coordination through simple systems thinking.

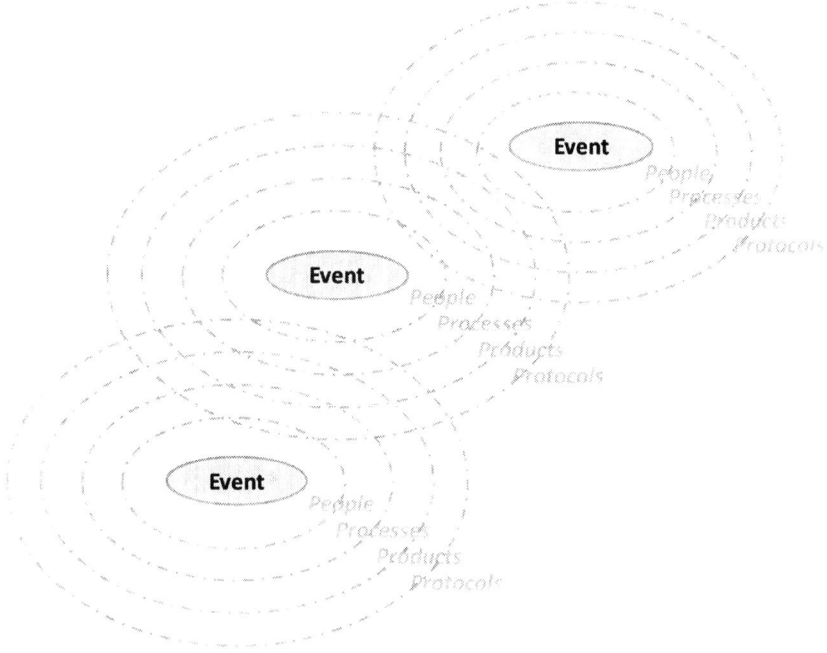

Figure 6.2 - Simple systems thinking for training event coordination

Systems thinking is based on the fundamental principle that events do not normally occur in isolation. Any action inevitably results in reaction somewhere else. Effective coordination should ensure that those effects are predicted and managed to minimise any negative impact. A useful tactic is to consider the coordination of training events through the filter of people, processes, plant (equipment / resources), products and protocols.

To take the simple example of a two day off-job training course organised for a group of production system operators we obviously have a "people" coordination issue. Taking employees off shift eventually impacts on other people e.g.

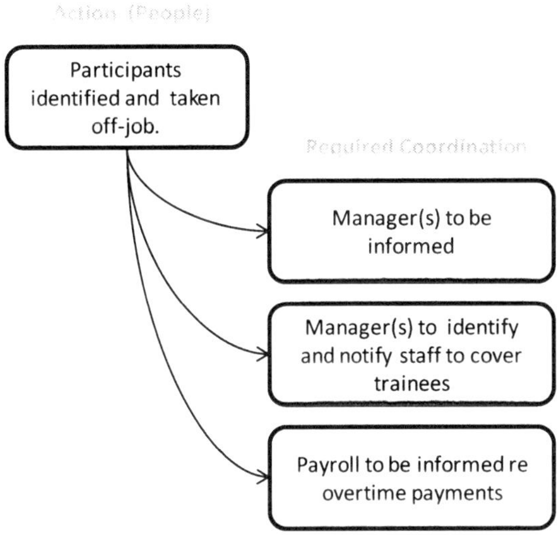
Action (People)
Participants identified and taken off-job.
Required Coordination
Manager(s) to be informed
Manager(s) to identify and notify staff to cover trainees
Payroll to be informed re overtime payments

Figure 6.3

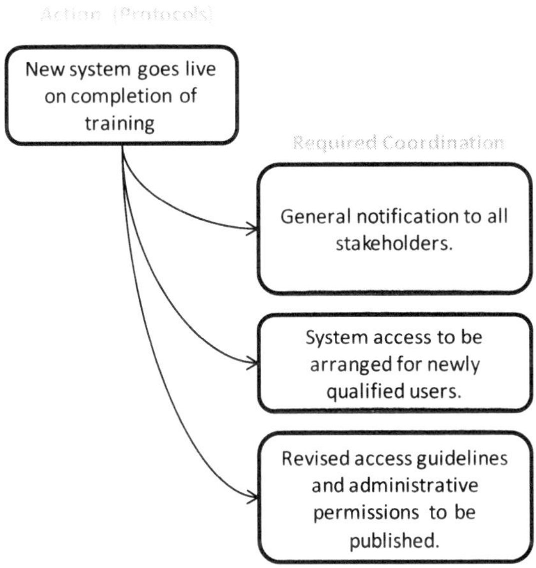
Action (Protocols)
New system goes live on completion of training
Required Coordination
General notification to all stakeholders.
System access to be arranged for newly qualified users.
Revised access guidelines and administrative permissions to be published.

Figure 6.4

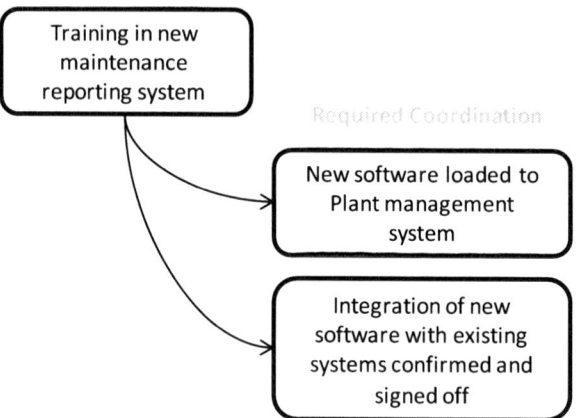

Figure 6.5

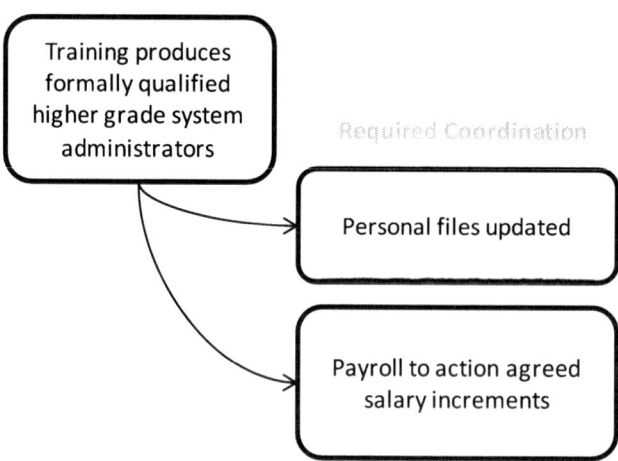

Figure 6.6

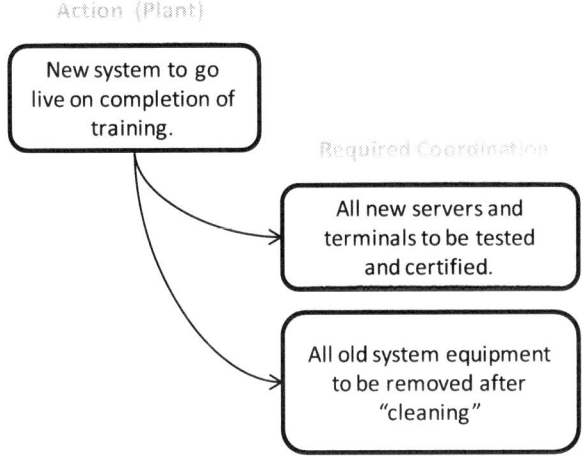

Figure 6.7

It would, of course, be fair to say that dealing with these "knock on" effects of a training course is not the responsibility of whoever is managing events. In terms of hands on accountability that may be true, but if these requirements are not flagged for coordinated treatment, the impact of the training is likely to be severely damaged. The delivery of training carries with it the responsibility to ask:

- What / who is impacted by this?
- Who needs to know about a given impact?
- When do they need to know? (lead time etc.)
- What things can or need to happen simultaneously?
- Which things are critically dependent i.e. critical path?

For small-scale learning events the impacts are likely to be limited and the resulting coordination needs likely to be correspondingly simple. On the other hand, large-scale events may need a complex coordination plan.

Reporting.

Immediate post-delivery reporting will inevitably be limited in scope. Beyond simply recording that delivery has occurred, it can only focus on the first two levels of Kirkpatrick evaluation i.e. how the learners felt about the delivery and how they fared in terms of achievement – if this information is available. Despite its limitations this information is potentially significant for a number of stakeholders. Accurate and timely reporting is therefore crucial. Figure 6.8 illustrates the various stakeholders or targets for immediate reporting.

Depth of reporting will depend on organisational requirements, and these will generally reflect the level of investment. For 'must do' compliance training training reporting seldom goes beyond achievement data and levels of satisfaction with the training delivery. Major investments will however usually call for in-depth reporting. If no organisational template exists the classical format is always a safe bet i.e.

- Executive summary
- Introduction
- Body / narrative
- Conclusion
- Recommendations
- Appendices / supporting information

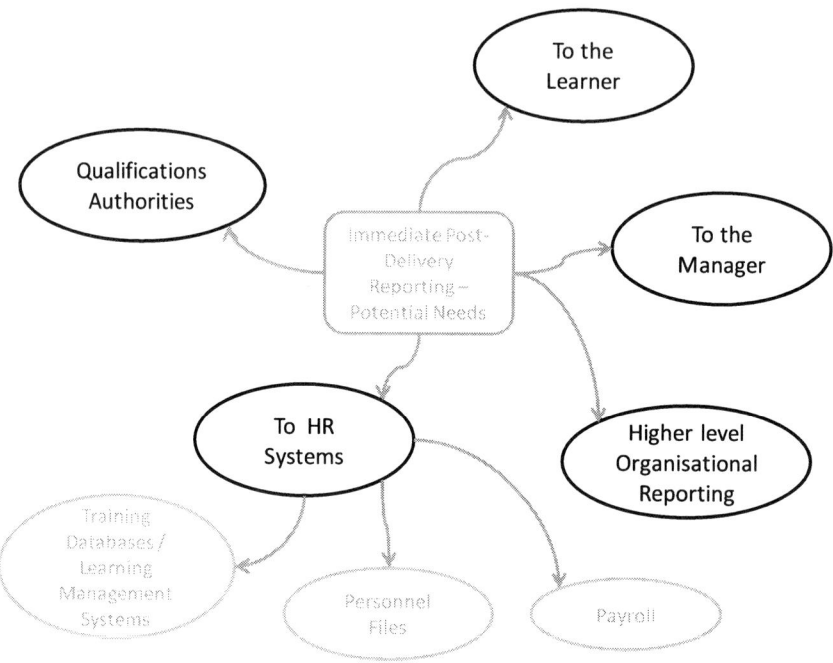

Figure 6.8 – Post Delivery Reporting Targets

- **Learner needs** – most of us have at some time experienced the frustration of having to wait for the results from courses. As providers of learning events we must view the learner as the primary customer. Every effort must be made to get results through as quickly as possible. This should be a fundamental quality check on both internal and external delivery options.

- **Line Manager needs** – a key stakeholder, the line manager has a strategic interest in the learner's achievement. He may intend to make use of the new skills immediately but cannot do so until official confirmation of competence comes through.

- **Higher level reporting needs** – most organisations will have regular corporate reporting that gathers data from all sources in order to measure progress. L&D reporting would figure significantly within the HR input.

- **HR systems needs** – training outcomes need to be formally recorded on a centralised system. This would normally be achieved through a training database or increasingly by means of a learning management system. Attendance and achievement may also be recorded on the individual learner's personal file. In some cases, satisfactory achievement may be linked to a salary increment. In this case payroll will need confirmation. Conventions will vary here, notification is likely to be the responsibility of the line manager but in some organisations this task might fall to HR.

- **Qualifications authorities** – training may be linked to external qualifications systems or frameworks. Most qualifications authorities are passive i.e. they do not actively seek information on achievement, only updating learner records on receipt of authorised information. Conventions will vary once again here. Notification may be the responsibility of the learner, with training staff or may sit with HR.

Budgeting.

In the final analysis, if you can't afford to do it, then you can't do it. Budgeting therefore has to follow very quickly on the heels of planning to judge whether the project is a feasible proposition. Once the outline plan is in place, every effort must be made to find out what it will cost. This is not necessarily straightforward because a number of the cost components may not be immediately obvious e.g. the cost of taking people out of production. Then there are costs that are probably visible only to the accountants e.g. the loss of interest on the funds provided.

However, for most organisations, costing out a training course can be more or less standardised and built into a spreadsheet for rapid calculation. A typical Excel-based course cost calculator follows. It would be a simple matter to link this to an overall training budget analysis.

Organising.

Good organisation boils down to a thorough analysis of what needs to happen to implement the plan, who should do it and by when. This should be drawn up as a standard checklist. All that remains is for somebody to link tasks to resources and then to track the listed events to ensure that they happen. Most often this task falls to a departmental administrator but reporting points should be built in so that HR / L&D managers can be confident that all is proceeding as planned. A typical course organisation checklist follows.

Programme / Course Cost Calculator.

Programme / Course Title: Front Line Management (Operations)

Course Duration (hours): 24

Participants	Business Unit Department	Participant Salary (£hourly rate)	Salary Costs	Travel Costs		Accommodation Costs		Meals Costs		Venue Costs	Role Cover Costs*
				Daily**	Total	Daily	Total	Daily	Total		
Learner 1 Smith J	No. 2 Mill D shift	42	1008	12	36	120	360	75	225	1200	
Learner 2 Brown W	Despatch D shift	36	864	6	18	120	360	75	225		
Learner 3 Jenkins H	Despatch D shift	36	864	12	36	120	360	75	225		
Learner 4 Williams K	Goods inward	40	960	12	36	120	360	75	225		960
Learner 5 Allen C	Warehouse 1	48	1152	12	36	120	360	75	225		
Learner 6 Griffiths L	No 1 Mill D shift	32	768	24	72	120	360	75	225		
Learner 7 Clark N	Boilerhouse D shift	32	768	12	36	120	360	75	225		
Learner 8 Davidson G	Health & Safety	36	864	12	36	120	360	75	225		964
Learner 9 Edwards M	Maintence Crew D shift	36	864	0	0	0	0	25	75		
Learner 10 Fox K	Chemical Plant D shift	32	768	12	36	120	360	75	225		
Learner 11 Murray M	Enviro Safety Team D shift	42	1008	18	54	120	360	75	225		
Learner 12 Guy A	Warehouse 2	42	1008	12	36	120	360	75	225		1008
Learner 13 Johnson F	Security Team D shift	48	1152	6	18	120	360	75	225		
Learner 14 Kelly N	Apprentice Management	36	864	6	0	120	360	75	225		1152
Learner 15 (enter name)			0		0		0		0		
Learner 16 (enter name)			0		0		0		0		
Learner 17 (enter name)			0		0		0		0		
Learner 18 (enter name)			0		0		0		0		
Learner 19 (enter name)			0		0		0		0		
Learner 20 (enter name)			0		0		0		0		
Internal Trainer 1 (enter name)			0		0		0		0		
Internal Trainer 2 (enter name)			0		0		0		0		
Internal Trainer 3 (enter name)			0		0		0		0		
External Trainer 1 BDC Consulting Ltd		100	2400		0		0		0		
External Trainer 2 BDC Consulting Ltd		100	2400		0		0		0		
External Trainer 3 (enter name)			0		0		0		0		
Totals			17712		450		4680		2775	1200	3984

* Role cover costs = hourly rate for cover x duration (hours)

** Travel costs may vary depending on where participants live or are accommodated in relation to the venue, car pooling, minibus arrangements etc.

*** Role cover. Left blank = not required

Course Organisation Checklist

Course / Programme Element :　　　　　**Dates:**

Item	Detail	Required Completion Date	Date Completed	Notes / Special Requirements
Course advertising	Intranet feature: E-Mailout: Flyers: Notice boards:			
Participant confirmation	Full names: Employee numbers: Contact info: Roll closed off:			
Joining instructions	To all participants: Variant to managers:			
Attendee allowances authorised				
Venue booking				
Lunches / refreshments				
Accommodation booking				
Breakfasts /evening meals				
Travel	Flights: Rental vehicles: MMA authorised: Other:			
Equipment / resources	Trainers specification			
Trainers / facilitators booked				
Guest speakers confirmed				
Course records completed				

Recording and learning management systems.

Accurate recording of learning events and their outcomes is an extension of the reporting function and is critical for the strategic management of organisational learning. It is particularly important for learning that requires qualification, re-certification orprogrammed refresher training. It is also essential for a strategic approach to role selection and succession planning. This begs the question of how learning should be recorded.

Small scale organisations will generally take a somewhat casual attitude to training records. Individual and collective memory is often sufficient in the context of a small workforce – people "just know" who has done what and when. However, as a company begins to grow this approach becomes increasingly untenable. Eventually a learning management system (LMS) must be introduced if chaos is to be avoided. The question for every organisation is the same i.e. "given our size and the complexity of our learning requirements, what learning management system do we need?"

Research shows that the acquisition of learning management systems tends to be an ad hoc affair but generally follows a familiar process. Initially an administrator in the small business will be tasked with developing and managing a simple spreadsheet to record training. Spreadsheets are calculation tools and are ill-suited to functioning as a database. Consequently, as the organisation grows the transition of records to a database tool becomes obligatory. Often this is no more than a migration to something like Microsoft Access. Eventually, organisational learning needs expand to the point that the call goes out to 'integrate' training records with other systems, specifically with the HR management system. There are now numerous human resource information management systems (HRIM) that provide training database functionality of varying degrees of sophistication. Full blooded HRIM systems represent a significant financial investment for businesses so procrastination tends to be the order of the day until the situation becomes critical. The first solution is usually an attempt to source a database tool that will talk effectively to the HRIM but in practice these "clip on" database systems seldom work well.

Even those large organisations that have acquired an HRIM with training management built in will eventually find themselves frustrated by the HRIM solution if they grow to a size where they develop in-house learning development or, as is increasingly the case, they choose to build their own learning campus. The degree of sophistication needed to service learning needs at this level inevitably means a 'stand-alone' LMS. Large organisations with complex learning management and development needs will thus find themselves eventually grappling with identifying the most appropriate system, either to develop or, more likely to buy in. The task of finding the right product is usually allocated to the L&D professional working with the IT department and (most likely) external consultants. Neither L&D nor IT are likely to be sufficiently expert to specify requirements precisely. Nonetheless they should have an adequate grasp of the LMS landscape to manage as consultation and procurement process with potential providers.

Essentially, we can describe the LMS landscape as offering functionality on four levels. Selecting the appropriate level requires answers to the following two questions.
- What do we need the system to do for us now? (present need).
- What are we likely to need in the foreseeable future? (scalability)

As always with IT the maxim 'design and build for the future as far as you can imagine it' holds true here. Identifying future organisational needs is never a simple matter of course. The pace of technological change is such that the capability of software improves exponentially. Nevertheless, at a basic level, the organisation needs to be able to:

- Assign learning needs to individuals and groups
- Assign specific learning events to individuals and groups
- Provide individualised records (training transcripts)
- Provide adequate status reports for wider management purposes

These fundamentals can be found in association with HRIM systems, but higher levels of sophistication generally require dedicated stand-alone design. The charts that follow provide a summary of the four levels of LMS provision and should assist with thinking clearly about prospective requirements.

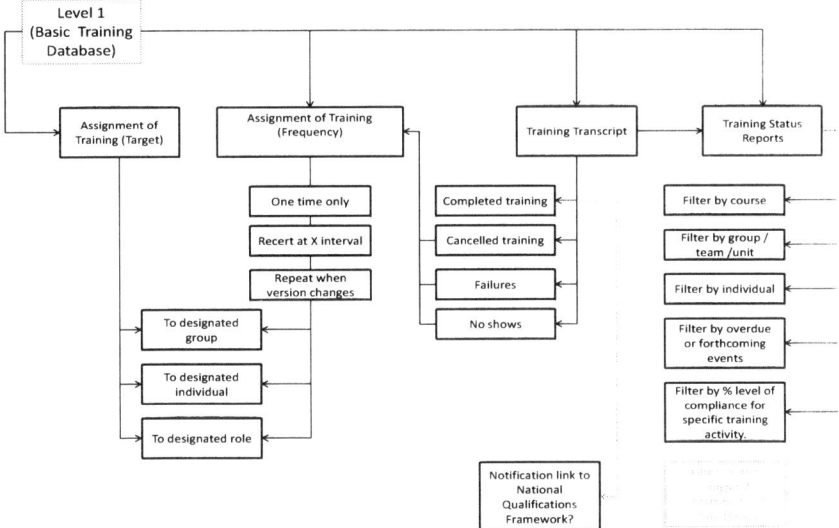

Figure 6.9 -Typical required functionality – LMS level 1

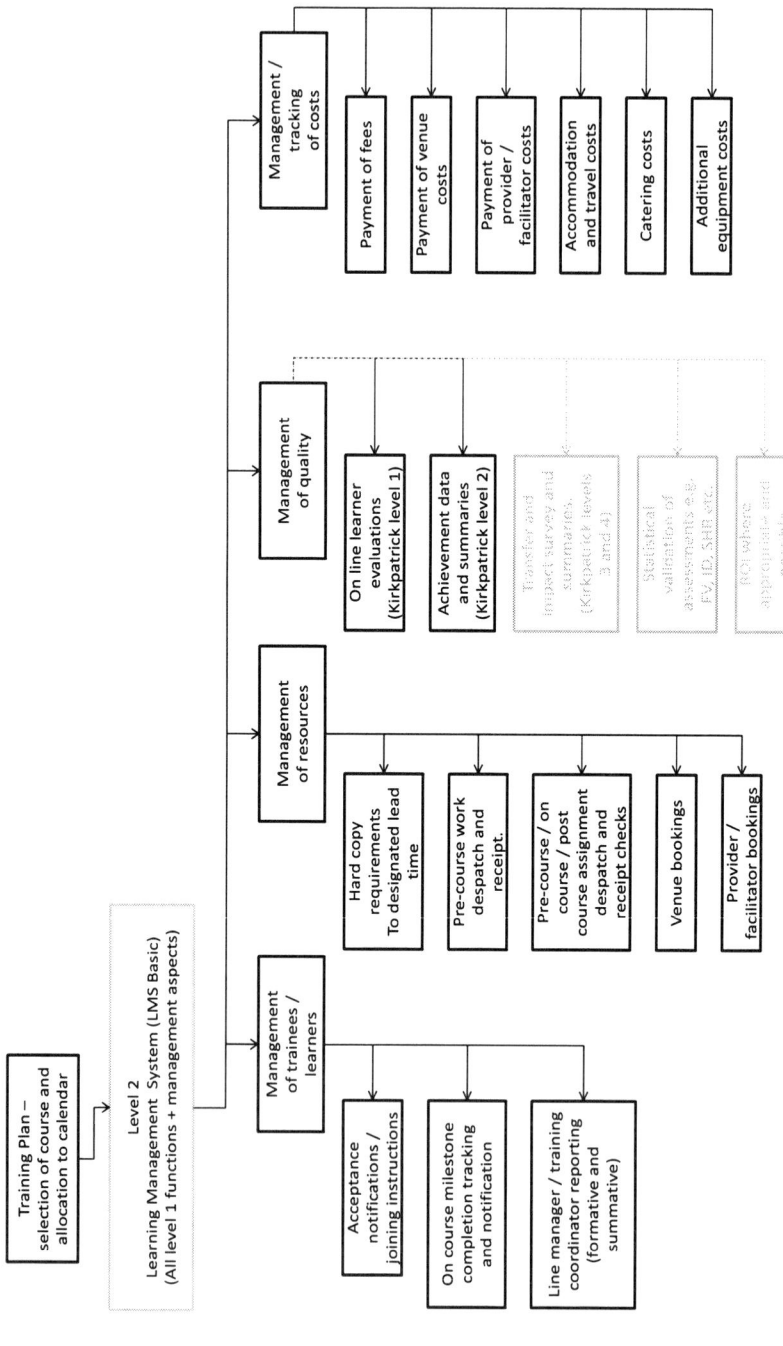

Figure 6.10 -Typical required functionality – LMS level 2

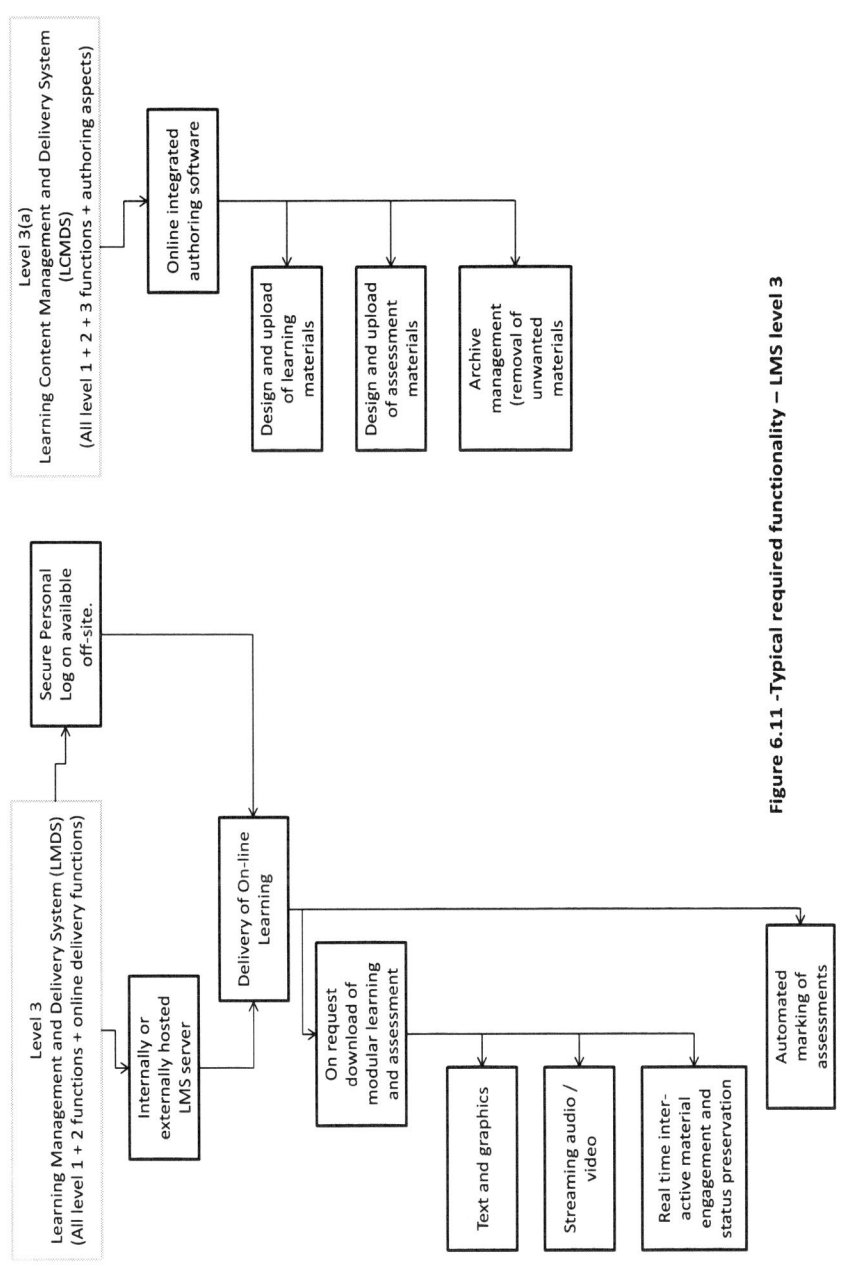

Figure 6.11 - Typical required functionality – LMS level 3

The figure contains the following labelled boxes:

Level 3(a)
Learning Content Management and Delivery System (LCMDS)
(All level 1 + 2 + 3 functions + authoring aspects)

- Online integrated authoring software
  - Design and upload of learning materials
  - Design and upload of assessment materials
  - Archive management (removal of unwanted materials

Secure Personal Log on available off-site.

Level 3
Learning Management and Delivery System (LMDS)
(All level 1 + 2 functions + online delivery functions)

- Internally or externally hosted LMS server
- Delivery of On-line Learning
  - On request download of modular learning and assessment
    - Text and graphics
    - Streaming audio / video
    - Real time inter-active material engagement and status preservation
  - Automated marking of assessments

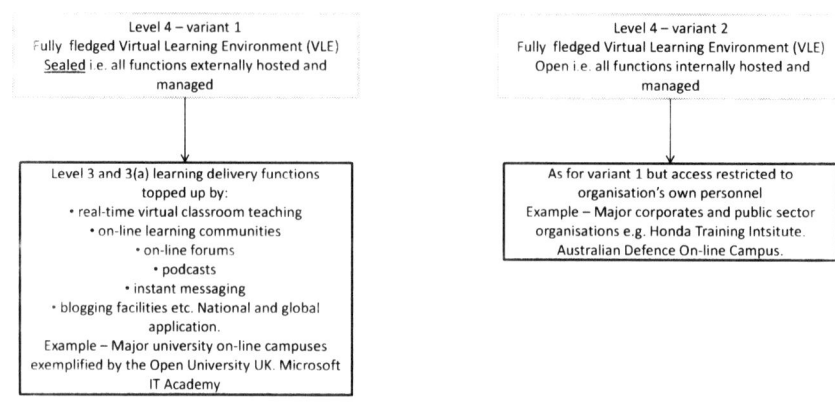

Figure 6.12 -Typical required functionality – LMS level 4

7. EVALUATION OF LEARNING EVENTS

WHAT IS EVALUATION?

Evaluation is not a simple concept. At its heart lies the notion of "value" and therein lies the problem. The value potentially offered by a specific training course or learning programme depends heavily on perception and need. For example:

- An instructional designer pilots a new course. He focuses on how well the course delivers on the immediate learning outcomes i.e. does it do the job? Value here is linked to effectiveness.

- An external training provider delivers a course to a client company. They will most likely focus on how satisfied the learners profess to be. This is because the majority of organisations seldom go further than the end of course "happy sheet". Value here is linked with the ability to keep the client happy.

- A business unit manager sends his shift managers on a people management course. He is most likely to focus on how well learning can be transferred back to the workplace. Value here is linked to the practical application of learning.

- An HR manager sources a training course to up-skill first line people managers in the business. She is most likely to focus on whether the course produces the kind of managers needed by the company. Value here is linked to improving operational performance.

- A finance manager is asked for the third year in a row to find funds for a repeat learning programme. He is likely to need convincing that the cost benefit ratio is acceptable i.e. is the dollar investment adequately offset by an increase in performance or efficiency directly attributable to the programme? Value here is related to the notion of value for money or "payback".

- A CEO reviews performance against the business goals and objectives and asks to what extent training has been able to drive the business forward in key directions. Value here is linked to strategic business impact.

- A learner completes a training course in order to be eligible for promotion. His focus is likely to be on whether the learning actually gets him to where he wants to go, rather than on the new skills or knowledge. Value here is centred on personal benefit.

All of these perceptions of "value" are commonly seen and quite legitimate. Consequently, as far as possible, we should employ an appropriate model or metric to gather sufficient data for meaningful comment on all of them. This is the process of evaluation.

The answer to this is simple enough i.e. to meet all or some of the needs described above. If a learning event does not "add value" to some degree it should not continue. "Learning for learning's sake" may be a worthy sentiment but very few organisations would support it practically. Resources are usually just too scarce and shareholder inquisition too sharply focused. Evaluation provides the justification for learning activity.

Perhaps a better question would be "why don't we do it?" Despite the obvious requirement, evaluation of workplace learning is generally acknowledged to be minimal and of poor quality. A 2004 report entitled "Learning Analytics Best Practices"(1) revealed the following:

- Only 30% or organisations actually measure the impact of training on business performance.
- Only 50% evaluate the impact of training on job performance.
- The majority of companies only use end-of-course "happy sheets" which focus on learner satisfaction
- While a lot of training related data is collected by HR departments very little time is spent on analysing it.

Why should this be so? The answer is perhaps quite complex, but there are very evident barriers to meaningful evaluation e.g.

- **It is too difficult**. Beyond the relative ease of designing and administering the end of course reactionnaire and analysing simple achievement data, it becomes increasingly harder to collect and analyse meaningful higher level data. The skills required are usually only found in organisations with dedicated L&D teams.

- **There is little opportunity to measure or sample ongoing performance**. This is particularly true of "public" off-job training, where participants are drawn from a range of organisations. It is practically difficult, if not impossible for the provider to gather data on downstream job performance or change in behavior. If the company chooses to evaluate downstream performance the in-depth understanding of the learning intervention is likely to cloud results.

- **There is no apparent management support**. Oddly enough this is a very common scenario. Completion of training is so often seen as a tick the box commitment. Interest is seldom sustained sufficiently to commit to tracking and analysing performance long-term.

- **It is not cost effective**. Very often the sheer complexity of data gathering and analysis to produce meaningful statistics drives up evaluation costs to the point where a "gut feeling" is preferable.

- **It is not actually necessary**. A significant proportion of organisational training is related to compliance e.g. safety related issues. This is training that must be done and must be done to a prescribed standard.

Consequently, the principal question posed by any evaluation process i.e. "is this worth continuing" is not relevant. The issue here is cost effectiveness; can we achieve the required standard for less input of time, money and other resources?

WHAT SHOULD WE EVALUATE?

While we might find fault with organisations that fail to evaluate anything, we should also question the wisdom of policies that require everything to be evaluated. Numerous occasions arise when evaluation is quite simply a waste of precious time and resources. So, before heading down what can be a difficult and complex road, we should establish clear guidelines. We should seriously question the "value" of evaluation when:

- **The learning event is not to be repeated**. Since the primary goal of evaluation is programme improvement, the evaluation process here simply produces useless data. In these situations, energy and resources are best directed at ensuring quality "up front" e.g. making certain course specification, design and delivery are of the highest quality. External providers will nevertheless often conduct low level evaluation (participant reaction) to gain some measure of their trainer performance.
- **Stakeholders exhibit little interest.** This might seem indefensible, but there are circumstances in which stakeholders cannot be bothered with evaluation reports e.g. the organisation is entirely consumed by working through significant change, or perhaps the training is associated with compliance that is universally regarded as an unnecessary burden.
- **Learning outcomes cannot be meaningfully measured.** This is particularly true of "soft skills" training or learning that is ultimately personality dependent. A good example might be the ubiquitous "time management" course. Research shows that people are naturally inclined toward order and structure, or they are not. We may well see apparent changes in behaviour in the weeks following the course only to find that individuals "revert to type" sooner or later.
- **Participants have no opportunity to practice what they have learned.** This is perhaps the most commonly experienced failure of organisational training systems. The course or programme may well have been of excellent quality but because no attempt has been made to examine and, if necessary, change the environment to which the learner returns, the skills acquired are not used or maintained.
- **There is little or no opportunity to gather data.** Transfer of skills to the workplace and performance improvement can only be meaningfully calculated if there is adequate information regarding previous and new levels of output. Consequently, if organisational record-keeping and analysis is poor, there is a limit to what evaluation can achieve.
- **Learners have been compelled to participate.** "You can take the horse to water, but you can't make him drink". All trainers are familiar with the scenario where the few negative individuals severely distort both the general participant experience and the ensuing evaluation data.

- **There are numerous variables affecting post-course performance.** There are very few situations in which we can positively state that attendance at a particular course has been entirely responsible for a clear improvement in performance. Generally there are identifiable factors that could also contribute to improvement e.g.
  - Particularly supportive managers or work teams that help the individual to embed the new skills.
  - New or upgraded equipment coming on line.
  - New systems or processes being introduced.
  - Salary increments accompanying a new qualification level, resulting in improved motivation.

It should be no surprise that stakeholders are frequently skeptical of very positive evaluation reports. They will be aware of the range of variables involved and that statistics can be dubiously interpreted. This does not render them necessarily false, but perhaps unreliable. Hence Disraeli's cynicism "there are lies, damned lies, and then there are statistics".

So what's left? What should we evaluate? Logically, the converse of all the above contraindications will be valid reasons to evaluate. The two most powerful justifications will undoubtedly be repetition of the course or programme and stakeholder interest. If a course is to be continually repeated we should be looking for continuous improvement. If stakeholders have shown commitment and sanctioned resources, they certainly have a right to demand evidence of "value".

HOW DO WE DO IT? - ESSENTIAL PROCESS STEPS AND COMMON MODELS.

So often we find that the evaluation of organisational learning is accompanied by muddled thinking. Clarity is only achieved by working through a rigorous process to ensure that we know what we're doing and why we're doing it. Figure 7.1 overleaf illustrates the essential process steps that should precede and accompany evaluation. If we can assume that the course or programme has been built on a foundation of sound needs analysis and effective design, we can take step 1 as a given.

Step 2 – stakeholder needs.

All learning events will generate associated stakeholders. The mapping process (see section 6) will identify them and reveal their levels of interest and influence. Each needs to be carefully considered in relation to the key question "what information is this person or department primarily interested in?" If in doubt the best policy is to ask. You may have to describe, in some detail, just what information the evaluation process can actually reveal.

Collating individual responses to this key question will enable the development of the evaluation task list. This in turn will allow you to work economically. There is little point in laboriously calculating the $ return on investment for a stakeholder who is only interested in how many achieved the qualification.

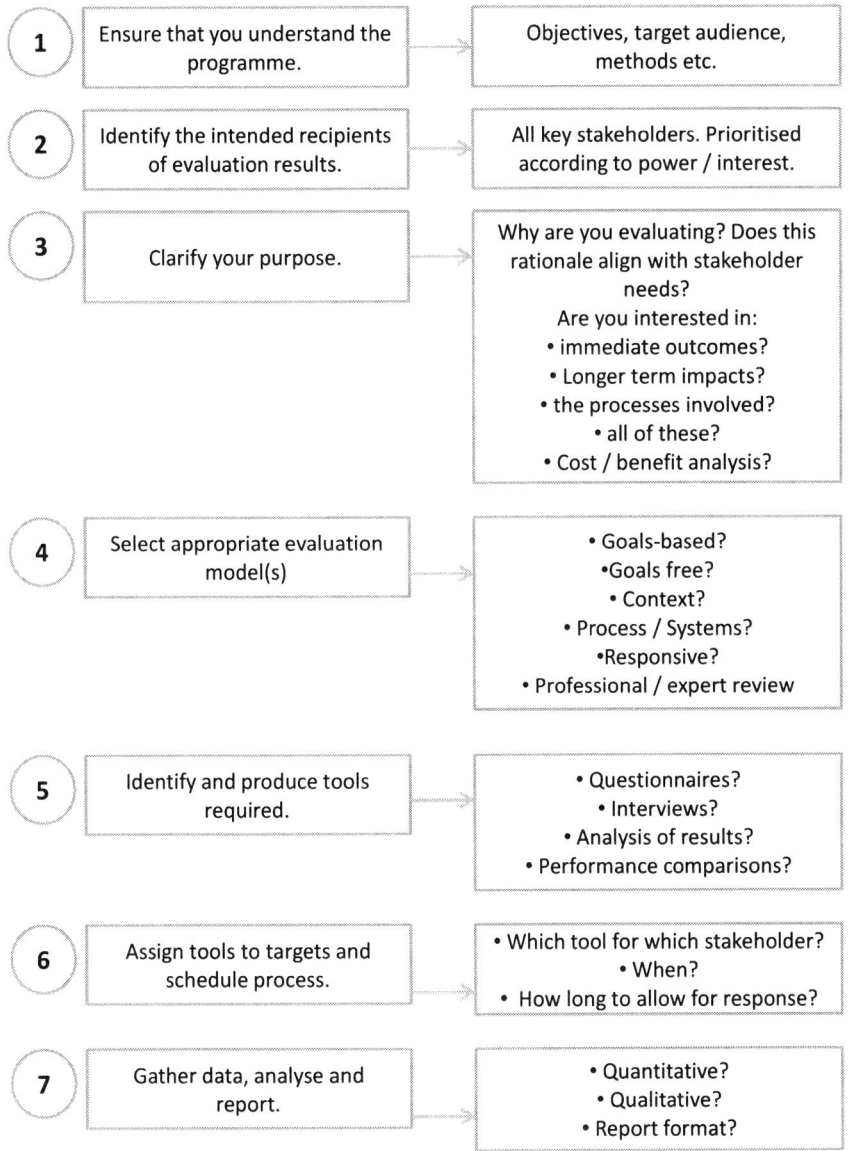

Figure 7.1 – Evaluation – essential process steps

Step 3 – clarification of purpose.

Stakeholder needs will provide a large slice of evaluation purpose, but these are seldom the same needs as those of the HR department and certainly not those of an L&D specialist. Stakeholder needs are largely coincidental with business needs. The issue for the business is centred on effectiveness and end results i.e. did the course or programme equip the participants to do what was needed by the business? The L&D specialist invariably has different priorities. For her, the issue is more likely to be associated chiefly with quality of the process and the nature of the learning experience for the participant.

At a tactical level, the evaluator needs to decide on the scope of the evaluation i.e. *"what aspects of the learning event do I need to examine?"* (breadth) and *"what level of analysis do I need to apply to each of these to satisfy my stakeholder's needs?"* (depth). The desired scope must then be qualified by *"what is actually possible?"* i.e. in terms of resources, time and access to data sources.

The first question should be addressed by considering whether you are primarily interested in:
- Outcomes relative to intention i.e. did the course or programme achieve what it set out to do? This is "product" evaluation
- How the programme actually worked as a learning experience. This is very much centred around internal quality considerations and is generally referred to "process" evaluation.
- Whether the course or programme is actually correctly adjusted to needs and appropriateness. "Needs" obviously refers to local organisational requirements but also to wider contexts such as the needs of the labour force in general. Governments have vested interests in this wider "macro" view. This is commonly referred to as "context" evaluation.
- Any measurable benefit relative to cost i.e. the $ return on investment. This is really only possible in relation to "hard skills" learning.
- Reporting on all or a combination of these priorities.

Step 4 – selection of appropriate model(s).

Exploring the range of evaluation models and techniques can be a daunting experience, but becomes less so once we understand that many are intended for the full depth examination of long term educational curricula and consequently of limited relevance to business needs. In addition, most of the models overlap each other to some extent. For example they all give some consideration to whether or not the learning achieves its purpose or specified outcomes.

To address general business needs we need only consider 4 models:
- Donald Kirpatrick's 4 level model – fundamentally a product focussed approach.
- Jack Phillips' ROI model – focussed on cost benefit analysis.
- Daniel Stufflebeam's CIPP model – essentially geared toward process process evaluation.
- Warr, Bird and Rackham's CIRO model.

The Kirkpatrick Model.

Kirkpatrick began to develop his fundamental ideas around evaluation as long ago as the late 1950's, but it was not until the publication of his *Evaluating Training Programmes* in 1994 that his model was taken up enthusiastically by the world of business. It is now undoubtedly the most frequently used framework, for the very simple reason that it is easy to understand and can provide HR and senior managers with the justification data they need. Fully implemented, Kirkpatrick's model tells the client organisation whether or not the course or programme has delivered to the business the required knowledge, skills (and perhaps attitudes) i.e. the "product" is to specification. Figure 7.2 summarises the Kirkpatrick 4 level model.

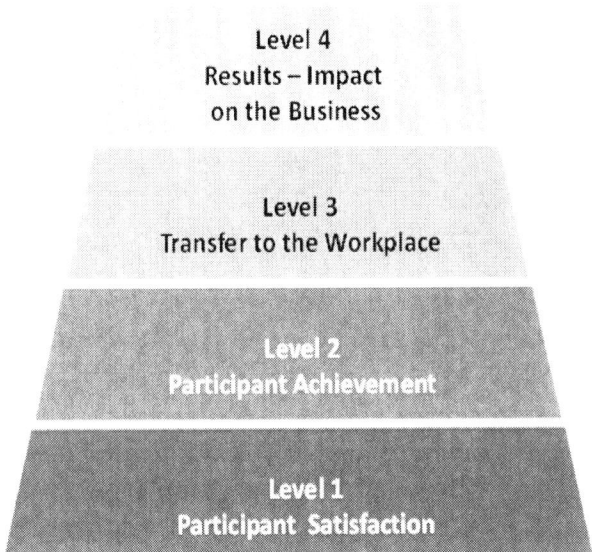

Figure 7.2 – Kirkpatrick : the most commonly used evaluation model

Although Kirkpatrick is the most widely used model, even those companies which work very hard at evaluation find the process increasingly difficult as they attempt to move up the levels. A recent review (2012) of the top 125 organisations confirms this. "The Kirkpatrick Levels of Evaluation are more widely used: Level 1 (96 percent), Level 2 (95 percent), Level 3 (90 percent), Level 4 (82 percent)." (2) Usage of levels 3 and 4 at these rates is truly exceptional. The majority of businesses generally find it just too difficult or lack the expertise.

The table that follows summarises the typical tools and their relative usefulness against the four levels.

Level	What is evaluated	Typical tools and methods	Usefulness and practicability
1	**Participant satisfaction.** Kirkpatrick refers to REACTION. This level usually attempts to capture how learners responded to all aspects of the programme e.g. content, delivery, environment, administration etc.	The usual approach is to administer an end of course "happy sheet" or "reactionnaire". This is a summative approach. A more thoughtful method is to evaluate formatively i.e. at strategic points during delivery. Post-training surveys are often used to avoid the "rush to get away' syndrome – but return rates can be poor.	Needs careful design if useful information is to be obtained. Easy to administer and analyse. Rapid feedback to stake-holders. Enables repeat programmes to be quickly adapted.
2	**Participant achievement.** Kirkpatrick uses the simple term "learning". This may be a before and after comparison or, in the case of completely new learning, a simple measure of performance against outcomes, objectives.	Hard skills upgrade can be effectively measured through a pre-course benchmarking and an end of course test or assessment. New knowledge, skills will require a valid and reliable assessment focussed on learning outcomes.	Relatively easy to obtain. Essential information for all stakeholders, especially the learner. It is important to remember that this is a moment in time reflection of learning – it will not reliably indicate retention.
3	**Transfer to the workplace.** Kirkpatrick refers to subsequent "behaviour". Perhaps the acid test of learning i.e. can the learner perform or apply the new knowledge or skills in the real world of the workplace?	Direct observation in the workplace. Interviews with learners and with managers. Follow-up performance analysis.	Can be difficult to obtain reliable data or information. Numerous other variables can intrude e.g. the associated performance of other team members, opportunities to actually use the new skills etc. Time consuming and therefore expensive.
4	**Impact on the business.** Kirkpatrick uses the term "results".	For acutely "hard skills" it is possible to track impact through to improvement in output and the bottom line. This requires extensive performance observation and analysis and the screening out of other obvious variables.	Most organisations have management systems that record ongoing performance. Problems occur when trying to tease out the actual effect of a learning programme from the host of other variables. It is virtually impossible to measure the impact of soft skills development meaningfully.

Typical Kirkpatrick level 1 tools.

The end of course "reactionnaire" is the most commonly used evaluation tool, but probably the least valuable. Efficacy is totally dependent on good design and seeking information that learners are actually able or qualified to provide.

Surveying course participants to capture their reactions to the total learning experience can produce useful and valid information e.g. acceptability of:
- Pre-course administration
- Travel arrangements
- Quality of accommodation
- The venue
- Refreshments

None of this information comments on the quality of the learning – but if we accept that all these things can have a negative impact on participant attitude, and therefore eventual achievement, any opportunity to improve administrative and environmental factors should be welcomed.

Useful feedback can also be gathered regarding the perceived relevance of individual topics to the learner's workplace roles and the level of delivery. However, this information should be treated with caution simply because learners may not be able to comment meaningfully. For example, if a course is intended to prepare individuals for taking up a new role, they may not be able to gauge the relevance of specific knowledge or skills. Reaction to the level of learning delivery is useful but negative comment could be interpreted in two ways e.g. course design is at fault and has "missed the mark" with the target audience, or alternatively, the level is actually appropriate for the subject matter and it is the audience that is inappropriate i.e. we have the wrong people on the course.

Badly designed 'reactionnaires' often attempt to measure trainer 'likeability'. This has dubious merits because the real issue should always be trainer effectiveness. It is often the case that learners have to be pushed hard if outcomes are to be achieved in the given timeframe. This is not likely to make trainers immediately popular. However it is certainly appropriate to ask whether the trainer appeared to know the subject and was able to respond effectively to queries and requests for fuller depth. The issue of appropriate style is also worth investigating when external trainers or facilitators are used. Internal trainers should of course already be tuned into organisational culture and be able to hit the mark more or less immediately. External trainers will need to attune to their audience, but if they are professionals they will quickly adjust their style appropriately. If they cannot do this, they should not be used for further training.

The following pages provide an example of a typical Kirkpatrick level 1 reactionnaire; in this case for a supervisor refresher workshop on basic leadership skills. This example seeks information about each of the major topics covered in terms of its perceived relevance to the role and the level of delivery. Given that the participants were already established in the role, their comments would be well informed by the realities they faced on a daily basis. This gives the data a high level of validity.

With this example we can assume that evaluation would be formative i.e. carried out at strategic intervals during the workshop. Summative evaluation, at the end of the course, seldom provides well considered comment. Learners are usually keen to get back to work or to get on the road. In addition, formative evaluation captures opinion while the topic is still fresh in the mind.

The structure here is typical and straightforward:

- A set of clear instructions. This would normally be reinforced by verbal instructions from the trainer.
- A list of the major topics.
- Rating scales for each of the topics. In this case a simple scale of 1-5 is preferred because this makes analysis by spreadsheet very simple and provides an eventual overall percentage rating of participant satisfaction.

Simple descriptor ranges such as "strongly disagree, disagree, agree, strongly agree" are often used – but these do not lend themselves quite so readily to spreadsheet analysis.

- An "open response" section where learners can offer comment on any aspect not addressed directly in the evaluation. This section most often presents suggestions for improvement or more personal feedback to the trainers themselves.
  For practical purposes the reactionnaire is authored as a Word document and issued in hard copy. This allows the trainer / facilitator to ask for sections to be completed as the delivery progresses (formative evaluation). The great advantage of this tactic is that evaluation is staggered, focused on a specific topic and avoids the end of course rush for the door. The information gathered is thus of greater credibility and depth.

An example of a spreadsheet summary tool follows the level 1evaluation document.

Kirkpatrick level 2 tools.

Level 2 is concerned with what learners have achieved, primarily in terms of the specified outcomes. Consequently, evaluation here must be based on some kind of assessment tool and the subsequent analysis of results. Given the sheer range of assessment devices we cannot point to typical tools. Achievement might be measured by written tests, observation of practical processes, one-on-one interviewing to probe understanding, learner presentations or perhaps post-course assignments involving elements of research or application in the workplace. The critical criterion must always be well designed valid and reliable assessment (see section 5) focussed on the learning outcomes.

Application of knowledge or skills in the workplace takes the concept of achievement through to engage with Kirkpatrick's level 3 i.e. the ability to transfer learning to the real world of work. The key issues to be addressed at level 3 are:

- To what extent have individuals put the new learning into practice?
- To what extent are they aware that their behaviour has changed and why i.e. do they attribute the change to the course or programme they have attended?
- Is there a discernible improvement in performance, and if so, can it be measured?

In practice there are very few situations where the effects of training can be completely isolated and objectively quantified. When they do occur it is usually in relation to clearly observable "hard" skills for which there is an existing performance bench mark. New operating techniques or redesigned processes are the obvious examples here. Evaluation is a simple matter of gathering performance data on several occasions and quantifying improvements in output and / or quality over several observations to allow for the "bedding in" of new skills.

No.	Topic		1	2	3	4	5
8.	Maintaining control – the TRAP concept.	Relevance				X	
		Level				X	
9.	Principles of performance management. SMARTA objectives.	Relevance				X	
		Level				X	
10.	Performance management – appraisal interviewing and recording	Relevance					X
		Level					X
11.	Team building – motivation and morale	Relevance				X	
		Level				X	
12.	Team membership roles – Belbin types.	Relevance				X	
		Level				X	
13.	Principles of coaching and mentoring.	Relevance				X	
		Level				X	
14.	Implementing change.	Relevance				X	
		Level				X	
15.	Maintaining personal effectiveness – delegation and time management.	Relevance					X
		Level					X
16.	Production reporting.	Relevance				X	
		Level				X	

General comments on course content:

Basic Management Skills	Supervisors' 2 Day Refresher – Level 1 Evaluation					
No.	Delivery Quality	1	2	3	4	5
17.	The quality of visual aids e.g. PowerPoint presentations.					X
18.	The quality of hand-out materials when used.			X		
19.	The general pace and momentum of delivery.					X
20.	The style and manner of the presenters.					X
No.	Course Administration – please provide detail of specific concerns	1	2	3	4	5
21.	Pre-course administration (course information, bookings etc.)		X			
22.	Joining instructions.			X		
23.	Travel arrangements.				X	
24.	Suitability of accommodation and meals.			X		
25.	Venue				X	

Basic Management Skills	Supervisors' 2 Day Refresher – Level 1 Evaluation

Additional comment. If you have any specific recommendations for improving this course please outline them here. Alternatively, please leave a contact number if you would like the course trainers or designers to follow up with you personally.

Supervisors' Refresher Workshop Level 1 Evaluation

Maximum Respondent Total: 65

Topic / Issue	Rating for Relevance							Rating for Level						
	Relevance Score					Total	%	Level Score					Total	%
	1	2	3	4	5			1	2	3	4	5		
1 Day 1 – Introduction. Setting up the workshop and explaining its objectives.			3	44	5	52	80			3	36	15	54	83.076923
2 Day 1 – Senior Manager's overview.			3	16	40	59	90.769231			3	24	30	57	87.692308
3 Day 1 – The concepts of "responsibility" and "accountability" as an extension of leadership and management skills.			3	28	25	56	86.153846			3	36	15	54	83.076923
4 Day 1 – Understanding ethics, values and morals in leadership. The necessity of leadership integrity. Relationship to the Company Code of Conduct.			3	20	35	58	89.230769			3	24	30	57	87.692308
5 Day 1 – Adjusting leadership style and focus according to circumstances.			15	16	20	51	78.461538			9	20	25	54	83.076923
6 Day 1 – Overview of basic communication principles - CART.			9	24	20	53	81.538462			9	24	20	53	81.538462
7 Day 2 – Formal briefing skills for hand-over and take-over of shifts.			6	16	30	52	80			6	20	25	51	78.461538
8 Day 2 – maintaining control - the TRAP concept.			6	16	35	57	87.692308			6	20	30	56	86.153846
9 Day 2 – Principles of performance management. SMARTA objectives.			6	16	35	57	87.692308			3	24	30	57	87.692308
10 Day 2 – Performance management - appraisal interviewing and recording.			6	20	30	56	86.153846			6	24	25	55	84.615385
11 Day 2 – Performance improvement - principles of coaching and mentoring.			9	28	15	52	80			3	36	15	54	83.076923
12 Day 2 – Maintaining personal effectiveness - delgation and time management.			9	16	30	55	84.615385			6	24	25	55	84.615385
13 Day 2 – Production reporting.		2	6	20	25	53	81.538462		8	12	20		40	61.538462
				Overall perception of relevance =			84%				Overall perception of level =			83%

Overall level of satisfaction = 83%

Topic / Issue	Presentation Quality Rating						
	1	2	3	4	5	Total	%
14 Quality of visual aids e.g. PowerPoint presentations.			9	24	20	53	81.538462
15 Quality of hand-out materials when used.			3	24	25	52	80
16 General pace and momentum.			3	28	25	56	86.153846
17 Style and manner of presenters.				20	40	60	92.307692
						340	
			Overall perception of presentation quality =				85%

The more we move toward "soft" skills the harder evaluation becomes, because we move from objectivity to subjectivity. The commonly used tools here are:

Interviews – potentially of a wider range of people including the learners themselves, their managers or supervisors, their co-workers, their teams (if they are managers). Careful thought must be given to interview design if useful information is to be secured. There is an undoubted tendency for people to say what they feel is wanted, or conversely to be unduly negative. Consequently interviewees should be encouraged to speak plainly about their perceptions. Questioning should obviously be related directly to the original learning outcomes or objectives but should also attempt to define the environment to which the learners have returned and its effect on their ability to employ new knowledge or skills.

While interviewing can be time-consuming, it offers the great advantage of allowing issues to be pursued to their root cause with those directly concerned. The interview itself can be conducted in a number of ways. Options include:
- One-to-one, face-to-face.
- Interview groups, face-to-face.
- Telephone interviewing.
- Video-conferencing.

Formats too may be widely varied e.g.
- Structured – set questions with accompanying guidance notes.
- Partially structured – set questions and a degree of free exploration.
- Unstructured – most often simply allowing the respondent to talk freely about their perceptions of the learning event and its consequences.

Interviewing also poses some problems for meaningful evaluation. They generally return qualitative data which can pose difficulties in terms of valid interpretation. Unless completely independent people are used, interviewers may also need to grapple with their own possible "bias" i.e. unconsciously steering the interviewee toward their own views. Consequently, if possible, those involved in the design and delivery of learning events should not be involved in their evaluation.

Surveys – offer a convenient means of data collection but they suffer from severe limitations. Firstly, issues that emerge from their analysis may have to be followed up by further surveys or interviews and this can quickly alienate respondents. Secondly, return rates can be poor, often resulting in data being extrapolated from a very meagre base. Thirdly they are difficult to design. Fourthly, what may be "comprehensive" to the evaluator can be "unnecessarily complex" to the respondent, resulting in rushed and ill-considered responses.

A useful blueprint for designing surveys to measure the degree of successful transfer has been developed by Donovan et al. (3) This tool gathers data related to four key concerns:
- Ability to use knowledge and expertise
- Motivation to use knowledge and expertise
- Work environment supporting use of knowledge and expertise
- Trainee characteristics

These four concerns are further broken down into a total of sixteen key questions which can be further elaborated as required. The tool is summarised in the table that follows (source: Higher Education Funding Council for England).

Staged assessment / performance measurement – an attempt to measure not only transfer of new learning to the workplace but also the degree of permanence. One-off immediate snapshots may be positive but are ultimately unreliable. A series of planned measures over a realistic time-frame will provide real "proof" of behavioural change. This requires real commitment from management and is consequently often neglected. To overcome this, managers can be encouraged to build immediate performance improvements into employee targets for the next performance period.

Kirkpatrick level 3 – 16 factor measurement of learning transfer to the workplace.		
Ability to use knowledge and expertise	Personal capacity for transfer.	How individuals' workload, schedule, personal energy and stress levels facilitate or inhibit transfer of learning into the workplace.
	Transfer of design.	The degree to which skills and knowledge taught in training are similar to performance expectations as well as to what is needed to perform more effectively. Similarity of methods and materials to those used in the work environment.
		Does the training programme clearly link learning with on-the-job performance and demonstrate how to apply new knowledge and skills?
	Opportunity to use learning	Does the organisation provide individuals with opportunities to apply new skills? Is there adequate provision of resources to apply new skills such as equipment, information and materials as well as financial and human resources?
Motivation to use knowledge and expertise	**Motivation to transfer learning**	Are trainees motivated to utilise learning? To what degree do individuals feel able to perform and believe new skills will help them to more effectively perform on-the-job?
	Performance – outcomes and expectations	This is a measure of whether individuals believe that applying learned skills and knowledge will lead to recognition / rewards they value. Does the organisation create an environment in which individuals feel good about performing well?
	Transfer effort – performance	Do individuals believe that applying skills and knowledge learned in training will

	expectations	improve their performance? How have efforts to utilise new skills made a difference in the past and will such efforts affect future productivity and effectiveness?
Work environment designed to support use of knowledge and expertise	**Personal outcomes – positive**	What positive outcomes exist for the individual as a result of applying training on the job?
	Personal outcomes – negative	Are there any outcomes for the individual as a result of not applying training on the job? Negative outcomes include: reprimands, cautions and penalties. It also indicates whether it is noticed or not if employees do not use their training.
	Peer support	Do colleagues mutually appreciate and encourage the use of new skills learned in training? Do colleagues expect new learning to be applied and do they show patience when new skills/techniques are tried out?
	Supervisor/man ager support	To what extent are managers/supervisors involved in: clarifying performance expectations after training; identifying opportunities to apply new skills and knowledge; setting realistic goals based on training; working with individuals on problems encountered while applying new skills; and providing feedback when individuals successfully apply new abilities?
	Supervisor/man ager sanctions	Do individuals perceive negative responses/opposition from managers/supervisors when applying new skills? Do they assist in identifying opportunities to apply new skills and knowledge?
	Openness to change	This factor surveys individuals' perception of their work groups' resistance to change, willingness to invest energy for change, and the degree of support provided by the workgroup to individuals who use techniques learned in training.
	Feedback – performance coaching	Do individuals receive indicators from people in their work environment (colleagues, managers, employees) about their job performance? These indicators may be formal and/or informal such as constructive input, assistance and feedback from people.
Trainee characteristics – secondary elements	**Learner readiness**	How well were individuals prepared for training? Did they have the opportunity to provide input prior to training? Did they know what to expect during training and did

		they understand how training was relevant to their work performance and job-related development?
	Performance self- efficacy	Are individuals confident and self-assured about applying new abilities and overcoming obstacles that hinder the use of new knowledge and skills?

Kirkpatrick level 4 tools.

Measuring the impact of new knowledge or skills on the business as a whole is obviously fraught with difficulty. So many internal and external variables impose themselves on the question that practically any claim for the efficacy of training could be open to dispute. Successful organisations will have a wide range of business performance indicators that can be used to demonstrate apparent effects of new learning e.g.

- Production volumes / output
- Improved turn-around times
- Reduced customer complaints
- Reduced failure rates
- Improved levels of compliance
- Achievement of quality standards
- Growth in market share
-

It is easy to see how training could contribute to all of these, but difficult to prove precisely to what extent. Meaningful evaluation at this level requires clear thinking before any impact claims are made. Each specific learning event should be quantified against all the other potential variables that could have contributed to the apparent result. The key process questions are:

- Does evaluation at level 2 and 3 suggest that the learning outcomes for the course or programme have been achieved? If not, then there is little point in pursuing evaluation at level 4. If the answer is yes other questions need to be answered.
- What should the impact of the learning be on the business e.g. improved output? Improved customer satisfaction etc.?
- What else has changed in the operating environment that might also contribute to these impacts? What are the other variables in this equation? If nothing else has changed then we can reasonably assume that any improvement will be due to the learning input. If the environment has experienced other changes we must analyse at a deeper level.
- Can we quantify the impact of each of the variables involved? If yes, then how? If no then we can only justify a claim that the learning event contributed t the impact.
- Does the learning event offer opportunities for quantitative and qualitative impacts e.g. improved output (quantitative) and improved employee morale (qualitative)? If so, how can these be demonstrated?

In most situations more than one variable will be apparent and improvements are likely to be due to some combination of their effects. In these cases we have little choice but to fall back on perceptions of the relative impact of each variable. A simple survey to all those directly involved can yield useful (but probably unreliable) indicators of the impact of training.

If, for example, a company's shift managers were trained in process analysis and improvement, we would certainly be entitled to expect an eventual improvement in output or quality, or both. If, on their return they collectively agree on and implement process changes, but nothing else changes in the working environment, we can certainly attribute any improvement to their new knowledge. However, if management decided to implement other changes at the same time, attribution of impact becomes much more subjective. Asking all staff involved (except the shift managers, who would naturally be biased toward the effect of their own input) to record their views on the relative importance of the contributing factors, at least allows us a sense of what has really occurred. In the simple survey example below we can see that in addition to training the shift managers (re-design of process) management is seeking improvement through a number of other initiatives.

	Important				Not important
Improvement Factor	5	4	3	2	1
Re-design of process.					
New equipment.					
Re-defined product specifications.					
New shift cycles.					
Improved bonus scheme.					

In addition, the effects of learning and development on the individual can have positive impacts unrelated to the immediate bottom line. For example, research shows that personal development and the ability to contribute positively motivates staff and improves retention. This is an impact that can be measured over the longer term through devices such as climate surveys.

The Phillips Model – Return on Dollar Investment (ROI)

As Kirkpatrick's 4 level evaluation model evolved, he came to realise that there would inevitably be occasions when learning programmes would need to be justified to senior management in terms of "bangs for the buck" i.e. value added in dollar terms. Despite this, he did not pursue $ROI with any particular vigour, primarily because in the majority of cases the actual effects of learning are so difficult to isolate, and investment can be rewarded in ways equally or perhaps more valuable than monetary considerations.

The challenge of developing a relatively straightforward methodology for $ROI was taken up by Jack Phillips in the 1970's. Because the Phillips ROI analysis requires evaluation data from the Kirkpatrick levels it is often referred to as a "fifth level" of the Kirkpatrick system as shown at figure 7.3.

In fact, the Phillips model is not merely an "add-on" to Kirkpatrick. It regards the evaluation process as an extended procedure which commences with developing an evaluation strategy, and moves through data collection and extensive data analysis toward an eventual impact study or report. This is illustrated at figure 7.3.

Although the Phillips model is chiefly identified with the calculation of $ROI, perhaps its real point of difference is its emphasis on evaluation strategy and planning. Philips asserts, quite rightly, that much evaluation is attempted without any thought being given to why we are doing it and what we intend to achieve as an outcome. Most trainers and most managers are driven, consciously or unconsciously by the old adage "you can't manage what you don't measure" – therefore we must always evaluate. Only clear thinking at the front end of the process will make full and proper use of the data generated. In addition, as Phillips himself has reminded us, not everything can be evaluated or indeed should be evaluated. Evaluation objectives are often driven by an insatiable management demand for financial metrics resulting in often extravagant ROI claims which do not stand up to informed scrutiny. This is why Phillips urges us to "educate management" as to what is actually possible.

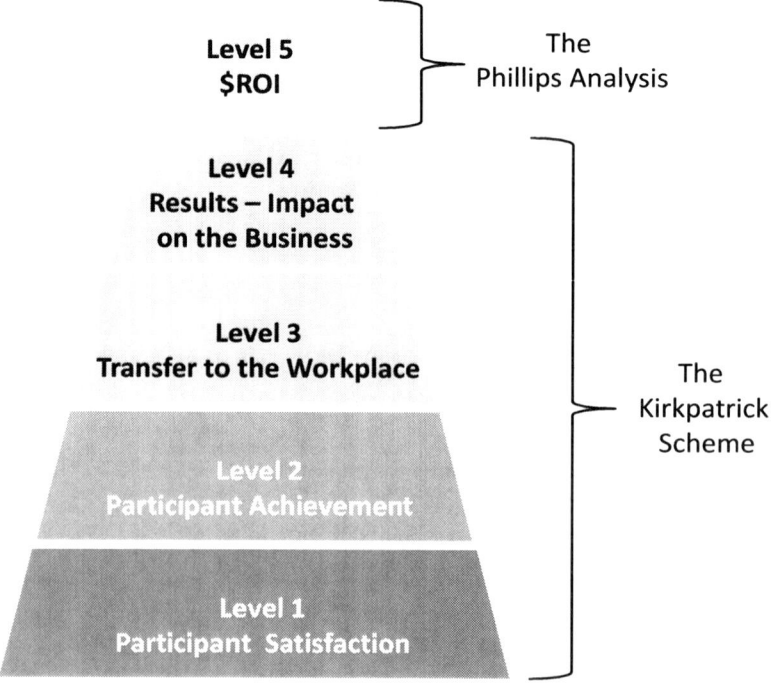

Figure 7.3 – Kirkpatrick + Phillips "5th level"

The calculation of $ROI is clearly not a simple process. Generally, it requires significant investments of time and skilled resources to generate meaningful results. Furthermore, it is often impossible to capture sufficient valid data to complete the process properly. Phillips has acknowledged this and provided guidelines for when the pursuit of evaluation through to level 5 is actually worthwhile. Attempting level 5 evaluation of all learning events would prove excessively costly (4). The guidelines recommend that level 4 (impact on the business) and level 5 (ROI) should only be attempted for:

- Programmes that are intended to be continually repeated (extended life cycle).
- Programmes that are clearly linked to critical business objectives.
- Programmes that have (for whatever reason) attracted significant senior management interest.
- Programmes that have incurred high costs.
- Programmes that are highly "visible" throughout the programme e.g. flagship initiatives.
- Programmes that are delivered to large numbers.
- Programmes that are exclusively "soft skills" oriented.

These recommendations have been converted to a "rule of thumb" to guide HR departments in formulating their evaluation strategies. This is illustrated at figure 7.4.

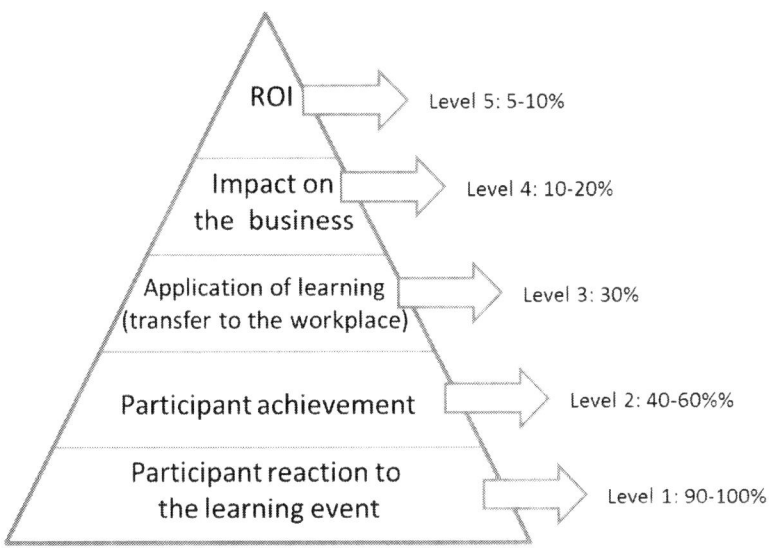

Figure 7.4 – Guidelines for targeting evaluation activity

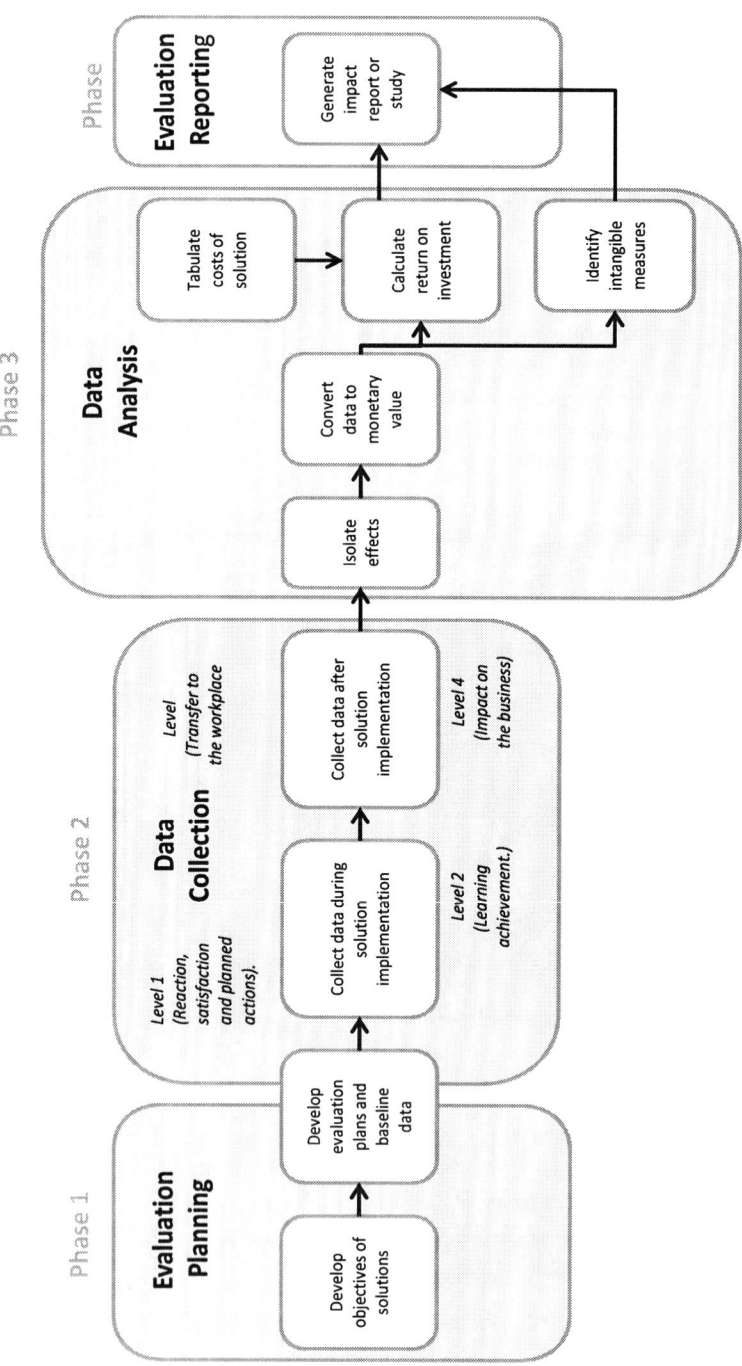

Figure 7.5 – The Phillips evaluation model

Using the Phillips model.

Working through the full Phillips model should be treated formally as a project in itself. The complexities involved will need careful planning, resourcing and management. As an example we will work with the following scenario:

ABC Widgets Inc. has been suffering from constantly increasing numbers of customer complaints and the associated costs of returned product. This is having significant impacts on profitability and must be addressed if customer loyalty is to be retained. Senior management task HR to implement training for all senior production operators and shift managers in quality control processes in all its plants.

Phase 1 (evaluation planning) is critical for eventual success. Rigorous questioning of sponsoring stakeholders is needed to establish clear business objectives for the proposed training programme (the "solution"). These objectives should not be confused with the learning outcomes written to support training delivery. The question here is "what should be the eventual impact on the business issue / problem?" This will generate objectives such as:
- To reduce customer complaints by at least 80%
- To reduce returned product by at least 90%
- To eliminate on-site product rework by 80%
- To ensure customer sign up to new season contracts

These business objectives are the yardstick by which the value of the training input will eventually be measured.

We now need to identify the data required if we are to measure performance against business objectives. Principally we are looking for improvements against a range of quantifiable factors. We can't measure improvement unless the "base-line" data is available. Consequently we should plan to obtain accurate data related to complaints, returns and reworking.

Phase 2 – Data collection includes collecting information at the traditional Kirkpatrick levels 1 to 4 but paying particular attention to levels 2, and 3. We need to track through these levels because level 5 evaluation is pointless if:
- There is little evidence of learning achievement (level 2).
- Learning has been achieved but has not been successfully transferred back to the workplace.
- There is no reliable data for performance subsequent to the training input. It is always advisable to collect performance data at staged intervals following training. This is to ensure that there has been sufficient opportunity for the new knowledge and skills to become adequately embedded. It may be necessary to monitor performance for as long as six months to measure the level of transfer accurately.

Collection methods will of course vary according to the specific situation but might include hard data measures such as:
- Continuous monitoring of production or output
- Reductions in product reject or returns
- Reductions in customer complaints
- Reduction in unit costs

- Increased sales
- Reductions in workplace injuries

Hard data such as this is relatively easy to gather and analyse, but we should be very careful when linking observed improvements to training or learning programmes. Hard data collection should always be accompanied by interviewing or survey tools designed to reveal the effects of any other potential contributing factors.

For example, let us suppose that a company's call centre staff have recently been trained in new complaint handling protocols intended to reduce the total handling time. Analysis of handling times over the next 3 months reveals an apparent reduction of 30%. This looks like a significant endorsement for the training programme. However, when we look closer we find that new software has simultaneously been installed on the call centre systems and when staff are questioned about its performance, they all say that it has helped to speed things up.

The only way now to tease out the actual effect of the training would be to keep a proportion of the staff working with the old software, but this is hardly likely to be acceptable to management. In these situations claims for the efficacy of training have to be tempered by including the impact of other significant variables. For this example we would probably be content with claiming that the combined effect of new protocols and new software has resulted in a 30% reduction in handling times. Evaluation is very often forced to a pragmatic compromise.

To be sure of reasonably reliable data we need to monitor and sample performance through to a point where improvement tails off to a consistent plateau. Sampling immediately following training may well reveal a fall in performance as employees struggle to incorporate new learning into existing systems.

Some time may also be needed for the workplace environment to adjust to the new skills or processes being brought back by trainees. Figure 7.6 illustrates the concept of staged sampling.

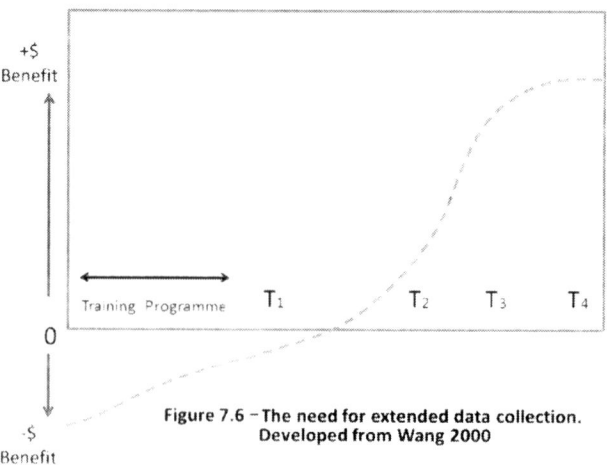

Figure 7.6 – The need for extended data collection. Developed from Wang 2000

Phase 3 – data analysis involves a number of potentially complex exercises aimed at generating monetary equivalents that can be fed into a formula for the calculation of ROI. As already noted, the validity of any eventual claim will depend on isolation of the learning impact from other variables. If this is not possible it may be sensible to abandon the consideration of $ROI and to concentrate on softer measures.

Assuming that isolation is possible, the nest step is convert performance data into $ values so that direct comparisons can be made. At first glance this can appear to be a daunting proposition but the cost of most workplace activity can be measured in terms of staff time x hourly rate, resources expended etc. and then averaged out as unit cost. So, for example, customer complaints can be costed by examining the number of responses that have to be made and any follow-up activity, multiplied by staff costs and any travel etc. associated with "damage limitation" activity. Similarly the costs of training can be precisely tracked and calculated using a standard course cost calculator (see section 6) and adding in the costs associated with time spent on the evaluation process itself.

All this can be very time consuming. Consequently, companies sometimes find themselves "evaluating the evaluation" and if the final results are likely to be unreliable, they will often prefer to go with "gut feel".

Once we have monetary values we can move to the calculation of the $ROI. This is achieved by using the simple formula:

ROI = total programme benefits – total program costs (net benefit)
$$\frac{\text{total programme benefits – total program costs (net benefit)}}{\text{total programme costs}} \quad \text{x } 100$$

Returning to our ABC Widgets scenario the spreadsheet at Figure 7.7 shows the calculation of baseline data to produce a first quarter cost for the quality issues of $129840. Training is conducted and performance measured again at the end of the 3rd quarter. This produces a cost of only $22430. In this case there are no other discernible impacts so we can attribute a benefit of $107410 to the training. Subtracting the total costs of training realises a net benefit of $54810. Thus we have:

ROI = $54810 / $52600 x 100 = $104%

This means that for every training dollar spent the return is $1.04 i.e. in this case a "break even" investment, which at first glance does not seem to be much reward for all the effort of running a training programme. A more satisfying picture emerges however once we remember that while the training cost is a one off investment, the benefits continue to accrue. Assuming that new levels of performance are maintained the ROI quarter on quarter very rapidly accumulates until by quarter 10 it is standing at 1533%. Any Chief Financial Officer would be content with this result.

The spreadsheet calculator overleaf (Figure 7.7) illustrates this cumulative process at work.

ABC Widgets Inc. ROI for Quality Control Processes Training

Baseline data - First Quarter

Customer complaints	
No. received	84
Average cost staff time, immediate follow-up	50
Average cost staff time, travel etc re visit to customer	760
Average total cost per complaint	810
Total cost re complaints	68040

Returns	
No. of units returned	2760
Average cost per unit for inward freight / handling	14
Average cost per unit for break down	3
Average cost per unit for return to component stocks	3
Average total cost per unit returned	20
Total cost re returned units	55200

On site rework of QC rejects	
No. of units reworked	1320
Average cost of extraction from line	1
Average cost per unit for break down	3
Average cost per unit for return to component stocks	1
Total cost per unit reworked	5
Total cost re reworked units	6600

Total costs re quality issues	129840
Gross benefits	**107410**
Total cost of training	**52,600**
Net Benefits	**54,810**

Post Training Data (3rd Quarter)

Customer complaints		% improvement
No. received	12	85.71428571
Total cost re complaints	9720	

Returns		% improvement
No. of units returned	322	88.33333333
Total cost re returned units	9660	

On site rework of QC rejects		% improvement
No. of units reworked	610	53.78787879
Total cost of reworked units	3050	
Total costs re quality issues	####	

ROI = net benefit / programme costs x 100

Immediate Return on investment Q3	104%

Cumulative ROI (Ensuing Quarters)

	Prog. Cost	Benefit	ROI
Q4	52,600	162,220	308.403
Q5	52,600	269,630	512.6046
Q6	52,600	377,040	716.8061
Q7	52,600	484,450	921.0076
Q8	52,600	591,860	1125.209
Q9	52,600	699,270	1329.411
Q10	52,600	806,680	1533.612

Figure 7.7 – Example of Phillips ROI calculation (accumulating).

The Kirkpatrick + Phillips model remains the most widely used method to evaluate workplace training. This is undoubtedly because its principles mesh comfortably with the practical requirements of the business world. Fundamentally, commercial organisations want to know three things about training i.e.

- Did it work?
- What did it cost?
- What kind of return will we get on the investment?

Kirkpatrick + Phillips will provide answers to all of these. Nevertheless, this approach is often criticised for not addressing "context" and "process" issues i.e. it simply assumes that the training delivered is appropriate, relevant and at the right level (context) and, furthermore, that the design methodology for administration, delivery and assessment are valid and reliable (process). However, such criticism is valid only if evaluation does not sit within a comprehensive framework for learning and development. When organisational learning is conducted within such a framework, the context and process issues should have been dealt with at the "front end". This is commonly referred to as "FEA" or front end analysis. Kirkpatrick is only meaningful if the FEA has been professionally accomplished

The CIPP Model.

Kirkpatrick is fundamentally a "goals based" approach. It is concerned entirely with outcomes and impacts. While this generally suits the business world it is not always the only concern. Kirkpatrick focuses primarily on the "what" of learning i.e. what has been learned? What has been transferred? What is the impact on the business? What did it cost? etc. For some learning programmes, and for certain organisations, the "how" of learning will be just as important. There are many occasions where the focus is legitimately centred on process rather than outcomes.

This shift of focus is most obvious with educational institutions and with very large corporations that run in-house "cradle to grave" development programmes. Evaluation here tends to concern itself with the way learning integrates into other development activity and with the "quality" of the whole experience.

In the early 1970's Daniel Stufflebeam recognised that educators and trainers were more likely to be concerned with ongoing improvement of their programmes and courses than with $ROI. The continuing rebuttal of the ROI focus is that it "understands the cost of everything and the value of nothing" – cost and value are not necessarily related. Consequently, Stufflebeam evolved a truly holistic evaluation philosophy which requires every contributing factor to be taken into account. In this sense it subsumed the "front end". More importantly perhaps, Stufflebeam recognised that the Kirkpatrick method did not produce worthwhile data on what was needed for the continuous improvement of the various processes involved.

While this shift to a "goals free" philosophy sits easily with the educators, it is generally not well received in the cut and thrust of business environments. The complexity of Stufflebeam's approach generally means that only education and training professionals can understand and make use of the data produced. Consequently it is often regarded as "incestuous" and unnecessarily heavy on L&D resources. Stufflebeam's CIPP system is fully at home in the world of major curriculum development but would be an uncomfortable fit in the environment of short duration industrial training. For large organisations that are committed to the long term development of staff and have significant L&D resources permanently on board, a combination of systems often evolves to meet the full range of needs. We see this, for example, with the US and British Armed Forces.

Using the CIPP model.

In essence, the CIPP model is simple. In practice it is a complex and exhaustive process requiring considerable commitment of time and skilled resource. The basic concept is illustrated at figure 7.8.

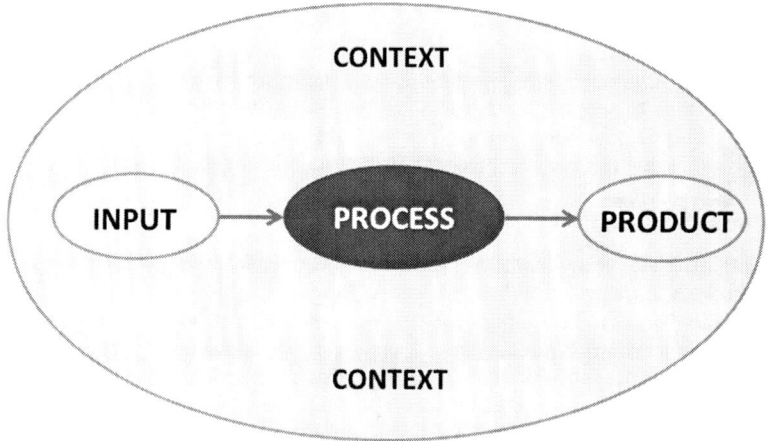

Figure 7.8 – The CIPP evaluation model

The four essential components are:

CONTEXT – as the graphic shows, "context" relates to the ongoing evaluation of the total environment in which learning takes place. It is the essential rationale in which every aspect of learning is rooted. At the front end we question the relevance, level, and general "fit" of the proposed programme or course itself. These key concerns are then addressed to the input, process and product phases to provide commentary on suitability, achievement and need for improvement.

INPUT – evaluation here is concerned with the wide range of variables that flow into the stream of the learning event e.g. what the learner brings, what the trainer brings, what the environment contributes, the quality of the course design and tools etc.

PROCESS – the concern here is with method, the "how". Evaluation tools need to be applied to programme administration, support systems, communication and feedback mechanisms etc.

PRODUCT – the focus here is essentially on what the learner ends up with at the end of the course. As such it comments on achievement (Kirkpatrick level 2) and on the use learners might make of their new knowledge and skill (Kirkpatrick level 3) but does not venture into evaluation of transfer, impact or ROI.

The design of a CIPP evaluation strategy can be complex and will vary considerably according to specific situations. The following table provides a very basic "blueprint" for typical inclusions.

CIPP Component	Typical Issues for Evaluation
Context	• Is there actually a need for this course? • Is the course related directly to demonstrated job needs? • Is the course set at the most appropriate level? • Does the course have full stakeholder support? • Can the course be adequately resourced and delivered? • What is the relation of the course to other courses? Is it part of a larger qualification etc? Is it part of a modular sequence etc? • Is the course a one-off or a repeated event? • Is there sufficient time for development? • Are there particular power / interest groups that need to be involved? • Does the course align with organisational culture?
Input	• Who is the target learner? • What is the existing knowledge and skill level of learners? • Has the course been fully specified with relevant learning outcomes? • Is the course designed to suit the needs of the target audience and their learning styles? • Is there an appropriate theory – practical balance • Is the course fully resourced in an appropriate manner? • Are the trainers appropriately qualified and fully prepared? • Is the learning environment fully conducive to quality learning? • Is there any post-course work? If so, is this realistically achievable? • Is there a facility for post course trainer discussion? How effectively does this work for continuous improvement?
Process	• Is the administration of the course well organised and efficient? • Is the workload of learners realistic? • Are learners able to contribute effectively? • Are learners able to comment on course delivery, formatively or summatively? • Are there appropriate mechanisms to deal with individual learner support needs?

Product	• Is there a clear indicator of end of course (summative) achievement? Hoe effective is this?
	• Is there a formative assessment procedure? How effective is this?
	• How is individual achievement measured?
	• Is achievement norm referenced or criterion-referenced? Does this provide an adequate picture for all stakeholders?
	• Are learners able to see clearly how they will apply their new knowledge and skills?
	• How is achievement reported? Does this satisfy the needs of all stakeholders?
	• Has the reputation of the course and course providers been affected in any way? If so, how?

Successive revisions and expansions of the CIPP approach have produced a model which is truly daunting in scale and more or less only of use with long term learning strategies. A more comprehensive checklist of ideal evaluation CIPP content can be found at _http://www.wmich.edu/evalctr/archive checklists/cippchecklist.htm_ This reveals something of the complexity that has proved so generally disconcerting. Businesses need proof that the training dollar is being well spent. Stufflebeam's often quoted maxim _"the purpose of evaluation is not to prove but to improve"_ clearly sets him at odds with the Kirkpatrick approach.

The CIRO model.
Perhaps there is an obvious question to ask here i.e. "Is there a possibility of a compromise between the apparent extremes of Kirkpatrick and Stufflebeam?" The answer may lie with the CIRO model proposed in 1970 by Warr, Bird and Rackam.(5) CIRO focuses on context, input, reaction and outcomes thus neatly combining core elements of both Kirkpatrick and Stufflebeam.

The CIRO model is more sharply focused on fewer evaluation targets than CIPP. Context here directly addresses key factors such as effective ITN (identification of training needs) and the proper specification of learning through objectives or learning outcomes. These must be properly aligned to organisational culture and strategy. Input evaluation targets the design and delivery of training and related assessment activity. Reaction, as with Kirkpatrick, seeks data on the nature of participant experience of the course.

Perhaps the most interesting aspect of the CIRO model is its acknowledgement that the outcome of a learning event cannot simply be judged by a one off sample. The requirement here is for at least three enquiries:
- Immediate outcomes – end of course measures that gather data on changes to knowledge and skills before a return to the workplace.
- Intermediate outcomes – attempt to measure the degree of transfer to the real world of work
- Ultimate outcomes – data associated with the eventual impact on business performance

So perhaps CIRO does indeed offer an opportunity to approach evaluation in a more balanced way and could certainly include $ROI within its intermediate and ultimate outcomes considerations.

Step 5 – identify and produce tools required

Selecting the most appropriate tool for the evaluation of training depends fundamentally on the answers to four key questions:

- What level (e.g. Kirkpatrick) of evaluation do you need to go to?
- What kind of information / data do you need?
- Who or what are your best sources?
- What kind of approach will work best with each individual source e.g. face to face, on-line survey etc.

The question of evaluation level needs careful consideration in the light of what is desirable and what is possible. Training managers can often be pressurised to report evaluation at level 3 and 4 when it is not possible to gather sufficient valid data for any kind of meaningful analysis. In these cases it is essential to "educate" stakeholders about what is achievable or necessary. There are some absolutes e.g. all high cost or long duration programmes should be fully evaluated to level 4 and to level 5 (ROI) if possible, and once the value of a repeated course has been established evaluation should be scaled back to level 2.

Having decided which evaluation level is both appropriate and feasible, thought must be given to the kind of information you need to fully satisfy the objectives associated with the target level. The choice more or less comes down to either fact or opinion. Factual information will be verifiable through hard data sources such as operational performance trends or other business metrics. This is "quantitative" data i.e. data that can be analysed and presented numerically. As such, quantitative data is regarded as being objective. Information that based on personal opinion or perception is "qualitative" and is essentially subjective in nature. Qualitative information can be assembled and presented numerically to indicate trends of perception e.g. the organisational climate survey or perceptions of programme quality at level 1. We can also make factual statements in regard to qualitative data e.g. that it is a fact that 88% of respondents felt that the course was pitched at the right level. In practice, the best evaluations will use both types of information to support eventual conclusions. Quantitative data on its own may present a confused picture that can only be clarified by qualitative commentary.

Whether we select quantitative or qualitative tools depends largely on the precise information we are seeking. Figure 7.9 overleaf illustrates the kind of thinking process required.

The table overleaf lists the tools typically chosen to obtain information against specific target data. As the table indicates, the most commonly used tools for evaluation data collection are:

Surveys – paper-based or on-line. On-line surveys offer distinct advantages in that they can be used to access learners who are geographically dispersed and they will return information in electronic format which can speed up the process of data collation and analysis. However, the design input can involve considerable effort and certainly requires some expertise. They can be used to collect both quantitative and qualitative data.

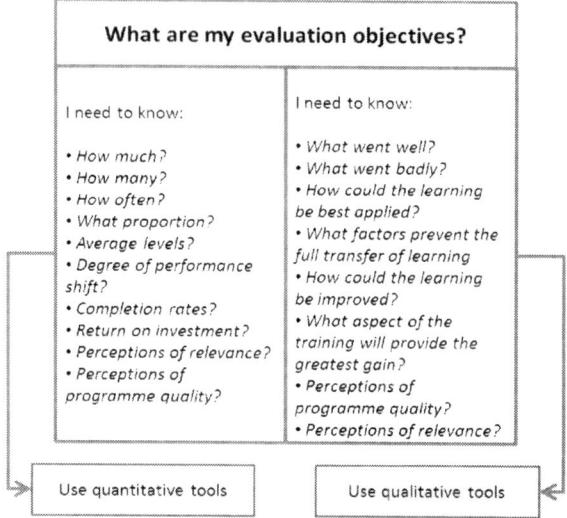

Figure 7.9 – selecting evaluation tools

The chief disadvantage of surveys is that there is no opportunity to "drill down" into issues. The respondent is largely constrained by the survey format. This is why it is wise to include a format that will allow individual respondents to add informal comment to expand on their opinions if they so wish.

Interviews – very much the opposite strategy to surveys. Providing we know what information we are seeking, comparatively little effort is required to assemble a range of interview questions and we do not need to be expert in the intricacies of survey formatting. In addition, when face to face with the interviewee we have every opportunity to explore issues as far as necessary. Problems arise however with gathering and managing the data. Most interviewers will now use sound recording.

Survey design principles.

Survey design is undoubtedly something of an art and should be handed to the professionals if large scale, complex data collection is needed. Nevertheless, there is no reason why smaller scale surveys cannot be adequately designed by HR or L&D professionals once some basic principles are understood i.e.
- What makes a good question?
- What is the appropriate response mechanism for the information I am seeking?
- How should I structure the content to the best advantage (layout and sequence)?

A good survey question is brief, objectively and simply phrased, and specific to a single issue.

Evaluation of Learning Events - Selection of Tools			
Kirkpatrick Level	Target Data	Typical Useful tools	Primary Data Generated
Pre-course	Base-line operational performance.	Relevant business metrics.	Quantitative.
	Learner knowledge / experience levels.	Individual surveys.	Quantitative / Qualitative.
		Learner / Line Manager interviews.	Qualitative.
		Skills audits.	Quantitative.
		Peer reviews.	Qualitative.
1	Course administration / joining instructions.	Learner Reaction survey.	Quantitative.
	Pre-course materials.	Learner Reaction survey.	Quantitative.
	Venue.	Learner Reaction survey.	Quantitative.
	Accommodation + Meals.	Learner Reaction survey.	Quantitative.
	Travel arrangements.	Learner Reaction survey.	Quantitative.
	Course structure.	Learner Reaction survey. One-on-one selective interviews.	Quantitative.
	Course content (relevance).	Learner Reaction survey. One-on-one selective interviews.	Quantitative / Qualitative.
		Post-course survey in the workplace, learner and line manager	Quantitative / Qualitative.
	Course content (level).	Learner Reaction survey. One-on-one selective interviews.	Quantitative / Qualitative.
		Post-course survey in the workplace, learner and line, manager	Quantitative / Qualitative.
	Course delivery (pace and style).	Learner Reaction survey. One-on-one selective interviews.	Quantitative / Qualitative.
		"Pulse-taker" one -on-one informal soundings.	Qualitative.
		Peer assessments by direct observation.	Qualitative.
2	Immediate learning achievement.	Completion rates	Quantitative.
		Analysis of formative / summative assessment results.	Quantitative.
		Learner on course presentation or teach back.	Quantitative / Qualitative.
3	Transfer to the workplace / behavioural change.	Learner / Line Manager interviews on-job.	Qualitative.
		Relevant operational metrics.	Quantitative.
		Individual surveys.	Qualitative
		Direct observation and monitoring against baseline data at staged intervals.	Quantitative
		Action planning (learners) plan how skills will be integrated and demonstrated. Implementation monitored by manager and evaluator.	Qualitative.
		Action learning e.g via a skills related post-course project	Quantitative / Qualitative
		Request for validation (managers asked to confirm detail of skills transfer)	Quantitative / Qualitative
4	Impact on the business	Standard business metrics	Quantitative
		Climate surveys (re effects on morale etc)	Qualitative
5	Return on Investment	Phillips method where reliable baseline and post course performance data is available	Quantitative

Brevity is always desirable - after all we are intruding on the respondent's time. We must be economical while ensuring absolute clarity. *"Brevity's goal is to create the shortest way to ask a question without losing its intent. It is not always about reducing the length of the question".(6)*

Achieving **objectivity** is largely a question of neutral language and avoiding any format that might "lead" the respondent to particular answers. Questions cease to be objective when they:

- Are visually unbalanced e.g. in questions with several options, one response clearly has far more words than the others or employ obviously different kinds of language (leading questions).
- Force the respondent to answer in an unnecessarily restricted manner e.g. a yes / no choice when he may have wanted to qualify his response.
- Contain "emotive" words that give a positive or negative impression (loaded questions) e.g. *What are your thoughts about the upgrade to the No.2 Fibreline?* The word "upgrade" implies improvement. This should be replaced by "changes made" which is neutral.
- They are "complex questions" i.e. questions that actually contain more than one issue e.g. *"Now that you have been trained to a greater level of technical expertise, how ready are you to take charge of the production team".* The two issues of technical expertise and willingness to lead are not necessarily related. Furthermore there is an in-built assumption that a greater level of expertise was in fact achieved.

Simplicity is actually hard to achieve. It requires constant scanning and questioning of the language used. Guiseppe Larossi insists on the following guidelines:

- Use words and expressions that are simple, direct, and familiar to all respondents.
- Avoid technical jargons or concepts.
- Use the same definitions throughout the survey.
- Avoid negative or double negative expressions.
- Avoid the use of absolute terms in the question e.g. "always", "never". Terms such as these can of course be used as part of a response scale.

Being **specific** is mostly a question of precision in identifying the actual issue and avoiding ambiguous language. We need to understand that individual respondents will interpret words and phrases differently if there is any room for ambiguity. Consequently, terms such as "often", "sometimes", "frequently", "occasionally" should be avoided. It is far better to direct the respondent e.g. *"How many times a day do you use the new reporting software?"*

There are no particular preferences for open or closed questions. Each is valid and useful depending on the type of information required. For a full depth analysis of techniques for writing effective survey questions see Schaeffer, Cate and Presser. "The Science of Asking Questions." *Annual Review of Sociology*, Vol. 29: 65-88 2003 available through:
http://www.annualreviews.org/eprint/rU4UOoizjrXROhijkRIS/full/10.1146/annurev.soc.29.110702.110112

Providing an appropriate format for the respondent to answer is obviously critical. There are numerous formats available, but for learning evaluation purposes they are generally limited to a favoured few e.g.

- Multi-Point Rating (e.g. Strongly Agree to Strongly Disagree)

	Strongly Disagree	Disagree	Agree	Strongly Agree
On my return to work, my manager and the team were keen to see how my new skills could be used.	☐	☐	☐	☐

- Semantic Differential

	Never		Sometimes			Always	
	1	2	3	4	5	6	7
I am always consulted for my opinion on what skills need to be refreshed or improved.	☐	☐	☐	☐	☐	☐	☐

In the above example the range of response is numerically coded (1-7). This tactic will make the processing and analysis of data much easier.

- 5-point rating with comment

The quality of training provided by the facilitators was:

Outstanding	☐	Please explain why you have given this rating.
Above Average	☐	
Average	☐	
Below Average	☐	
Poor	☐	

- Selection (single or multiple options)

Please consider the functions of the Fibreline Operator role shown below. In your view, which of these have been positively improved by the recent refresher training undertaken by your shift?

- Check supply and use of steam to DO tower ☐
- Controlling standpipe dilution ☐
- Controlling consistency ☐
- Correct reaction to analyser results ☐
- Interpreting DCS information to ensure optimum operation ☐
- Interpreting feedback from online instruments ☐
- Monitoring top scraper operation ☐
- Controlling lift out procedure ☐
- Shut down and start up after maintenance ☐

Note that the selection format can serve two purposes e.g. responses to the above example will also reveal aspects of training that have not had a positive effect and may consequently need improvement before the next course.

- Open response (short answer).

  What additional knowledge or skills should be included in future health and safety refresher training for shift supervisors? Please give your response in the space below.

The delivery of evaluation surveys poses similar problems to any other survey e.g. rate of return, quality of response, valid interpretation of data etc. Nevertheless, the fact that we can generally work through the management "chain of command" will usually ensure that things get done in a timely manner. Actual delivery method largely depends on scale and geographical issues. If a large sample from a dispersed population is needed, an electronic method will work most effectively provided the target population all have access to computers. The usual methods are either by Email attachment or via a web-based solution. Many organisations now routinely use web-based survey design tools to put their evaluations on-line. These sites offer a wide range of question formats which ease the design burden, but ultimately they seldom match the sophistication that can be achieved through direct local design. Good examples of on-line survey design facilities are:

- Survey Monkey
- Opinio
- Survey Gizmo
- Zoomerang

Hard copy, paper-based surveys remain an option for small scale, locally delivered surveys. Manual handling and completion can make this a cumbersome and time consuming process however. Even more time-consuming is the telephone survey. While this guarantees completion and has the advantage of allowing the respondent to clarify what is meant by a question, it is extremely resource heavy and the frequent inability to contact targeted respondents can be very frustrating.

Interviews. Compared to the obvious efficiencies offered by survey tools, face-to-face interviews with individual respondents are a significantly more costly option. Consequently we need to be very clear about what we are trying to achieve by interviewing and very confident that the exercise will be successful.

As with surveys, face-to-face interviewing can gather both quantitative and qualitative data. However, before opting for an interview strategy we should be mindful of the fact that quantitative data is generally best collected by survey. The primary advantage of interviewing is that it allows us the freedom to "open up" the interviewee's responses to obtain a fuller understanding of their perceptions and feelings around targeted issues. So there is a very good case for interviewing being directed primarily toward qualitative evaluation. There is also a clear rationale for using qualitative interviewing in partnership with surveys to validate the hard data collected. For example, interviews can be used as an exploratory step to gather information on what kind of quantitative survey questions should be asked. Alternatively, interviews can be used following a quantitative survey to explore and validate the reality of hard data.

Experience shows that face-to-face qualitative interviewing is particularly suited for:

- Evaluating learning that is likely to have varying outcomes for individual participants.
- Identifying and variations in programme delivery at various sites or at different times.
- Exploring variations in individual experiences of the learning programme.
- Adding weight to quantitative data conclusions that may be disputed

There are three types of qualitative interviews commonly used for evaluation purposes, characterised by the degree of formality and structure they employ. These are:

- **The standardised structured interview.** This technique is based on a strictly structured "script" which poses exactly the same questions, in the same order, to the interviewee and allows no flexibility to deviate or explore beyond the script. Despite the tight control (standardisation), this approach is still regarded as qualitative because the questions are open-ended. A major advantage of this technique is that it does not require high levels of interpersonal skill on the part of the interviewer. It also lends itself to telephone delivery.
- **The guided interview**. A less structured approach where the interviewer works to a general outline of the issues to be explored. The interviewers can vary the order of issues addressed and the wording of the questions. Consequently it opposes the notion of standardisation. Interpersonal skills of a high level are needed here. The interviewer needs to "read" the interviewee's behaviour and language to detect just how far to explore specific issues.
- **The informal conversational interview**. These interviews tend to be opportunistic, often generated through initially casual conversations around a training course or programme. Consequently there is no interview plan or prepared questions. Evaluators may deliberately seek out casual conversations of this nature, knowing that the "interviewee" is likely to be more at ease and willing to reveal more of their true feelings or opinions.

Step 6 – assign tools to target stakeholders and schedule. This stage is relatively straightforward. All that is now required is to identify who is the most likely source of the information you need, and what methods are most likely to succeed in obtaining it. Internally conducted evaluation processes (e.g. by the HR department), will often identify sources very early in the planning process. External evaluators, on the other hand, will need continued guidance on who to consult and how to approach them.

Much depends on the scale of the evaluation exercise. If stakeholders are numerous and geographically dispersed, strategies involving interviewing may become unworkable unless interview teams are trained to ensure a fully moderated approach. Simply delegating the task to local managers via a script is likely to produce significant reliability issues. In these circumstances a well-designed survey is generally a far better option, perhaps followed up by "sampling" interviews to validate interpretation of survey data.

Careful consideration should be given to scheduling repeat or follow up interviews / surveys to ensure that the transfer or learning over time is properly captured (see figure 7.6).

Step 7 – Analysis of data and reporting. Raw data must be given meaning if it is to be of any practical use. This entails analysis, interpretation and presentation in an appropriate format. Quantitative data lends itself to statistical analysis and numerical presentation. Conversely, qualitative data generally focuses on discerning meaningful patterns or trends that are revealed in verbal or written responses. Quantitative analysis is a more obviously linear process with discrete steps e.g. data collection, data processing, data analysis etc. Qualitative analysis usually involves a continual build up on all fronts, with analysis often starting from the time the first data is returned. This reflects the fact that each response potentially questions other responses and may reveal fresh issues.

Qualitative analysis. The fundamental questions addressed by qualitative analysis are:

- Are there any common themes or patterns emerging from the responses to specific questions?
- If there are clear trends or patterns, do the responses offer any explanation for them?
- Are there clearly identifiable alternative trends to the main pattern?
- Does the data corroborate other findings, opinion or assumption?
- Do any of the responses indicate that more data is required?

Unlike quantitative evaluation, the "open-ended" nature of much qualitative evaluation will tend to generate considerable amounts of information, often with little apparent relationship to the issues being investigated. While the open and expansive nature of qualitative questioning is in itself a virtue, it presents real difficulties for analysis. Attempting to "discipline" the data can lead to suspicions of distortion. Nevertheless, reduction must occur to some degree just to render the data digestible. Miles and Huberman describe the process of qualitative analysis as a three stage exercise; data reduction, data display and final drawing of conclusions.(7)

Typically, a single item of qualitative data might comprise relevant parts of transcribed interview notes, excerpts from "field notes" or records of comments gathered from individuals or groups. Embedded in this complexity will be the "nugget" of valid evaluation information being sought. Honing down such rich information is often made even more difficult by the fact that the person analysing the data may have been directly involved in its collection and therefore unlikely to approach the task with complete objectivity.

Reduction of data is best achieved by each item (or part item) to an organised framework of required evidence. The framework must reflect precisely the evaluation objectives. Essentially, this exercise is a variant of "coding" or "filtering" and does not involve any attempt to interpret. This approach can be illustrated via the following typical scenario.

ABC Widgets Ltd has recently concluded a 12 month programme of first line management training for its production shift managers. External consultants were engaged to produce and deliver a programme tailored directly to learning needs specified by the company. The learning outcomes were drawn directly from full depth role maps (see section 2, figure 11, for an extract example) and prioritised according to identified mastery requirements. Consequently there is real clarity around the learning that needs to be achieved and transferred to the workplace. The consultants have provided evaluation at level 1 (learner reaction) and level 2 (learner achievement on course). Given the cost of the programme the HR manager has decided that evaluation at level 3 (transfer to the workplace) should be done internally to ensure maximum objectivity.

Evaluation was carried out using a variety of qualitative interviews, surveys and observation exercises with production managers, the shift managers themselves, and the production operators they supervised. This work produced a wealth of information, much of which referred generally to production and organisational culture issues. Before any meaningful interpretation could occur, this data would need to be reduced to what was actually relevant to the level 3 evaluation objectives. The role map was used to provide a logical basis for filtering the data. Full or partial statements were allocated to the various "codings" resulting in a structured and manageable data set that would allow focused analysis and interpretation.

Figure 7.10 illustrates the data filtering structure for this example. This shows the high level scheme. In practice it would no doubt be necessary to allocate each of the separate coded areas to a separate worksheet. Consequently using a tool like Excel is sensible since it allows for limitless expansion and any quantification that might arise from the information.

Figure 7.11 illustrates how the high level data filtering plan can proceed to the next level of detail. In this case the first primary area of required evaluation focus (shift planning) has been opened up and "drilled down" to the related secondary (shift liaisons and hand-overs). This is allocated its own evaluation code, and a reference to the role map. Data items (or extracts) relevant to this specific issue are then inserted and given their own references. Finally an ID in allocated to the source of each data item. Each primary area (or perhaps each secondary area if the evaluation is sufficiently complex) can be allocated its own worksheet. Identifying trends and patterns then becomes a relatively straightforward matter.

Although figure 7.11 is only an extract we can already begin to see that training in this area is regarded as effective, but there are individual aberrations that may need further investigation. If the rest of the data for this area of focus is similar we could justifiably claim that training has been generally effective. The aberrations may simply be representative of the normal curve for reaction to change – but this would need further enquiry.

ABC Widgets Ltd. First Line Management Programme Level 3 Evaluation

Required Evaluation Data					
Primary	Related Secondary	Eval Code	Role Map Ref	Data Item	Item Ref
Operations - shift planning		O1			
Operations - operational standards		O2			
Operations - problem solving		O3			
Operations - routine review and forward planning		O4			
Operations - routine reporting		O5			
Health & Safety - managing compliance		HS1			
Health & Safety - contibuting to H&S culture		HS2			
Environmental Safety - managing compliance		ES1			
People Management - managing performance		PM1			
People Management - motivation and morale		PM2			
People Management - dealing with conflict		PM3			
People Management - planning operator succession		PM4			
Developing Capability - identifying training needs		DC1			
Developing Capability - managing shift skills matrix		DC2			
Communications - ensuring effective shift and inter shift communication		C1			

Figure 7.10 – example of data reduction / filtering plan for level 3 qualitative evaluation

ABC Widgets Ltd. First Line Management Programme Level 3 Evaluation

Data Focus - Operations - shift planning

Required Evaluation Data					
Related Secondary	Eval Code	Role Map Ref	Data Item	Item Ref	Source ID
Effective liaising with outgoing and oncoming shift managers.	O1.1	1.1	"Yes, I think I have a much clearer idea of what is needed fo the HOTO. I start to plan this and make my about two hours before the ned of the shift. Seems to working well."	O1.1/1	SMA1
			"I think I've got a good handle on this now - though I was uncertain at first. I try to stick to the formats we learned on the FLM programme but sometimes I get derailed by other shift managers who won't play ball".	O1.1/2	SMA3
			"Thank God we've got a standard system now. Before we all had the training handovers were pretty hit and miss. I'm not saying we've got it nailed yet, but it all seems so much more professional now".	O1.1/3	SMC2
			"I can't really see the point. We managed perfectly well before. I still prefer the old way".	O1.1/4	SMD 3
			" No doubt about it. This is the way to do things. We are so much better organised now. I hear there are one or two shift managers who are still not on to it, but they'll have to fall into line eventually."	O1.1/5	SMB1
			"Generally, I can see a real improvement in handover effectiveness. We are getting far fewer start of shift incidents as a result."	O1/1/6	PM/L1

Figure 7.11 – extract from qualitative reduction / filtering worksheet for one area of evaluation focus

It will be immediately apparent that qualitative evaluation can be a complex and time consuming exercise, requiring a good deal of willpower to complete thoroughly. This is perhaps why it is so seldom done. Very often, senior managers will opt for "gut reaction" observation. Evaluation at this level is expensive and we should genuinely question its viability.

There are no specific rules for presentation of qualitative data for stakeholder consumption. The solution will depend on what we need to demonstrate. However, more often than not, data can be presented in matrix form as an effective summary of a key evaluation issue. For example, with our ABC Widgets scenario we would most likely want to probe both Shift Managers and the Line Production Managers concerning their perceptions of which aspects of the training have had the most positive impact on the way they now do things in the workplace. We could simply produce a list and ask respondents to tick a box. This would produce quantitative information which is very easily presented in percentage terms. Unfortunately, as an evaluation strategy, this is of little use because we need to know why the respondents think as they do. Once filtered out from the general responses, this information can be assembled as shown overleaf at figure 7.12. Presentation in this format renders the data easily digestible and allows any trends or patterns to emerge

The final stage involves examining the data to draw whatever conclusions might be justified by the evidence available. For example, looking at the extract shown at figure 7.12 we can draw the following conclusions with some confidence in their validity:
- Across the board, performance management was the training component most commonly cited for positive impact back in the workplace.
- While respondents had mixed views on which training component had the most positive impact, the training provided for dealing with conflict was the most commonly cited.
- For all training components cited, respondents indicated that the new skills and techniques have enabled a higher level of performance. They also indicated that previous to the training input skills were at a low level. This should be taken as a need to re-design the way in which shift managers are inducted and prepared for their role.

Obviously we are looking at an extract only. There would no doubt be corresponding evaluation data focused on what had failed to transfer successfully to the workplace, and this would drive a review of training content and methods.

Clearly, the analysis of qualitative evaluation data is a relatively subjective process. Nonetheless, if the presentation is sufficiently open e.g. includes verbatim rather than edited statements, readers are more likely to accept the validity of any conclusions. Evaluation usually requires moving from conclusions to recommendations for improvement. Consequently it is essential that the recommendations should transparently reflect the data.

Quantitative analysis. The analysis of quantitative data eventually resolves itself into statistics of some kind. The field of statistics has evolved into a complex science with many of the advanced techniques being beyond the grasp of the humble HR department.

Data matrix 1: Front Line Manager Programme - Level 3 Evaluation			
Respondent Group	**Positive Impact Components Cited**	**Most Positive Impact**	**Reason Why (verbatim)**
Line 1: A Shift Managers	• Performance management • Problem solving techniques	Performance management	Now have strategies and techniques to get the best out of each individual
Line 1: B Shift Managers	• Performance management • Staff development • Dealing with conflict	Dealing with conflict	Team has previously been dominated by aggressive individuals. Can now stop this behaviour and ensure a calmer atmosphere
Line 1: C Shift Managers	• Dealing with conflict • Performance management	Dealing with conflict	Had no idea how to do this before training. Now able to approach it confidently with proven processes
Line 1: D Shift Managers	• Shift planning • Problem solving techniques	Problem solving techniques	Can now share the problem solving load with operators. Better solutions and improved ownership in the team
Line 1: Production Manager	• Communications • Shift planning • Dealing with conflict	Communications	Production problems now emerge much earlier because the shifts are communicating effectively. This means that we deal with issues well before they become significant
Line 2: A Shift Managers	• Planning operator succession • Identifying training needs • Dealing with conflict	Dealing with conflict	Have had a lot of interpersonal problems in recent years which have never really been dealt to. Now we have the skills we can work on defusing these issues and focussing on the job
Line 2: B Shift Managers	• Motivation	Motivation	Basically we have very good people who are well paid. Getting more out of them means something other than a financial incentive. This training gave us useful strategies
Line 2: C Shift Managers	• Performance management • Identification of training needs	Identification of training needs	Poor performance is sometimes actually under-performance resulting from lack of skills. Can now audit individual skill levels and put appropriate measures in place
Line 2: D Shift Managers	• Performance management • Health and Safety compliance • Problem solving techniques • Motivation	Health and Safety compliance	We are a high performing shift all round – but this has meant cutting corners and bending the rules around H&S. Consequently we have the highest level of reportables. Have now improved understanding and systems significantly

Figure 7.12 –Example of data analysis presentation in matrix form.

Fortunately, most of the "number-crunching" related to the evaluation of learning can be expressed via a limited range of relatively straightforward mathematical functions that can be driven through a dedicated Excel spreadsheet. The most commonly encountered (and perhaps most useful) methods include:

- Tallies or frequencies
- Percentages
- Measures of central tendency (mean, mode, median)
- Expressions of variability (standard deviation, range etc.)

Tallies or frequency analysis simply quantify the number of times a specific response occurs or aligns with a given category e.g.

- 58 of the respondents had undertaken training within the last two years.
- 20 of the participants withdrew from the course after the first day because they felt the level was too high for them at present.
- 14 participants were required to resit the anatomy assessment.

Tallying usually provides the base numbers for calculating percentages. These are extensively used because they are more easily understood than raw numbers. It is far easier to grasp statements such as:

- 12% of the participants were excluded from the course following pre-course medical examinations
- 22% of the participants were awarded distinctions

Percentages are also useful for expressing frequency distribution. For example if we wished to show the participation rate in a particular course, over a number of years, for various regions, a simple table with percentages makes this very clear e.g.

Health Service Region	Yr 1	Yr2	Yr3	Yr4	Yr5	Yr6	Yr7	Yr8	Yr9	Yr10	Total	% Participation
					Yearly Participation							
Northland	22	18	16	11	20	12	24	21	8	14	166	14.43478261
North East Bays	6	8	5	9	4	3	5	12	3	6	61	5.304347826
Ragnor	12	23	24	20	22	26	24	19	18	16	204	17.73913043
Stapleton	12	12	13	12	14	11	8	11	10	6	109	9.47826087
Western	6	7	5	9	12	7	4	6	9	3	68	5.913043478
Central Plateau	2	8	6	3	2	2	3	2	4	2	34	2.956521739
Eastern	12	16	15	18	16	17	12	13	13	10	142	12.34782609
Princeton	32	30	34	28	29	30	28	26	28	24	289	25.13043478
South Western	5	5	7	5	9	5	7	6	19	9	77	6.695652174
									Total Participants		1150	100

Figure 7.13 – Example of tallying and expressing participation rates as percentages

Normal practice would include rounding off percentages to the least number of places required for reasonable accuracy. This would certainly make the example above easier to digest.

When we need to know what is typical of a certain group or programme we need to use a measure of central tendency. The most commonly used measure must be the mean or average of a data set. An obvious use of "averaging" would be the typical score obtained by a group of learners in an examination. This is obtained by simply summing all the scores and dividing the total by the number of participants. This could be applied question by question as well as for the assessment as a whole. The table below gives an example of this simple analysis. Note that the average score for the group has been converted to a percentage because this is easier to grasp.

Participant	Q1	Q2	Q3	Q4	Q5	Q6	Q7	Q8	Q9	Q10	Participant Total
Smith	3	5	3	6	4	5	9	6	5	5	51
Brown	5	6	4	8	3	5	10	7	4	6	58
Jones	4	8	4	8	3	4	11	5	5	5	57
Jenkins	5	5	4	9	2	5	10	8	3	4	55
Green	6	4	3	6	3	6	10	9	3	5	55
Thomas	7	6	6	6	4	6	8	9	2	6	60
Walker	2	3	4	7	5	5	9	8	5	6	54
Harris	8	7	5	10	4	8	7	6	3	5	63
Robinson	4	5	5	7	3	4	10	8	3	3	52
Johnson	5	6	4	8	5	7	9	8	6	5	63
Allen	3	4	3	7	3	8	6	7	5	6	52
Group total	52	59	45	82	39	63	99	81	44	56	620
Average score for question	4.73	5.36	4.09	7.45	3.55	5.73	9	7.36	4	5.09	
Maximum score for question	8	10	6	12	5	8	12	10	8	6	
Average score for exam											56.36363636
Maximum score for exam											85
Average % score											66.31016043

Figure 7.14 – Example of expressing central tendency by the mean performance

The mean is also a useful tool for summarising and presenting data generated from rating scales. Even if a semantic scale is used, a numerical value can be attached to each descriptor thus allowing translation into a quantitative form. The example extract below shows how this might work.

Evaluation Issue	Strongly Disagree (1)	Disagree (2)	Agree (3)	Strongly Agree (4)	Total Responses	Mean Rating
1. The course covered all the required skills thoroughly.	22	31	6	0	59	1.73
2. I now know how to apply these skills back on the job.	13	24	10	12	59	2.35
3. These skills will need a regular refresher	2	8	32	17	59	3.08

We calculate the mean rating for each evaluation issue by multiplying the number of responses in each rating column by the associated numerical value, summing these and then dividing that sum by the total number of responses. Thus for the first issue the mean rating is calculated as follows:

$$22x1 \ (22) + 31x2 \ (62) + 6x3 \ (18) + 0x4 \ (0) = 102 \ / \ 59 = \underline{1.7}$$

As any trainer will know, the problem with averages is that they present a picture that may misinform, simply because they can be severely distorted by a few extreme results at either end of the range.

The **mode** is another useful measure of central tendency that is not affected by extreme values to the same extent as the mean. It denotes the most commonly occurring response or value. This can be very useful when we are trying to define the "typical". The mode is identified through simple tallying. The **median** is of limited value in evaluation. It does no more than indicate the mid-point of a data set.

Quantitative data can also be analysed and described in terms of its "spread". This can be done very simply through defining the **range** e.g. "over 5 successive tests with unchanged test items, results have ranged from 34% to 96%." Unfortunately this gives little indication of how all the scores are dispersed along that range line. Calculating the **standard deviation** of a data set gives us the clustering or "shape" of the data around the mean. Standard deviation derives from the concept of the normal curve of distribution and this has already been discussed in section 2.

Standard deviation (SD) is particularly useful in assessing the reliability of data i.e. we could rely on similar performance in the future. A low SD tells us that the data is closely clustered about the mean (see data set A in figure 7.15).

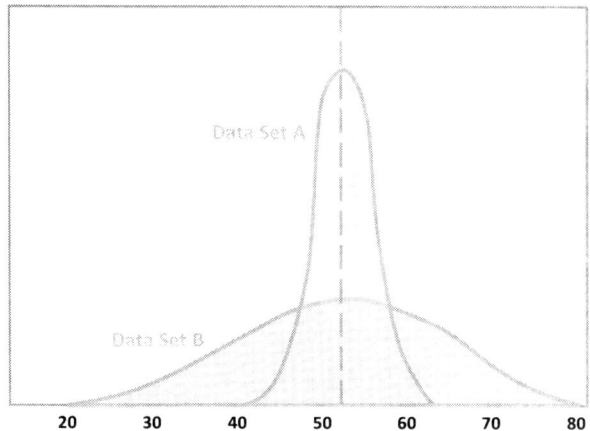

Figure 7.15 – Data showing same mean but different standard variations.

This means that the great majority of people are responding in a broadly similar fashion. Alternatively, data set B has a high SD from the mean and this indicates widely varying performance. There are certainly circumstances where a high SD is acceptable and to be expected e.g. when we are deliberately seeking to "separate the sheep from the goats". The issue here for evaluation is always *"does this data support what we are trying to achieve through the learning programme – or does it indicate something is wrong?"*

Figure 7.16 illustrates standard deviation used to aid the evaluation of the ongoing consistency and reliability of a course assessment. In this scenario a pilot assessment has been administered and has produced the desired distribution in this case i.e. it provided a balance between really testing the most able, while also allowing them to distinguish themselves from the less able. The distribution approximates to a normal curve with an SD of 8.5. This is to be regarded as the "bench mark" for the courses that follow.

	Participant Scores by Course																						SD
Pilot	38	43	45	45	47	47	48	50	51	51	52	53	53	56	57	59	60	60	63	64	68	72	8.514312
Course 1	22	28	31	35	42	44	46	46	49	50	51	51	53	54	54	56	59	67	72	78	80	84	16.38392
Course 2	37	39	42	43	43	47	48	51	51	52	52	53	55	58	59	59	61	62	64	66	72	78	10.54531
Course 3	39	42	43	44	47	47	49	49	50	51	51	52	53	55	56	59	60	61	63	64	68	76	9.126931
Course 4	34	40	42	44	46	48	48	49	50	50	52	52	52	54	54	56	58	59	60	65	69	69	8.823056
Course 5	32	39	39	44	45	45	49	50	50	51	53	53	53	55	55	58	59	62	63	64	65	66	9.134872
Course 6	34	35	38	43	44	46	47	49	49	52	52	54	54	55	57	58	60	60	63	66	67	69	9.921336
Course 7	36	37	39	42	43	43	46	49	50	51	51	51	54	56	58	58	59	61	61	63	67	68	9.433866
Course 8	33	37	37	38	41	41	43	44	48	48	50	53	55	56	56	59	60	60	62	63	67	69	10.59609
Course 9	34	34	38	38	39	40	44	45	45	47	51	51	52	53	56	57	59	59	61	62	62	63	9.639834
Course 10	40	42	43	46	46	47	48	48	50	51	51	53	54	54	56	58	59	59	60	61	67	74	8.306494
Course 11	19	22	25	26	28	32	43	45	45	48	50	50	52	53	56	58	59	60	62	63	66	74	15.59887
Course 12	37	39	40	40	43	44	46	47	50	51	51	53	54	55	58	59	61	61	63	67	68	68	9.777282

Figure 7.16 - Standard deviation used to compare assessment reliability

We can see immediately that the course 1 assessment did not go well. The SD is double that of the pilot. This may have been a delivery issue or even poor assessment by the next course things were back on track. Another aberration occurred with course 11 which would require investigation and explanation.

Graphs provide useful alternatives for displaying data. The table at figure 7.16 can be easily translated into a bar chart (figure 7.17) which, for some readers, offers an easier insight into the issues. There is a vast array of graphing tools available in Microsoft Excel.

There are numerous possibilities for analysing and presenting evaluation data. The priority must always be the most effective way to summarise the data and make its meaning transparent to the reader.

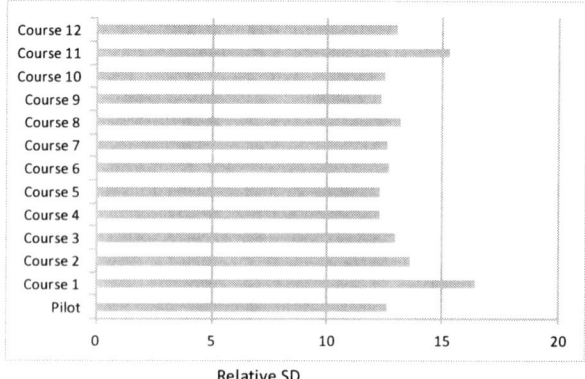

Figure 7.17 – Simple bar chart used to visualise relative standard deviations.

Step 8 – Reporting

There is no standard format for an evaluation report. Ultimately the breadth and depth of detail and the mode of presentation will depend on stakeholder needs. Long duration, costly programmes will no doubt excite senior management attention and will need significant justification. Conversely, proven courses will probably get by "on the nod". Most often, stakeholders are drawn directly to the evaluation conclusions and their validity. If you are making some fairly bold statements be sure that the supporting data is immediately available and not buried deep inside an appendix. Otherwise raw data is best kept separate as an annex to the report, available for those with the time and interest to peruse it.

Above all, beware of misusing data. Conclusions should reflect what the data actually shows, not what you want it to say. We should always be guided by Disraeli's cynicism concerning statistics.

The typical structure of an evaluation report is not dissimilar to other formal reports. The format below would serve most purposes.

- Title page
- Table of contents
- Executive summary
- Programme objectives and purpose
- Evaluation methodology
- Findings and analysis
    - Perceptions of relevance
    - Learner reaction
    - Learner achievement
    - Transfer to the workplace (if covered)
    - Impact on the organisation (if covered)
    - Return on investment (if covered)
    - Sustainability
- Recommendations
- Annexes – data and relevant supporting documentation

In conclusion.

One thing should be abundantly clear from the detail of this section i.e. evaluation becomes increasingly difficult as we climb the Kirkpatrick levels. This is true to such an extent that many organisations simply do not bother with levels 3 and 4, reporting only at levels 2 and 3. The effect of this strategy is to draw attention away from strategic intent i.e. a desired impact on the business. Yes, higher level evaluation will often be exhausting and difficult but whenever possible it should be attempted. If not, businesses run the risk of being drawn into false apprehensions of what is actually occurring. Charles Handy describes this as the Macnamara fallacy:

"We start out with the aim of making the important measurable, and end up making only the measurable important. The first step is to measure what can easily be measured. This is OK as far as it goes. The second step is to disregard that which can't

easily be measured or to give it an arbitrary quantitative value. This is artificial and misleading. The third step is to presume that what can't be measured easily really isn't important. This is blindness. The fourth step is to say that what can't be easily measured really doesn't exist. This is suicide."(8)

8. BUILDING A LEARNING AND DEVELOPMENT FRAMEWORK

As the term "framework" immediately suggests, we are essentially discussing something structural. It also implies support and integration for what might otherwise be freestanding and unrelated elements. A well designed L&D framework should therefore provide structure, support and integration for all the learning activities undertaken by the parent organisation.

Big picture purpose.

A fully conceived learning and development framework should address the broad needs of organisational development (OD); especially succession and planning for key roles. To achieve this the framework should provide an appropriate balance of support for the critical high level OD drivers. These are modeled at figure 8.1.

Figure 8.1 – High level organisational drivers for learning and development.

The model reflects the belief that organisations can only prosper if their people are enabled to develop technical, management and leadership capabilities in line with their responsibilities and accountabilities. Defining the precise balance of these components is the prerogative of senior management at the strategic level and the human resources department at the operational level.

Experience shows, however, that the progressive development of people capability is seldom sustained, or lacks commitment, if it is not linked continually to the company vision and values. These must therefore provide the core of the L&D framework.

Organisational Core – the underpinning foundation of the organisation.
- A clear understanding of what the organisation exists to do – VISION.
- A clear understanding of how the organisation will deliver on its vision – AIMS and STRATEGIES.
- A clear understanding of how we treat each other, our customers, the environment and of how we go about our work – VALUES.
- A clear understanding of the organisation's alignment to formally articulated standards – ETHICS.

Business as usual effectiveness. – the hands-on knowledge and skills required to maintain operations sufficiently to deliver successfully on current contracts. This would include learning in such areas as:
- Operational / production skills
- Health and safety
- Operational risk management.
- Problem solving.
- Reduction of waste.
- Managing rosters and shift patterns.
- Immediate performance management (plant, process and people).
- Local production planning.
- Implementation and management of incremental change.
- Stakeholder liaison and management
- Quality management processes

Strategic Management – generic higher level management skills focused on moving the organisation, and its operations forward (in contrast to maintaining the status quo). This would include learning in such areas as:
- Business risk management.
- Strategic and business planning.
- Human resource planning.
- Significant change management.
- Strategic partnering and stakeholder management.
- Longer term performance enhancement – competitive manufacturing.
- Customer focus.

Leadership – knowledge and skills that allow the individual to motivate and support people toward their best efforts. This will involve learning in such areas as:
- Essential qualities and personal characteristics required for effective leadership.
- How to adjust leadership style and focus according to a given situation
- Self- awareness and self- critique.
- Signposting – providing vision and direction.
- Supporting individuals and teams through significant change.
- Developing people.

Specific purposes. At the operational level a well-designed framework should:

- Provide a comprehensive overview of the learning activities that have been agreed by key stakeholders as relevant and necessary to the success of the company i.e. **what** learning we do. This summary should be the subject of on-going review in order to ensure alignment with business needs.
- Provide clarity regarding the principles that inform learning and development within the organisation i.e. **why** we do the learning that we do.
- Provide an overview of the learning and development management methodology by which learning activities are accommodated, regulated and integrated i.e. **how** learning activity is structured.
- Provide procedural guidance for the delivery of each of the major learning strands and components i.e. how learning opportunities should be awarded, delivered, assessed, evaluated and reported.
- Define clearly the nature of internal alignments to strategic and business planning.
- Define clearly the nature of any external alignments e.g. to qualification frameworks, codes of practice, legislation etc.
- Provide clear policy to clarify the principles on which learning and development opportunities will be identified and allocated.
- Provide clarity around the roles and responsibilities of all stakeholders.
- Provide a rationale for the organisation's adopted strategy for balancing the various L&D input streams i.e. the relative values attached to on-job training, off-job formal training and qualifications, and continuing professional development activities outside the workplace. Figure 8.2 shows these streams balanced in favour of on-job training, but of course this weighting might not be applicable to all organisations.

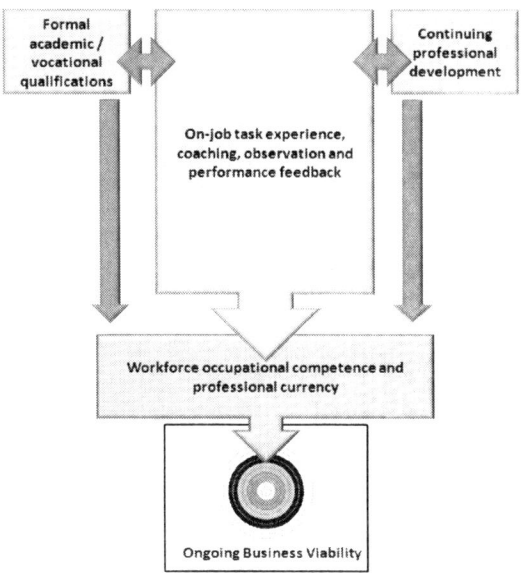

Figure 8.2 – Strategically balanced L&D focus

Adding value.

It is widely accepted that the global economy has changed radically with the new millennium. For most organisations, continued growth can no longer be guaranteed and has largely been replaced by the mantras of business sustainability and survival. Lavish L&D budgets are certainly a thing of the past. The call now is to "leverage every training dollar". In this sense Senge's concept of the learning organisation now has a leaner look about it. Many L&D departments are still driven by the idea of overall knowledge gain without really examining exactly how this gain aligns to business goals. Consequently, much of that gain gathers dust and is ultimately deemed to be irrelevant.

This view was confirmed by Bob Mosher in the American Society for Training and Development's 2009 white paper "Keep Learning Mission Critical". Mosher commented:

"The reason why a lot of learning departments are struggling right now is because they are focused on knowledge gain. That sounds like a noble thing, but the reality is that a lot of organisations are shifting to productivity, not knowledge gain. There is not a middle manager who would argue that knowledge is a bad thing, but we live in a world now where knowledge for knowledge's sake is not helping."

Properly formulated framework policy can ensure that organisational L&D remains "mission critical" by requiring training budget expenditure to be justified by business case alignment to organisational strategy and business goals.

Transparency and due process.

In many organisations, claims on the training budget are often the subject of dispute. Invariably there will be a shortfall and hard decisions have to be made. The "stranding" of learning activity allows the business to clarify its priorities for all concerned. Combining clear priorities with due mandatory process effectively discourages abuse of the system by the more proactive individuals or departments. Without this transparency the training dollar may be mis-directed or used to placate the "squeaky wheels".

Educating the organisation

Only the presence of a freely accessible framework document (e.g. through the company intranet) will create, over time, a satisfactory level of awareness around the strategic intent of learning and development. It will also help to break down the "silo" mentalities that can steadily accrete at department level. Managers and staff need to think holistically, beyond their own immediate needs, if the adopted L&D philosophy is to be understood.

When approached with queries regarding learning and development issues, the astute L&D manager will continually refer individuals to the framework document.

This has the effect of generally educating the organisation to the bigger picture. It also deflects a great deal of unnecessary distraction and repetitive explanation.

WHO SHOULD BUILD A FRAMEWORK?

It is tempting to argue that small to medium enterprises which engage in limited training activity do not need to be encumbered with a framework. At first glance the task can appear to be daunting, but in reality the investment of time, energy and expertise required is proportional to the size of the organisation's learning and development activity. Pausing to consider the specific purposes of an L&D framework described earlier, we can see that it is simply good business practice for any organisation to create an environment of structural clarity, disciplined process and meaningful integration relative to the level of activity.

Consequently it is fair to say that HR should readily accept this responsibility, regardless of organisational size.

HOW DO WE GO ABOUT IT?- TYPICAL DESIGN AND STRUCTURE.

Structural complexity will of course vary according to the scale of learning and development activity supported by the parent organisation, but the following structural components would be present in most framework documents.

- **Purpose statement** – an explanation of the aims and objectives of the framework. Typically this would reflect the general and specific purposes already described.
- **Fundamental principles** – a set of statements outlining the agreed key concepts that underpin the framework e.g.
  - The justification of all learning activity (other than compliance). through TLNA processes linked to strategic and business planning.
  - Adherence to the Systems Approach to Training (SAT).
  - Alignment of internal training to external qualifications wherever possible.
  - The agreed balance of focus.
  - Roles and responsibilities.
- **Identification of supported learning and development** – through stranding analysis.
- **Policy and procedures** related to each identified learning and development strand.
- **Development pathways** – recommended routes and methods of learning and development for individual departments or business units.
- **Guidance on individual development planning** – an explanation of the adopted principles and processes that should guide managers and individual team members when assessing and planning development activities.
- **External linkages** – mapping of learning activity to qualifications, industry or government codes of practice, compliance standards etc.
- **Quality assurance** – a description of the processes to be used to maintain the quality of learning activity. This would include the frequency and

levels of evaluation to be undertaken.

- **Annexes and appendices** – supporting information for any of the above components.

Stranding.

This is critical to the eventual effectiveness of the framework. Thorough analysis here enables all stakeholders to grasp the complexity of what actually goes on across the whole organisation, and the rationale for prioritisation.

The number of identified strands will vary but strand 1 will always be related to compliance i.e. to the training that must be done by law. After that, learning and development will usually be allocated to separate strands according to the degree of relevance to business need and consequent ease of justification. Figure 8.3 shows a typical stranding matrix. In this case six distinct areas of supported activity have been identified. The extremes are strand 1 (compliance) and strand 6 (externally delivered elective personal development with no demonstrable relevance to the business). Given the need now for "mission critical" L&D we might wonder why this latter learning activity would be supported at all, but the fact remains that many companies will "indulge" staff in this way as a means of retaining their skills and enthusiasm. Note that the various strands are supported by relevant technical competency frameworks and a generic leadership framework. Since these are frameworks within a master framework they are often referred to as "nested" frameworks.

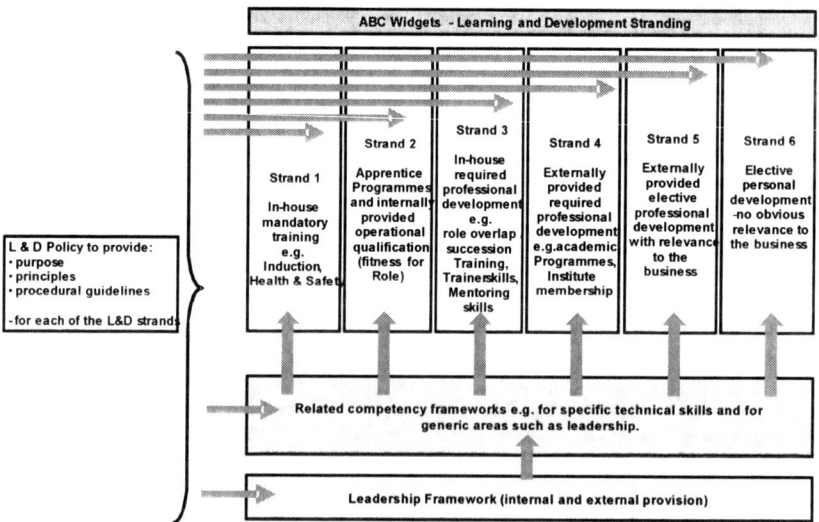

Figure 8.3 – Typical stranding for a Learning and Development Framework

Policy and procedures.

Each strand needs to be supported by clear policy and procedures i.e. an explanation of how learning activity will be administered, and any required processes. The following should be covered for each strand:

- **Learner selection** – guidance on eligibility for individuals and / or departments. This might include thresholds and limitations on numbers.
- **Application procedures.** Non-mandatory, significant learning events would typically require a business case to demonstrate alignment with business needs.
- **Learning design, delivery, assessment and moderation** – a description of how learning will be provided.
- **Evaluation** – a description of the type and level of evaluation tools to be applied.

Development pathways.

Many organisations suffer unduly from the "Cheshire Cat" syndrome i.e. *"If you don't know where you are going, then any road will do!"* Managers and their staff so often dread the annual appraisal because they have no sense of what kinds of development might be sanctioned by the organisation. Individual development planning must be underpinned by legitimate development pathways for each of the major departments or business units. This is particularly important for effective succession planning.

From their very first day in the company, individuals need to be able to see the road ahead, with all the significant milestones they will need to pass as they progress. Producing these will mean close collaboration between HR and a range of managers at various levels in each department. Generally they can only reflect standard achievement programmes and qualifications. One off events would be identified within individual development plans.

Figure 8.4 overleaf shows a typical development pathway graphic, in this case for a Supply Chain operating with 4 separate groups; sourcing, sales and ops planning, customer services, logistics and warehousing. The first consideration is to identify these teams and the operational levels within them, from entry level through to group manager. Managers and HR then work to identify typical learning programmes / qualifications that would signal appropriate professional learning at the various levels. These are then aligned to levels within the national qualifications framework. This analysis was completed for three streams of development i.e. operational knowledge and skills, business effectiveness and improvement, and leadership / management skills.

For the Supply Chain manager and team members this provides a clear view of the kinds of formal learning that aligns to operational levels. However, it is always important to stress that this kind of scheme should never be regarded as prescriptive. Experience and other qualifications should always be investigated by comparison.

Individual development planning.

We have already recognised that organisational learning and development must be "mission critical". The sharp end of this for managers is the task of planning individual development planning. Many managers still labour under the misapprehension that every team member must be constantly engaged in professional development. In practice this is seldom necessary and unlikely to attract sufficient resources.

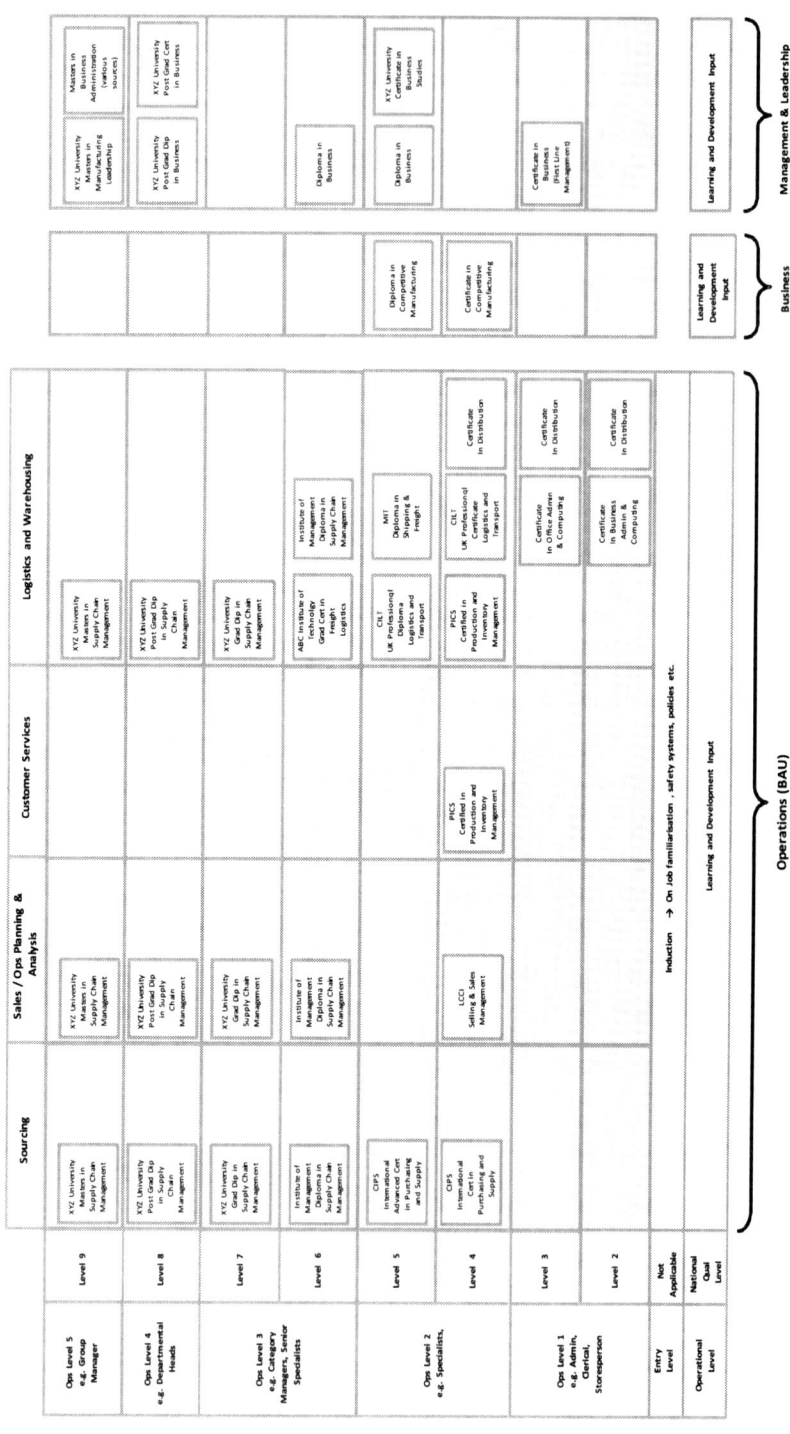

Figure 8.4 – Example of a development pathway for Supply Chain mainstream staff.

We can approach this issue from two angles. Firstly, when considering the individual's need to be engaged in development it is wise to be mindful of the normal curve of distribution. At any given moment, a small minority will be eager to pursue development activity and an equally small minority will be supremely uninspired by the prospect. The great majority sit in the middle and are, for the present, quite content with things as they are. Managers should recognise this and, as far as possible, work with it.

Secondly, we should consider business needs. These will emerge through the setting of key accountabilities or performance objectives. Once again we should never assume that every objective assigned to an individual will require associated development. For the most part, individuals will already possess sufficient knowledge and skills to achieve their objectives. The issue of development should arise only when it is clear that they do not.

Different organisations will inevitably develop their own templates for planning individual development. Generic tools are rarely effective. Most however will address:
- career goals and any associated development
- business goals and required development
- development associated with any adopted competency frameworks
- monitoring procedures

An example of a typical individual development plan template follows. This is a comprehensive template and indicates something of the work that has to be done to perform this function properly. It is also easy to see why managers will struggle if they have too many direct reports. The classic 1 to 9 span of control ratio makes obvious sense.

The 70:20:10 model.

The example IDP template shown above should serve to remind managers that there are alternative development strategies to simply sending people on courses. Not only is this very often wasteful of the training dollar, it is often ineffective. Managers should at least understand the advantages offered by alternative strategies.

The 70:20:10 model for learning and development is based on research that shows that the bulk of organisational learning actually occurs in the workplace while doing the job. Across the whole spectrum of learning this has been shown to equate to approximately 70%. Next in terms of significance is local coaching, mentoring and networking. This equates to around 20%. Only around 10% of organisational learning can be directly credited to formal off-job training course or learning programmes. Of course this model is a normalised representation of the real world and the ratios will vary according to organisation type. At the extremes some organisations will do everything on-job, others will outsource everything. The majority however, will operate some kind of blended approach.

The lesson here for managers is to actually ask the question "is there a better way to support development for the individual than sending them off on a course?" Figure 8.5 illustrates the 70:20:10 concept.

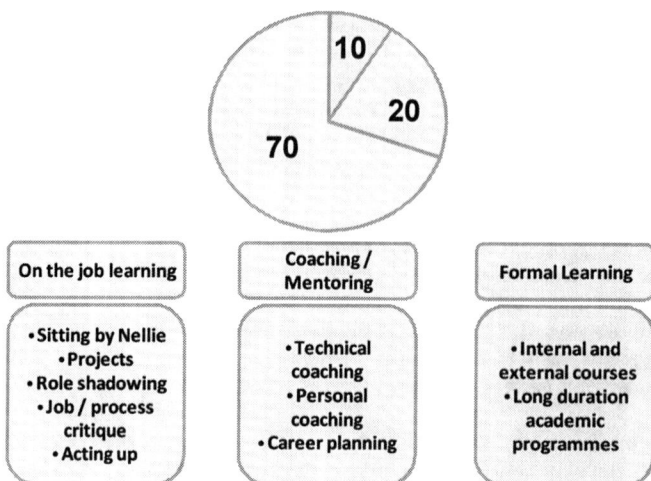

Figure 8.5 – Individual development: the 70/20/10 concept.

The major advantages of on-job learning are:
- It takes place in the real world
- It uses the real thing / addresses real issues
- It occurs at business speed
- It is followed by immediate practice
- Retention of knowledge and skills is known to be far higher

An excellent overview of the 70:20:10 model can be found at:
http://www.deakinprime.com/deakinprime/resources/pdf/whitepapers/DeakinPrim e_70.20.10_WhitePaper.pdf

These obvious advantages may be offset by several, frequently encountered disadvantages e.g.
- Because it is real world training it will be subject to everyday operational imperatives e.g. stoppage for maintenance, operational emergencies etc.
- Staff selected to train or coach may not possess either the aptitude for training or the willingness to become involved.
- Training or coaching may be provided by a range of different staff members e.g. if the trainees is a day worker being taught by staff assigned to shifts. This may well result in inconsistencies of procedure and standards.

External linkages.

A well designed framework recognises that organisational learning does not exist in a vacuum. Inevitably, certain aspects of L&D provision will need to engage the wider world. The most obvious example will be any training delivered that is ultimately governed by legislation e.g. health and safety. The framework document should set out the nature of any linkages between learning activity and external influencing factors.

Individual Development Plan : Period ( ) to ( )

ABC Widgets Ltd

Your name:

Development Area:

Manager / Key contact:

Career goals. *See note 1

Long Term:

Short Term:

Development activities required to assist with reaching career goals. *See note 2

Specific Development Activities	Projected Key Performances	Resources / Access Required	Steps to Knowledge (where necessary)

Formal learning required to assist with reaching career goals. *See note 3

Course / Learning Event	Provider	Projected Cost	Target Completion	Target Completion	Result / Outcome

Development activities required to assist with fulfilling key accountabilities (KA's) or performance objectives. *See Note 4

Activity				

Formal learning required to assist with fulfilling key accountabilities (KA's) or performance objectives. *See Note 4

Course / Learning Event	Provider	Projected Cost	Target Start	Target Comp.	Result / Outcome

Leadership development focus *See Note 5

Measure	Suggested key accountabilities	Suggested Training Required	Leadership Competencies Addressed

Name	Team	Signed (individual)	Date

Name (Team Member)

Comments: This IDP may be subject to change, depending on the viability of your career aspiration, performance of the team member of the business.

Review *See Note 6

Review 1 (Enter date) *See Notes 7

Name of Manager / Position

			Done

Signed (Team Member)

Signed (Manager)

Review 2 (Enter date)

Any recommendations / actions...

Signed (Team Member) .... Date ....

Signed (Manager) .... Date ....

Review 3 (Enter date)

Any recommendations / actions...

Signed (Team Member) .... Date ....

Signed (Manager) .... Date ....

Notes

Career goals – must be matched following discussion between team member and manager. These can be difficult to formulate for individuals who are presently content in their jobs. In these situations it is best to focus on maintenance. Consequently, agreements such as 'To continue in present role, maintaining or enhancing current skills' or 'could do' will probably suffice.

Development activities – it is important to ensure most of the most effective development takes place on the job. Prior consideration should be given to on the job coaching, job exchange, projects, job shadowing, attending etc.

Formal learning – if needed. Next column to be filled out though organisation resources, or externally provided learning interventions may be appropriate. In these cases careful consideration must be given to available budget and the hidden costs of attending some or all kinds of production etc. Share responsibility for running activities; many often spread its more valuable to include and have effective options.

Key accountabilities / performance objectives – these will be established for individuals on an annual basis and may contain objectives linked in order to close skills and performance gaps this year.

Leadership development focus – is a major step toward the organisation. Note that are born or made, if our company's greatest leaders can either be a single manager. I trust particular beliefs but it does make a difference. It is mostly up that we support developing actively, who may be considered should be prepared in order to acquire. Development activity and opportunity.

Review and the time for individual employees in current position. Note the specific actions around the end of the program review or retirement. Should be in a four year review based.

The most common external linkages will be:

National qualifications frameworks (NQF). Most developed countries have set up a standardised system of multi-level qualifications for vocational education and training (VET) and higher academic learning (HE). These ensure transferability and portability within the host nation and internationally through reciprocity agreements. Typical examples are the British NQF administered through the Qualifications and Curriculum Authority (QCA), the South African NQF administered through the South African Qualifications Authority (SAQA), the Australian AQF administered by the Australian Qualifications Framework Council and the New Zealand NQF administered by the New Zealand Qualifications Authority. Typically, national qualification frameworks are organised into eight or ten levels of learning achievement. Some countries are also aligning the final years of mandatory secondary education to these levels.

For many organisations, particularly those in the public sector, alignment to the national qualifications framework is mandated by government. Others are forced to engage if compliance requirements stipulate that individuals must hold an NQF qualification to do their work. Others may choose to link their internal training to national qualifications to ensure a minimum level of best practice and to provide added value for their employee development.

Each NQF is governed by "level descriptors" which provide an indication of typical qualification equivalence and the general competence and behaviours that can be anticipated by individuals achieving specific levels. Each qualification that sits on the NQF is closely moderated to ensure that learning outcomes and associated assessment activity aligns comfortably with these descriptors. The table that follows shows a typical example of level descriptors; in this case those of the European Qualifications Framework for Lifelong Learning.

This is an example of the continuing move to integrate national frameworks into regional frameworks to assist with portability and the free movement of labour. African countries are following a similar strategy.

In addition to identifying individual development requirements, many organisations use the level descriptors of their NQF to help define the required performance levels of their staff and to assist directly with recruitment.

Institutes or Professional Associations. These are organisations (usually non-profit) that exist to further the interests of a particular profession, to regulate the behaviour of members of the profession and to safeguard the interests of the public they serve. Many will develop and promote their own professional qualification systems and these may become the absolute benchmark for the profession e.g. chartered accountants and chartered professional engineers. Membership is often graded from Associate level through to Fellow status. Moving through the grades is usually linked to qualifications obtained, recorded and approved continuing professional development activity (CPD) and contributing activity within the Institute. The larger institutes will also provide access to online learning activities, information archives, networking and discussion forums.

European Qualifications Framework Level Descriptors	KNOWLEDGE In the context of the EQF, knowledge is described as theoretical and or factual.	SKILLS In the context of the EQF, skills are described as cognitive (involving the use of logical, intuitive and creative thinking) and practical (involving manual dexterity and the use of methods, materials, tools and instruments).	COMPETENCE In the context of the EQF, competence is described in terms of responsibility and autonomy.
LEVEL 1 The learning levels relevant to Level 1 are:	Basic general knowledge.	Basic skills required to carry out simple tasks.	Work or study under direct supervision in a structured context.
LEVEL 2 The learning levels relevant to Level 2 are:	Basic factual knowledge of a field of work or study.	Basic cognitive and practical skills required to use relevant information in order to carry out tasks and to solve routine problems using simple rules and tools.	Work or study under supervision with some autonomy.
LEVEL 3 The learning levels relevant to Level 3 are:	Knowledge of facts, principles, processes and general concepts, in a field of work or related study.	A range of cognitive and practical skills required to accomplish tasks and solve problems by selecting and applying basic methods, tools, materials and information.	Take responsibility for completion of tasks in work or study. Adapt own behaviour to circumstances in solving problems.
LEVEL 4 The learning levels relevant to Level 4 are:	Factual and theoretical knowledge in broad contexts within a field of work or study.	A range of cognitive and practical skills required to generate solutions to specific problems in a field of work or study.	Exercise self-management within the guidelines of work or study contexts that are usually predictable, but are subject to change. Supervise the routine work of others, taking some responsibility for the evaluation and improvement of work or study activities.

	KNOWLEDGE	SKILLS	COMPETENCE
LEVEL 5 The learning levels relevant to Level 5 are:	Comprehensive, specialised, factual and theoretical knowledge within a field or work or study and an awareness of the boundaries of that knowledge.	A comprehensive range of cognitive and practical skills required to develop creative solutions to abstract problems.	Exercise management and supervision in contexts of work or study activities where there is unpredictable change. Review and develop performance of self and others.
LEVEL 6 The learning levels relevant to Level 6 are:	Advanced knowledge of a field of work or study, involving a critical understanding of theories and principles.	Advanced skills, demonstrating mastery and innovation, required to solve complex and unpredictable problems in a specialised field of work or study.	Manage complex technical or professional activities or projects, taking responsibility for decision-making in unpredictable work or study contexts. Take responsibility for managing professional development of individuals and groups.
LEVEL 7 The learning levels relevant to Level 7 are:	Highly specialised knowledge, some of which is at the forefront of knowledge in a field of work or study, as the basis for original thinking and / or research. Critical awareness of knowledge issues in a field and at the interface between different fields.	Specialised problem-solving skills required in research and / or innovation in order to develop new knowledge and procedures and to integrate knowledge from different fields.	Manage and transform work or study contexts that are complex, unpredictable and require new strategic approaches. Take responsibility for contributing to professional knowledge and practice and / or for reviewing the strategic performance of teams.
LEVEL 8 The learning levels relevant to Level 8 are:	Knowledge at the most advanced frontier of a field of work or study and at the interface between fields.	The most advanced and specialised skills and techniques, including synthesis and evaluation, required to solve critical problems in research and / or innovation and to extend and redefine existing knowledge or professional practice.	Demonstrate substantial authority, innovation, autonomy, scholarly and professional integrity and sustained commitment to the development of new ideas or processes at the forefront of work or study contexts including research.

Equivalence. Learning and development is characterised by constant change. Consequently, qualifications undergo change, if only in name. This in turn creates potential confusion in terms of how the old or "legacy" qualifications relate to the new. Frameworks should establish the accepted level of equivalence. Similar issues will arise with overseas qualifications e.g. when companies recruit offshore.

Legislative compliance. The framework document should clarify precisely the legislative requirements that any internal and externally provided training may need to meet. All too often precious training resources are wasted because providers are not appropriately briefed on the standards required.

Codes of Practice. Many professions regulate themselves through voluntary best practice agreements. While these are not mandatory, they exercise a disciplinary effect on organisations who wish to be associated with best practice. The framework should indicate which of these have been selected for voluntary compliance.

Preferred providers. A comprehensively designed external framework will often include a list of preferred providers for each training activity. Alternatively, the preferred provider may be identified within specific policy statements attached to the stranding write-up.

Why align?
Careful consideration should be given to organisational alignment to external frameworks when this is not mandatory e.g. to satisfy compliance. The key questions to be answered are:
- What exactly are our needs?
- Will this framework meet those needs?
- What are the full implications of alignment?

This is particularly true in regard to national qualification frameworks. These tend to be bureaucratic, cumbersome and slow-moving. They offer many advantages, but, as experience has shown, they can have detrimental effects if their requirements are not fully understood. It is essential to understand that these frameworks are built around sets of assessment standards which define a minimum acceptable level of competence. As such, they are criterion-referenced and do not identify the relative levels of competence between individuals.

Neither do they provide training programmes or specify curricula. All of this is left to the organisation. This has led, on many occasions, to training being provided simply to meet the assessment standards rather than what the organisation actually needed. Thus we see "the assessment tail wagging the training dog". Organisations must always give priority to their precise needs, design their learning systems to meet those needs and only then look to alignment. This may result in additional assessment standards being written, but this can usually be undertaken by the appropriate Standard Setting Body.

Figure 8.6 overleaf illustrates the thinking process that needs to be worked through. It also demonstrates that a training system unique to the organisation is always an option.

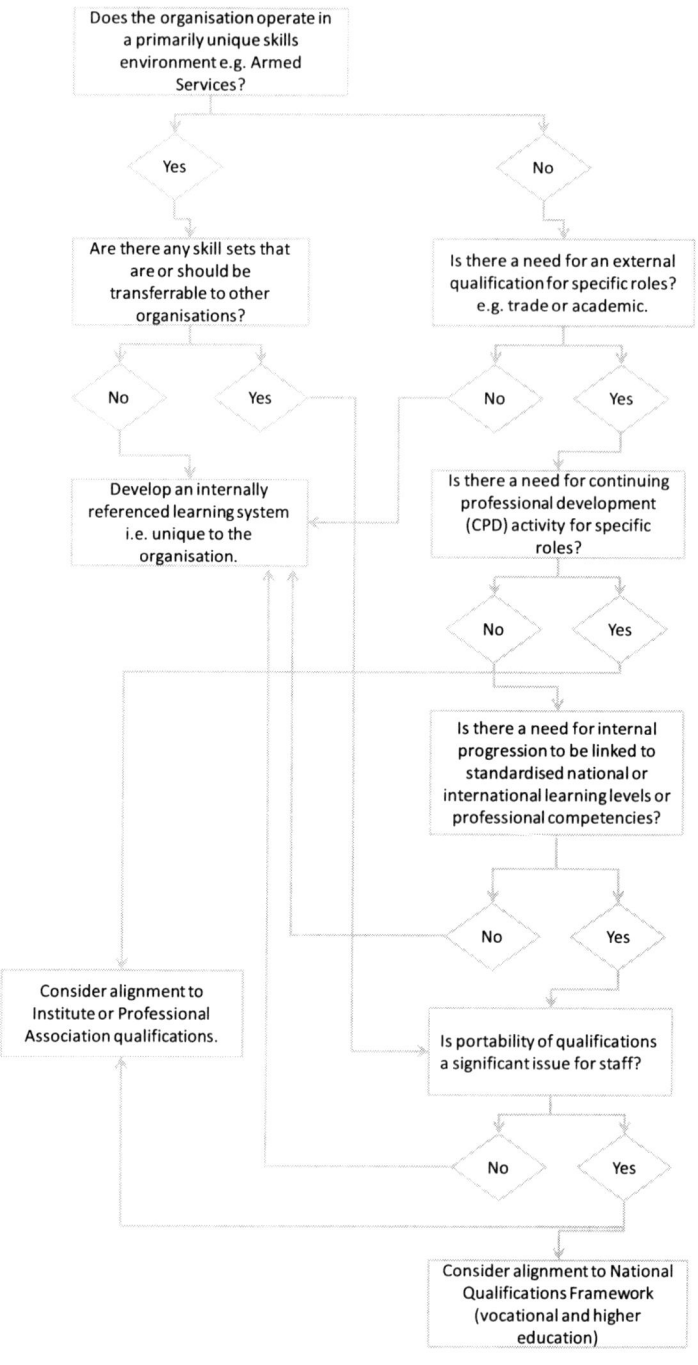

Figure 8.6 – Considerations for external alignment of organisational learning

Quality assurance.

The means by which organisational learning activity will be quality assured, validated and evaluated is a critical aspect of framework design. At framework level there is no need to identify individual programme evaluation tools. The framework document should focus on policy and process. This will entail identifying the "planned and systematic activities implemented in a quality system so that quality requirements for a product or service will be fulfilled." (ASQ definition). Figure 8.7 shows a typical QA cycle.

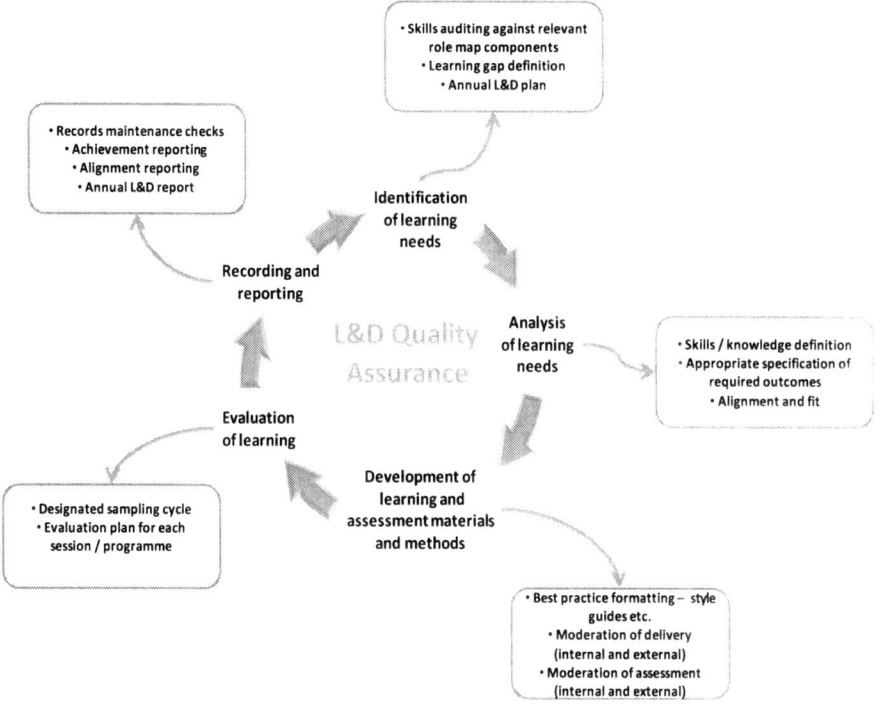

Figure 8.7 – Typical L&D quality assurance cycle.

Clearly, each of the processes indicated here will link to specific tools and checklists. The full QA cycle would only need to be implemented for new programmes. Once a programme becomes established, a more selective cycle can be applied.

9. ENSURING ORGANISATIONAL CAPABILITY AND CAPACITY

We are often told that productivity in the workplace is related directly to the "3 C's" i.e. to capability, capacity and contribution. While this formula may slip alliteratively off the tongue it is essential to understand the distinctions between the terms.

Capability: built into the word itself is the term "ability" and this is the core of capability at both organisational and individual levels.

At the organisational level capability refers to a sum total of human resource, equipment, physical resources, intellectual resources, financial resource etc. required to achieve business objectives. Organisational capability is a complex equation but can be summarised as "having the right stuff" to the do the job. At the level of the individual employee, capability is fundamentally a matter of possessing the appropriate skills and experience, but it is still a matter of the "right stuff".

Capacity: significantly different to capability. Organisations may well possess all the resources necessary to achieve a particular objective but, for the time being, these resources are fully dedicated to other projects. The company possesses the capability but not the capacity. It is a matter of sufficiency. Thus we can say that capacity is a matter of "having *enough* of the right stuff".

Contribution.
Capability is itself further conditioned by the human factor. Organisations may possess all the required resource to dedicate to a specific project but, for whatever reason, either teams or individuals are not disposed to contribute to their full potential. Capability is therefore reduced and eventual productivity negatively impacted. This concept has given rise to the 3C's formula.

Workforce productivity = The 3 C's – Capability x capacity x contribution

The degree to which individuals and teams are enabled to perform and exercise their capability to the fullest extent is largely a matter of leadership and effective management techniques. Contribution therefore sits outside the scope of this book. Nevertheless, in the contemporary workplace it is the HR department that is most often charged with identifying leadership development requirements and coaching managers in performance management skills and supporting systems. Consequently HR must accept a high level of responsibility for tracking capability and capacity building through to maximized contribution.

The aging workforce.
Both capability and capacity are threatened (for the forseeable future) by the demographic trends evident in the developed world. In the coming decades, HR

professionals must face up to the potentially crippling problems caused by the 'baby boomer' generation disappearing from the workforce. Often referred to as the 'silver tsunami', the post second world war generation are retiring in their millions. Their successors, generation X are considerably fewer in numbers. Consequently recruiters are effectively fishing in a smaller pond. This difficulty is further compounded by the fact that there are now a lot more fishermen out there. The newly emerging super-economies e.g. China, Korea, India, Brazil, Indonesia etc. have entered the bidding war with a vengeance. They can, and they will pay whatever it takes to secure the best talent.

Figure 9.1 below illustrates the quantum issues associated with the baby boomer exit and the consequent natural succession issues. While this reflects the situation in the United States, it is more or less replicated across the developed world and is actually more extreme in some European countries and Japan. Population picks up again with the millenials, but the business world, and society in general, must contend first with the very serious shortfall accompanying the progress of the 'Xers'.

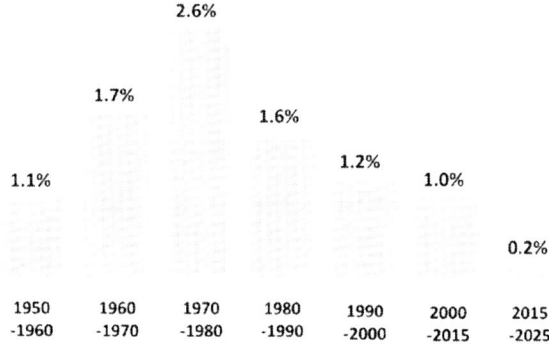

Figure 2.12 - Annual rates of labour force growth in developed economies. (Source US Bureau of Labour Statistics).

For the foreseeable future recruiting skilled people will at times be a cut-throat affair, but not just because of the rarity factor. The very nature of what we call 'skilled' is changing before our eyes. Automation and information technology are fast decreasing the ranks of the 'blue collar worker'. The 21st century skills portfolios look radically different and are effectively disenfranchising a large proportion of the smaller generation available to replace the baby-boomers. The situation may be mitigated to some degree by bringing the larger millennial generation through more quickly to more senior positions but this will obviously generate issues around required levels of experience and maturity.

Ensuring adequate succession into skilled roles will therefore require constant aggressive focus on business needs and the ability of the market to provide. More significant perhaps is the very obvious need for organisations to focus on a 'grow your own' philosophy'.

ENVIRONMENTAL SCANNING.

HR departments must gear up to maintain a 'listening watch' on their workforce profile relative to business needs. Consequently the discipline of environmental scanning must become a critical routine that drives normal HR planning processes. Figure 9.2 below shows typical high level analytical process tools that will define the nature of the landscape in which the business must operate, including broad issues relating to workforce profile. Variations of PEST (political, economic, social, technological) analysis are used to open up the macro environment. Organisations will adapt the tool to meet their specific needs e.g. in the case below STEEPLE is being used (social, technological, economic, environmental, political / people, legal and ethical).

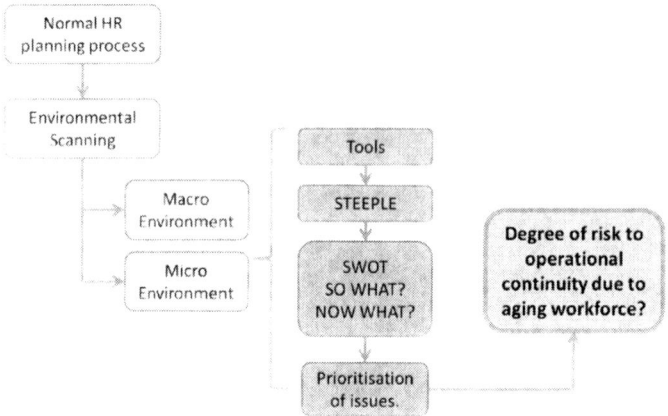

Figure 9.2 – Workforce planning high level processes

This should be followed by SWOT analysis to narrow down the focus, particularly in terms of the organisation's capability to deal with threats and opportunities alike. Effective SWOT analysis should be backed up by SO WHAT? and NOW WHAT? thinking to drive action planning.

WORKFORCE PROFILING BY EXTRAPOLATION – DEFINING THE SIZE OF THE PROBLEM.

Profiling the workforce must go beyond a snapshot of the present. Proactive response to the aging workforce and skills shortages can only be achieved through a calculated vision of what the future looks like. How should we go about this?

Of course we can never predict precisely. The question for HR centres around an acceptable degree of reliability. This will vary according to the type of organisation. Let us take, as an example, a manufacturing company whose core business is stable with only incremental changes to product lines and customer base. In this situation we should be able to assume that the informing workforce metrics from the last decade will look (overall) very like those for the next. We should be able to extrapolate forward and build a reasonable accurate set of expectations.

The historical data we need to collect (in this case from the last ten years) should yield answers to the following key questions:
- What is the average age of retirement? (assuming there is no national mandatory age)
- What is the number of medical retirements occurring in each of the 10

previous years? These can then be repeated in the extrapolation exercise.

- What is the number of deaths in service occurring in each of the 10 previous years? Again, these can be repeated in the extrapolation.
- What is the number of dismissals occurring in each of the previous 10 years? Again repeated.
- What is the number of resignations (people moving on) in each of the previous 10 years? Again repeated.

These data can then be built into a spread-sheet which will reveal the size of the problem we must prepare to deal with. Fig 9.3 below illustrates this process.

Total Workforce =	1582																				
Assumed retirement age	67																				
		2014		2015		2016		2017		2018		2019		2020		2021		2022		2023		Acc % of
		No.	%	No	%	No.	%	No.	%	No.	%	No.	%	No.	%	No.	%	No.	%	No.	%	workforce.
Number reaching retirement age.		21	1.33	30	1.9	47	2.97	48	3.03	58	3.67	33	2.09	43	2.72	32	2.02	35	2.21	49	0	21.93426043
Annual resignation (repeat 2004-20014)		15	0.95	12	0.76	17	1.07	16	1.01	9	0.57	22	1.39	11	0.7	12	0.76	32	2.02	15	0.95	9.288758968
Annual dismissal (repeat 2004-2014)		2	0.13	1	0.06	3	0.19	2	0.13	0	0	1	0.06	4	0.25	2	0.13	1	0.06	0	0	1.011378003
Annual death in service (repeat 2004-2014)		0	0	2	0.13	3	0.19	1	0.06	0	0	0	0	1	0.06	4	0.25	1	0.06	0	0	0.758533502
Annual medical retirement (repeat 2001-2014)		3	0.19	2	0.13	4	0.25	0	0	4	0.25	2	0.13	0	0	8	0.51	5	0.32	4	0.25	2.022756005
																				Total % workforce turnover		35.01568691

Figure 9.3 – Extrapolation of historical data to gauge staff turnover

Here we can see that the assumed retirement age (based on the previous 10 years) is 67. Combined with the other key data this organisation is facing a 35% turnover of staff over the next 10 years. This would probably be regarded as relatively low, due mostly to the low rate of resignations. However, this should be regarded as '2 dimensional' data, in that it reveals a basic quantitative perspective, but little or nothing about the relative criticality of roles that are losing staff, the so-called 'hot spots'. This requires a more in-depth analysis at the level of individual employees. This can be achieved by a simple survey tool, best deployed at line manager / supervisor level and then collated by HR. An example of such a tool is shown below at Figure 9.4

Role - Example										
					Risk Rating					
Risk Factors	1	2	3	4	5	6	7	8	9	10
Difficulty in finding suitable replacement.	0	0	0	0	5	0	0	0	0	0
Length of induction and training.	0	0	0	0	0	0	7	0	0	0
Time to come up to full speed.	0	0	0	0	0	0	0	8	0	0
Complexity / difficulty of training.	0	0	0	0	0	0	7	0	0	0
Availability of suitable training / trainers.	0	0	0	0	0	0	0	0	9	0
Current age of incumbent.	0	2	0	0	0	0	0	0	0	0
Health status of incumbent.	0	0	0	4	0	0	0	0	0	0
Likelihood of iminent retirement / resignation of incumbent.	0	2	0	0	0	0	0	0	0	0
Column Totals	0	4	0	4	5	0	14	8	0	0
Final total / 80	35									
% exposure	44									

Interpretation of scores	Score	Risk Rating
	80+	Extreme
	70-79	High
	60-69	
	50-59	Moderate
	40-49	
	30-39	Low
	20-29	
	0-19	Insignificant

Figure 9.4 –Example of roles at risk 'first rating'.

The risk factors shown here are typical for this kind of exercise but others may be applicable. Some information may be imponderable e.g. health status. Individuals may be apparently in perfect health at the time of survey only to suffer health issues in the near future. Similarly, individuals may choose not to reveal some information (such as retirement intentions) in which case neutral scores should be returned. The risk factors are rated 1-10 and the total aligned to risk rating bands. This produces a 'first rating' as a percentage for a particualr individual in a specific role. If there are several incumbents the first rating for the group can be aggregated to provide an overall risk rating.

We can see from the above example that this role has associated high risk factors related to the length and complexity of required training and the difficulty in finding a suitable trainer. Fortunately, the role incumbent is relatively young, seemingly in good health and has no apparent plans to retire or move on. Consequently the risk associated with this role is no more than moderate. Other criteria could be added into the mix depending on organisational context.

Ratings of 'high' or 'extreme' mean that urgent action is required to ensure that succession planning and appropriate training or development is put in place to mitigate the risk to a satisfactory level.

The term 'first rating' is used because, subsequently, we must look at additional factors such as the required level of contingency. What level of 'back up' do we need to ensure optimal levels of cover. Typically, for example, shift-based production line roles would need two others to be fully trained, one to provide initially for holiday of sickness cover and one other to be available in the event of first line cover being unavailable. This contingency factor effectively acts as a 'multiplier' of the risk.

WHOLE OF WORKFORCE PROFILING FOR ROLES AT RISK (HEAT MAPPING).

Every role in the organisation is important – if not why would they exist? Some roles however are more critical, in as much as they are highly specilised and potentially difficult to replace. Succession into these roles needs to be managed proactively in order to identify those that are "at risk" e.g. through imminent retirement or possibly health issues. The process of building a roles at risk profile at business unit or organisational level is commonly referred to as 'heat mapping' and is designed to identify all the 'hot spots' that need urgent attention. Each role in each work place area needs to be surveyed to gather data which is then assembled into a consolidated map. Fig 9.5 overleaf shows a typical example.

Referring to this example, if we look at the Run Time Operator role we can see that we have six trained in the role when we need ten to cover risk adequately. This gives us a risk multiplier of 1.66. The first rating was475 and so we end up with a final rating of 111.66 which is graded extreme. The multiplier in each case is calculated by dividing the optimum number trained by the actual number trained. We use this figure thyen to multiply the first rating to achieve the final rating. Colour coding is then used to provide a visual summary. The result of this exercise is a risk profile of the workforce giving us very clear priorities for training delivery and the key data we need to feed into a strategic training plan.

Work Area	Operator Role	Extreme	High	Moderate	Low	Insignificant	Current Establishment	Optimum Skilled	Current Skilled	First Rating	Risk Multiplier	Final Rating
Power Generation	Senior Contro Room Operator						5	8	5	39	1.6	62.4
	No 2 Control Room Opperator						6	9	6	39	1.5	58.5
Compound Prep	Senior Mixer / Tester						5	8	10	31	0.8	24.8
	No. 2 Mixer / Tester						5	10	8	38	1.25	47.5
	Zone Supervisor						5	10	5	47	2	94
	Run Time Operator						5	10	6	67	1.666667	111.6667
	Spare Operator						1	2	1	59	2	118
	Bulk materials Handler						5	8	5	49	1.6	78.4
	Goods Inwards Receiver						5	10	5	51	2	102
	Training Spare						1	2	1	28	2	56
Heating / Front End	Zone Supervisor						4	8	20	39	0.4	15.6
	Hot Delivery Operator						4	8	20	39	0.4	15.6
	First Belt Operator						8	16	20	47	0.8	37.6
	Roller Setter						8	16	16	42	1	42
	Spare Operator						1	2	1	38	2	76
	Sampler / Tester						1	2	1	35	2	70
Hardening	Zone Supervisor						5	10	10	30	1	30
	Run Time Operator						5	10	13	37	0.769231	28.46154
	Water Cooling Operator						5	10	10	46	1	46
	Sampler / Tester						5	10	6	65	1.666667	108.3333
	Spare Operator						1	2	5	61	0.4	24.4
	Training Spare						1	2	1	44	2	88
Finishing / Warehouse	Zone Supervisor						5	7	6	30	1.166667	35
	Knife Setter						5	8	6	30	1.333333	40
	Packing Operator						5	7	10	25	0.7	17.5
	Stacker Driver						5	10	20	29	0.5	14.5
	Spare Operator						2	2	1	39	2	78
	Customer ID Operator						5	7	5	43	1.4	60.2
	Goods Outward / Stock Management						5	7	8	44	0.875	38.5
											Total risk rating	1618.962
											Average risk rating	59.96154

Figure 9.5 Typical organisational / business unit 'Heat Map' – roles at risk analysis

The heat mapping and extrapolation exercises are essentially concerned with maintaining the status quo i.e. ensuring operational capability on the basis of current concerns. The strategic business plan may reveal additional or new skills to be developed or acquired and this will require long-sighted initiatives aimed at identifying the best talent. With mounting skills shortages these initiatives will most likely be increasingly internally focussed.

An internal focus will require individual managers to think multi-dimensionally, considering personality profiles, skills profiles, performance histories and personal development ambitions and how these might line up against the departmental role portfolio. This is where role maps and comprehensive competency frameworks can be really helpful. They provide the necessary clarity of expectation against which individuals can be assessed for other roles, especially if those roles differ in kind as well as degree.

This 3 dimensional understanding of teams can be greatly assisted by simple tools such as '9 box' analysis. This technique utilises a matrix which maps individuals in terms of performance to date against likely future potential. This process locates individual team members on a 'character' landscape which can then underpin decisions on the level and kind of development activity that should be undertaken. Figure 9.6 illustrates the tool.

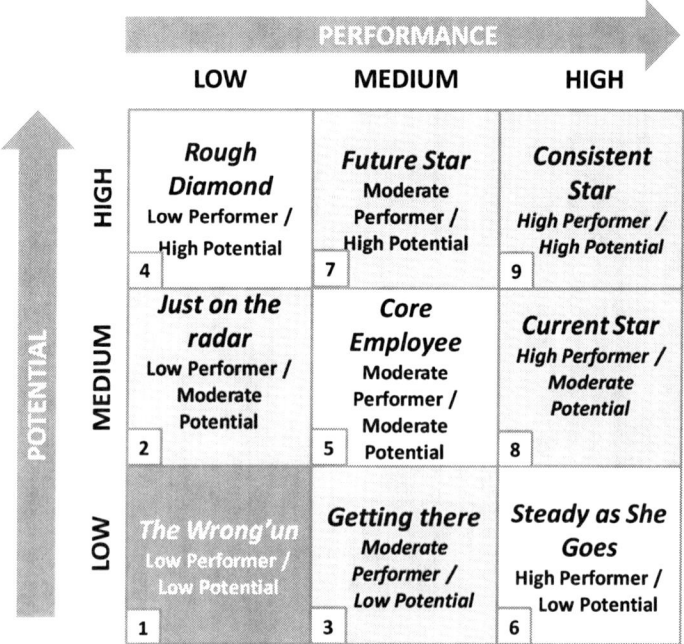

Figure 9.6 – Nine Box Tool for Succession Planning

Using the tool is apparently straightforward. Managers simply review the performance of their team members, consider their potential and then place in one of the nine boxes. In practice however these deliberations are quite complex, especially in terms of assessing potential. The subtext here is always the question "potential for what?" Again, this is where a comprehensive role map or competency framework will clarify the situation greatly.

The 9 box analysis invariably starts life as a snapshot of the current situation but in the hands of a proactive manager becomes a tracking tool and a means of prioritising development needs. It is also of huge assistance to HR / L&D. So often HR is approached for development assistance by managers who have done little or no analysis. They can then be coached to do the groundwork using the 9 box tool and to return with much more targeted and appropriate requests.

The table below lists the general advice HR/L&D should be offering once the 9 box analysis is done.

Employee Category	Development Strategy
The Wrong'un.	**Low performer, low potential.** If this history is consistently observed, it's time to admit that we have the wrong person for the job. Poor recruiting is most likely the issue here. Performance manage this person out of the team. Development is likely to be entirely wasted.
Just on the radar.	**Low performer, moderate potential.** This person can do rather better but isn't. Investigate the cause. If necessary consider some degree of coaching toward the modest improvement expected or performance manage to expectations. Don't set the bar too high.
Getting there.	**Moderate performer, low potential.** This person is probably reaching their ceiling in the current position with no apparent ability to progress further. Consider peer coaching but again don't set the bar too high.
Rough Diamond	**Low performer, high potential.** This person can be very frustrating. They have considerable ability but for whatever reason are not living up to their potential. This is a significant waste of talent and needs investigation to unearth the issues. Causes can vary from boredom to disenchantment or relationship issues. If stagnation is the cause, performance management should focus on potential career development or role exchange accompanied by appropriate development activity.
Core Employee	**Moderate performer, moderate potenntial.** The 'middle of the roader' probably fairly happy with their lot? Development should be targeted on a limited raising of the game in the same role. Performance targets should require some stretch but not be unrealistic given limited potential.
Steady as she goes.	**High performer, low potential.** You are getting the best out of somebody who has little potential to go further (at least in the current role). No significant development input required. Maintenance objectives only.
Future Star	**Moderate performer, high potential.** This person has more to give and is clearly willing to give it. Consequently, development should be geared to an

	exploration of what standard could be attained and aligning appropriate resources.
Current star	**High performer, moderate potential.** Clearly highly motivated with some room for further development into new areas or additional performance. Important not to stretch him too far, so as to avoid discouragement and a fall-off in performance.
Consistent Star	**High performer, high potential.** This person is at his peak and the question is "how long can that be sustained?" Much depends on personal circumstances and the individual's personal and professional standards. While there is clear potential for higher level performance (probably in a new role) would that be a matter of a higher level in a similar field or a different discipline e.g. moving from operations into a leadership function? Be aware that if neglected this person could be a flight risk.

Linking specific role risks to overall exposure.

In order for learning and development to support the organisation strategically, the relative risks posed by the loss of personnel need to be accumulated and analysed to provide a general picture of risk exposure.

Figure 9.7 shows a matrix approach to capturing the nature of this general exposure.

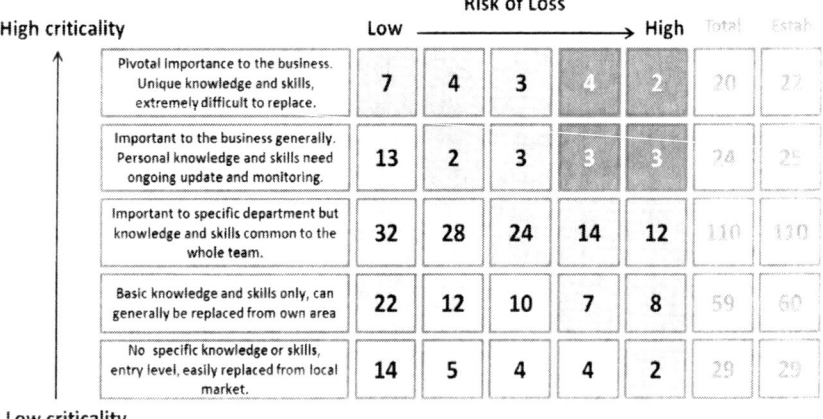

Figure 9.7 - Role succession – general exposure analysis

After individual roles have been risk assessed, totals can be plotted on to the grid according to their level of criticality to the business and the level of risk they currently pose. The example above captures exposure for a company with a current headcount of 242 against an establishment of 246. Running with a staff shortfall of 4 may not be significant, but 3 of those are critical roles and judged to be at high risk of disappearing. This should be regarded as an unacceptable situation and management, together with HR should working urgently to address it.

Bench strength.

The potential loss of critical personnel can be mitigated by shoulder tapping the heir apparent (if one is available). A far better approach is to go for strength in depth. The sporting analogy of players on the bench, ready and willing to take the field, is useful here. The stronger your bench the more likely you are to win the game.

Bench strength will show itself at the level of individual role analysis in response to the question "how difficult is it to find a suitable replacement?" Improving bench strength is largely a matter of:

* Multi-skilling across a department.
* Up-skilling individuals to ensure that there is sufficient acting up / step up capacity.

A useful tool for managing bench strength is the team skills matrix. This can be set up and maintained as a "behind the scenes" device used exclusively by managers or training staff, or it can be used openly to encourage team development. Actual use will depend on team maturity and the specific operational context. Figure 9.8 shows a typical skills matrix, in this case for a team of airport security officers against the skills involved for aircraft guard duties.

Team Skills Matrix - Ref (Aircraft Guard Duties)

Number of skills =   8 (enter number)

Staff Member	Skill 1 HC	Skill 2 M	Skill 3 M	Skill 4 M	Skill 5 HC	Skill 6 M	Skill 7 M	Skill 8 HC	Total	Current Aggregate
Officer A	5	5	5	5	5	5	5	5	40	5
Officer B	4	4	4	3	4	4	4	4	31	3.875
Officer C	5	4	4	4	4	4	5	4	34	4.25
Officer D	4	5	4	4	4	4	4	4	33	4.125
Officer E	3	3	3	3	3	3	3	3	24	3
Officer F	2	2	2	1	3	2	2	2	16	2
Officer G	5	5	4	4	5	3	4	5	35	4.375
Officer H	1	2	2	2	1	3	2	2	15	1.875
	29	30	28	26	29	28	29	29		

(Current Skill Specific Ratings — Performance Category i.e. Mastery, High Conformity, Low Conformity)

Rating Descriptors	
5=	Expert standard. Can be used to train others in this skill.
4=	Highly competent. Can be left to supervise others in this area.
3=	Competent - at the minimum required standard.
2=	Improving - but remains under the minmum standard.
1=	Very weak. Needs constant supervision.
0=	Has no discernible ability in this area whatsoever.

Skill Descriptions	
1=	Radio Communication with Sergeant and Operations
2=	Notify Operations when aircraft on blocks and push back.
3=	Check IDs of people entering the cabin
4=	Wand people every time they enter the cabin to procedure standard.
5=	Notify the aircraft search team of the progress of the cleaners on board
6=	Wand and check the cleaners and caterers prior to them entering the aircraft.
7=	Notify engineers if any problems found during aircraft screening .
8=	Public relations with airline staff and passengers.

Figure 9.8 – Simple team skills matrix

Role mapping has revealed the activities / skills associated with the aircraft guarding task and these have been categorised according to performance criticality e.g.

- M = mastery
- HC – high conformity
- LC = low conformity (not applicable here).

Each Security Officer has been observed and rated for current skill level on a 0-5 scale with the required minimum organizational standard set at level 3. Operating below this level equates to *under* performance, but not necessarily to *poor* performance. We can immediately see that Officer A has achieved all round expertise, closely followed by Officers B,C and G. These Officers might be considered for training others or acting as on-shift "buddies" to those less skilled. Officer E has achieved minimum competence across the board but Officers F and H are seriously under-performing, thus putting operations at risk. There may be good reasons for such under-performance e.g. they may be new starters. Nevertheless the matrix indicates a situation that has to be rigorously managed.

Some teams (and perhaps some managers) will be uncomfortable with a numerical rating tool. In these situations a "friendlier" approach can be adopted through the box completion method. Figure 9.9 gives a typical example.

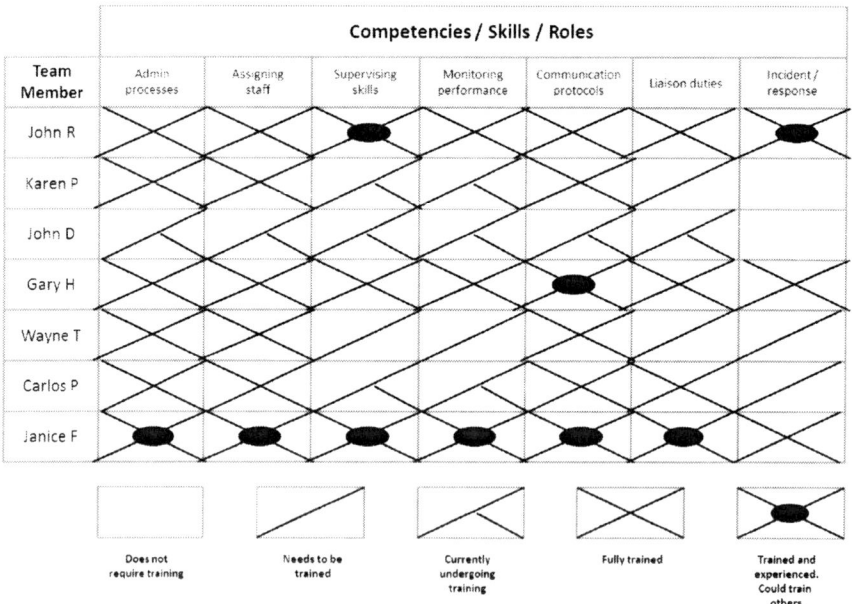

Figure 9.9 – Box completion training matrix

This method generates the same overall appreciation of team skills levels and areas of exposure as that shown in figure 9.8. However, it is fair to say that individuals tend to prefer it to being "scored". It is largely a matter of team sensitivity.

We can see immediately that there is an unacceptable level of exposure in the area of incident response with more than 50% of the team not up to speed in what will be a critical area. We should also be concerned that only Janice can be relied upon as an effective trainer across the board, but even she is doubtful for training in incident response.

Assisting supervisors and managers to build and maintain these matrices should be a priority for the L&D professional. Perhaps more than any other practical tool they facilitate a strategic approach to bench strength and the reduction of risks to operational continuity.

Selecting for progression or 'acting up'.

Figure 9.9 tells us that Karen and John will not be trained in incident response. The reason for this may well be that they are not sufficiently effective under extreme pressure. They may be perfectly competent, even perhaps exemplary under routine conditions but become overly stressed when presented with crisis situations.

This highlights the issues managers face when trying to identify those who are actually capable of progressing to higher level or critical performance. Too often we simply assume that because somebody excels at their current level they will inevitably perform well at the next. The question that should always be asked before individuals are identified for progression is "Does the next level, or the additional role differ in kind rather than just degree?" If the progression is simply a scaling up of existing skills, the individual stands a very good chance of succeeding, with appropriate support of course. If however, the new role is a significant shift away from existing skillsets, more searching analysis must be done to determine the individual's potential. The classical example of failing to ask this question is seen when operator / production staff are promoted to supervisor level. Being an outstanding operator does not necessarily equip the individual to be a front line manager.

Laurence Peter researched the tendency to promote purely on the basis of current rather than potential achievement during the late 1960's. (1) The main tenets of his work were subsequently enshrined in "the Peter principle" which states, simplistically, that in any organization where promotion is based on performance at the current level, individuals are likely to be appointed eventually to a level beyond their actual competence. The long term effect of this, if unchecked, may well be accumulating organisational incompetence. HR undoubtedly has a part to play in improving management ability to resist this pernicious tendency, through increased awareness of the issues and the use of appropriate tools and processes.

RESISTING THE PETER PRINCIPLE.

Management awareness.

The key message for management here is that a clear distinction must be made between current performance in the current role and potential to perform well in a different role. These things should never be regarded as synonymous. Assessment of current performance should not be a problem if the organisation makes full use of appropriately focused performance management systems. Any evidence of the individual's ability to respond positively to development opportunities will also be useful.

Assessing potential is more complex but in essence is a simple enough task i.e. to match the requirements of the new role to the individual's overt and latent capability. The value of in-depth role mapping becomes obvious here but we need to remember that role maps describe functionality, the range of tasks associated with the role. They generally do not describe required behaviours, the manner in which the individual engages with colleagues and stakeholders to achieve objectives. These requirements are often presented as values statements, codes of practice, leadership competency frameworks etc. When taken as a whole these various documents can define the "gap" which must be crossed for effective transition into the new role. With this in mind managers can focus enquiry on the 3A's – does the individual possess:

- The required **ABILITY** – the knowledge and skills. Alternatively, are we confident that he / she will respond well to any required training.
- The required **APTITUDE(S)** – the innate predisposition toward the essential nature of the new role. For example a leadership role requires a fundamental and abiding interest in people and (ideally) a gregarious nature. Highly introverted, solipsistic individuals are unlikely to succeed as leaders in the long term. Similarly, individuals with no aptitude for numbers will not do well in a new role that specifies significant responsibility for the department budget.Aptitudes will certainly show reveal themselves in current performance but if the new role is significantly different aptitude assessments through psychometric testing may be needed.
- The required **ATTITUDE** – a measure of the individual's historical and current willingness to contribute constructively and their enthusiasm for the new role.

MAXIMISING CAPABILITY ACROSS TEAMS.

When dealing with individuals, ensuring that performance is maintained at the desired level is fundamentally a matter of good leadership and sound performance management techniques. At team level the picture is rather more complex because managers must develop an integrated strategy for maximising the sum total of individual competence and contribution. This cannot be an ad hoc process. It must be carefully thought through.

Job / role rotation.
All organisations need specialists. These are people whose skills are relatively rare and highly developed. Particular attention must be paid to succession or adequate cover if their roles impact critically on operations. Generally this will be a matter of selecting the most appropriate employee to be taken through a developmental programme aimed at embedding the core knowledge and skills.

With non-specialist roles managers can choose to adopt a systematic strategy leading toward a minimum level of multi-skilling among team members. The system must be under-pinned by a realistic assessment of the risk to operational continuity and what is needed to mitigate that risk to an acceptable level. In an ideal world every team member would of course be skilled in every team role and able to cover successfully for any co-worker. The real world is rather different because no two roles are identical. Designing a job rotation system will always be the 'art of the possible'.

Apart from the obvious benefit of reducing the risk of operational discontinuity, role rotation offers several other important advantages to managers e.g.

- Assists with the identification of capability that may otherwise have remained invisible.Increases self-esteem and consequently morale through the acquisition of higher or broader skill levels.
- Helps to relieve potential boredom and the possibility of employees becoming 'stale'.
- Offers continuing fresh critique on processes and plant.
- Can improve safety. Employees who remain in the same role for long periods of time can become complacent.
- Avoids the 'great person syndrome' where critical knowledge or skills are monopolised by individuals as a means of increasing their standing in the team or the workplace generally.

With such benefits on offer, the case for role rotation would seem to be undeniable. However, there are potential negatives that need to be carefully considered and which may eventually render this strategy inoperable e.g.

- Potential dips in productivity and quality as employees 'come up to speed' in their new rotation.
- Potential employee resentment. Inevitably there will be a sizeable proportion of the workforce that prefers to stick to one role and has little interest in learning another.
- Potential misunderstandings with Unions or employee representatives who might regard rotation as a form of 'harassment'.
- Disparity in the size of roles making scheduling over complex.

In effect, the adoption of rotation is a cost-benefit issue. Partial systems are always an option. Figure 9.10 shows a simple partial system for one shift in a manufacturing environment.

	Role Rotation Plan- A Shift												
	Role	Jan	Feb	Mar	Apr	May	Jun	Jul	Aug	Sep	Oct	Nov	Dec
Level 3	Stock Preparation	Specialist - cover by DR											
	Level 3 Spare Operator	Covers all shifts- all level 3 non-specialist roles											
	Dry End Operator	JW	JW	MH	MH	CB	CB	JW	JW	MH	MH	CB	CB
	Wet End Operator	CB	CB	JW	JW	MH	MH	CB	CB	JW	JW	MH	MH
	Recycle Operator	MH	MH	CB	CB	JW	JW	MH	MH	CB	CB	JW	JW
Level 2	Winder Operator	KL	KL	KL	FS	FS	FS	KL	KL	KL	FS	FS	FS
	Level 2 Spare Operator	Covers all shifts- all level 2 non-specialist roles											
	Tester Dryer Asistant	FS	FS	FS	KL	KL	KL	FS	FS	FS	KL	KL	KL
Level 1	Millhand	JG	JG	HD	HD	DS	DS	BA	BA	RP	RP	SM	SM
	Load platform Assistant	SM	SM	JG	JG	HD	HD	DS	DS	BA	BA	RP	RP
	Stacker Driver	RP	RP	SM	SM	JG	JG	HD	HD	DS	DS	BA	BA
	Warehouseman	BA	BA	RP	RP	SM	SM	JG	JG	HD	HD	DS	DS
	Shunter Driver	DS	DS	BA	BA	RP	RP	SM	SM	JG	JG	HD	HD
	Level 1 Spare Operator	Covers all shifts- all level 1 non-specialist roles											

Fig 9.10- Typical role / task rotation matrix

In this case rotation between most roles will occur every 2 months but certain roles do not rotate because they are too specialised or they are individuals who are highly experienced, skilled across all the roles and able to step into any position to cover for sickness or release individuals for training.

Rotation will only work well if employees and their representative bodies are prepared to accept it. This may require some effort by managers to persuade all concerned of the very real benefits.

CAPABILITY HEALTH CHECKING.

Regardless of which specific systems and tools are used to improve or maintain capability, organisations must continually monitor the big picture, courageously, 'warts and all'. This is akin to regular health checks and follow-up corrective action. Figure 9.11 shows the key questions that should underpin such an examination.

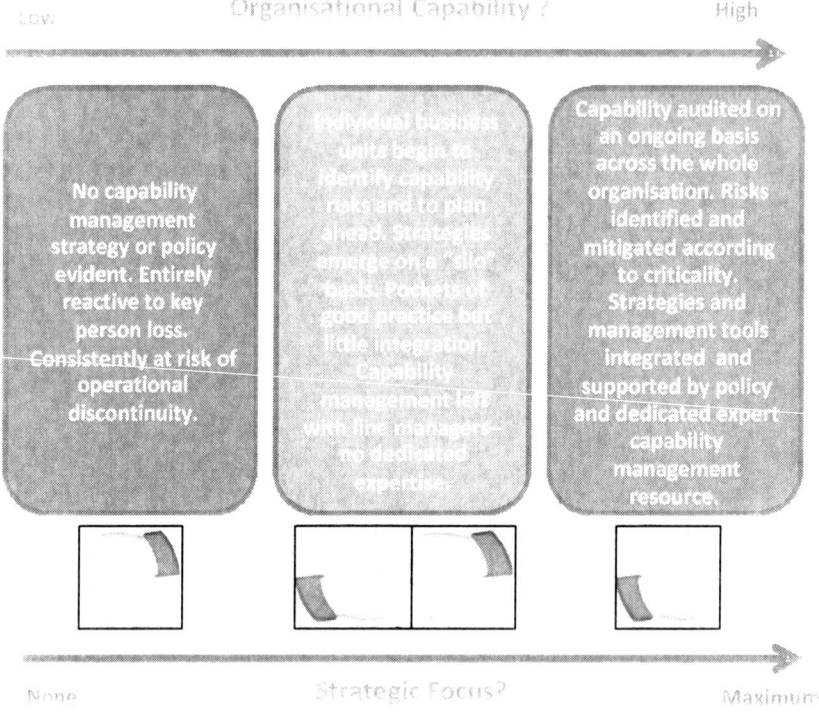

Figure 9.11 – Capability health checking : key questions

Achieving a thumbs up on a capability health check will depend heavily on in-house HR expertise linked to sound L&D practice and to management development at all levels. This level of responsibility and accountability epitomises the emerging role of HR as a strategic business partner.

10. BUILDING AND SUSTAINING A LEARNING CULTURE

GOING BEYOND THE L&D FRAMEWORK

A well designed framework will help to ensure that the training spend is aligned to business strategy and will provide a transparent structure in which organisational learning can occur. What it will not do, unaided, is to guarantee that the organisation leverages its learning activity to move continuously to new dimensions of performance and continues to learn from the act of learning itself. If this is to happen to any premeditated extent it will be due to the presence of an underpinning organisational understanding of how higher order learning occurs and a philosophical commitment to enabling such learning.

So what does this understanding and philosophical position look like?

WHAT IS "ORGANISATIONAL LEARNING"?

As long ago as the 1970's Arie de Geuss, in his role as head of Royal Dutch Shell's strategic planning group, identified the emergence of knowledge and its successful acquisition and management within organisations as the principal factor in commercial success. While all the other factors appeared to be subject to constant change, the need to remain at the cutting edge through continuous organisational learning remains constant - *"The only enduring source of competitive advantage is an organisation's relative ability to learn faster than its competition."* Other prominent industry leaders rapidly concurred and perhaps went further by giving learning an absolute status e.g. Jack Welch's insistence that *"An organisation's ability to learn and to translate that learning into action rapidly, is the ultimate competitive advantage."*

The ever-increasing pace of change has further accentuated the need to be one step ahead in the knowledge stakes and has resulted in the enshrinement of "organisational learning" as a core value. But what does it actually entail?

The 1990's witnessed a rapid growth in the awareness of the seminal importance of knowledge and the learning process to organisational success. Defining precisely what this meant has however proved difficult. In the lingering vacuum numerous academics, theorists and educationalists have stepped in to provide largely idealistic and philosophical interpretations. These were seldom linked to the stark realities of the business world and its strategic and operational needs. The challenge for humble HR or L&D professionals is to find their way through the academic fog to a pragmatic understanding that they can "sell" to the whole organisation as a workable foundation.

Perhaps the most useful (albeit high level) definition of organisational learning has come from Thomas Sattelberger, former chief human resources manager for Deutsche Telekom: *"Organisational learning is purposeful, intentional learning in order to stay or become capable of surviving under changing or unstable environmental conditions by transforming intentionally the ability of the organisation to face the future successfully".*(1) This focuses our attention on the primary need of organisations to use learning to survive and exercise control over their present and future state. But what should they be learning?

Knowledge or competence?

From the theoretical and philosophical exchanges of the 1990's an ongoing debate has arisen concerning the virtues of "knowledge" and "competence". Unfortunately, the term "knowledge" is essentially abstract and non-specific. We have, for some time now, been surrounded by talk of the "knowledge economy" and "knowledge management", but the brutalism of the contemporary global economy now demands that learning be sharply focused on knowing what needs to be done to produce ever more efficiently. As noted earlier, Bob Mosher, of Learning Guide Solutions has been at pains to articulate this through his concept of "mission critical" learning and development.

This hardened view has shifted the ground seismically toward "competence" i.e. knowing how and being able to do - as opposed to just knowing. Organisational learning is now generally understood to be driven by business survival strategy (remaining competitive) and as a primary means of driving the business forward. So organisational learning is the means by which organisational competence is achieved. Unfortunately, however, a moment of reflection will reveal that the effective linkage of learning to eventual competence is a hard one, both complex and challenged by subliminal cultures.

Figure 10.1 illustrates something of the processes that should occur within an organisation to drive learning toward competence. At any one time we can detect several interacting knowledge streams that are rarely managed in a conscious manner.

- **New knowledge acquisition** – generally the most immediately visible stream because it is linked (or should be) to current strategic business needs and therefore at the forefront of organisational consciousness. As new knowledge enters the organisation it is usually activated immediately as a competence and to a varying extent flows into the stream of explicit organisational knowledge.
- **Explicit organisational knowledge** – the current sum of knowledge that is "out in the open" and available to all. In addition to items of new knowledge this continuum incorporates existing activated knowledge and skills, policies, procedures, manuals, systems etc. This is the stuff that organisations "know that they know".
- **Implicit organisational knowledge** – this is the stuff that generally sits below the surface i.e. is truly subliminal. Generally, organisations do not know they know this stuff until a pertinent need arises and demands specific answers.

In many ways this situation is the L&D version of the Johari Window. (3) If the organisation is to maximise its knowledge potential and therefore its competence, it must find ways to bring the "unknown" into the "known arena" and to ensure that new skills are become explicitly integrated rather than being allowed to drift into the implicit domain where they may never be used. Achieving this in a systematic way is a primary function of knowledge management.

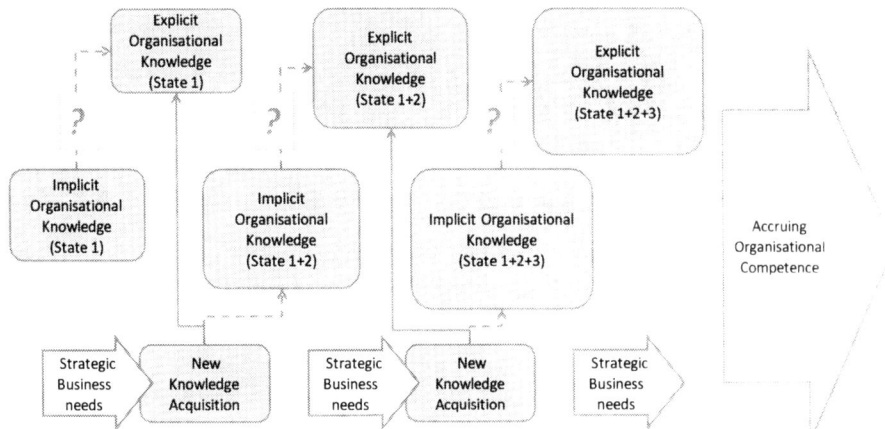

Figure 10.1 – the organisational learning chain

Unfortunately, very few organisations "manage" knowledge in any consciously strategic way. So often, people go on courses and return without anybody actually noticing. Their new learning is either ignored because it is either seen as irrelevant, or it challenges the status quo. More often than not there are no mechanisms to ensure that managers are properly briefed on the new skills they should anticipate from their returning staff. Consequently they are seldom in a position to deploy that new learning successfully. Again, we seldom see any requirement for newly trained staff to "cascade" the general principles to their team or to the wider organisation.

Perhaps the cardinal sin is the failure to bring the full range and depth of individual knowledge and skills out into the open, the explicit area. This can be largely achieved through regular staff skills and experience auditing. How often do we see companies bringing in consultants at huge expense to drive projects that could have easily been completed by their own staff – but nobody bothered to ask them? This is a serious waste of resources, but worse still, it demotivates staff, who will inevitably feel undervalued.

So why does this situation continue? Why do so many organisations fail to systematically manage their knowledge assets? The obvious answer is that management is simply not aware of what needs to be done. Alternatively, a nascent awareness may be there, but a whole range of negative factors can prove to be significant obstacles. Typically, managers and staff may be:

- Too focused on knowledge minutiae and so miss the big picture e.g. as illustrated by figure 10.1 above.
- Focused on short term returns and lacking long term stamina.
- Genuinely unable to find the time and resources to deal with the complexity of knowledge management.
- Involved in "silo" thinking or "turf wars" and consequently unable to share across business unit or departmental boundaries.

- Concerned that revealing own knowledge and skills will result in more work being allocated.

Obstacles like these are not insurmountable but will certainly require long term dedication from a sponsor department e.g. HR. David Skyrme suggests the following conditions as essential if effective knowledge management is to evolve.

- The organization has to be focused on the development and exploitation of its own knowledge
- Top management has to see that knowledge is the main asset of the company, and also has to start initiatives and support for the processes of knowledge management
- Techniques and processes of the knowledge management have to be clearly defined
- Creating, sharing and use of knowledge management has to be a natural part of organisational processes and an integral part of everyday work processes
- There has to be cooperation, not competition of the groups within the organisation
- Knowledge has to be accessible to anyone who can contribute to it or use it
- There have to be good communication channels and technological infrastructures that allow knowledge management activities (4)

Maximised or "true" learning.

Perhaps the most significant of Skyrme's essential conditions is the requirement for the organisation to focus on the "development" and the "exploitation" of its own knowledge. To understand the full implications of this principle it is best to separate the two concepts.

Superficially, most businesses certainly appear to be committed to the "ongoing development" of their people. Indeed, most organisations will espouse this as a central business value. But is the development of people actually synonymous with the development of knowledge? To what extent does the completion of a learning event by individuals or teams contribute to the development of organisational knowledge? If the event has been successful in imparting new knowledge there must certainly be a positive contribution to the quantum of knowledge, but the question of knowledge quality is less obvious. How far do organisations actually go to rework individual and team learning to higher levels where it might be truly beneficial at an enterprise wide level? How does quantum transform to quality?

An answer to this question has evolved through the work of early work of Gregory Bateson and more significantly the later thinking of Chris Argyris and Donald Schön. Their research into learning methods led to the concepts of single and double loop learning.

Figure 10.2 illustrates these processes and their relationship to each other.

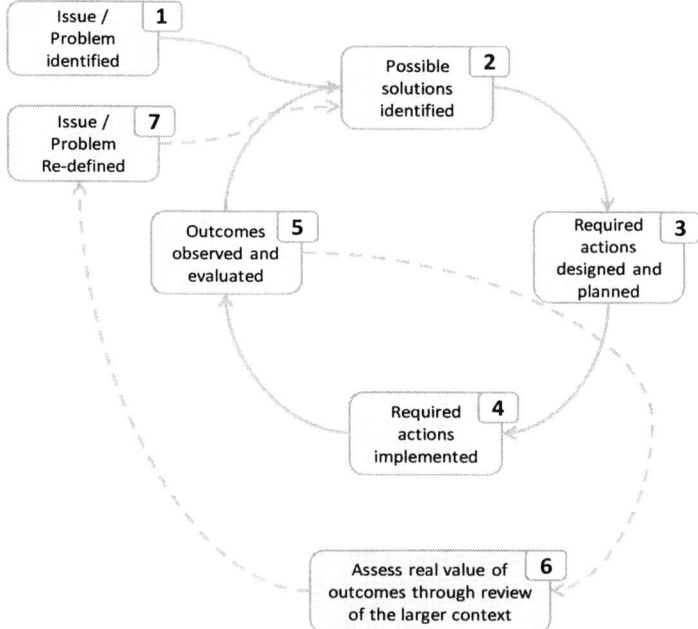

Figure 10.2 – The Single to Double Loop Learning Concept

Single loop learning.

This is the base level of learning or problem-solving and generally involves only incremental improvement or possibly no actual improvement at all. A good example would be the cyclist who repeatedly punctures a tyre on a certain part of his training route. He learns to repair the puncture and (incrementally) becomes expert at doing this. He has learned to solve the problem of the puncture by repair, and clearly, as an expert he is *doing it right*. He has focussed on procedures and skills and with continued practice has achieved mastery of them. However, he has failed to address the larger context i.e. "why do I keep getting punctures? Are there changes I could make that would allow me to avoid getting punctures?"

Double loop learning.

This occurs when we look at the outcomes of immediate solutions and take a step backwards to get a wider view. This is often referred to as "reframing". When our cyclist eventually tires of mending punctures he may ask himself *"I have learned to fix punctures but the problem recurs, so am I doing the right thing? What else have I learned here?"* The answer will probably be two-fold i.e.
- If he keeps riding that particular part of the route he will keep getting punctures.
- If he keeps using tubed tyres he will keep getting punctures.

Coming at the problem afresh generates new solutions e.g. changing his route or perhaps better still, changing to solid training tyres.

This second loop involves looking at the issue and trying to find patterns and underlying causes. This is the substance of classic root cause analysis and the "5 why technique". In the business world double loop thinking can ascend to the strategic level and shows itself in the big picture questions *"How can we do what we do better?"* and *"How can we do new and better things with what we have?"*

Triple loop learning.

Figure 10.3 adds a third loop to the double loop thinking concept. We can picture our cyclist taking the decision to switch to solid training tyres to avoid continuous punctures, but then pausing and reflecting on why he didn't spot this much earlier. He begins to evaluate his thinking and his learning processes to see whether he can "learn to learn" faster. This stage is focused on looking at outcomes and questioning the assumptions we make. The typical questions we ask are "what is going on here? How did we arrive at this solution? Do we need to refine or restructure how we go about learning?" Organisations that are prepared to build this kind of thinking into their behaviour, as a habit, find themselves capable of making significant shifts in their approach and in so doing accelerate their learning processes and their ability to adapt and change.

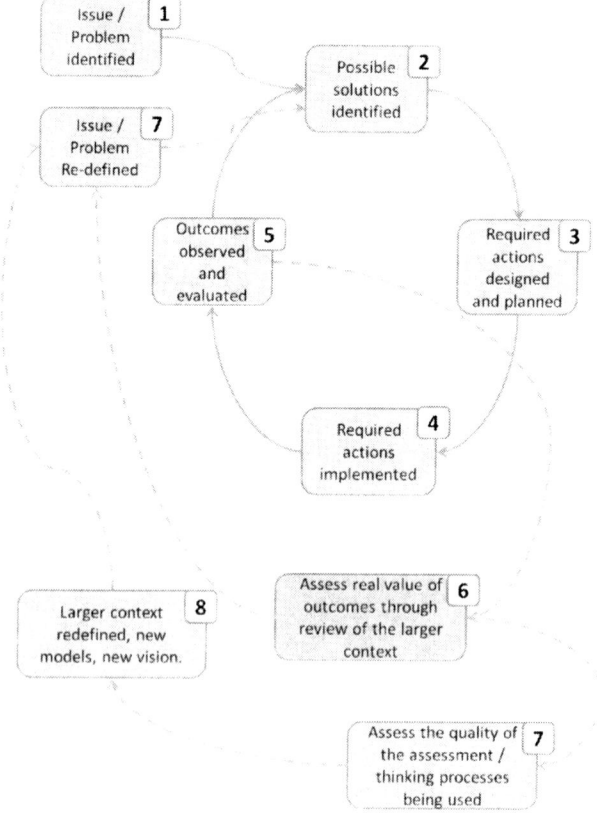

Figure 10.3 – Triple Loop Learning Concept

The "learning organisation".

So, if triple loop learning represents the maximising of learning opportunities, how are organisations to raise their game to this level across the board?

Peter Senge attempted to answer this question in a holistic manner in his influential 1990 book *The Fifth Discipline*. Senge has described his approach to organisational learning as "idealistic pragmatism", by which he means that high level concepts and principles must ultimately be expressed in practical applications and outcomes for business. Therein lies the challenge.

For many hard-nosed executives, Senge's concept of the "learning organisation" is no more than utopian dreaming. This is hardly surprising given Senge's often quoted definition:

"Learning organisations are places where people continually expand their capacity to create the results they truly desire, where new and expansive patterns of thinking are nurtured, where collective aspiration is set free, and where people are continually learning to see the whole together."(5)

However, those that take the trouble to probe behind the surface idealism will find more solidly grounded pragmatic thinking. Senge's fundamental rationale is that organisations must learn to survive. This is *adaptive learning*. Successful and on-going adaptation can only be achieved if organisations can discover *"how to tap peoples' commitment and capacity to learn at all levels"*. This clearly targets those businesses that fail to ensure that learning is aligned and integrated at all levels. More often than not, isolated elements of the organisation receive development or specific training and this is not subjected to the "vertical slice" principle i.e. examining what associated learning needs to happen up and down the organisation to ensure that everybody moves forward together.

Successfully integrated adaptive learning is an absolute, but Senge goes further in maintaining that an additional dimension is needed i.e. that of *"generative learning"*. Adaptive learning will enable us to question what we are doing and to seek continuous improvement in our core processes. It enables incremental change but in the face of ever increasing competition, organisations may need transformational change to re-invent themselves, to *"create their own futures"*. This requires the ability to detach from the everyday reality of the organisation and to investigate not just better ways of doing what we normally do but also the possibility of doing something completely different. Increasingly, organisations that can achieve this are referred to as "ambidextrous".

Charles O'Reilly and Michael Tushman identified this in an article for the Harvard Business Review:

"To flourish over the long run, most companies need to maintain a variety of innovation efforts. They must constantly pursue incremental innovations, small improvements in their existing products and operations that let them operate more efficiently and deliver ever greater value to customers. An automaker, for example, may frequently tweak a basic engine design to increase horsepower, enhance fuel efficiency, or improve reliability. Companies also have to make architectural

innovations, applying technological or process advances to fundamentally change some component or element of their business. Capitalising on the data communication capabilities of the Internet, for instance, a bank can perhaps shift its customer-service call centre to a low-labour-cost country like India. Finally, businesses need to come up with discontinuous innovations—radical advances like digital photography that profoundly alter the basis for competition in an industry, often rendering old products or ways of working obsolete."(6)

The conceptual link to Argyris and Schön's triple loop thinking is immediately apparent, but what is perhaps most valuable about O'Reilly and Tushman's observations is the need for organisations to maintain momentum in all areas of learning to support innovation. This is where Senge's organisational learning theory can be especially helpful. It offers us no magic bullet, but clearly defines the issues we have to deal with and the kind of culture we must strive to create. To be truly ambidextrous (in the sense described above) businesses must transform themselves into learning organisations. This can only be achieved if the following five "disciplines" are developed, valued, rigorously applied and eventually inculcated as organisational culture:

- Personal mastery
- Mental models
- Building shared vision
- Team learning
- Systems thinking

Personal mastery. In a sense this is the "raw material" of Senge's vision of the learning organisation. When all is said and done, it is not organisations that learn but rather the people within it. The quantum and quality of organisational learning depends absolutely on the ability of individuals to embrace learning and to lift it beyond mere personal 'competence'. The mastery of knowledge and skills associated with a specific competency can generally be easily specified and assessed, but on its own this will not guarantee learning momentum. Unfortunately, learning is often viewed as a succession of potentially linked acquisitions of knowledge and skills items, limited to an acknowledged standard and achieved within an approved timeframe. This view presents learning as component based, rather like the bricks that make up a wall. But without mortar, the bricks are more or less useless, the dimensions and longevity of the wall inevitably compromised.

The "mortar" of organisational learning is provided not by the mastery of individual learning components but by the individual's mastery of himself. For Senge, personal mastery involves achieving a mindset whereby the individual views himself as being in a state of constant transition; reflecting on each learning event and redefining his capability and future needs. Consequently, the individual should come to see learning as an ongoing process rather than a finite product. Mastery is achieved when individuals willingly subscribe to Kolb's experiential learning as a positive discipline driven through powerful and honest reflection.

"People with a high level of personal mastery live in a continual learning mode. They never 'arrive'. Sometimes, language such as the term 'personal mastery' creates a misleading sense of definiteness, of black and white. But personal mastery is not

something you possess. It is a process. It is a lifelong discipline. People with a high level of personal mastery are acutely aware of their ignorance, their incompetence, their growth areas. And they are deeply self-confident. Paradoxical? Only for those who do not see that 'the journey is the reward'." Senge 1990.

It is easy to see why organisations have so often failed to address this fundamental need. Either they are simply not aware that they can play a part in 'shaping' their people in this way, or perhaps they feel inadequate in the face of the time, effort and resources that may be required? In addition the 'zen like' feel of concepts such as personal mastery do not sit easily with the harsh realities of 21st century business.

Mental models. Closely linked to personal mastery is the ability to detach oneself from the *"deeply ingrained assumptions, generalisations, or even pictures and images that influence how we understand the world and how we take action"* in order to assess their continuing value and relevance objectively. Senge refers to this as the discipline of working effectively with mental models. If we are unable to do this, appropriate courses of action can be stalled or derailed.

"The discipline of mental models starts with turning the mirror inward; learning to unearth our internal pictures of the world, to bring them to the surface and hold them rigorously to scrutiny. It also includes the ability to carry on 'learningful' conversations that balance inquiry and advocacy, where people expose their own thinking effectively and make that thinking open to the influence of others." Senge 1990.

Senge is here describing a level of emotional and intellectual maturity that all would probably aspire to, but perhaps only a few attain? This is the true meaning of 'openness' and while it is clearly a considerable asset at the individual level, organisations or teams cannot really move forward until a certain 'critical mass' has been achieved. Fostering and nurturing openness at the team level is a stern test of leadership and relationship building. The very best leaders will focus on modelling openness and receptivity to the views of others. They will also manage team interactions (perhaps even manipulate them) to help individuals develop this capability.

The key to mastering this particular discipline is the willingness to be wrong, accepting that this is a positive donation to group enterprise.

"I have to be prepared to be wrong. If it was pretty obvious what we ought to be doing, then we'd be already doing it. So I'm part of the problem, my own way of seeing things, my own sense of where there's leverage, is probably part of the problem. This is the domain we've always called 'mental models.' If I'm not prepared to challenge my own mental models, then the likelihood of finding non-obvious areas of leverage is very low". Senge – Navigating Webs of Inter-dependence.

Building shared vision. When attempting to navigate in unknown territory, the first principle is to fix your position. If you don't know where you are starting from you can't calculate a bearing to take you somewhere else. So, as Max de Pree was fond of saying, *"The first responsibility of the leader is to define reality".* The second responsibility must surely be to define the objective, where we are headed.

For most employees, in most organisations, 'vision' is something that sits alongside the 'mission statement' on the company intranet, or is perhaps proudly displayed in the reception foyer. In an extensive survey of US companies William Schiemann found that only 14% were able to say with any confidence that their employees had a good understanding of organisational vision and strategy. However, for Senge, even a 100% understanding of the vision and mission statements would not be enough. These are, after all, merely words. The initial vision statement has to be opened up, interpreted in detail to provide a clear view of what the future will look like. Leaders at all levels must willingly accept the responsibility of constantly refreshing and, if necessary, re-defining that image for all their people. Senior leaders must ensure that the vision can be articulated in this way and is being stitched into the very fabric of the organisation in a consciously managed way.

"Many leaders have personal visions that never get translated into shared visions that galvanise the organisation. What has been lacking is a discipline for translating vision into shared vision. The practice of shared vision involves the skills of unearthing shared 'pictures of the future' that foster genuine commitment and enrolment rather than compliance." Senge 1990.

Team learning. At the heart of Senge's thinking around teams is the old adage "an effective team will always be greater than the sum of its parts". However, to be truly effective, teams have to find ways of working together profitably, allowing each individual to contribute fully. This is Tuckman's 'norming' which must precede 'performing'.(7) Optimised performance of course depends on individuals achieving personal mastery and working toward the shared vision, but it also depends on individual growth being translated into team growth. This can only occur if teams have created, and are able to sustain what David Bohm has called 'a larger intelligence'. This is not necessarily a conscious creation. More often than not, teams learn that sharing experience, problem-solving as a group and learning together inevitably brings higher quality outcomes. Eventually, this 'dialogue' becomes instinctive and solutions become team driven, regardless of individual specialisms.

Leaders can and must encourage processes that will clearly demonstrate the added value of team learning. They can deliberately 'norm' the process of team application to any significant issue and ensure that all team members find ways to contribute.

Systems thinking. When asked what systems thinking is, Peter Senge often resorts to the analogy of the family. The actions of one family member inevitably impact on others because they are connected as parts of an interactive whole; a system. We can easily fall into the trap of believing that only immediately adjacent parts of the system are affected. This may be true in terms of time, but not in terms of potential significance. To understand the actual impact of actions and events we need to have 'system maps' which allow us to track effects from initial cause, through the system connections, to the point of eventual dissipation. We should also never forget that any given system interacts with others, thus allowing potential onward transmission. In this sense we can see that nothing exists in total isolation and we cannot fully understand issues if we regard them as isolated. The relationship to chaos theory and complexity theory is obvious, although not yet fully elaborated.

Senge maintains that if we wish to create true learning organisations, we must develop a working consciousness of the various systems at work within them and how each is populated i.e. the parts of the system where individuals variously reside and develop their perspectives and mental models. Only then can leaders and teams begin to learn about issues and to solve problems in a way that engenders truly systemic thinking. Relying on the 'smart' individual to solve problems will never be as good as 'collective intelligence'.

"You need to triangulate. You need to get different people, from different points of view, who are seeing different parts of the system to come together and collectively start to see something that individually none of them see." Senge – Navigating Webs of Inter-dependence.

Without the discipline of systems thinking, the other four disciplines ultimately count for little. Those disciplines are themselves are an inter-dependent system. Organisations that have gone some way toward systems thinking stand a much better chance of developing the self-perpetuating collective intelligence that characterises the learning organisation.

THE REAL WORLD – CHALLENGES TO IMPLEMENTING THE LEARNING ORGANISATION.

So is the learning organisation, as Senge sees it, an achievable proposition? To any pragmatic person, rooted in the real world of business, the answer would surely be "No. At least not in its entirety". There are several reasons for this.

Economic and business imperatives.
Although the majority of larger organisations are at least paying lip service to superficially attractive concepts like shared vision and team learning, these ideas seldom extend beyond boardroom buzzwords. They fail to gain traction principally because they clearly represent a long-term investment with no clearly defined return, which must compete with the clamour for short-term predictable gain.

Senge's vision of organisations is essentially post-capitalist. It is not driven entirely by the bottom line, but by a more holistic sense of business organisations as communities. This simply does not fit comfortably with contemporary business priorities. When researching for his 1995 book *The State We're In* Will Hutton noted that the raison d'être of most British companies was overwhelmingly one of financial gain. He also comments that "the targets for profit are too high and the time horizons are too short". There is no reason to suppose that businesses across the world have a different take on things. Despite the global financial crisis of 2008, initiated by the sub-prime lending scandal with the resultant collapse of huge financial institutions, little appears to have changed. The rise of China as an economic powerhouse looks like perpetuating the capitalist creed, albeit under Communist branding. For an idealistic minority this is a simple matter of unfettered corporate and shareholder greed. For those charged with actually running businesses, the drive for quick profit is more likely to be defined as a 'survivalist" strategy.

Of course Senge would argue that long term survival does not depend on profit alone. Sustainability must also be founded on the quality of the organisation's human and intellectual capital and ultimately its ability to reinvent itself in order to "create its own future". Nonetheless, no matter how appealing his arguments may be, the fear of losing out in the present in order to profit in the future seems just too daunting a prospect.

Lack of organisational competence.
We simply cannot escape the fact that Senge's ideas seem essentially simple but when opened up are in fact extremely sophisticated. Even those who would willingly aspire to master the five disciplines are likely to be faced with a herculean task. At corporate and individual levels building a learning organisation would be a truly transformational undertaking, only achievable, if at all, over a number of years. Cultural change, on this scale, will require wholesale levels of understanding and commitment previously only encountered in evangelistic business theorists, who traditionally live out their days as 'voices crying in the wilderness'.

In addition to the intellectual (and spiritual) competence required, transforming to a true learning organisation will require phenomenal feats of leadership in which key managers perform more as facilitators and teachers, rather than directors. And of course we should not forget the ordinary team member. How does a leader shift the working man's rationale of the workplace from one of simply 'earning a living' to the contributive and inclusive learning community that is deemed necessary. The levels of employee engagement that would need to be developed and sustained are a daunting prospect even for the most optimistic and talented leader.

Inner tensions.
For many observers, Senge's learning organisation, if ever implemented, might be subject to systemic tensions that could prove difficult to resolve and manage comfortably. In particular, there is an apparent antagonism between the need to develop a shared vision and the aspects of continual 'dialogue' called for within the disciplines of personal mastery and mental models. Is it actually possible to maintain a shared vision when the organisation invites the constant questioning of its culture, strategy and values? For Senge's supporters this is simply the status quo for a healthy, progressive organisation that is truly geared to learning. On the other hand, the die-hard pragmatists would argue that all organisations encounter the need, from time to time, to simply 'stand still and consolidate'.

Tensions arise too around the uncertain political and social implications of Senge's theory. Many managers take the view that his vision of the learning organisation is a simple variant of communitarian ideology. This is a comparison that is difficult to dispense with entirely. The commonplace reaction is quite predictable e.g. 'we exist to do business, not to be an instrument of social and political change'.

Given the challenges to implementing the learning organisation described above, what can we hope to achieve? Is the learning organisation a luxury we simply can't afford – or a necessity we simply can't afford not to afford?

A MIDDLE WAY – A LEARNING CULTURE OR A LEARNING ORGANISATION?

To paraphrase an old adage, half a utopia is better than none! Senge's learning organisation may be ultimately unattainable, but given the universal acknowledgement that continuous learning is an absolute for success and survival, there can surely be no excuse for not trying? For most senior leaders the ideal of the learning organisation is just too ambitious in today's world, despite its long term strategic appeal. The elephant appears just too large to eat at one sitting. An alternative strategy is, of course, to eat it one piece at a time – but how to do this?

The solution may lie with understanding the difference between 'organisational learning' and a 'learning organisation'. This has been the subject of a good deal of academic debate in recent years. Anders Örtenblad has summarised the position very succinctly.

"The two most common ways to distinguish between organisational learning and the learning organisation, in existing literature, are that the learning organisation is a form of organisation while organisational learning is the activity or process of learning in organisations, and that the learning organisation needs effort while organisational learning exists without any effort."(8)

Furthermore it seems that organisational learning is not an activity but a natural process, simply because organisations must learn in order to survive. There is a clear understanding that organisational learning happens of its own accord. The issue is really centred on the quality of learning, not its justification. The evolution of organisations into learning organisations on the other hand is not a natural process. If it happens at all, it is the result of a long term, sophisticated strategy.

"Organisational learning is as natural as learning in individuals ... the "learning organisation" can be distinguished as one that moves beyond this 'natural' learning, and whose goals are to thrive by systematically using its learning to progress beyond mere adaptation."(9)

The question that arises then is - 'how can we utilise what is a naturally occurring process to move toward a learning organisation?' Taking a fresh look at Senge's five disciplines, it seems sensible to approach them as a strategic developmental sequence rather than a simultaneously integrated change project. We should be mindful of the much quoted Sun Tzu axiom *"Strategy without tactics is the slowest route to victory. Tactics without strategy is the noise before defeat."*

Figure 10.4 overleaf offers a view of how we might strategise to begin the transformation to a learning organisation. Naturally this is a schematic and somewhat artificial sequence in a much as the components would not develop totally independently of one another. Each component would of course loop around to reinforce others. The suggestion here is that development focus would be best prioritised in this sequence.

In this sense, figure 10.4 maps out a 'campaign' strategy for the learning organisation champions within the business, whoever they might be.

Everything must begin with strategic intent. Therefore transforming to a learning organisation must begin with shared vision. From the very outset everybody in the organisation needs to know what the learning organisation will look like and why they need to go there. Continual development and reinforcement of these key messages should form the backbone of the development enterprise.

From strategy we derive tactical priorities, and this is where the remaining disciplines can be factored in as a logically dependent sequence. Essentially this sequence can be divided into two distinct phases:

Phase 1 – shifting to a true learning 'culture'. To ensure a good foundation, the first priority should be to work towards an organisational understanding and adoption of maximised learning i.e. double and triple loop learning mechanisms. This will not be achieved overnight and will require the steady 'conversion' of key stakeholders i.e. those who will be able to influence others in their turn. In-house systems, such as six sigma, lean manufacturing, TQM etc can all be targeted as forums in which higher level learning can be introduced.

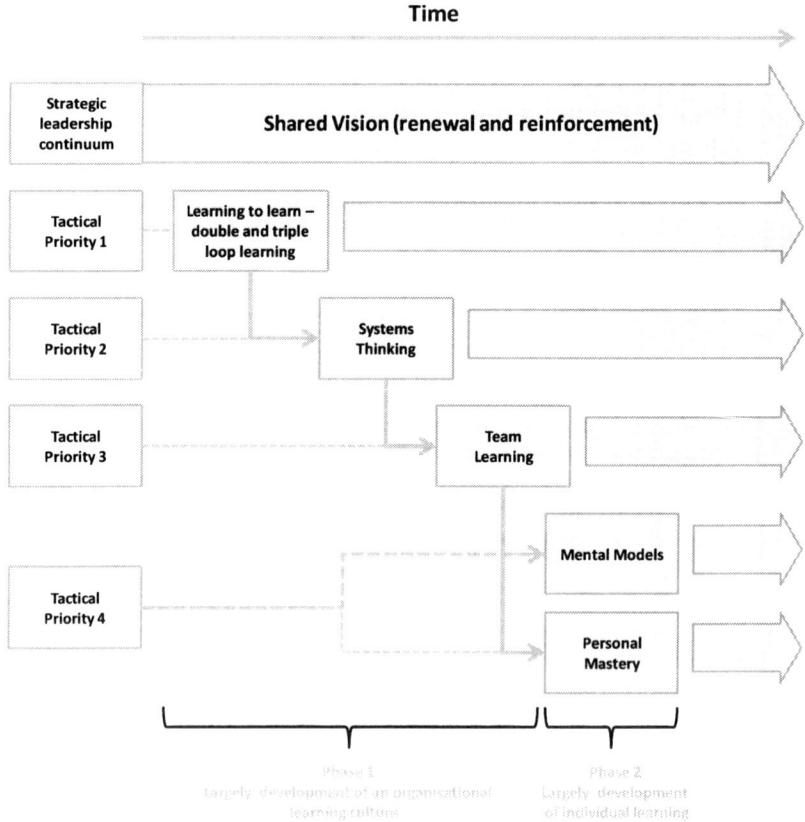

Fig 10.4 – "Campaign Strategy" - Learning Culture to Learning Organisation

Triple loop learning, by its very nature will support and link naturally to the second priority, systems thinking. Learning at this level is often referred to as "transformational learning" in that it drives a complete revision of what learning means, how it should be done and how it might be applied in the organisation.

Addressing the issue of application will cause managers to engage with systems thinking. Within that triple loop they should be asking obvious questions such as "how does learning in area X impact on other areas within the organisational system?" Working with system maps will clearly aid this analysis. True transformation begins to occur however when the higher level questions are asked e.g. "How can we maximise the impact of learning through the system?" This level of enquiry lifts learning impact from the reactive to the proactive i.e. the organisation begins to 'design' the learning culture.

Recognition of the organisation as a system will inevitably reshape the concept of team i.e. from 'silo-ised' departmental groups to a much more integrated view of working together. When previously distinct teams begin to infiltrate each other's territory, armed with triple loop mentalities and attitudes true team learning, the third tactical priority. This is what Senge means when he says *"The smartness we need is collective, not individual"*. Once this collective learning becomes normalised behaviour organisations can legitimately lay claim to a 'learning culture'.

Phase 2 – completing the transformation to a 'learning organisation'.
Once true team learning is established, within a systems thinking culture, individuals, teams and eventually the organisation itself would inevitably be drawn into the consistent questioning and revision of mental models in an 'organised' fashion. This would be an 'organic' process, of indeterminate duration and difficult to capture in terms of monitored progress. Nevertheless, skilled and vigilant champions should be able to encourage development at all levels.

As discipline is attained over mental models, personal mastery can fully evolve. In this scheme personal mastery expands somewhat on Senge's original concept in that it assumes mastery of all the other disciplines as well as the individual's ability to open himself to truly reflective experience and learning. This is transformation at the individual level which of course is the primary driver of organisational transformation. Learning to learn, systems thinking and team learning are disciplines that can, to a large extent be facilitated by appropriately skilled advocates. Reaching the goal of personal mastery, and objective management of mental models' will however be much more dependent on personal maturation, and consequently be much more of a personal journey. Progress toward this goal will of course be assisted by the other disciplines, but will certainly be more difficult to facilitate. Skilled mentoring over an extended period would most likely prove to be the best tactic.

Taking action – key roles. In an ideal world strategies could be evolved to engage the whole organisation in transforming to a true learning organisation. Perhaps it is true that complete success cannot be achieved any other way?

"Building the learning organisation is inevitably a collective exercise. Everyone has to help draft the blueprint; everyone has to carry both hammer and nails. There is no place to sit around and just watch the building go up."(9)

Unfortunately however, we do not live in an ideal world. The stark reality of the business world means that total engagement at any point in time is a practical impossibility. The constant demand for immediate results and a demonstrable dollar return on investment will pretty well crush any attempt to establish building a learning organisation as a formal long term change project. If transformation is to happen to any extent then it is far more likely to occur on an informal basis through the 'stealth' tactics of enlightened leaders and specialists. But where are these enlightened individuals to come from? There are really only two sources; senior management and HR /OD specialists. It follows, of course that "enlightenment", in the sense of understanding learning organisations, does not come pre-packaged with the standard portfolio of management or HR skills. Anybody looking to set an organisation down this difficult path would need to have undergone the transformation themselves at the personal level. Such individuals are relatively rare.

The role of senior management.
Senior managers are not necessarily the most influential people in an organisation, but they certainly have the potential to be. Hopefully, leadership exists at all levels within an organisation but the opportunity to establish strategy and create momentum and sustain transformation must surely lie chiefly with senior executives.

The leadership role is essentially catalytic, not idealistic. The goal may be distant but senior managers can actively intervene to help teams and individuals on their way. For example, the enlightened manager can:

- Analyse departmental function to identify opportunities where problem-solving and decision-making processes can be challenged to ensure double and triple loop learning.
- Constantly provide the triple loop example by leading individuals and teams through the maximisation of learning e.g. by instilling questions such as "what have we learned here?" and, more importantly, "what have we learned about how we are currently learning?"
- Ensure that each element of progress is thoroughly communicated and understood.
- Facilitate team learning by ensuring that learning is transformed from the implicit state to the explicit.
- Encourage the challenging of mental models by ensuring that a true diversity of minds is set to work on issues.
- Ensure that the organisational horizontal and vertical systems are mapped and their necessary integration understood.
- Enforce a systems thinking culture by ensuring that decisions made, actions taken and lessons learned are actively driven through the systems maps to ensure maximum alignment.
- Coach / mentor potential champions to expand the transforming force within the organisation.

All this presupposes that senior managers possess the vision, the conceptual framework and the considerable intellectual and inter-personal skills required. This is a very big ask as David Skyrme has acknowledged:

"The challenge facing managers today is to make the effort needed to learn some of the new skills and techniques, and to put in processes that engage their workforce in programmes of continuous capability development. Learning should be integrated into the doing, as part and parcel of everyday work. It should also be energising,

stimulating and fun. Getting the best out of everybody, including yourself, to meet the challenges ahead." Making the effort to acquire new skills is all well and good but generally "we don't know what we don't know". How are managers to find out what they don't know? Where is that awareness to come from?

The role of HR/L&D professionals.

The answer to this last question must surely be "from HR - and in particular from the L&D specialist". We would not expect business managers even to be aware of the learning organisation concept, let alone actually understand and support it. We should, however, expect this of an L&D professional. After all, it is directly associated with their core discipline. HR is seldom able to drive organisational change directly. Generally it must operate through the offices of conventional leadership. This can only be done through the exercise of fluent and subtle influencing skills. It is tempting to regard this as 'educating management' but is more akin to describing an alternative future which can only be driven home by a powerful and clear vision.

Vision on its own will never be enough. The Canadian Public Service Agency analysis describes an intimidating portfolio of skills that appears to sit outside the the L&D remit e.g.
- Visioning
- Strategising
- Planning
- Consulting
- Researching: probing and surveying the organisation
- Communicating
- Influencing
- Facilitating (11)

We can surmise from all this that the L&D role could, and perhaps should be, that of principal change agent. As such, the heady vision must be backed up by calculated strategies and detailed tactical measures. Organisational transformation cannot be achieved by HR alone. HR professionals, of any ilk, must take on the challenge of evangelising the prospect of the learning organisation as the inevitable way forward, but they must also be prepared to familiarise themselves with the commercial and business imperatives faced by managers.

"Senior managers need to understand the language associated with learning organisations, just as HR practitioners need to learn the language of corporate management if they are to contribute to formulation of organisational strategy. Both senior managers and HR professionals need to share an understanding of those principles and practices of learning organisations which can be important elements of a business strategy. They need to share a common language if discourse is to be effective and their actions need to be more closely aligned with this discourse."(12)

REFERENCES

Section 1.   1.   See Peter Senge. *The Fifth Discipline: The Art and Practice of the Learning Organisation.* 1990

2.   See Stephen George. *The Baldridge Quality System.* 1992

3.   See Jarvis, Lane and Fillery-Travis. *The Case for Coaching.* CIPD 2004.

4.   See Pliny the Elder – *Naturalis Historia* A.D.77

5.   See David Kolb. *Experiential Learning: Experience as a Source of Learning and Development.* 1984

6.   See Charles Greer, *Strategy and Human Resources* page 105. 1995

7.   See IBM Executive Brief: *Learning governance – aligning strategy with organizational outcomes.* Page 2. 2005

8.   For a succinct explanation of ADDIE and IDS see http://www.learning-theories.com/addie-model.htm

Section 2.   1.   See www.fire.org.nz/About-Us/Publications/Other-Reports/Pages/Strategic-Plan-2006-2010.asp

2.   See Peter Senge *The Fifth Discipline* page 9. 1990

3.   Interview with Don Soderquist at ethix.org 2008

4.   Ibid.

5.   See Lombardo, Eichinger *Career Architect Development Planner* Lominger 2010

Section 3.   1.   See *A Taxonomy for Learning, Teaching, and Assessing: A Revision of Bloom's Taxonomy of Educational Objectives.* Lorin Anderson, David Krathwohl. Allyn & Bacon; (2000)

2.   See *Developing and writing educational objectives* RH Dave, 1970

Section 4.   1.   See: www.admin.cam.ac.uk/offices/education/curricula/aims

2.   See Kolb, D. A. 1981. Learning Style Inventory: Self-Scoring Inventory and Interpretation Booklet. Boston, MA: McBer & Company.

3.   See Smith, M. K. (2001). David A. Kolb on experiential learning.

4.   See Hargreaves, D., et al. (2005). About learning: Report of the Learning Working Group.

5.   See Massa, L. J.; Mayer, R. E. (2006). "Testing the ATI hypothesis: Should multimedia instruction accommodate verbalizer-visualizer cognitive style?" Learning and Individual Differences.

6.   See McCarthy. B *Teaching Around the 4MAT* Cycle 2005

7.   See Piaget, J. (1977). The Grasp of Consciousness.

8.   See Vygotsky, L.S. (1978). *Mind and society: The development of higher psychological processes.*

9.   See: *Siemens Connectivism: Learning as Network Creation* 2005

	10.	Ibid.
	11.	See Mosher B. ASTD white paper 2009 cited in Lydia Cillié-Schmidt *Blue print for the Learning and Development Function*. Human Capital Review 2011.
	12.	See Knowles, M. 1970. *The Modern Practice of Adult Education*. Englewood Clift.
	13.	See VCAL information sheet February 2014

Section 5.   1.   See John D Bransford et al *How People Learn.* 2000
             2.   See:
                  http://wenku.baidu.com/view/9c8c4263ddccda38376b
                  afb6.html

Section 7.   1.   A summary of the survey's key findings is available free of charge, by request to Global Learning Alliance.
             2.   See http://www.trainingmag.com/article/training-magazine-ranks-2012-top-125-organizations.
             3.   See Donovan, P; Hannigan , K. and Crowe, D. (2001) 'The learning transfer system approach to estimating the benefits of training: Empirical evidence', *Journal of European Industrial Training.*
             4.   See Phillips J, and Stone R *How to Measure Training Results* 2002
             5.   See Warr, P., Bird, M. & Rackham, N. (1970*). Evaluation of management training.*
             6.   See Larossi, G., 2006. *The power of Survey Design: A User's Guide for Managing Surveys, InterpretingResults, and Influencing Respondents.* Washington, DC, The World Bank.
             7.   See Miles and Huberman *Qualitative Data Analysis* 2nd edition 1994
             8.   See Charles Handy *The Age of Paradox* Harvard Business School Press, 1994

Section 9.   1.   See *The Peter Principle: Why Things Always Go Wrong* William Morrow & Co. 1969

Section 10.   1.   See *Facing up to the Learning Organisation Challenge* Chapter3. CEDEFOP 2003
             2.   Bob Mosher. Quoted in *Blueprint for the Learning and Development Function* Lydia Cillié-Schmidt. Human Capital Review 2009.
             3.   See Jesse Russell, Ronald Cohn.2012. *Johari Window.* Books On Demand.

             4.   See David Skyrme *Knowledge Networking: Creating the Collaborative Enterprise.* Oxford. Butterworth Heinemann.
             5.   See Peter Senge *The Fifth Discipline. The Art and Practice of the Learning Organisation.* Doubleday.1990
             6.   See http://hbr.org/2004/04/the-ambidextrous-organization/ar/1

7. See Bruce Tuckman. *Developmental sequence in small groups*". Psychological Bulletin 1965

8. See Anders Örtenblad *On Differences Between Organisational Learning and the Learning Organisation*. The Learning Organisation Vol. 8. 2001

9. See M.Dodgson. *Organisational Learning: a Review of Some Literatures*. Organisation Studies Vol 14. 1993

10. See *A Primer on the Learning Organisation* Canada Public Service Agency February 2007

11. Ibid.

12. See The Changing Role of HRD practitioners in learning-oriented organisations. Sambrook, Stewart and Tjepkema. 2003

RECOMMENDATIONS FOR FURTHER READING

The publications listed below are cited simply as a means for deepening and broadening understanding of the learning and development field. They represent a variety of views of and approaches to the various L&D component skills.

General

Anthony Landale (1999). Gower Handbook of Training and Development. Gower Publishing, Ltd.

Raymond Noe, Colin Winkler. (2009) "Emplyee Training and Development". McGraw Hill.

Diane Arthur (1995). "Training and Development". Managing Human Resources in Small & Mid-Sized Companies. AMACOM Div American Mgmt Assn.

Shawn A. Smith and Rebecca A. Mazin (2004). "Training and Development". The HR Answer Book. AMACOM Div American Mgmt Assn.

Cohn JM, Khurana R, and Reeves L (October 2005). "Growing talent as if your business depended on it". Harvard Business Review.

Michael M. Lombardo and Robert W. Eichinger (1998-12-06). "HR's role in building competitive edge leaders". Human Resource Management (John Wiley & Sons, Inc.) Rosemary Harrison (2009). "learning and Development". CIPD Publishing.

Training / Learning Needs Analysis

Roland and Frances Bee (1994). "Training Needs Analysis and Evaluation". CIPD Publisihing.

Paul Donovan, John Townsend.(2004) "The Training Needs Analysis Pocketbook".Management Pocketbooks.

Sharon Bartram, Brenda Gibson. (2000). "The Training Needs Analysisn Toolkit".HRD Press.

James Smith. (2011) "Training Needs Analysis - What You Need to Know". Amazon Kindle Book.

Tom Holden. (2002)"Training Needs Analysis in a Week". Chartered Management Institute.

Robyn Peterson.(1992)" Training Needs Analysis in the Workplace". Kogan Page.

Anamika Kishan Chawhan (2012)"Training Need Analysis: Conducted TNA in a robust form at Tata BlueScope Steel,Pune, India"Lamber Academic Publishing.

Irwin Goldstein, Kevin Ford.(2001)"Training in Organizations: Needs Assessment, Development, and Evaluation with InfoTrac"

Jean Barbazette. (2006) "Training Needs Assessment – Methods, Tools and Techniques" Pfeiffer.

Allison Rossett. (1987) "Training Needs Assessment". Educational Technology Publications.

Deborah Tobey. (2005) "Needs Assessment Basics". ASTD Press.

Programme or Course Development.

Rita Smith. (2011) "Strategic learning Alignment". ASTD Press.

Walter Dick, Lou Carey. (1985) "The Systematic Design of Instruction". Scott Foresman.

Reginald Melton. (1982) "Instructional Models for CourseDesign and Development". Educational Technology Publications.

Cat Sharpe. (2005) "Course Design and Development" ASTD Press

George Piskurich. (2006) "Course Design Made Easy". ASTD Press

Saul Carliner. (2003) "Training Design Basics". ASTD Press

Gary Morrison. (2011) "Designing Effective Instruction". John Wiley & Sons. Cjarles Reigeluth. (1999) "Instructional Design – Theories and Models". Lawrence Erlbaum Associates.

Rita Richey, James Klein, Monica Tracey. (2011) "The Instructional Design Knowledge Base". Routledge.

Leslie Briggs, Kent Gustafson, Murray Tillman. (1991() "Instructional Design: Principles and Applications". Educational Technology Publications.

Bobby Elliott. (2009) "E Pedagogy".Scottish Qualifications Authority at http://www.scribd.com/doc/932164/E-Pedagogy

Patti Shank and Amy Sitze.(2004) "Making Sense of Online Learning" Pfeiffer and Company.

William Horton.(2000) "Designing Web-based Training"Wiley.

Helen Beetham, Rhona Sharpe. (2007) "Rethinking Pedagogy for the Digital Age". Routledge.

Abbie Brown, Timothy green. (2006) "The essentials of Instructional Design". Pearson Merrill Prentice Hall.

Assessment Design.

Walvoord, B. E. (2010). Assessment clear and simple: A practical guide for institutions, departments, and general education (2nd ed.). San Francisco: Jossey-Bass.

Thomas Haladyna. (2004) "Developing and Validating Multiple Choice test Items". Lawrence Erlbaum Associates.

Steven J Osterlind. (1998) "Constructing Test Items". Kluwer Academic Publishers.

Howard Wainer, Henry Braun. (1988) "Test Validity". Lawrence Erlbaum Associates.

Ruth Pickford , Sally Brown. (2006). "Assessing Skills and Practice". Routledge.

Richard Freeman, Roger Lewis. "Planning and Implementing Assessment". Routledge Falmer.

Delivery of Learning.
Tony Pont. (2003). "Developing Effective Training Skills". CIPD Publishing.

Robert Pike. (2002) "Creative Training Techniques Handbook". HRD Press.

James Davis, Adelaide davis. (1988) "Effective Training Strategies". Berrett-Koehler Publishers.

Jack Gordon, Ron Zemke. (1988) "Designing and Delivering Cost-effective Training". Lakewood Books.

Carolyn Nilson. (2003) "How to manage Training". AMACOM.

Suzy Siddons. (1997) "Delivering Training". The Cromwell Press.

Geri McArdle. (2007) "Training Design and Delivery". ASTD Press.

George Piskurich. (2004). "The ASTD Handbook of Training Design and Delivery". ASTD Press.

Evaluation of Learning Activities.

Leslie Rae. (1999). "Using Evaluation in Training and Development". Kogan Page.

Jack Phillips. (2004). "Make Training Evaluation Work". ASTD Press

Jack Phillips. (2005). "ROI at Work". ASTD Press.

Jack Phillips. (2003). "Return on Invetsment in Training and Performance Improvement Programs". Taylor & Francis Group.

Robert Brinkerhoff. (2006). "Telling training's Story". Berrett- Koehler Publishers.

Donald Kirkpatrick, James Kirkpatrick. (1975). "Evaluationf Training Programs". McGraw Hill.

Donald McCain. (2005). "Evaluation Basics". ASTD Press.

Jody Fitzpatrick, Blaine Worthen, James Sanders. (2004) "Program Evaluation". Allyn & Bacon.

Michael Quinn Patton. (1980). "Qualitative Evaluation Methods". Sage Publications.

Anthony Crandell Hamblin. (1974) "Evaluation and Control of Training". McGraw Hill.

Stephen Brown, Constance Seidner. (1998). "Evaluating Corporate Training: Models and Issues". Springer, London Ltd.

Dana Robinson, James Robinson. (1989). "Training for Impact". Jossey Bass Publishers.

Building a Learning and Development Framework.

Steve Whydett, Sarah Hollyforde. (2003) "A Practical Guide to Competencies". CIPD Publishing.

Building and Sustaining a Learning Culture.

Linda Honold. (2001) "Developing Employees Who Love to Learn". Davis-Black Publishing.

Reginald Hayes. (2008) "Developing Employees and Enhancing Employee Performance". Booksurge.

Klas Mellander. (1993) "The Power of learning". McGraw Hill.

Nancy Dixon. (1999). "The Organisational Learning Cycle". Gower Publishing.

Reza Sisakhti. (1998). "Effective learning Environments". ASTD Press.

Michael Marquardt. (2011). "Building the Learning Organisation". Nicholas Brealey Publishing.

Peter Kline, Bernard Saunders. (1993). "Ten Steps to the Learning Organisation". Great Ocean.

Alan Belasen. (2000). "Leading the Learning Organisation." State University of New York Press.

Index

A

ability
  individual's, 255, 273
  learner's, 109, 138
  organisation's, 9, 259
abstract conceptualisation, 74–75, 77
adaptive learning, 265
affective domain, 41, 43–45, 63
affective learning, individualised, 48
analysis, qualitative, 211
Analysis of learning, 10, 242
Anderson, 41–42
Annual Review, 17, 30
application, 26, 42, 47, 49, 62, 81, 111, 118–23, 130, 138, 183, 273
applied learning, 110–11, 151
applied learning principles, 111–12
applying new skills, 190
Appropriate active verbs, 44–45, 60
assessment
  authentic, 116–17
  formative, 116–17
  multi-choice, 128, 130
  single, 116, 118
  summative, 116–17
assessment analysis, 139–40, 147
assessment design, 114
assessment materials, 90, 97, 242
assessment methods, 87, 112–13
assessment outcome, 60, 138
assessment reliability, 219
assessment reliability analysis, 140, 143
assessment results, 114, 139–40
assessment rubric, 150–52
assessment standards, 240
assessment tools, 4, 115, 117, 130, 183
Assessment Type Formative, 118–23
assessment validity, 138
Assignment of Training, 170
associated actions, 12, 17–19, 25, 27, 46
associated activities, 25–28
Associated learning mode, 4
Associated Objectives, 12, 17, 46
Aural learners, 80

B

Basic Management Skills, 184–86
bench strength, 253, 255
Bloom, 41–43, 62, 64, 114, 118–24
Bloom's analysis, 40–41, 43, 61
Bloom's taxonomy, 42–44, 111
Budgeting, 154–55, 166
Building and Maintaining Relationships, 24–25
business environments, 7, 200
business goals, 12, 17–18, 46, 174, 225, 230
business managers, 12, 274
business objectives, 196, 243
business organisations, 269
business performance, 175, 203
business planning, 223–24, 226
business strategy, overt organisational, 32
business units, 12, 17, 226, 228, 247, 249, 261

C

capability, 33, 53, 71, 170, 243–44, 257–58, 266–67
  organisational level, 243
  organisation's, 245
capability health, 258
capacity, 7, 33, 146, 243–44, 253, 265
career goals, 230, 232
CIPP Model, 200–201
CIRO model, 203
Cognitive, 47–48
cognitive domain, 41–44, 47, 49, 61–62
Cognitive Learning levels, 61, 118–23
Cognitive Level, 42, 49–50, 62, 124
competence, 19–23, 29, 40–41, 43–44, 56, 58, 114, 117, 165, 240, 255, 260, 266, 270
  functional, 22
  unconscious, 20–21, 26
competency, 9, 19, 21, 23, 29, 266
competency frameworks, 19, 23, 29, 227, 251
competitive advantage, 8–9, 259
compliance training, 30–31, 39, 110
Comprehension, 42, 118–23, 130, 133, 138
conformity
  high, 26, 28, 253–54
  low, 26, 28, 253–54
connected E-learning groups, 109
conscious competence, 20–22, 26
consolidation, 20–21
context, 18, 22, 31, 34, 60, 72, 80, 109, 112–13, 131, 150, 153, 156, 200–203, 238–39
Continuing professional development (CPD), 7–8, 224, 237, 241

costs, 7, 52, 54, 67–69, 71, 84–86, 104–6, 166, 171, 175, 178–79, 198, 200, 212
criticality, 22–23, 25–26, 90, 252, 258
cultures, 15–16, 29, 54, 73–74, 86, 100, 106, 159, 266, 270, 272

D

data
  qualitative, 188, 204–5, 210–12, 214
  quantitative, 204, 210–11, 214, 218
data analysis, 193, 198, 208, 211
data reduction, 212–13
delivery costs, 85–87
departmental business plans, 7, 17–19
design, 4, 10, 81, 83–85, 87, 95–97, 110, 113–15, 119–20, 122, 169–70, 172, 181–82, 188–89, 201–3
  good, 127–28, 181
develop E-learning programmes, 106
developers, 49, 55–56, 66–67, 71, 85, 87–88, 92, 105–6, 110
Developing Capability, 213
development
  associated, 230
  civic, 151
  driving E-learning, 107
  external, 52
  individual, 34, 230–31
  personal, 32–33, 40, 192, 227
development activity, 2, 6–7, 200, 226, 230, 250
development framework, 27, 222, 227
development hour, 84
Development Input, 229
development of learning experiences, 4, 54
Development pathways, 226, 228–29
development plan, 35
development planning, 11, 34
  individual, 32, 34, 226, 228
development processes, 16, 55–56
development project, 53, 89, 106
development team, 40, 52
development time, 84
development work, commissioning E-learning, 107
discrimination, 148–49
distance learning, 71, 76, 85, 160
distribution, 97, 128, 140–43, 219, 229
  normal, 140–41
domains, 41, 44, 50, 55–56, 110, 267

E

educational programmes, 3
Effective management of learning delivery, 153
E-learning, 1, 85, 104–7, 110, 157

generic competency frameworks, 23, 29
golden ratio, 94–96
graphics, 85, 93–94, 96, 98, 172, 201
group learning experiences, 4

H

handouts, 90, 95–97, 103
hard skills mastery learning, 60
HC (High Conformity), 26–28, 253–54
higher level learning, 110, 272
High Performer, 142, 250–52
HR, 8–10, 12, 14, 17, 53–55, 58, 87, 104, 107, 110–11, 166, 226, 228, 251–52, 274
HRIM, 169
HR/L&D, 155, 251
HR professionals, 1, 11–12, 244, 274

I

Identification of learning, 10, 242
impact, 25–27, 54–55, 83, 87, 156, 161–62, 164, 175, 181, 191–97, 200, 202–3, 220, 268, 273
Implicit Organisational Knowledge, 260–61
indicators, 142–43, 190, 192
Individualised remote learning, 66–67
individual learning components, 266
individual learning outcomes, 69
Individual learning styles, 74, 76–77, 79–81, 108
individual performance, 36, 115, 148
Individualsurveys, 206
interviewers, 188, 205, 210
interviewing, 188, 197, 209–11
interviews, 122, 131, 178, 181, 188, 205, 210–11

K

key materials, 90
Kirkpatrick, 31, 155, 180–81, 192–93, 200, 203–4
Kirkpatrick levels, 31, 171, 183, 189, 191, 193, 201–2, 220
knowledge, fundamental, 45, 54
knowledge gain, 111, 225
knowledge management, 9, 260–62
Kolb, 3, 74–76, 82, 109
Kolb model, 3–4, 74–75
Kolb's model of preferred learning styles, 74–75

L

L&D, 1, 6–7, 14, 16–17, 22, 30, 35, 104, 107, 110, 154–56, 166, 169, 251, 255
leadership, 8–9, 24–25, 29, 47–48, 132, 154, 187, 223, 227–28, 243, 267, 270, 274
learner acceptability, 55, 74

organisational learning initiatives, 16
organisational learning strategies, 2, 104
organisational training systems, 176
organisational transformation, 273–74
organisational values, 15–16
organisational vision, 12–14, 268
organisation checklist, 166, 168
organisations, larger, 11, 269
organisation types, 39, 230
outcomes, 2–3, 55–58, 60, 65–67, 69, 113, 115, 151, 178–79, 181–83, 189–90, 193, 200, 202–3, 263–65
outsourcing, 55, 58, 84–85, 87, 110

P

pedagogies, 106–8
performance, 25–26, 28, 35–37, 64–65, 121–22, 139–40, 174–75, 177, 181, 183, 189–90, 196–98, 233, 250–52, 254–56
  poor, 35–36, 254
performance expectations, 19, 23, 58, 189–90
performance levels, required, 26, 237
performance management, 18, 25, 43, 184, 214, 223, 251
personal mastery, 266–67, 270, 273
Phillips, 193–94, 200
Phillips model, 192–93, 196, 200
plan
  annual business, 17
  individual development, 2, 228
planning, 19, 24–25, 27, 30, 46–47, 49, 62, 122, 124, 154–55, 193, 195–96, 222, 228, 230
planning process, 18–19, 211
  strategic, 17, 27, 30, 32, 34–35
planning requirements, 46, 49, 62
policies, 87, 130–32, 155, 176, 226–27, 229, 242, 258, 260
portability, 237, 241
PowerPoint, 98–99, 103
PowerPoint presentations, 98–99, 101, 185, 187
preferred learning styles, 4, 55, 74–76, 80–81
presentation, 73, 97, 102–3, 113, 120, 125, 211, 214, 220
presenters, 98–100, 103, 185, 187
process evaluation, 179
process information, 77, 80–81
process steps, essential, 177–78
professional development, 8, 40, 227–28
professions, 39, 237, 240
programme specification, 56–57
program's learning objectives, 151
psychomotor domain, 41, 43–45, 48, 62, 64
purpose statement, 115–16, 226

Q

Training Transcript, 170
transfer, 57, 110, 123, 171, 181, 188–89, 193, 195–96, 202–3, 211–12, 214, 220
transfer learning, 183, 189
transformation, 1, 271, 273–74
Typical L&D quality assurance cycle, 242

U

understanding learning organisations, 274
Up-front costs, 52, 106

V

validity, questionable, 119–22
values, 2–3, 5, 12–16, 29, 31, 42–43, 47–48, 80, 82, 138, 174, 176–77, 200, 223,
    267–68
value statements, 15–16
variables, 52–53, 84, 114, 129, 159, 177, 181, 191, 198, 201
VCAL (Victorian Certificate in Applied Learning), 111
Virtual Learning Environment (VLE), 173

W

workbooks, 86, 90, 94–97
work environment, 188–90
workplace/situation, 151

ABOUT THE AUTHOR:

Brian is a learning and development professional with some 40 years of wide-ranging experience. Much of that time has been spent attached to the UK Ministry of Defence where he was employed in a training and development role across all three armed services, but primarily with the Army.

During that career he has been tasked with the design and delivery of training and development across numerous subjects and levels of audience. He has also been privileged to manage large teams of lecturers and trainers of graduate calibre, and to be closely involved with a number of strategic level L&D projects.

After leaving Defence in 1995 he worked in a freelance capacity in the UK on educational projects in the tertiary education sector and assisting industry and emergency services with the design of internal assessment systems. In 1998 Brian emigrated to New Zealand with his family and took up a post with the newly created training support division of the New Zealand Fire Service. Working initially on the creation of new programmes, he was selected to project manage an initiative aimed at the complete rebuild of the Service's training and progression system.

Moving on from the Fire Service he worked independently as a consultant, focusing particularly on the design, development and delivery of leadership and management skills training for organisations in New Zealand and across the South Pacific.

In 2011 Brian took up his present post as Learning and Development Manager for an Australasian Pulp and Paper company. He is currently working on the introduction of the systems approach to training and the enhancement of leadership capability across the business.

CPSIA information can be obtained at www.ICGtesting.com
Printed in the USA
LVOW10s1956220915

455250LV00026B/860/P